Being Gods

Christian Deification as Restoration of the Divine Nature

By Michael Roden

BEING GODS

CHRISTIAN DEIFICATION AS RESTORATION OF THE DIVINE NATURE

MICHAEL RODEN

Being Gods: Christian Deification as Restoration of the Divine Nature
by Michael Roden.

Copyright © 2024 by Michael Roden.

All rights reserved. No part of this book may be reproduced or used in any manner without the prior written permission of the copyright owner, except for the use of brief quotations in a book review.

Omnia Gratia Publishing
An imprint of Infinite Passion Publishing

Website: https://michael roden.weebly.com

For Zacchaeus, Sarah, Nick and all the divine children of every age. Special thanks to John for the books.

First Edition.

10 9 8 7 6 5 4 3 2

Printed in the USA.

Library of Congress Cataloguing in Publication Data

Roden, Michael

Being gods: Christian Deification as Restoration of the Divine Nature/ Michael Roden

ISBN-10: 0-9652996-5-1
ISBN-13: 978-0-9652996-5-7

Bible Translations and Abbreviations

Unless otherwise indicated, all Bible passages are from the *The New Revised Standard Version* (**NRSV**), copyright ©1989 by the Division of Christian Education of the National Council of the Churches of Christ in the United States of America. Used by permission. All rights reserved.

Other English translations used include:

NRSVUE: New Revised Standard Updated Edition (Copyright © 2021 National Council of Churches of Christ in the United States of America.)
KJV – King James Version (1604; public domain)
NKJV – New King James Version (Copyright © 1982 by Thomas Nelson, Inc.)
ESV – English Standard Version (*ESV Study Bible*. © 2008. Wheaton, IL: Crossway Books.)
WEB — World English Bible (Public domain Bible based on the American Standard Version of the Holy Bible first published in 1901 the Biblia Hebraica Stutgartensa Old Testament, and the Greek Majority Text New Testament.)
WEY — The Weymouth New Testament (by Richard Francis Weymouth, 1912. Public domain in the United States.)

Patristic Writings

ANF – *Ante-Nicene Fathers. The Writings of the Fathers Down to A.D. 325.* (Ed., Alexander Roberts. Vols. 1-5. Buffalo: Christian Literature, 1886-1905. Repr., Grand Rapids, Mich.: Eerdmans, 1989.)
NPNF — *Nicene and Post-Nicene Fathers. A Select Library of Nicene and Post-Nicene Fathers of the Christian Church.* (Edited by Philip Schaff and Henry Wace. 28 vols. in 2 series. 1886–1889. Repr., Grand Rapids, Mich.: Eerdmans, 1989.)
Philokalia — *Philokalia.* (Ed., G.E.H. Palmer. Vols. 1-4. London: Faber and Faber, 1981.)

CCEL – Christian Classics Ethereal Library (online: www.ccel.org)
ECW - Early Christian Writings (online: www.earlychristianwritings.com)
NA – New Advent (online: www.newadvent.org)

Table of Contents

Introduction 1
    Deification in the Early Church 1
    Rediscovery of the Lost Doctrine 6
    Deification East and West 15
    Definition of a Fully Restorative Deification 19
    Method and Aim 23
    Chapter Sequence 26
    A Note on Inclusive Meaning behind the Patriarchal Language 30

1. The Biblical Foundations of Deification 32
    "You are Gods" 32
    Created in the Image of God 37
    The Exchange Formula 41
    Participants in the Divine Nature 46
    Conclusion 50

2. Eternal Life and Immortality 52
    Immortality in the Patristics 52
    Immortality in the Hebrew Literature 60
    Eternal Life in Jesus' Teaching 62
    Immortality in Paul 64
    Conclusion 66

3. Sonship and Deification 68
Adoptive Sonship in the Patristics 68
Adoptive Sonship in Paul's Teaching 74
    Galatians 4:5 74
    Romans 8:15 76
    Ephesians 1:5 78
Begotten Sonship in Jesus' and John's Teaching 81
Sonship in the Hebrew Bible and Apocrypha 91
Conclusion 93

4. The Nature of God 96
Divine Simplicity 96
God as Being 99
God as Spirit 101
God as Father 102
God as Love 104
Conclusion 106

5. Creation and Deification 108
Christian Negative Attitudes Towards the World 108
The General View of Creation 113
The Double Creation 121
The Dual Nature of Human Beings 130
Conclusion 136

6. The Fall of Gods 140
The Fall of Gods 140
The Fall for Origen 145

A Note on Dissociation 148
The Undescended Soul 150
Conclusion 156

7. Preexistence of Souls 159
In Origen and the Patristics 159
In Jesus' Teaching 168
Preexistence and Predestination in Paul 172
In the Hebrew Bible and Apocrypha 176
Plato and Preexistence 183
Conclusion 186

8. The Holy Spirit and Natural Theology 188
Natural Theology 188
The Holy Spirit in the Hebrew Bible 192
In Jesus' Teaching 195
In Pauline Literature 197
Conclusion 201

9. Deification and Salvation 203
Beyond the Cross 203
The Simplicity of Belief 210
Original Sin Revisited 212
Existential Guilt and Its Concealment 226
Conclusion 230

10. Living as Gods in The World 234
Experience of the Deified Self 234

Contemplation 240
Selfless Yet Universal: Jesus' Example as a God 245
The Way of Love 248
Conclusion 252

11. The End of the World 256
Realized Eschatology 256
The Internal Kingdom 264
The Last Judgment 268
Resurrection 271
The Light of Revelation 276
Conclusion 279

12. Apokatastasis: The Universal Restoration 283
Universalism in the Bible 283
Apokatastasis in Origen 290
Hell 297
Heaven 310
Oneness 314
One in the Son and Christ 318
Conclusion 325

Conclusion: Where Humanity Meets Divinity 328

Appendices 336
Restoration and the Patristics 336
Categorization of Approaches 343
The Essence-Energies Distinction 350

Bibliography 354
Index 363

Partial Chronological List of Christian Patristics and Theologians Who Taught Deification

Justin Martyr (c. 100-165 CE)
Tatian the Syrian (120-180)
Theophilus of Antioch (120-183)
Irenaeus, Bishop of Lyons (130–202)
Clement of Alexandria (150-215)
Tertullian of Carthage (160-220)
Hippolytus of Rome (170-236)
Origen of Alexandria (185-254)
Cyprian of Carthage (200-258)
Gregory Thaumaturgus of Neocaesarea (213-270)
St. Anthony the Great of Thebes (251-356)
Eusebius Pamphilus (265-339)
Athanasius of Alexandria (296-373)
Hilary of Poitiers (310-367)
Gregory of Nazianzus (328-390)
Basil of Caesarea (330-379)
Gregory of Nyssa (335-399)
Ambrose of Milan (339-397)
Augustine of Hippo (354-430)
Cyril of Alexandria (370-444)
Diadochos of Photiki (400-486)
Leo the Great (400-461)
Dionysius the Areopagite (450-532)
Gregory the Great (540-604)
Thalassios the Libyan (580-640)
Maximus the Confessor (580-662)
John of Damascus (676-749)
Symeon the New Theologian (949-1022)
Anselm of Canterbury (1033-1109)
Thomas Aquinas (1225-1274)
Gregory Palamas (1296-1359)

(Dates should generally be considered approximations.)

Introduction

Deification in the Early Church

> *We carry mortality about with us, we endure infirmity, we look forward to divinity. For God wishes not only to vivify us, but to deify us.* — *St. Augustine*[1]

Augustine's words here echo the views of nearly every Christian theologian from its beginnings up through the Protestant Reformers. God intended human beings for deification, to become "gods." As Augustine writes elsewhere, God "makes his worshipers into gods."[2]

This aspect of Augustine's teaching is a far cry from viewing human beings as miserable sinners by nature. There is at least the potential and capacity within lowly, debased humanity for something immeasurably, even infinitely great, majestic, and Godlike. This divine aspect of humankind is hidden in plain sight from our realization until we come to believe and accept it for ourselves, at which time we see it everywhere.

Deification (Greek, *theosis*) has always existed as a core teaching in Christianity, from its earliest theologians onward, but for the past few hundred years it has gone underground. It was not that the Reformers (Luther, Calvin, Wesley, etc.). themselves did not carry on the tradition and think deeply about how God meant us to

---

[1] Augustine, *Sermon 23B*, in *Sermons*, trans. Edmund Hill (NY: New City Press, 1997), 11:37.

[2] Augustine, *City of God*, 10.1. Translated by Marcus Dods. From *Nicene and Post-Nicene Fathers, First Series*, Vol. 2. Edited by Philip Schaff. (Buffalo, NY: Christian Literature Publishing Co., 1887.) Revised and edited for New Advent by Kevin Knight. <http://www.newadvent.org/fathers/1201.htm>

be gods and how such deification was the epitome of Christian salvation. They, like nearly all Christian theologians in the fifteen hundred years before them, saw deification as the culminating stage of Christian salvation, the ultimate goal of every believer and indeed of creation itself. Unfortunately, deification would in ensuing years be deemphasized and lost sight of in favor of lesser, more mundane and disconnected dogmas. And not only in the West, among Protestants and Catholics, but also in the Christian Orthodox East, deification slipped into the esoteric underground with the monks and mystics.

For over 1500 years, deification had been the *sine qua non* of Christian theology, the essential teaching around which all else revolved. We will point out how instrumental the idea was to the development of the Christian doctrines from its earliest centuries, through the church councils and onward into Medieval times. It was undeniably the underlying foundation upon which Christian theology was built, the often invisible hand (because behind the scenes as common knowledge) by which it was shaped. For instance, the reason for the insistence on Jesus as "God" in the early church councils was because it was commonly accepted that only a God can deify human beings. And the reason Jesus also had to be fully human is because it is through his taking on humanity that we are deified.

We will find that the Bible, particularly the New Testament, is filled with mediating images for deification, images that help transition human subjectivity into divine subjectivity. These range from humans having been "created in the divine image and likeness" of God to becoming "gods" and "children of God," to having "eternal life" and being "begotten from above," to "participation in the divine essence and nature." The preponderance of these images seem to confirm that deification was the *telos* or overarching purpose of Christianity from earliest New Testament times.

Early theologians picked up on these images and noted their great significance. Justin Martyr, also known as Justin the Philosopher (c. 100-165 CE),[3] writes: "we have learned that those

---

[3] All such early dates should be considered scholarly approximations.

only are deified who have lived near to God in holiness and virtue."[4] Justin is here distinguishing specifically between Christian deification and the *apotheosis* or elevation to nominal godhood of Greek and Roman emperors and national heroes. In Justin's eyes, Christian morality, holiness, and virtue was meant to lead to true godhood, not in name only and not just metaphorically, and this way of deification was open to anyone and everyone.

Irenaeus (c. 130-202), Bishop of Lyons and noted heresiologist, brought all the elements of a system to the teaching of deification, and his opinions ultimately became the prevailing view. We will hear from him extensively in this book. He is perhaps most famous for having introduced what has become known as the exchange formula for deification:

> [T]he Word of God ... through His transcendent love, became what we are, that He might bring us to be even what He is Himself.[5]

According to this formula or, better, encapsulation of Christianity, Jesus, originally a god, became human so that we humans might be gods. Thus, deification was the meaning behind the incarnation, and Jesus' entire existence on earth was meant to recapitulate and correct for Adam's fallen existence which had denied Adam of godhood. For each of these early fathers, deification ("becoming gods") was both the goal of the religion and the essence of what God intended all human beings to be. And their arguments for such universal deification are all steeped in Judeo-Christian scripture rather than Greek philosophy.

Hippolytus of Rome, who lived between 170-236 CE, wrote a nice summation of the effects of deification:

> And thou shalt be a companion of the Deity, and a co-heir with Christ, no longer enslaved by lusts or passions, and

---

[4] Justin Martyr, *First Apology Ch. 21. Ante-Nicene Fathers.* Translated by Alexander Roberts and James Robinson. (*ANF* 1:170).
[5] Irenaeus, *Against Heresies*, Book 5, Preface (*ANF* 1:526), tense modified.

> never again wasted by disease. For thou hast become God: ... because thou hast been deified, and begotten unto immortality. This constitutes the import of the proverb, 'Know thyself;' i.e., discover God within thyself....[6]

When Greek philosophy is brought to the discussion, it is for the sake of comparison and elucidation. Thus, when we come truly to know ourselves, as with Socrates' encapsulation of philosophy ("Know thyself"), we will know that we are gods. This is the will of God himself so that we might relate to him. For who can have a genuine relationship with God except beings like himself?

Clement of Alexandria (150-215), a noted Christian scholar and contemporary of Irenaeus, wrote that:

> [H]e who listens to the Lord, and follows the prophecy given by Him, will be formed perfectly in the likeness of the teacher — made *a god going about in flesh*.[7]

Clement believed that even during this present life we can come to know and experience our godhood. Even in our daily lives we could each be "a god going about in flesh."

Anthony the Great of Thebes (251-356), the founder of monasticism in Eastern Christianity, saw deification as the divine purpose of God, "who has created all things that man may be saved and deified."[8] Deification *was* salvation, its end result, to these early Christians. Like most patristics, Anthony taught that our immortality and incorruptibility as gods comes from the soul:

> A true man is one who understands that the body is corruptible and short-lived, whereas the soul is divine and

---

[6] Hippolytus of Rome. "Refutation of All Heresies 10: 30." *Ante-Nicene Fathers*. Ed. Alexander Roberts. Vol. 5. Buffalo: Christian Literature, 1886. 153. Print.

[7] Clement of Alexandria. *The Stromata, or Miscellanies*. "Book VII, Chapter XVI," (*ANF* 2: 553). My emphasis.

[8] Antony the Great. "On the Character of Men and on the Virtuous Life 168." *Philokalia*. Ed. G.E.H. Palmer. Vol. 1. London: Faber and Faber, 1981. 355. Print.

immortal and, while being God's breath, is joined to the body to be tested and deified.[9]

The reason for our earthly existence is for our immortal soul "to be tested and deified." Our purpose in this life is to reattain knowledge of our soul, which is already "divine and immortal." The soul is the divine-breathed part of ourselves, the part that came directly from God and is most like him. It is by identifying with this immortal soul rather than with the body that human beings will receive their deification. Therefore, deification is at its root a change of mind and identity that has real effects.

We will in Chapter 10 detail some of the processes put forward by church fathers as leading to deification. These methods include contemplation (Gk., *theoria*) by which the mind that immerses itself in the attributes of God becomes a god, a method shared by patristics both East and West. This is linked with our moral and ethical practice, which again allows us to become like God by cultivating the Godly qualities and attributes, as with some of Jesus' main and most comprehensive teachings. The idea is expressed here by Anthony:

> Those who pursue a life of holiness, enjoying the love of God, cultivate the virtues of the soul.... [K]nowledge of God, self-control, goodness, beneficence, devoutness and gentleness deify the soul.[10]

Without deification, we lose sight of the rationale for the rules, virtues and practices emphasized by Christian teaching. We are left with only rules and regulations, stripped of their underlying rationale — to be a god, and share the blessings thereof. Church rituals and sacraments like baptism and the Eucharist are likewise intended for our deification. In baptism, Christians are "christened," anointed into

---

[9] Antony the Great. "On the Character of Men and on the Virtuous Life 124." *Philokalia*. Vol. 1: 348. Print.
[10] Antony the Great. "On the Character of Men and on the Virtuous Life 34." *Philokalia*. Vol. 1: 334. Print.

Christhood, and in the Eucharist or holy communion, believers take Christ within themselves. The sacraments were intended to be mediating practices for deification.

The idea that human beings could somehow be called "gods" may sound outlandish to modern religious sensibilities. But that is precisely because we have lost sight of this core ancient doctrine of deification. With the loss of its *telos*, its ultimate aim and purpose, Christianity lost what made it and human beings in general transcendent. Deification faded from general awareness and Christianity became something else.

This loss of emphasis was tragic regarding our understanding the Christian message, as articulated by St. Maximus the Confessor (580-662) who writes:

> The only real disaster that can befall us is the failure to attain deification.[11]

Much of Christianity has lost this holy understanding, but modern historical scholarship has for the past hundred years or so has been rediscovering its central importance to the religion.

Rediscovery of the Lost Doctrine

It is only in the last century or so that the ancient Christian teaching of deification has been rediscovered, after having gone underground for the centuries just prior. Biblical scholarship in the late nineteenth century happened upon the great significance of deification in Christianity in an ironic way. The esteemed Protestant historian of religion Adolph von Harnack (1851-1930) had a dampening effect on deification scholarship for much of the twentieth century with his characterization of deification as a "fringe"[12] religious idea derived from Hellenistic mystery cults that

---

[11] Maximus, *On the Lord's Prayer*, cited in Russell 2004: 295.
[12] Harnack, *History of Dogma*, Vol. II, Ch. 5, Section 3, p. 318.

intruded itself upon the purity of the humanistic biblical message. Harnack recognized the ubiquity of deification among Christian theologians through the centuries, but he attributed this to Greek philosophical influence rather than to the scriptural underpinnings pored over by those theologians. (We will examine these scriptural foundations thoroughly, beginning in chapter 1.)

Such was Harnack's impressive grasp of Christian history that many of his colleagues followed suit during the early twentieth century. In the decades that followed, his view of deification and of Hellenistic influence in general was, surprisingly, found to be thin and contrary to the weight of the evidence. Deification in particular has since been found to have arisen from scriptural considerations of the early patristics rather than philosophical or cultic sources. Mosser sums up how recent research obviates the early criticisms:

> It was unimaginable to Harnack, Bousset, or their followers[13] that the doctrine of deification could have more than the most tenuous connection with earliest Christianity and the Second Temple Jewish soil from which it sprang. But careful study in the decades since has demonstrated that the doctrine of deification does not represent the climax of a syncretistic affair between Christianity and Hellenism. Hellenistic 'influence' is indeed detectable, but it is primarily linguistic and secondary. As expressed in the earliest patristic interpretations of Psalm 82, the patristic notion of deification represents a remarkable instance of fidelity to the early Jewish roots of Christian belief.[14]

A flurry of research into the subject has since affirmed that Harnack, et. al., were mistaken in their assumption that Christianity was merely appropriating its deification teaching from Greek philosophical ideas. Christian theologians, beginning with Justin

---

[13] "M. Werner, B. Drewery, and many others follow the line of Harnack's thinking, categorizing *theosis* with decline and with doctrinal hardening" (Finlan and Kharlamov, 2006: Intro, 8-9).
[14] Mosser 2005: 73.

Martyr, Irenaeus, and Origen, among others, depended solely on scripture for the development of the doctrine. They relied on the New Testament writings and the Hebrew Bible along with Jewish scriptural commentary or *midrash*, [15] Wisdom and apocalyptic writings to develop their understandings of deification, which distinguished Christian deification from its surrounding Greco-Roman context. Ancient Greco-Roman culture had reserved a kind of nominal deification or *apotheosis* for emperors and national heroes. Plato's idea was a smidge less elitist perhaps, but still difficult for the common person, requiring three successive lifetimes of philosophical contemplation. Christian deification, which arose primarily from Judeo-Christian sources, seemed to offer the promise of godhood to anyone who desired and believed in it.

Jeffrey Finch notes that a specific form of deification piqued Harnack's criticism: that proposed by Athanasius in the fourth century which he called a "physical theory of redemption." Harnack rejected what he saw as Athanasius' mechanistic understanding of deification, whereby the introduction of divine substance into the world via Christ's incarnation was thought to transform human substance. [16] Finch states that "recent historical research has revealed the Harnack school's critique to be a shortsighted 'reduction' of the patristic doctrine of divinization to the acquisition of incorruptibility (*aphtharsia*) only." [17]

Early challenges to Harnack came in the East from the Russians Ivan Popov[18] and Vladimir Lossky and in the West from French researcher Jules Gross. In 1938, Gross wrote "the first comprehensive and chronological analysis" of deification, encompassing "Patristic, Hellenistic, mystery religion, biblical, and

---

[15] Jewish *midrash* is an ongoing written rabbinic commentary on the Hebrew Bible, considered by many adherents to be sacred teaching.
[16] Finch 2006b: 108.
[17] Finch 2006b: 106-107.
[18] See Gavrilyuk, "How Deification was Rediscovered in Modern Orthodox Theology: The Contribution of Ivan Popov" in *Modern Theology* 38:1 Jan. 2022, pp. 100-127.

postbiblical sources."[19] Scholarly consensus is that Gross successfully answered Harnack, et. al., on this question by carefully examining the biblical basis of deification within the greater Greco-Roman cultural context and the patristic tradition up to John Damascene (676-749 CE). Gavrilyuk notes Gross' significance: "Responding to Harnack and others, Gross contended that far from being an instance of intellectual capitulation to pagan Hellenism, deification was a legitimate development of the biblical ideas of divine filiation [sonship] and incorporation into Christ."[20]

More recently, Norman Russell expanded upon Gross with his detailed study, *The Doctrine of Deification in the Greek Patristic Tradition* (2004). Russell carefully contextualizes (so far as possible in a single volume) the idea of deification in light of the panoply of surrounding thought systems (from the Pythagorean to the Hermetic to the midrashim to the Valentinian). David Meconi comments about this landmark work that "the greatest contribution of Russell is the splendid attention with which he works through how standard deifying taxonomy changes and has adapted to related theological trends throughout the millennia."[21]

Russell concentrates primarily on the Greek or Eastern patristics, and only cursorily notes the Western or Latin fathers and the biblical foundations of deification in his 2004 work. Although focusing more on the context than on the New Testament writings themselves, he does trace the scriptural pillars back to John 10:35, Psalm 82:6, Genesis 1:27, and 2 Pet 1:4.

Russell's proposed categorization method and his inconsistent use of it has been rightly criticized.[22] Most confusing is Russell's continual description of deification as a "metaphor"[23] (even while labeling most of its usage in the Byzantine tradition as "realistic" or "ontological"), which serves only to muddy the

---

[19] Finlan and Kharlamov, 2006: Intro, 9. Gross' study, originally in French, was translated into English in 2000 as *The Divinization of the Christian According to the Greek Fathers.*
[20] Gavrilyuk 2009: 649.
[21] Meconi 2006: 5.
[22] E.g., Keating 2006: 390; Litwa 2012: 10. See my Appendices for more on this.
[23] Russell 2004: 8.

categories. Even in the Pauline and Johannine traditions deification is said to be "metaphorical"[24] though perhaps this might have been clarified had he simply said that it is *expressed* metaphorically rather than in technical philosophical language. After all, biblical expressions of sonship to God and recovering the divine image seem intended to work as mediating images and concepts intended to lead believers into a *lived experience* of godhood via primarily moral and ethical means coupled with contemplation.

Deification teaching has been spreading like wildfire through the academic community in the last several decades. There are a myriad of valuable works on Eastern deification and patristics, far too many to list here, including those by Bishop Kallistos Ware, Panayiotis Nellas, and John Zizoulas. Andrew Louth has for decades penned excellent books and articles on the Eastern patristics and this tradition.

Western Approaches

Inspired in large part by all this activity in the East, Western scholarship has sought — and, surprisingly to some, found — a major theme of deification in the Western (Catholic and Protestant) fathers and theologians. Recent research has discovered deification teaching within the writings of Tertullian, Hilary of Poitiers, Ambrose, Augustine, Leo, Jerome, Anselm, and Aquinas, thus firmly established in the Catholic tradition. Even the Reformers Luther, Calvin, and Wesley in the 1500s up to the 1700s taught of deification as the ultimate goal and effect of Christian salvation.

In 1932, Myrrha Lot-Borodine (1882–1957) a Russian émigré living in Paris, wrote a series of articles introducing Eastern deification to the West.[25] For Lot-Borodine, God was basically

---

[24] Russell 2004: 11.
[25] Heleen Zorgdrager describes Lot-Borodine as "an esteemed medievalist," and adds the detail that "deification came to her attention during a conversation with Fr Georges Florovsky at Berdyaev's home." Berdyaev and the Russian philosopher/poet Soloviev had done much to reintroduce the idea in the East.

inaccessible in his essence to the human mind, and so she assented to Gregory Palamas' essence/energies distinction.[26] However, "She criticizes the 'rather angelic than apostolic' virtues of monks," preferring a more ecstatic and erotic approach, and "she clearly prioritizes the personal over the ecclesiastically mediated journey towards God."[27]

Twentieth-century Western researchers undertook a reassessment of the teachings of individual Greek fathers including Origen (Walter Volker 1931), Maximus the Confessor (by Hans Urs von Balthasar in 1941), and Gregory of Nyssa (by Jean Danielou in 1944). Though not entirely about deification, these studies helped spark its retrieval in the West. Deification itself was later studied in individual fathers Gregory of Nazianzus (Winslow 1979), Athanasius of Alexandria (Norman 1980), Irenaeus of Lyons (de Andia 1986), Maximus the Confessor (Larchet 1996), and Cyril of Alexandria (Keating 2004).[28]

St. Augustine (354-430) remains the most prominent classical theologian of the Western tradition in both its Catholic and Protestant strains. In 1986 Gerald Bonner published his still-influential historical study, "Augustine's Concept of Deification." New sermons have been discovered since, some of which touch on deification and one that is based upon it.[29] Augustine, like his Latin forebears, treats the idea of deification as if it were natural and standard within the Christian teaching. David Meconi writes about the centrality of deification in Augustine's thought and how he echoes the exchange formula found in most patristics:

---

[26] Zorgdrager 2014: 227.
[27] Zorgdrager 2014: 228.
[28] These and other studies are listed in Russell 2004: 6.
[29] *Dolbeau* 6 or *Mainz* 13. Puchniak (2006: 122-123) writes of this letter: "In what is a homiletic exposition of Psalm 81, [Augustine] gives voice to a rich theological anthropology. In so doing, he connects the concept of a 'deifying God' (*deificatorem deum*) to the soul's spiritual warfare, the biblical vision of salvation history, and the gathering of members of the ecclesial 'Body of Christ.'"

> [I]n order to make gods of those who were merely human, one who was God made himself human.[30]

We in the modern world are more prone to be surprised by such language than was he. The idea was so commonplace it was rarely disputed during Augustine's time, a time of increasing orthodoxy. McGuckin summarizes:

> The language of deification was never quite as dominant in the West, where it did not carry the main burden of redemption theory as it did with the Greek fathers, but it is a notion certainly found in parts of Augustine (*Sermon 192; Exposition of Ps. 29; Exposition of Ps. 146*) who uses it to denote the transformative effects of grace.[31]

The Latin-speaking Augustine sees things a little differently from the Greek-speaking fathers. For Augustine, God was "fundamentally intelligible, i.e., accessible to the mind."[32] Conversely, for the Greeks and Eastern Orthodoxy in general, there existed a rather unyielding barrier of apophaticism, a cloud of unknowing, that they speculated would forever stand between the Father and the human mind.

Augustine continually stresses the double love command of Jesus, which pushes active ethicism and valuation to the center of his soteriology or view of salvation, thus associating the idea of deification with the synoptic tradition and Jesus' teaching. I see in such mutual intelligibility and ethicism the epitome of Western deification, which should be thought of as a real deification into actual godhood. We will explore this association further and emphasize along with Augustine the sonship and reformation of the *Imago Dei*, the divine image of God granted us at moment of our creation.

---

[30] St. Augustine, *s.* 192.1; Hill, *Sermons* (III/6), 46; cited in David Meconi, *The One Christ: St. Augustine's Theology of Deification* (2013: xii).
[31] McGuckin 2007: 110 n. 1.
[32] Russell 2009: 118.

The highly influential Italian Medieval scholastic St. Thomas Aquinas (1225-1274) writes clearly and logically about the need for an ontological and essential commingling of Creator and created — despite the Father's transcendence. This is another area where the Western idea of deification will find its differentiation from the Eastern version. A. N. Williams, in *The Ground of Union: Deification in Aquinas and Palamas* (1999), compared the scholastic and methodical Aquinas with the more experiential Gregory Palamas, an influential Eastern monk who lived a few generations later. Among her major contentions, Williams indicates that Aquinas is open to the possibility of human beings coming to "see" the essence of God. Indeed, he announces it directly, as we will see. Townsend likewise finds that Thomas at one point clarifies that participation in God is a participation in God's very essence and concludes that Thomas has "no less than a comprehensive vision of deification deeply integrated into the whole of his thought."[33]

Among recent research into the rich vein of deification among Christian thinkers, the well-received anthology *Partakers of the Divine Nature: The History and Development of Deification in the Christian Tradition* (2007), edited by Michael J. Christensen and Jeffrey A. Wittung, contains a wide range of articles, some of which "venture into previously unexplored fields."[34] This volume includes essays on the patristic fathers (including J. A. McGuckin on the Cappadocians and Elena Vishnevskaya on *perichoresis* or mutual indwelling in Maximus the Confessor), an article on deification of the philosopher in ancient Greece by John R. Lenz, and one on deification in Paul by Stephen Finlan. The West is not neglected, as there are articles on St. Anselm (Kerr), Martin Luther (Linman), John Calvin (Billings), and John Wesley (Christensen), as well as one on famed Catholic theologian Karl Rahner (Caponi). Studies focused on Western proponents of deification support the idea that they were more likely to speak of an *essential* union of Creator and created than were the Eastern Palamites.

---

[33] Townsend 2015: 233.
[34] Gavrilyuk 2009: 654.

Two of the contributors to the above volume edited their own volume, *Theosis: Deification in Christian Theology* (2006). Besides having a helpful introduction, articles include those on theosis and Old Testament anthropology (Glazov), 2 Peter (Finlan), second-century apologists (Kharlamov), Athanasius and Irenaeus (Jeffrey D. Finch), Augustine (Puchniak), T. F. Torrance (Habets), and the Russian philosopher Soloviev (Finlan), whose nineteenth-century writings on "Godmanhood" sparked the rediscovery of deification in the East prior to Harnack. Interestingly, in his article "Reforming Theosis," Myk Habets [35] writes that early American preacher Jonathan Edwards (1703-1758) himself asserted "an ontological union" that is more radical than the Palamite version of union only with the energies.

Kharlamov went on to edit a sequel as well. In *Theosis: Deification in Christian Theology*. Vol. 2. (2011), Stephen Finlan contributes an article on "Deification in Jesus' Teaching," a rare but welcome topic. It also includes an English translation of an article by Russian historian Ivan Popov. In another article, Mark Medley finds the theme of deification in four contemporary Baptist theologians (Clark H. Pinnock, Stanley J. Grenz, Douglas Harink, and Paul S. Fiddes), and details how they do not seem to adhere to the Eastern essence-energies distinction (which we will examine later).

A recent anthology focuses entirely on the Western fathers. *Deification in the Latin Patristic Tradition* (2019), edited by Jared Ortiz. In the first essay, Ortiz examines the deification teaching behind the sacraments. Janet Sidaway contributes an excellent chapter on deification in the early Western theology of Hilary of Poitiers (c. 310-367). The last chapter, by Norman Russell, compares Greek and Latin deification without the misconceptions that have plagued the discussion since Harnack. The similarities are much closer than some in the recent past, particularly in the East, are liable to admit. There are also essays on Perpetua and Felicity, Tertullian, Novatian, Ambrose, Leo the Great, and Boethius (among others). Ron Haflidson contributes an article on Augustine's interesting idea of deification as rest ("We Shall Be That Seventh Day").

---

[35] Habets 2006: 150-151.

Deification East and West

It was common in the early twentieth century for Eastern commentators to assume that deification was a particularly Eastern doctrine of Christianity, largely neglected in the West. Much was made of the fact that Augustine, the main proponent in the West, emphasized "justification" in Christian salvation, thus influencing later Christian fundamentalism, which largely neglected Augustine's stated outcome of salvation by deification in favor of only the legal requirements to appease God, thus collapsing the basic process of deification (from purification to sanctification to glorification) down to the first step, thereby distorting the goal.

By the late twentieth century, the sharp distinction between East and West regarding deification was found not to hold. Foundational Western theologians like Augustine, Anselm, and Aquinas were just as apt to view deification as the effect and reason for salvation as their Eastern counterparts. And in fact, the Western writers were more prone to emphasize a more *Godlike* deification if you will, an essential, natural, and ontological connection and overlap between humanity and divinity.

The main difference from the beginning was that the Eastern fathers wrote in Greek while the Western wrote in Latin. Although translations were hard to come by in the early centuries, certainly Augustine knew of many of the Eastern fathers and they of him and perhaps of Tertullian and Hilary in earlier centuries. The Greek or Eastern patristics included Irenaeus, Clement of Alexandria, Origen, Athanasius, Cyril, Gregory of Nazianzus, Gregory of Nyssa, the anonymous Pseudo-Dionysius Areopagite, Maximus the Confessor, and Gregory Palamas. The Latin writers include Tertullian, Hilary of Poitiers, Augustine, Leo the Great, Gregory the Great, and the Medieval Scholastics Anselm of Canterbury and Thomas Aquinas. We have mentioned that the Western Reformers Martin Luther (1483-1546), John Calvin (1509-1564), and John Wesley (1703-1791) not only spoke approbatively of deification within their theologies, but saw it with Augustine and the Eastern fathers as the outcome of and reason for salvation.

McGuckin provides an apt general description of the Greek or Eastern Christian understanding of deification:

> In the Greek Christian understanding, the concept of deification is the process of the sanctification of Christians whereby they become progressively conformed to God; a conformation that is ultimately demonstrated in the glorious transfiguration of the 'just' in the heavenly kingdom, when immortality and a more perfect vision (and knowledge and experience) of God are clearly manifested in the glorification ... of the faithful.[36]

Daniel Keating comments that McGuckin's synopsis can be applied to the Western fathers as well:

> This statement employs a set of biblical terms (sanctification, conformation to Christ, transfiguration, vision) in order to identify the content of deification and (intentionally or not) links up with the Western patristic tradition (Hilary and Leo) by speaking of deification in terms of glorification.[37]

We shall find that both the Latin and Greek halves of the ancient Roman Empire held to the major themes and processes by which humans are deified, so the differences in practical terms are nonessential. The resulting deification is called by various names, including glorification, divinization, illumination, being born again or begotten from above, attaining sonship, restoration of the divine image and likeness of God, participation in the divine nature, being raised from the dead, ascending to heaven, entering the kingdom of God, and possessing eternal life. With increasing purification, which one might think of as minimalism in living or thinking, comes sanctification (also known as illumination, which highlights its

---

[36] McGuckin 2007: 95.
[37] Keating 2015: 280.

cognitive emphasis), and with this comes deification, an elevated state of being for the human being.

The major flaw that Eastern authors see in the Western approach was that the first stage (purification) increasingly became encroached upon by a justification in a juridical sense, which went against the West's best tendency to posit a natural relationship between humans and God. Justification would be a more legal and formal, thus distancing basis for both deification and salvation than the moral and ethical one Jesus himself proposed.

While Augustine does speak of justification, he also emphasizes the moral and ethical duty (and desire) to love and to share the other attributes of God, so the difference is not so much among the patristics East and West as it is with what was made of the justification idea (collapsing the steps of the process to just this one) in recent centuries. I entirely agree with the Eastern fathers that salvation runs much deeper than juridical or legal categories can go, and that in fact the Christian God is not bound to such human categories and viewpoints.

Deification existed as a scriptural concept long before it acquired its technical language in 363 CE, when Gregory Nazianzus coined the Greek term *"theosis,"* which in Latin was translated *"deification."* Prior to the birth of that technical term, it was known simply as "becoming gods" and was fostered through the aforementioned mediating images. I will seek to show that none of these can be mistaken for anything *but* deification.

While the East was increasingly systematic in its approach to deification, effectively nailing down the doctrine in some respects, there was a negative side to this. It landed on certain now-questionable assumptions that seemed common sensical at the time the doctrines were solidified. One of these assumptions was that, despite becoming gods themselves, human beings were by nature forever different from God, limited and inferior, a view I intend to question in this volume.

This assumption, that we are different kinds of gods than God or Jesus, sometimes only nominally so, sometimes analogically, leads to other questionable assumptions, such as the idea that we are "adopted" and not begotten into sonship with God and therefore into godhood. Only Jesus' sonship was natural and "begotten"; ours is of an inferior kind. This view is based on the now outdated philosophical idea that a perfect being (i.e., God) can create only imperfect beings because they were born of change. Such a view does justice neither to ourselves nor to God. It makes for inequality from the start, and it has nothing to do with Jesus' teaching about sonship, which was all about us and not so much about him. In fact, I will show that neither has it anything to do with Paul's teaching about either sonship or deification. He uses this language of "adoptive" sonship for a different purpose altogether, to proclaim the adoption of Gentiles as Abraham's offspring and thus heirs of the promised blessings. It has nothing to do with deification itself, although it has been used as a basis for both Eastern and Western versions.

Some scholars see the Eastern versions of deification as being superior to the West's due to the fact that they make distinctions between the image and likeness of God and between the essence and energies of God. I will make the case that these distinctions, while possibly helpful for explaining the human perspective of deification's process, are not *essential* for a fully restorative doctrine of deification. In fact, the essence-energies distinction was formulated as a way around a more natural, ontological relationship, and such begottenness is indicated by the ubiquitous use of the familial language of sonship in the New Testament.

Paul Gavrilyuk comments on how the lack of rigidity of the theme in Western theology provides an opportunity to reexamine this ancient, lost idea in a new light:

> It is remarkable that despite its exalted status, the concept of deification is not mentioned explicitly in the dogmatic definitions of the first Seven Ecumenical Councils. The dearth of dogmatic precision has contributed to the concept's considerable fluidity.[38]

---

[38] Gavrilyuk 2009: 648.

Although deification teaching shaped the dogmas so hotly "debated" (sometimes with fisticuffs!) at these church councils, deification itself was common knowledge and so it escaped such scrutiny. Its consequent fluidity provides us in our modern scientific and psychological age a golden opportunity to derive new insights that may provide for a better understanding of this phenomenon with the help of scripture.

Definition of a Fully Restorative Deification

All it took for the West to rediscover that Augustine, Aquinas, and even Luther and Calvin had an understanding of deification was a more careful reading of them that was open to such ideas or language. Everyone in the world is blinded to some degree by presumptions based on preconceptions. These become fixed limits in and on our minds whereby we can no longer see what is really there to see, and we never think to ask if there is more to see than our preconceptions would allow. We decide too hastily, or leave it to the world to decide for us, what reality is, without asking and remaining open until all the pressing questions and intuitions are understood.

As time unspools, these preconceptions often fall away to become parts of history, but sometimes they are resistant even to being shown to be inaccurate. These preconceptions hastily established in the past out of the anxiety of uncertainty, affect how much or how little we are able to see and know in the present. Without periodic reassessment of these preconceptions, we unnecessarily limit the scriptural revelation, and miss the totally new way of thinking, seeing, feeling, experiencing, and *being* it teaches. The scriptural revelation unfolds as *we* evolve to meet and understand it. I believe this kind of reassessment is due for Jesus' teaching, and the Bible in general, even after two thousand years of intensive study and often brilliant theology. The Bible is infinitely deep and rich, and to experience just a bit of this is to begin to understand a depth and richness in ourselves and those around us that we had overlooked in the past.

Studying the patristics and modern commentators on deification, we learn quickly that most take a very conservative approach to the potential for human godhood. Humans are transformed, deified, but they never really shake their original human nature. They never really become actual gods. The underlying premise seems to be that because they were created human, true godhood will always remain tantalizingly out of reach.

For most of the patristics, we are made gods not by nature but by a later grace. We did not start as gods, however they understood that term, but rather become gods at some later point – generally not until the mass resurrection at the end of the world. This leads to certain questions. Did God create us incomplete, in process of development, or did he create complete, mature, divine beings like himself? Is it even conceivable that he set his newborn children on an obstacle course, a testing ground, with the goal in sight but hurdles to jump before we get to where he wants us in the first place? Or did a loving God create his children to experience complete joy and peace from the start? The test is this: If a loving human parent would default one way or the other, then a loving God would do so a thousand times more intently. As Jesus puts it, "If you then, who are evil, know how to give good gifts to your children, how much more will your Father in heaven give good things to those who ask him!" (Matthew 7.11). Thus, we must argue the latter, that God placed us in complete perfection, hence the obstacles we face must all be of our own making, and therefore our responsibility to look beyond.

These are not extraordinary questions, but rather, common sense questions that anyone might ask. How we answer such questions tells us what we truly believe about not only ourselves but God as well. How we were created, or with what nature, tells us not only who we are but who God is. We are growing closer to the truth ourselves as we narrow it down.

Western commentators are generally more open to humans becoming actual gods through deification despite Augustine's dictum that humans become gods by grace, not by nature. His stress was on the gratuitousness of the gift, the unearned quality of the reward, and the fact that human beings could never quite attain to real godhood on their own, without divine help. We as humans cannot deify ourselves, which is true enough, but the idea was taken too far when it was taken to mean that humans had a totally debased, debauched nature and nothing left of the *Imago Dei*, the divine image in and with which they were created.

A fully restorative deification makes clear that human beings do not make *themselves* gods, a major concern of many theologians East and West. Our godhood was a gift from God that *precedes* our earthly existence. We did not create our true and original divine being; although the children of God do share the Father's creativity.[39] But while on earth we are limited to the construction of a temporary self and world. We have made ourselves unaware of our own underlying eternal reality and believe we are the fleeting, worldly, anxious self we have constructed piecemeal over time. We can deny and forget but we cannot actually lose the grounded truth of our being. This underlying original truth is irrevocable and essentially inalterable. This corresponds to the teaching of many especially Eastern patristics that we did not lose the divine image in the fall, but only our likeness to God, which is under our control. We regain our freedom of mind along with our original identity, which remains forever as it always was, even while we believe that we are lesser beings.

We will see that scripturally deification is associated with our being called children, sons or daughters, of God. This speaks to a genetic (figuratively, not materially, speaking), begotten, essential and natural yet supernatural connection. It is an *ontological* connection in that it says that we and God share the same type or *order* of being, the same nature and essence. There is one nature

---

[39] I base this idea of our original selves as creators on such biblical ideas as Jesus' having said, "whatever the Father does, the Son does likewise" (John 5:19). It is also self-evident in the fact that we have complete freedom of mind to think and feel and create whatever we want, even to the point of making a reality for ourselves and living in it.

and essence because there is one God, and so all his creations must be like him. And this means that we are children of God even now, but we no longer realize it. In truth, there is only one type of *being*: God's. Although this is not the usual patristic understanding, I will seek to show that the Bible has more to say about this than has previously been understood.

In addition to being more comprehensible, a fully restorative view of deification is more comprehensive in that it interweaves every major thread of Christianity including its soteriology or views on salvation, its Christology, its eschatology or views on the end of the world or age, its mediating images, its anthropology and its processes or methods. The processes or ways to deification are the same in East or West, except that they have slightly different emphases. Moreover, a fully restorative view is comprehensive in that it must include every part of God's original perfect creation; it is truly universal.

A fully restorative view of deification is also different from the norm because it is more certain, more guaranteed, so much so that it might even be said to be *predestined* and *preexistent* (in the sense that it takes precedence over our earthly existence). We cannot lose the divine image, but we can delude ourselves into thinking we lost it. The ultimate goal of salvation is to be restored to the same graced state we were granted in the timeless beginning, albeit perhaps better appreciated. Salvation is a return to our own original but forgotten godhood, which requires revelation and realization rather than transformation per se.

This is a further advantage of a fully restorative deification, that it does not require any transformation — except of mind. A physical or mechanistic exchange of being is not required; there is no need to imagine an intermingling of substances (divine or human). The transformation by degrees of which Paul speaks, ending in our glorification, is a return to the spiritual being we always were and still are. Jesus proposes that we reattain our original nature and identity as children of God by loving like God — universally and completely. Deification is thus an entirely internal shift which determines how we understand reality itself, so that even our perception of the world begins to reflect our own divinity.

Method and Aim

After an examination into the biblical foundations of deification, the first half of this book will investigate the nature of our creation by God, asking whether we were created to be mortal or immortal (or on the razor's edge-between them, as some believed), how exactly we are supposed to think of ourselves as gods and children of God, and what is the true nature of God and consequently of ourselves who are created in his image.

We will arrange our discussion of creation in the middle of the book around contrasting views that were established in formative Christianity by Irenaeus in the second century and Origen in the third, before the church hierarchies chose one and nailed it down in the fourth century. Irenaeus' view influenced most of the fathers who followed, which was that God created incomplete, imperfect, and even infantile beings in need of development, born in the process of becoming, while Origen argued instead that God created perfect, complete, noncorporeal, spiritual minds, made in the manner of the divine image.

Throughout the study, I will be exploring the Bible and patristics specifically for those ontological aspects that inform us who we are as God-created or begotten beings. We will seek to distinguish these from the anthropological aspects that inform us who we are as humans. We are looking to map out an internal structure of the human being, highlighting those ontological or deiform aspects that are sometimes missed both by ancient patristics and modern commentators alike. I will contend along these lines that human beings carry a bipartite structure, a dual nature, divine and human, the divine more basic, primary, and foundational than the other. Therefore, our two natures are fundamentally unable to be fully integrated, and this is why the Bible, and Jesus in particular, presents us with such a stark choice between two realities and ways of being.

As we select and sort out these ontological aspects of the human being as found in the Bible, we are drawing closer to an understanding of the experiential aspects of deification: how human beings experience it. These aspects together comprise how we subjectively experience our increasing godhood, the internal process of deification, and its recovery in the one place we failed to look for it: within the depths of our own innermost being.

Jesus' teaching is strangely neglected in the history of deification teaching, but in fact it holds great promise for clarifying our thinking about this subject. If Jesus is truly a supernatural being who came into the world from the higher reality of heaven to save the world, then he would obviously be our foremost authority, the one who knows best whereof he speaks. Therefore, even to the most Christologically minded, his words (as far as we can ascertain and understand them) should carry the most weight. Paul and the gospel writers (Matthew, Mark, Luke and John) are Jesus' very early interpreters, the first theologians whose writings survived, Paul from just outside Jesus' inner circle, having met him in a blinding vision but never in person, the gospels (including John, in my view) most likely from vantage points within the inner circle, all agreeing on the major points of his ultimately deifying and thus radical teaching, but expressing them in a plethora of mediating images.

Jesus taught of an internal kingdom of God, a different kind of reality that transcends yet blesses the world. It is more than a new way of living; it is a new way of *being*. He urged his followers to love *like God* and be perfect and complete *like God*, capacities and potentialities humans in that time and place they did not know they had. He spoke of being sons and daughters of this entirely spiritual God, of having "eternal life," of our being one with this God and with each other in a transcendent state of mind, being, and interrelationship he called "the kingdom (or reality) of God" and "heaven."

Almost from the start, while still walking the earth, theology and Christology were already heaping layers of unnecessary complexity onto Jesus' own simple teaching and life story, thus effectively shunting aside his teaching about humankind in general in favor of dogmatic constructions *about him*. Therefore, one of my methods will be to examine his own words, which themselves help us walk back or simply bracket the elaborate Christology in favor of more fundamental, genuinely Jesus-derived principles. Historical biblical criticism has been of great help in determining Jesus' own true words and teachings as best we can.

To detheologize as much as possible means in part to trace the patristic arguments back to their original biblical sources, then reevaluate those sources to see if they might better be interpreted with greater simplicity in a more self-evident and experiential way. We are seeking the experiential aspects behind the dogma and the human or shareable aspects behind the Christology.

The main questions we will focus on are these: Will we truly know ourselves as gods, as Jesus and the patristics assert? If so, are we gods by nature (ontologically) or only later by acquisition and "adoption"? Either way, I will argue, we are gods by grace, but in the former way *also* by nature.

I will not spend much space on sacramentalism and ecclesiasticism, and will employ as little dogmatic theology as possible, although these are important aspects for the early fathers. They were building the fledgling church. I am more interested in the aforementioned aspects that apply to *any* individual, any human being, belonging to any denomination or to no denomination. The problem came when theology overstepped and insisted that Jesus' godhood was different from our own, his sonship unique to him and to no one else, a lesson I believe he neither taught nor intended that we learn.

A fully restorative model of deification, which teaches an actual deification and actual godhood, can help prevent the doctrine of deification from becoming just another piece of furniture in the Christian system. It is much more than fodder for researchers and theologians, or even only Christian believers. It is meant for everyone; its universality is one of its main characteristics and another of its key advantages. It means that every human being carries not only the potential, but the reality of godhood within themselves. And there are certain long-established but oft-overlooked ways of both recognizing and experiencing this godhood.

Chapter Sequence

This extended Introduction along with Chapter 1 is meant to provide a brief overview of Christian deification and to show how quickly and mightily it blossomed in the early church to become the centerpiece of its theology. Chapter 1 focuses on the biblical foundations of deification in the writings of the patristics. These biblical foundations include Jesus having called human beings "gods" in John 10:35, the idea that humans were created in the image and likeness of God (Gen. 1:26-27), and the revelation in 2 Peter 1:4 that Christianity aims to make us "participants in the divine nature." We will also survey the exchange formula for deification, a version of which can be found in nearly every Christian theologian: "Jesus, a god, became human so that humans might be gods."

In Chapter 2, we find further scriptural support as we investigate the views of the early theologians regarding when and how human beings receive immortality, a universally recognized hallmark of godhood. The prominence of "eternal life" in New Testament teaching points to the importance of deification, and it is spoken of as something we can experience in earthly existence simply by a radical shift of perspective. While most of the patristics believed that immortality came only with the general resurrection at the end of time, I will contend that in a fully restorative view, immortality is ours from the beginning but it goes unrealized when we identify exclusively with the body.

In Chapter 3, we examine how thinking of ourselves as children of God, a prominent idea in the Bible, is a mediating image for deification. Having heard this concept often, we miss the great significance and power involved in being children of God. Children of God would be divine beings, like God in essence and nature. Jesus teaches that it is by changing our minds to love like God that we realize our sonship (or daughterhood) as children of God. We will also clarify how the adoptive sonship language of Paul refers, not to deification as the patristics often saw it, but rather to an acceptance of Gentiles into the blessings promised to the descendants of Abraham. I will show that Paul himself taught an ontological sonship similar to Jesus' teaching of begotten sonship in the Gospel of John.

In Chapter 4, we look into the nature and essence of God, beginning with an explanation of divine simplicity, the nearly universally accepted theological principle whereby God is one with his attributes (love, goodness, beauty, and truth, etc.) and his attributes are all one in him as well. He is fully identified with them and they cannot be parsed out. I will argue that this applies to his creation as well. We can define God most simply as pure "being" (life itself without change), "spirit" (as Jesus states in John 4), "Father" (Creator or spiritual Source), and "love" (as in 1 Jn. 4:8, 16). Learning to conceptualize God in this way can reveal much about the perfect and perfectly abstract gods that we ourselves were meant to be.

Chapter 5 investigates the nature of our creation as gods. We will first examine, for context, the vociferously negative New Testament attitudes about "the world," which indicate that the world is not our true home or natural environment. The world as we know it cannot be God's original creation, being ruled over (it is asserted) by the devil and death. Jesus also taught that "the world" was opposed to both our "life" and "soul." This leads us to consider the probability of another, prior creation for our soul, a perfect creation of perfect spiritual beings. Origen proposed that this creation of perfect and perfectly free spiritual minds or intelligences preceded the creation of the world. We will see that there are valid scriptural reasons to believe this.

In Chapter 6 we delve specifically into the biblical idea of a fall or defection from the original perfect creation. As gods to begin with, there is only one way to fall, and that is downward on the ladder of being. I will posit that this fall from original grace erected psychological walls in the mind and resulted in a split self with two opposing natures competing mainly for our attention and devotion. The two very different realities of which Jesus spoke, the fallen world and the kingdom of God, are divergent states of being, ways of living, and ways of knowing reality. They are dissociated in the sense that each is hidden from the other; they can be fully experienced only alternately, not simultaneously.

Chapter 7 will consider the controversial topic of preexistence in the Bible, the idea (proposed by Origen and others, including many places in Augustine) that human beings existed as immortal gods and spirits *before* the world was formed and thus long before we were born. Whether we accept the possibility or not has ramifications for how we view deification. We will find that Jesus' preexistence is meant to reflect and spark our own. Such an idea would confirm that we are "not of the world," that is, not beholden to the world's version of our reality.

Chapter 8 examines how restorative deification can provide a solid foundation for natural theology, the ancient idea that spirituality is universal among all human beings, ubiquitous, and not confined to any one religion or only to religion. Next, we explore the role of the Holy Spirit as our natural inner guide back to our original reality and to our deification. Along with its teaching and reminding function, we will find that the mere presence of the Spirit is deifying because it spiritualizes the mind. Although not an entirely new concept with Jesus, it was elaborated upon and further personalized by him.

Chapter 9 will examine the importance of deification for Christian salvation in the Bible and in theologians from both East and West. Legal justification and absolution by the cross played but small parts in the overall picture until recent times. They are just two of at least a dozen ways St. Paul expressed the need for purification and sanctification for the purpose of glorification (deification). We will then explain how a fully restorative, ontologically grounded deification reinterprets the Augustinian juridical concept of "original sin" as a denial of our "original grace."

Chapter 10 will investigate the ways in which individuals are deified, some of the various processes and methods by which deification can be experienced. We will find that the two major categories of approaches, the positive and negative ways, often employed to distinguish Western from Eastern ways, respectively, are best used together in a kind of inner dialectic. We will detail how most patristics believed that the contemplation of Godly things and qualities would deify the mind, and we will further investigate how Jesus taught an ethical way to godhood through his instruction to love like God, the greatest commandment that fulfills the law, thus to share the full perfection of our Creator.

Chapter 11 will reassess what the scriptural "end of the world (or age)" means in light of a fully restorative deification. Observing how wildly popular the apocalyptic genre became in the two centuries just before Jesus arrived, we will find ample biblical evidence of a "realized" eschatology, an individualized experience of the end of artificiality that can happen any time, at different times for different individuals, and does not await a distant future. The same goes for associated eschatological concepts such as the kingdom of God, the last judgment, and the resurrection, each of which we will investigate in detail. We will also expound upon the great end-time vision, such as that found in the Book of Revelation: after all the spectacular cosmic drama comes a restoration of the original reality of spiritual light and perfect peace.

Chapter 12 will delve into perhaps the most controversial topic related to a fully restorative deification, that of *apokatastasis*, or universal restoration, the idea that all beings created by God will be saved and fully restored. We will find that, not only does it fit with the great themes of the Bible, it also fits with the idea of a perfect and perfectly loving God. Next we reexamine biblically the ideas of hell and heaven and reinterpret them based on what we have learned. Finally, we finish with Jesus' teaching of the oneness and mutual indwelling of souls with God and with one another (via a sense of corporate sonship and collective Christhood), which greatly reinforces the ontological argument.

In the Conclusion, we will expound upon the nature of humanity contrasted with divinity based on the evidence presented. The question is and always was: Which of our two natures is primary, and therefore should be predominant? Which do we follow most naturally when we seek only truth and to be ourselves? In the first of three Appendices, we will compare a fully restorative deification with a synopsis of patristic teaching on restoration. In the second we will seek to clarify where a fully restorative deification fits into deification typology, or whether it necessitates new categories. In the third we will examine the essence-energies distinction in more detail, pointing out that, while not necessary for a restorative deification, it might be advantageous in understanding its process and experience from a human perspective.

A Note on Inclusive Meaning behind the Patriarchal Language

It seems obvious, but should be made explicit, that although the original biblical and patristic language is almost entirely masculine and patriarchal, the teaching is meant to be generic, directed to all people of whatever gender — men and women, daughters along with sons always implied. Jesus had not been part of the world system that relegated femininity to secondary status. The Gospels tell us that women were among his closest disciples or students, including Mary Magdalene, Susanna,[40] and Salome.[41] The New Testament also notes several females who supported and helped establish the burgeoning church in various ways. Paul, too, from a slightly more traditional and patriarchal mindset, had specifically taught his audience to think beyond the male/female dynamic, while the extracanonical and proto-Gnostic Gospel of Thomas, compiled not long after the canonical gospels, proclaims the perfect union of male/female as a way of emphasizing our original spiritual therefore genderless beings.[42]

The words related to God and our own godhood in the New Testament all point to our inner being. "Being," "spirit," "soul,"

---

[40] Luke 8:1-3; Mary is also referred to in Mk. 16:9.
[41] Mk. 15:40-41; 16:1.
[42] In log. 22, Jesus speaks about making "male and female" one, along with the "inside and the outside" and "the upper and the lower." We will examine Thomas' light images, which also rise above such distinctions, in chapter 11.

"mind," and "heart" all refer to a deeper level than physical differences can go. Gender differences are meaningless to spirit and the higher mind. They are surface concerns, not core concerns, unless perhaps we think of gender differences in the Jungian sense as two complementary aspects of a complete being: the masculine principle (*animus*) being active and dynamic complementing the feminine (*anima*) which is open and receptive. Psychologically speaking, then, gender is a spectrum upon which each being seeks their own mean or balance in their striving for authenticity and genuineness, seeking their complement first in others before ultimately finding the completion within themselves.

Nothing in the realm of form has permanent bearing on our eternal being. Although the Bible calls God our "Father" and Jesus his "Son," this was simply the predominantly patriarchal language of ancient history, two millennia ago (nearly three in the case of the Hebrew Bible or Old Testament). But the revelations and insights peppering scripture far surpass the one-sided language in which they are couched. The revelations and insights are meant for every mind and every heart, for all, and so "sons of God" always indicates "daughters of God" as well, but both they and God inhabit a realm beyond surface distinctions altogether.

1

THE BIBLICAL FOUNDATIONS OF DEIFICATION

We begin with an examination of the major scriptural underpinnings around which the patristic teaching of deification coalesced. The three main passages (one of them cited by Jesus in John 10) recur again and again in the patristics as support for their thinking about deification. We will also survey the exchange formula for deification found in nearly every Christian theologian and patristic, teaching that our human nature was destined to cede to divinity as our true nature.

"You are Gods"

Jesus himself introduced the idea that ordinary human beings have a capacity for godhood. It all began with his rather offhand comment:

> Is it not written in your law, 'I said, you are gods'? [35]If those to whom the word of God came were called 'gods' — and the scripture cannot be annulled — [36]can you say that the one whom the Father has sanctified and sent into the world is blaspheming because I said, 'I am God's Son'? (John 10:34-36)

Jesus, here citing Psalm 82,[43] affirms that human beings can rightly be called "gods" (*theoi*) by holy scripture, and he reinforces this by saying that the scripture cannot be broken. He also equates this godhood of human beings with being sons or children of God (v. 36). It was thus Jesus who introduced the idea of human beings being called "gods" into Christianity.

This passage, along with Psalm 82 from which Jesus quotes, sparked a deifying fire in early Christian theology. Early Christian apologist Justin Martyr (c. 100-165 CE), also known as Justin the Philosopher, zeroes in on the universalism of the Psalm, understanding from it that:

> [A]*ll men* are deemed worthy of becoming 'gods,' and of having power to become sons of the Highest.[44]

Note again the symmetry between "gods" and "sons of God," signifying that they are seen as synonymous.[45] The patristics after Justin see "sons" and "gods" as being one and the same. Becoming children of God is a well-known mediating image in Christianity, taught by Jesus himself in all four gospels. Justin writes that the Word of God "makes mortals immortal, mortals god." [46] Life is lifted to a higher level, transcending the human situation all the way to divinity, because human beings are meant by God to be gods.

Early Bishop of Lyons and noted heresiologist Irenaeus (c. 130-202) interprets Psalm 82's "but you shall die like men" as applying to those who refuse to accept their own deification. They "have not received the gift of adoption" as children of God and thus they "defraud human nature of promotion into God." [47] Again, deification or "promotion into God" is what is expected of Christians, and writ larger, of all human beings.

---

[43] Some English versions number it as Psalm 81.
[44] Justin Martyr. "*Dialogue with Trypho* 124." *Ante-Nicene Fathers*. Ed. Alexander Roberts. Vol. 1. New York: C. Scribner's Sons, 1905, (*ANF* 1:262). My emphasis.
[45] "Sons of God" always means sons and daughters, without reference to gender.
[46] Justin Martyr. "Discourse to the Greeks 5." (*ANF* 1:272).
[47] Irenaeus. "*Against Heresies* 3: 19: 1," (*ANF*.1:448).

Early Christian theologians regularly referred to human beings as gods in their writings, after the manner of Jesus in John 10:34-35 and Psalm 82:6-7. Latin theologian Tertullian of Carthage (160-220 CE) also believed that Psalm 82 signified the eventual deification of human beings:

> We shall be even gods, if we shall deserve to be among those of whom He declared: 'I have said, you are gods,' and, 'God stands in the congregation of gods.'[48]

If humans can indeed be called gods, then this would render the original God, the Father and Creator, to be "the God of gods." What would God create except gods like himself, especially if he wanted beings with whom he could fully relate? We find indications of this all over the Psalms: "The God of gods, the Lord hath spoken" (Ps. 50:1); and again, "Confess to the God of gods" (Ps. 136:2); and again, "He is a great King above all gods" (Ps. 95:3). These are not only remnants of an older, polytheistic phase of the religion. Such passages have become in Jesus' mind (or at least John's) revelatory of the idea that God dwells with gods and children of God because they are like their Creator, the God of gods.

Also in the Hebrew scriptures (or Old Testament), the prophet Hosea (pre-722 BCE) declared that God's people, despite their current waywardness, would yet be called "sons of the living God" (Hos 1:10). There was an expectation even in this early stage of Judaism that human beings would eventually be considered divine beings, as gods and children of God, and the prophecy declares they would be countless, innumerable.

Note that Jesus in John 10:34-35 triply affirms that human beings can in certain circumstances rightly be called "gods" (*theoi*), first by citing the original Psalm 82, then by placing its authorship in his mouth ("I said"), then by reminding his (hostile) audience that "scripture cannot be annulled" (v. 35). The "gods" here are specifically "those to whom the word of God came" (v. 35), meaning (presumably) those who originally received the Word of God in the

---

[48] Tertullian, *Adv. Herm.* 5 (PL 2,202B; *ANF* Select Library).

form of the Torah, the core law of Moses. Jesus implies here that this early reception of the law is deifying, so that its devotees live as gods, i.e., in a blessed, revelatory state.

The gods are those human beings with whom the Word of God rested or found a home. Neyrey expresses the association in Judaism between living with the Word of God and being gods in this way: "receiving God's word (Torah) makes one holy, and if holy, then sinless, and if sinless, then deathless."[49] And if deathless, then gods. Immortality was considered a hallmark of godhood in both Jewish religion and the Greek and Roman philosophy of Jesus' time.

Note that Jesus identifies "gods" with sonship to God (Jn. 10: 36). The original Psalm Jesus cites here, Psalm 82, speaks of human beings as "gods" and "sons" or children of God who somehow made a wrong turn and fell into an inferior state of being:

> God has taken his place in the divine council;
> in the midst of the gods he holds judgment. ...
> [6]I say, 'You are gods,
> sons of the Most High, all of you;
> [7]nevertheless, you shall die like men,
> and fall like any prince.' (Psalm 82:1, 6-7)

The gods being addressed here are at least potentially immortal and in direct communication and participation with God. By Jesus' time, such passages were directing human beings to the idea that they were originally created to be gods, part of a divine council or family, but these gods somehow fell from this high and immortal status and identification to become mortal human beings.

We have already noted Clement of Alexandria (150-215) having stated that "he who listens to the Lord, and follows the prophecy given by Him, will be formed perfectly in the likeness of the teacher — made a god going about in flesh."[50] Clement, like the other patristics we have mentioned, was highly educated in both

---

[49] Neyrey 1989: 656.
[50] Clement of Alexandria. *The Stromata, or Miscellanies.* "Book VII, Chapter XVI," (*ANF* 2:553).

philosophy and scripture, yet scholarship finds that their ideas about deification as developed in their writings sprang primarily from their reading of scripture and Jewish understandings of it. Patristics have much to say about what it means that scripture calls us gods, whether in potential or fully-fledged, and what this means for our understanding about ourselves and our relationship with God.

Deification was gradually being systemized by all these fathers, but the first truly systematic theologian produced by the church, the great but misunderstood Origen of Alexandria (185-253), proposes the idea that our godhood actually *preceded* our humanhood. It had priority not so much in time, for our godhood was created in God's own timeless reality, but in primacy, in reality. We were gods first and foundationally, immortal minds (*logika*) and bodiless spiritual beings, and we will eventually know ourselves as gods again because the end will be like the timeless beginning. We will expound upon his views later.

Athanasius of Alexandria (296-373) equates sons and gods, stating that "we are sons and gods because of the Word in us."[51] Maximus the Confessor (580-662) writes about how "we may consort with God and become gods, receiving from God our existence as gods."[52] Basil the Great of Caesarea (330-379) sums it up well:

[B]ecoming a god is the highest goal of all.[53]

In the modern world we do not normally think of a reality populated by gods. We think of one God, and a monotheistic universe, but we have seen that God himself is surrounded by other gods in many Psalms, including the one cited by Jesus. God's oneness is inclusive of his creations, and so they must be divine like he is. God

---

[51] Athanasius of Alexandria. "*Against the Arians* 3: 25." *Nicene and Post-Nicene Fathers*. Ed. Philip Schaff. Vol. 4. New York: Christian Literature, 1892. 407. Print. Ser. 2.
[52] Maximus the Confessor. "Various Texts 1: 27-29." *Philokalia*. Ed. G.E.H. Palmer. Vol. 2. London: Faber and Faber, 1981. 170-171. Print.
[53] Basil of Caesarea, *On the Spirit* 9.23 (*NPNF* 2 8:16).

is still one; both religions remain monotheistic. However, scripture tells us it is God's will that his creations be like him, even to the point of being called *gods*. As Clement of Alexandria stated, "man becomes God, since God so wills."[54] And the Will of God, like the Word of God, is unbreakable. It *must* be done.

Historian Carl Mosser concludes:

> The earliest patristic writers understood Ps. 82:6–7 as a summary description of the creation and fall of humanity. God created humanity with the intention that they should be his immortal sons.[55]

This association of sonship with godhood remained strong with Western theologian Augustine (354-430), who expressed it directly:

> If then we have been made sons of god, we have also been made gods.[56]

We are gods but currently broken, having since fallen to mortal gods, gods in need of rehabilitation. We lost our immortality and incorruptibility and our claim to the infinite benefits of godhood. Now we firmly believe we are something different than what we really are. Yet, in truth we can only be what God wills us to be.

Created in the Image of God

Seeking further scriptural evidence of deification in the Genesis creation stories, the early Christian theologians landed on this passage from the Book of Genesis:

---

[54] Clement of Alexandria. "Instructor 3: 1." *Ante-Nicene Fathers*. Ed. Alexander Roberts. Vol. 2. New York: C. Scribner's Sons, 1905. 271. Print.
[55] Mosser 2005: 98.
[56] Aug. *On the Psalms* 50.2 (*NPNF* 1:178).

> Then God said, 'Let us make humankind in our image, according to our likeness'....
> ²⁷ So God created humankind in his image,
>   in the image of God he created them. (Genesis 1:26-27)

Human beings are created "in the image of God," which means that God is the archetype, the prototype, the model, after which human beings are made. Because God is not a body, this cannot be understood to be a physical resemblance; it must be one of spirit and mind instead. "Spirit" is simply a general descriptor of the invisible, inner reality of mind and heart and pure soul. Each of us is aware to some extent of the reality of mind — it is our subjective and internal world — but few realize it to be a separate reality.

Justin writes that humankind's original likeness to God contrasts with our present existence because it signifies a state of being without suffering and death:

> [M]en were made like God, free from suffering and death, provided that they kept His commandments, and were deemed deserving of the name of his sons, and yet they, becoming like Adam and Eve, work out death for themselves.[57]

Justin sees in the Genesis creation story an indication of what humankind was meant to be. He believed that Jesus came to restore to human beings the original image and likeness of God and the original deified state of Adam and Eve. With this restorative understanding, deification is a return to this pure and perfect state lost in the fall. Justin's disciple, Tatian (120-180), likewise saw Christianity as leading ultimately towards a recovery of Adam's lost original divine image and thus his immortality.

Irenaeus similarly taught that Jesus sought to restore the knowledge of this original image and likeness of God in humanity.

---

[57] Justin Martyr, *Dialogue with Trypho*, 124, (ANF 1:262).

> When he became incarnate, and was made man, he recapitulated in himself the long line of human beings, and furnished us, in a brief, comprehensive manner, with salvation; so that what we had lost in Adam; namely, to be according to the image and likeness of God, that we might recover in Christ Jesus.[58]

Irenaeus states that Jesus saves humankind by restoring to it what Adam lost, namely the divine image and likeness, by recapitulating for Adam, deciding and living on earth as Adam should have.

Some later patristics tended more clearly to distinguish between the image and the likeness, saying that humankind lost only the *likeness* to God via Adam's fall, but retained the divine *image*. I agree with such a distinction because the creations of God did not lose everything in the fall. They *remain* divine creations of God, immortal beings, sons/daughters and "gods." Thus, they retain the divine image in which they were created, which can never be lost to them. The likeness to God and the experience of this likeness is the part that they can accept or reject. Because of the goodness of God, they have free minds and are not forced to accept even their own greatest happiness and infinitude.

The distinction between image and likeness runs in the East through Clement of Alexandria, Evagrius, Diadochus, and Maximus. Following Augustine, Western tradition does not generally distinguish between the two terms. All the patristics agreed that the likeness could be reacquired via cultivation of and immersion in the divine attributes such as love, truth, beauty, and the highest good.

There are parallels to Genesis 1:27 elsewhere in Hebrew scripture. Ecclesiasticus (aka Sirach, c. 190 BCE) 17:3 states that when God created humankind, "He endowed them with strength like his own, and made them in his own image," indicating that humans were created with an inherent divine power. A similar understanding

---

[58] Ireneaus, cited in *The Scandal of the Incarnation: Ireneaus Against the Heresies, Selected and Introduced by Hans Urs von Balthasar,* trans. John Saward (SF: Ignatius Press, 1981), 56.

is found elsewhere in the intertestamental literature (texts written between the Old and New Testaments):

> God made man for incorruption
> and made him in the image of his own eternity. (Wisdom 2:23)

By the time the Book of Wisdom (also known as the Wisdom of Solomon) was written, within a hundred years before Jesus,[59] a burgeoning sense of eternal life was filtering into Judaism. The divine image from Gen. 1:27 is associated here with godhood and its characteristic "incorruption" and "eternity." To have been created in the image of God means that godhood is the true essence of humankind, imprinted deep on its being, *as* its being. This idea of the divine image being present in humankind went well beyond simply having dominion over the earth. It meant that humankind had a transcendent potential, a godlike origin, destiny, and overall reality.

Humankind having been created in the divine image presents us with a new way of conceiving and perceiving humankind and its deification. We are as timeless as God if we are created in his image and share in his reality. Just to share the reality God knows is to be like him. But to have been created in such a way as to be designed after him, in our mind and in our thoughts, is to transcend human nature altogether so that it is no longer an impediment and distraction but now serves the divine element.

The *image* is the structural element; it is our divine being, which cannot be lost. God willed it, and so it must still be true in his reality. The *likeness* is the process element, the experiential product of our choice whether or not to know ourselves as created. Our choice to restore the likeness to our awareness will also restore the divine image to our remembrance. We shall see that in Jesus' teaching the human being assimilates to God from the inside, by emulating and sharing the subjective mind and feeling state of God — specifically God's universally loving state of mind. This would

---

[59] This apocryphal book in the Wisdom tradition (with Proverbs, Ecclesiastes, and Job) was thought to have been composed in the mid-first century BCE.

seem to bring together the two elements and unify them in one teaching. Through reacquisition of the likeness to God by loving like God, says Jesus, we realize ourselves to be children of God, divine beings like God.[60] In Pauline teaching, we can refamiliarize ourselves with the image through "being renewed in knowledge" (Colossians 3:10) and "being conformed to the image" (Romans 8:29) that already exists as, not just an idea or even an ideal, but a reality within our higher mind. In fact, it *is* our higher mind.

This teaching that we were created in the image of God in Genesis 1:27 provided the foundation for thinking of ourselves as not only gods in waiting, but gods in ignorance: lost gods, gods who do not realize they are gods. The idea that people were created in the image and likeness of God means that they already have what they are searching for — *they already are* (in some hidden sense) *what they will be* — but they have yet to realize this. Soon, however, they will be able to say with Gregory of Nazianzus: "I too am an Image of God, of the Heavenly Glory, though I be placed on earth."[61]

The Exchange Formula

In about 180 CE, church father Irenaeus summed up the idea of deification in Christianity by writing that:

> [T]he Word of God ... through His transcendent love, became what we are, that He might bring us to be even what He is Himself.[62]

This came to be called the exchange formula, an encapsulation of Christian deification and of Christianity itself, describing in one succinct sentence the religion's *telos*, its ultimate mission: to

---

[60] Mt. 5:43-48; para. Luke 7:27-36. See discussion in chapter 3.
[61] Gregory of Nazianzus. "Oration 34: 12." *Nicene and Post-Nicene Fathers* (NPNF). Ed. Philip Schaff. Vol. 7. New York: Christian Literature, 1894. 337. Print. Ser. 2.
[62] Irenaeus, *Against Heresies*, Book 5, Preface, in *Ante-Nicene Fathers*, ANF01, tense modified.

transform humans into gods. Jesus, a divine being known as the Word of God or *Logos* (as in John 1:1), came to earth as a human being so that human beings might become gods.

This understanding remained a fixture in Christian theology for centuries, all the way through Medieval times and beyond to the original Protestant Reformers themselves in the sixteenth century and beyond. For many reasons, this mission statement contained in the exchange formula has since that time been lost. Some mystics, monks, and philosophers maintained the thread of the tradition. But it is making a comeback as evidenced by its prevalence in historical research of the past hundred years or so.

The biblical roots of the exchange formula lie in St. Paul's writing about how Jesus humbly and altruistically emptied himself of his preexistent divinity to become human and bring people to God:

> Let the same mind be in you that was in Christ Jesus,
> [6] who, though he was in the form of God,
>   did not regard equality with God
>   as something to be exploited,
> [7] but emptied himself,
>   taking the form of a slave,
>   being born in human likeness. (Phil. 2:5-7)

"The form of a slave" here is the human condition in comparison to the godly nature with which he began. Paul elsewhere expresses this same idea euphemistically, and it reads like the prototype of the exchange formula: "for your sakes he became poor, so that by his poverty you might become rich" (2 Cor 8:9). By this he means that Jesus willingly emptied himself of the richness of his divinity (for a time) in an effort to convince us of *our own* richness — that is, our own divinity.

According to this encapsulation of Christianity, Jesus had come down to earth, not simply to declare *himself* a god, as much later dogma puts it, but instead ultimately to impart godhood to others. It was a remarkable task, carried out by a remarkable individual. But Jesus in his superhuman humility never let his own realized divinity obscure our own. It was not a zero-sum game, but rather an infinite-sum game, because it belongs to literally everyone as Jesus first demonstrated.

Nearly every early Christian theologian had his own version of this exchange formula for deification. Cyprian of Carthage (c. 200-258 CE) offers his deification formula similar to that of Irenaeus:

> What man is, Christ was willing to be, that man also may be what Christ is.[63]

How does Cyprian see human beings as becoming "what Christ is," reaching Christhood, this highest status of divinity? Through imitating him, we will become like him. Our imitation of him eventually becomes reality for us. This method goes back to Paul whereby we take on the image of Jesus,[64] and many patristics picked up on it, calling it reattainment of the likeness of God. Such "Christification," as it is also sometimes called, was another early mediating image for deification shared by many church fathers.[65]

Most of the early theologians, like Clement, Origen, and Augustine a bit later, taught of acquiring the virtues of Jesus and therefore God through contemplation to achieve realization of our godhood.[66] Athanasius (c. 296–373) produced the most famous simplified version of the exchange formula:

> He was made human so that he might make us gods.[67]

It was unfortunate that Athanasius also favored a literal, physical substance-exchanging deification:

---

[63] Cyprian of Carthage. "Treatise 6: 11, 15." *Ante-Nicene Fathers*. Ed. Alexander Roberts. Vol. 5. Buffalo: Christian Literature, 1886. 468-469. Print.
[64] See esp. Romans 8:29; 1 Cor. 15:49; 2 Cor. 3:18.
[65] See the discussion at the end of chapter 12.
[66] See the discussion in chapter 10.
[67] Athanasius, *De incarnatione* Ch. 8, 54.3 (*CCEL*).

> The Word was made flesh in order that we might be made gods.... Just as the Lord, putting on the body, became a man, so also we men are both deified through his flesh, and henceforth inherit everlasting life.[68]

Athanasius like Cyprian believed that Adam's original life with God in Paradise was lost through material desires, which imprisoned the soul in the body and substituted complexity for the original divine simplicity of contemplation of God via participation in his purity.[69]

Athanasius used the exchange formula to stress the pre-existent divinity of Christ for Christological purposes in his fight against Arianism. Jesus had to be divine to make us divine because of the universally believed principle that only a begotten god can produce another god. But Jesus also had to be human to confer this godhood to us in the supposed substance exchange. The rarefied and ethereal "substance" of divinity would divinize the denser physical substance of our bodies and our human nature.

Clement of Alexandria (150-215), on the other hand, emphasized an information exchange model as the basis of his exchange formula:

> Yea, I say, the Word of God became man, that you may *learn* from man how man may become God.[70]

In an information exchange model as opposed to a substance exchange, Jesus is viewed as a *teacher* of godhood and an *example* of godhood for us. People can "learn" from him and his legacy in various ways how to become gods. Jesus is a revealer of godhood to humans and a representation or example of *their own* divine nature. But the idea of human beings having a preexistent divine nature (called the divine image) was diminished along with the instructive

---

[68] Athanasius, *Against the Arians*, 11.39 (*NPNF* Series 2, Vol. 4:329)., 3.34.
[69] See Russell 2004: 179.
[70] Clement of Alexandria. "Exhortation to the Heathen 1." Ante-Nicene Fathers. Ed. Alexander Roberts. Vol. 2. New York: C. Scribner's Sons, 1905. 174. Print. My emphasis.

model when this period of increasing orthodoxy (the 400s CE) distanced itself from the human called Jesus and his teaching in favor of later Christology and beliefs *about* him.

St. Augustine (354-430) produced several versions of the exchange formula, such as:

> To make human beings gods, He was made human who was God.[71]

Augustine veers toward the physical exchange of Athanasius in another of his formulae: "the Word became flesh, so that the flesh could partake of the Word."[72] The flesh is becoming the focus, the focal point for change, rather than the mind that identifies solely and mistakenly with the flesh.

Italian Medieval Scholastic Thomas Aquinas (1225-1274) in his own exchange formula writes:

> The only begotten Son of God ... assumed our nature, so that he, made man, might make men gods.[73]

Gregory Palamas (1296-1359) presented his own version of the exchange formula, stating from Thessalonica that the Word became incarnate "to turn human beings into sons of God and make them partakers of divine immortality."[74]

Deification was common knowledge for both Eastern and Western traditions. Both ultimately drifted toward the type of material or physical exchange formula that Athanasius inherited

---

[71] Augustine, Sermon 192.1.1, cited in Drever, Matthew (2014), "Deification in Augustine: Plotinian or Trinitarian?" in Khaled Anatolios, ed., *The Holy Trinity in the Life of the Church*. Grand Rapids, MI.: Baker Academic, p. 110.
[72] Augustine, *Enarr. in Ps.* 121,5 (PL 37,1622; *NPNF* Select Library). See also Aug., *City of God*, 9.15.2; 21.15-16.
[73] Aquinas, quoted in Weigel, George (2001). *The Truth of Catholicism*. New York City: Harper Collins. p. 9.
[74] Gregory Palamas, *Hom.* 16; cited in Russell 2009: 28.

from Irenaeus.[75] The exchange formula itself highlights how great the gulf was thought to be between the divine and human worlds. They were such vastly different realities that a major act of sacrifice (the incarnation) on the divine side was deemed necessary to bring them together. Thus, for most patristics, Jesus' sacrifice for humankind went beyond the cross to encompass his entire earthly existence, specifically his preexistent consent to become poor for our sakes and take the form of a servant. In turn, this great gulf between the two realities exhibits how lofty the divinity to which we are called.

Participants In the Divine Nature

Another major mediating scriptural concept for deification emphasized by early Christian theologians is that of participation in the divine nature, from the Second Letter of Peter:

> Thus he has given us, through these things, his precious and very great promises, so that through them you may escape from the corruption that is in the world because of lust, and may become participants in the divine nature. (2 Peter 1:4)

This phrase, *"participants in the divine nature,"* signals for some commentators (like Aquinas, as we shall see) a real, ontological connection with God, a sharing of his essence or nature (Greek, *ousia*). The author of the letter also highlights an "escape" from "corruption" here, which incorruptibility, we have seen, would be indicative of godhood. And the "lust" spoken of here is simply wayward desire, which arises from the urge to be something *other* and *lesser* than what we actually are by virtue of the inborn divine image.

---

[75] Irenaeus probably derived it from Theophilus of Antioch, as we will investigate later.

The verse indicates that when we assimilate the virtues or attributes of God, and in so doing restore our likeness to God, we become participants in his same "divine nature." For most patristics, particularly in the East, this means that we come to participate in a divine nature that does not naturally belong to us. Western theologians including Augustine and Aquinas generally followed this line of thought but in other places seem to affirm a degree of essential sameness between God and his creations, while Eastern fathers were more likely to envision a continual distancing of divine and human natures. Those in the East generally believed that despite our deification we would remain forever human, i.e., limited by an inferior state of being to God. Only Origen, Nazianzus, Nyssa, and a few others in the East had been more inclined, like the West, toward a greater closeness and less distancing between the two natures.

For Gregory Nazianzus (329-390), following Origen, Adam was deified by his inborn propensity toward God, and it is this natural kinship to which we long to return, to the soul as the "breath of God." But Nazianzus employs the qualification, "as far as man's nature can attain"[76] when speaking of our communion with God because of the seemingly self-evident presumption of the early fathers to assume that we began as human rather than divine. But should we presuppose that our present human appearance places *any* limits on our godhood except in our subjective experience of it? We are limited, not by God's will, but by our own choice. Nazianzus seemed to want to rehabilitate the genius of Origen while basing deification theology on Athanasius' more muted standard.

Gregory of Nyssa (335-399) expresses the significance of human participation in the divine nature when he insists that:

> To allow participation in God, there must, of necessity, be something in the nature of the participant which is akin to that in which it participates. This is why Scripture says that man was born in the image of God. It was surely that he could

---

[76] Gregory of Nazianzus. "Oration 21: 2." Nicene and Post-Nicene Fathers. Ed. Philip Schaff. Vol. 7. New York: Christian Literature, 1894. 270. Print. Ser. 2.

see as like does to like. For the vision of God is unquestionably the life of the soul.[77]

For Nyssa, this natural kinship with God comes from both the inborn divine image (Gen. 1:27) and the breath of God which birthed the soul (Gen. 2:7). A shared essence is necessary for our vision of God.

The Western fathers were more likely to envision an overlap between humanity and divinity in the mind, to which God was accessible. The early Western writers Tertullian, Novatian, and Hilary had all taught the shared substance between God the Father and the Son.[78] In fact, Hilary refuted the Arians' claim that the text 'I and the Father are one' (Jn. 10:30) referred to a union of will, not of nature.[79] A union of will was not sufficient to characterize the oneness of God with his deified creation. There had to be a substantial, or essential, connection for there to be both union and participation with God. Thus, there must be a shared substance and nature between God and his created gods.

For Hilary, the need to uphold the exchange formula of deification forced him to reject the Arians' subordination of the Son to the Father. As Ortiz states: "The common thread to his objection to them all was that none of their views of Christ's relationship to God the Father allowed the exchange formula to take effect."[80] The idea of deification thus shaped the patristics' doctrines in the Latin West as well as the East. Unfortunately, as the shared substance between Father and Son became the necessary emphasis, a detachment and distancing between Jesus' sonship and our own was emphasized with it.

The high Medieval period sees Thomas Aquinas (1225-1274) identifying the goal of human existence to be union and eternal fellowship with God. This goal is achieved through the beatific vision, in which a person experiences perfect, unending happiness by *seeing*

---

[77] Gregory of Nyssa, *Discourse on Children. Gregorii Nysseni Opera*. Ed. E Muhlenberg. Leiden. 1996.Vol. 3.2. p.79; McGuckin 2007:108.
[78] See Sidaway 2019: 119-20.
[79] See Sidaway 2019: 129.
[80] Sidaway 2019: 118.

(with the mind) the invisible essence of God. For Thomas, the vision occurs after death as a gift from God to those who in life experienced salvation and redemption through Christ. I will seek to show that there is abundant evidence that this beatific vision may occur transiently during one's earthly lifetime, prior to our final and full-hearted identification with it.

Aquinas emphasizes that participation in God would necessitate a sharing of his essence, because:

> [S]omething does not become something else by participation unless it participates in that something else by its essence... Hence, one does not become god by participation unless he participates in him who is God by essence. Therefore, the Word of God, that is the Son, by participation in whom we become gods, is God by essence.[81]

Participation in God *must* be by essence, or it is not true participation. It follows that we, like Jesus, cannot truly participate in God unless we share essentially the same nature as God, the Word, and the Son. Townsend comments: "This passage also brings out the christological and ecclesiological dimensions of deification, since Thomas says persons are deified through participation, or one might say incorporation, in Christ."[82] Thomas sees deification as a participation in essence as well as grace because, by his logic, one who participates by grace must participate in essence. In this sense, Aquinas goes farther than the Eastern Fathers, particularly his near-contemporary in the East, Gregory Palamas, were accustomed (or permitted) to go. Moreover, a sharing of essential being allows for a more intimate *relationship* between God and God's creation, reflecting the biblical insistence that we are related to God as his children.[83]

---

[81] Thomas Aquinas, *Super Evangelium*, c. 10. l.6, n.1460; cited in Townsend 2015: 224.

[82] Townsend 2015: 224.

[83] For more on the different views of Aquinas and Palamas, see the essay on the Essence-Energies distinction in the Appendices.

To participate in the divine nature is to be part of God, sharing even his nature and essence. If we fully participate in God's reality, even as he knows it, then we must be full-fledged gods, gods by grace *of* nature, seamlessly integrated into the divine Being, sharing that Being, sharing the essence and oneness of that Being, fully communicating and cooperating with that Being in such participation.

Conclusion

Just the idea that human beings can be called "gods," however this occurs, would seem to erase the impassable ontological gulf imagined to exist between God and his creations. Furthermore, the fact that we are called to be children of God suggests a real ontological relationship, that is, a real relationship on the same level of being. The idea that human beings were created in and with "the divine image" reinforces this real identity between our Creator and our higher selves, souls or minds. Finally, the idea that human beings are "participants in the divine nature" also suggests the sharing of one true nature, one singular essence, even shared mind and heart between our true God-created selves and God.

Almost no one sees it this way, ancient fathers or modern scholars. Most of the church fathers could not for various reasons follow their own logic all the way to full restoration of a full-fledged godhood, a perfect and complete state of being shared with God. Thus, there would be a restoration, but partial, i.e., not all the way to godhood. The fathers were limited in part by their perception that they needed to save their version of Christianity from competing Christian and Gnostic groups, which grew quite popular in the early Christian centuries in part because they brought up some good points alongside their extraneous ones. The march to orthodoxy also wanted to maintain a differentiation from Hellenistic philosophy, which from Plato through the Neoplatonism of Plotinus had taught of a divine element and underlying divine essence in human beings.

There may well be a psychological block against believing that godhood was our origin as well as our destiny. This is particularly likely if we were already gods when we decided no longer to be gods. Such a decision made with a god's power remains in effect until we change it, and it actively resists our change of mind back to this original state. In this sense, we created a monster where our godhood used to be. Nonetheless, there is a strong resistance to believing that God created actual gods, despite the scriptural and theological evidence, and that our deification represents a return to this original godhood. But it is not as strong as our underlying and deep-seated desire and yearning, derived from an even more ancient memory and state of being, with which we have hardly yet begun to reckon, to full restoration of complete and mature godhood.

Origen was one of the few Christian writers who thought along these lines. Some followed him at least part way in his thinking.[84] I hope to show that Jesus had seen it thusly also, in that the sonship/daughterhood he taught was a real, familial and yet transcendent connection with God. It is based on a real union and something we share, each in our essence and nature, with God. For Jesus' teaching of a real relationship with a very personal, yet utterly transcendent Father to make sense, *we* must be like this Father in a real, essential sense.

---

[84] They include early Augustine, Rufinus, Arius, early Theophilus, early Jerome, Didymus, Pamphilus, Eusebius the famed church historian, John Cassian, Evagrius, Diadochus, Gregory of Nazianzus and Gregory of Nyssa.

2

ETERNAL LIFE AND IMMORTALITY

Because of the close association of deification with immortality, the question of when and how human beings acquire immortality can help us determine when and how deification was thought to occur. We will begin by examining the idea in the patristics, and then go back to determine what scripture says about the matter.

Immortality in the Patristics

The hope of immortality is common to all Christianity, but it is in its deification teaching that we can gain a better understanding what exactly it means and how human beings can experience it. All the fathers associated immortality with deification, such as St. Hippolytus of Rome (170-236 CE), who confirms the identification:

> If, therefore, man has become immortal, [man] will also be God.[85]

With immortality comes divinity, and vice versa. We will find many instances of this as we go. But most patristics taught that immortality was a property given to humans only in the future, at the supposed general resurrection at the end of the world. It involved both the body and the soul which was attached to it. The soul was thought to remain in a state of suspended animation,

---

[85] Hippolytus of Rome. "Discourse on the Holy Theophany 8." *Ante-Nicene Fathers*. Ed. Alexander Roberts. Vol. 5. Buffalo: Christian Literature, 1886. 237. Print.

neither dead nor alive, from the moment of death until the physical resurrection. Most also believed our immortality is in some sense *earned* via a virtuous life, therefore conditional, while a fully restorative deification would say that immortality is instead *realized* via a virtuous life, or it becomes increasingly self-evident thereby, but it had been fully given at our creation. Although created, our being, like God's, is eternal. The only condition is whether we choose to be aware of this fact. We already have immortality in this sense, but do not realize it.

Justin Martyr did not view the human soul to be immortal by nature. As with most of the fathers who followed, we would not know our immortality until the resurrection at the end of time.

> The resurrection is a resurrection of the flesh which died. For the spirit dies not; the soul is in the body, and without a soul it cannot live. The body, when the soul forsakes it, is not. For the body is the house of the soul; and the soul the house of the spirit. These three, in all those who cherish a sincere hope and unquestioning faith in God, will be saved.[86]

For Justin, as for most theologians after him, the spirit is eternal and does not die. The soul is the part of the spirit that attaches to a body and lends it life. Nowadays we might refer to the soul as the mind, specifically the lower mind if it is attached to a body. Note that all three are "saved" by simply cherishing a sincere hope and faith. Technically, it is not the spirit (or higher mind) that needs saved, for as Justin says it is already deathless, and once the soul (or lower mind) is saved, so is the body.

Russell points out that: "Like Justin, Irenaeus teaches that man does not possess life but only participates in it." Humankind was not thought to have self-sustaining being (life-in-itself). Similar to the pre-Hellenic Jewish conception, their life was thought to be lent to them by God for these earliest theologians. For most of the fathers, it was only in the resurrection that immortality would become an ontological property of renewed human nature. For Irenaeus, it is

---

[86] Justin Martyr, *On the Resurrection* Chapter X, (*ANF* 1:298).

the incarnation of Jesus (as Word of God) into the world that made incorruptibility and immortality — two major characteristics of deification — possible for humankind. But the full manifestation of our immortality awaits our full moral assimilation to God, and even then, only at the resurrection at the end of time. Irenaeus thus envisions immortality as in some sense a continuation of physical existence.[87] Most Christians today do the same. But this only puts off into a distant future what might be ours now.

For Irenaeus, "we have not been made gods from the beginning, but at first merely men, then at length gods."[88] Irenaeus may have derived his idea of a compromise from Theophilus, Bishop of Antioch (d. c. 185 CE), who argued humans were created by God with the capacity for *both* immortality and mortality:

> But someone will say to us, Was man made by nature mortal? Certainly not. Was he, then, immortal? Neither do we affirm this. But one will say, Was he, then, nothing? Not even this hits the mark. He was by nature neither mortal nor immortal. For if He had made him immortal from the beginning, He would have made him God. Again, if He had made him mortal, God would seem to be the cause of his death. Neither, then, immortal nor yet mortal did He make him, but, as we have said above, capable of both; so that if he should incline to the things of immortality, keeping the commandment of God, he should receive as reward from Him immortality, and should become God.[89]

With all due respect to these wonderful patristics, this is a rather roundabout solution to the mortality vs. immortality dilemma. One problem with attributing such a compound solution to God is that it makes God appear indecisive, unable to choose whether he wants his children to be mortal or immortal. Consider

---

[87] Russell 2004: 107-108.
[88] Irenaeus. "Against Heresies 4.38.3-4." Ante-Nicene Fathers. Ed. Alexander Roberts. Vol. 1. New York: C. Scribner's Sons, 1905. 522. Print.
[89] Theophilus of Antioch, *To Autolycus*, "Book II, Chapter 27" (*ANF* 2:105).

also that a God with eternal thoughts could not possibly conceive of mortality, or some of his thoughts would not be eternal. In order for his thoughts to remain eternal, infinite and unlimited, he could have no thought that even hinted at limitation, let alone death. This middling solution also introduces an inherent dualism into the created order and a natural, God-given conflict within each being, which would seem to obviate divine simplicity and add problems and obstacles where none need be. There *is* an innate conflict within the human being. But this conflict cannot be called "natural." It is an ontological crisis.

Irenaeus, following Justin's idea that life is lent to us by God, goes so far as to speak of immortality as a whim of God, that he can rescind at any time:

> [A]ll things that have been made had a beginning when they were formed, but endure as long as God wills that they should have an existence and continuance. The prophetic Spirit bears testimony to these opinions, when He declares, 'For He spake, and they were made; He commanded, and they were created: He hath established them for ever, yea, forever and ever.'[90]

Note that Irenaeus' support for his argument speaks of God's creation as having been "established" "for ever, yea, forever and ever." He is referring to a Psalm here: "For he spoke, and it came to be; he commanded, and it stood firm" (Ps. 33:9). Contrary to Irenaeus' interpretation, the solidity and certainty indicated here suggests that God granted us true permanency of being, a being that stands firm forever, which suggests an ontological "life in itself," and therefore, a truly characteristic and innate immortality.

"Spirit" and "flesh" are so often opposed in the Bible because they are two very different types of life. One has nothing to do with the other, as far as their inherent essences go. Immortality is not a continuation of physical existence, but rather physical existence is an interruption, a lapse, in the state of immortality. If this is the case,

---

[90] Irenaeus, *Against Heresies*, 2.34.3, (*ANF* 1:411).

then what we thought was foreground (physical existence) is actually background, while what we thought was background (eternal mind or spirit) is actually foreground.

If we think of eternal life as a continuation of physical existence, then we are using physical existence as the measure, the standard. Should we use the temporal as the standard for the eternal, or should the eternal be the standard, and the temporal the contingent? Should the contingent and changeable be the foundation, or should the foundation be firm and unchangeable, established forever by God himself?

There was a generally accepted principle of thought in the ancient world that everything created is changeable by nature because its origin is in change, so that everything with a natural beginning must have a natural end. But would it not follow conversely that any changeable form of life must *not* be God's creation? Likewise, that which dies certainly *cannot* be God's creation, or God would be the source of death. The controlling principle should rather be: As God cannot be the author of death, that which dies *cannot* have been created by God. It is therefore relegated to the category of "illusion," a grand and intricate and all-too-real-seeming illusion perhaps, but an illusion nonetheless.

Of the early fathers, only Origen's idea of a preexistent immortal mind and spirit places the issue in proper perspective. God's creation is eternal, like God and all God knows. Therefore, it *must* preexist the world we see. Such a viewpoint has the advantage of corresponding with the ancient principle, derived from Plato, that immortality is endless in both directions: forward post-existence, in the "afterlife," but also backward into pre-existence "before the foundation (or creation) of the world." Created eternal and timeless, such created being truly has nothing to do with time, and is impossible to conceptualize in terms of time, whether past or future. As Origen states, "the Father is the origin and source of the Son or Holy Spirit, and no anteriority or posteriority can be understood as existing in them."[91] In this sense, the divine beings *always* existed, or

---

[91] Origen, *On First Principles*, 2.2.1, (*ANF* 4:270). Roberts-Donaldson English translation.

better, had being, even though they are said to have been created. They were like God even in terms of his having no beginning, for there was no time when they did not exist, even though it may seem impossible to us in time. My argument is that this would apply to our own natural state as well. If the Father is our Origin and Source, and we are created in his Image, then we share in his every characteristic, even his eternity going backwards.

Thus Origen believed that the mind, rather than the body, is the more direct and natural connection with God. The mind within a human being is in its natural, original state a true mirror image and reflection of the divine mind, that is, purely spirit. Immortality was given to us at the timeless moment of the mind's creation, which occurred prior to physical existence and prior to the fall (which also occurred in preexistence). We had the complete eternal joy of full godhood in our hands, but we threw it away. We denied our own reality. The mind is to Origen more ancient than the world and thus far more ancient than the body; like God, it preexists both.

The way back to our original likeness to God, which is volitive (according to our power of free will and decision), is through contemplation of this innate divine image via the principle that the mind *becomes* that which it contemplates. This is especially true if that which the mind contemplates already exists within the mind. With most other fathers, like Clement of Alexandria before him, Origen believed that prolonged fellowship with this inner divinity results in a progressive deification. This process continues after physical death if necessary.

Some early patristics did propose an immortality that is inherent in human beings. Athenagoras (127-190) was one of the first patristics to express a belief in natural immortality. Tertullian of Carthage (160-220), an early Western writer, defined the soul as having sprung directly from the breath of God, as in Gen. 2:7, thereby making it immortal. He adds, "Some things are known even by nature: the immortality of the soul, for instance, is held by many; the knowledge of God is possessed by all. I will use, therefore, the opinion of a Plato when asserting 'Every soul is immortal.'"[92] And Augustine (354-430) wrote a formal treatise on the immortality of the soul.[93] For him, the soul is immortal because it can apprehend truth, which is immortal (another Platonic idea). Augustine's influence led many Western theologians likewise to favor a natural immortality.

Among Eastern fathers, Gregory of Nazianzus used Plato's insightful phrase, "integrity of the true nature," to describe our foundational condition as human minds. Nazianzen artfully and subtly employs Platonic ontology but avoids the logical implications that led down the trail of connaturality Origen blazed in Christianity. For Nazianzus, Adam was deified by his inborn propensity toward God, and it is this natural kinship to which we long to return, to knowing the soul as the "breath of God" "but understood as a gift of God the creator, not the reassertion of any divine element innate within creaturely nature." [94] My argument is that this inborn propensity and kinship to God is still a gift even if received at creation, and that what is given later (in human existence) is a secondary salvific gift of restoration and resumption of the reality behind this innate propensity and kinship. The first gift is the real gift, the gift that includes all other gifts, but we threw it away in a moment of unappreciation, so that the second gift was necessary for us to re-appreciate and thus restore the first gift. The first gift is our connatural reality; the second is a gift of renewed awareness.

Athanasius' physical view of deification lends itself most comfortably to a physical impartation of immortality and the need for a physical resurrection. Along these same lines, in the fourth century the mother of Jesus, known as the Virgin Mary, was declared to have been made glorious and incorruptible through her unique

---

[92] Tertullian, *On the Resurrection of the Flesh*, Ch. 3. Translated by Peter Holmes. From *Ante-Nicene Fathers*, Vol. 3. Edited by Alexander Roberts, James Donaldson, and A. Cleveland Coxe. (Buffalo, NY: Christian Literature Publishing Co., 1885), p. 547.
[93] See Augustine, *On the Immortality of the Soul*. Ludwig Schopp, trans. 1947 by The Catholic University of America Press, Inc.
[94] McGuckin 2007: 102.

physical closeness to the Son of God.[95] This seems a rather roundabout and primitive way of seeing the matter, although in its way beautiful, whereas we could simply aver that the spiritualization already exists in our minds.

I will argue later that such a dual nature as that proposed by Theophilus of Antioch, Irenaeus, and Athanasius can only be our current condition, our fallen state. We are encouraged throughout the New Testament to choose between the two, which choice is made easier by realizing that one alternative is eternal life with God while the other (mortality) is the twisted product of fallen and self-deluded minds. Whichever side of this dual nature we choose for ourselves, the other will seem an illusion. Thus, it cannot truly be a dual nature if given by God. Only one side can be true and must take its natural priority in our minds if we are ever to escape the inner tension such duality produces.

Elowsky recounts a contrary view to Origen's in the Antiochene Theodore of Mopsuestia (350-429), critic of Alexandrian allegorical speculation, who believed "There was no age before the Fall in paradise when human nature existed in an immortal state" largely because God would not have created Adam immortal only to rescind this gift just six days later. Therefore, our future immortality at the resurrection will be entirely new to us. Adam was originally created mortal to preclude any sense of self-glorification. Thus, Theodore's view was not restorative; rather, the resurrection presented human beings with an entirely new life.[96]

However, Theodore's objection is more truly an argument *for* our having been created immortal. Theodore is correct to say that God would not rescind Adam's (and our) immortality. God's gifts to us — including life — are truly gifts and eternal gifts, permanently and fully given. They are ours now, at our disposal so to speak, to do with as we please. This is exactly why, if immortality was given to us from the beginning, then *we must still have it*. We are already immortal as minds created by God, even if we do not consciously realize. This immortality is not in our physical existence, obviously,

---

[95] Popov 2011: 56.
[96] Elowsky 2011: 154-155.

but it must still exist within our true being. Our immortality is ours forever. It cannot be rescinded by the One who gave it. It *can*, however, be forgotten, denied and dissociated by the mind given the original gift because the mind was also graced with a certain autonomy, the power of free decision, thought, and experience. We can earnestly believe we are bodies instead, and always will be. We have the choice because we are the ones who introduced it. And all of it — the choice, the reality, the realization — is a product of our mind. God gave us the latitude to accept or reject his original gift by the incredible power of our mind.

Maximus sees it similarly, that our original nature as mind and being was graced with immortality, while specifically goodness and wisdom were the divine qualities subject to our free will, our decision. Sharing this goodness and wisdom by participation was the way humans share the essence of God. We do it subjectively just by willing to do so, because it is part of our original nature to do so, not to mention our joy, while God *must* do so because his Mind does not waver. He does not possess the same power of decision he so graciously granted to us, out of respect for our freedom of mind.

The question isn't whether human beings are capable of deification. Indeed, this seems to be common knowledge among all the patristics we have cited. The question here is whether God created his children, his image and likeness, to be mortal or immortal. Did God create *human* beings or *divine* beings, or a mixture of both? Let us look to the Bible for its answer.

Immortality in the Hebrew Literature

Looking at the Old Testament, we do not find the word "immortality" or its cognates. The concept, however, is broached in different ways. In the Genesis creation story deathlessness was conferred at the beginning (with the breath of God in Gen. 2:7 and the divine image in Gen. 1:27) and then lost in the fall. And so, immortality according to this line of thinking would be closer to our original nature than would the current human (fallen) condition. This would mean that our true nature is immortal and divine, but something intervened to impede and nearly prevent our awareness.

The Book of Ecclesiastes expresses the basic duality according to their respective origins: "and the dust returns to the earth as it was, and the spirit returns to God who gave it" (Eccles. 12:7). The material and the spiritual are so different because they originate from different realities. Genesis 1:2 had spoken of a preexistent chaotic matter which had not come from God but rather was shaped and organized by his Spirit. From where had this preexistent "formless void" come? It had to have come from God's initial creation: i.e., *us*. More on this later.

The Book of Deuteronomy declares that human beings share the eternity of God:

> The eternal God is your dwelling place,
> and underneath are the everlasting arms. (Deut. 33:27)

There is a sense here that eternity is our true nature and our home, for we were created out of God, not out of dust or the void. The Book of Proverbs contains indications as well: "The wise man's path leads upward to life, that he may avoid Sheol beneath" (Prov. 15:24). Sheol in the Hebrew Bible, conflated with "hell" in early English Bibles, simply means nothingness and deadness.[97]

By the time of the intertestamental Book of Wisdom, thought by scholars to have been written in the first century BCE, immortality is a given:

> But the souls of the righteous are in the hand of God,
> and no torment will ever touch them....
> ⁴For though in the sight of men they were punished,
> their hope is full of immortality. (Wisd. 3:1, 4)[98]

In this book, immortality is associated with righteousness (1:15), a point it holds in common with both Plato and Paul, and humankind

---

[97] See the section on "Hell" in Ch. 12.
[98] See also Wisd. 5:15.

is created "for incorruption" and made "in the image of [God's] own eternity" (2:23-24), such as we find in Genesis 1:27 and our creation in the divine image, reinforcing that we began as gods.

In the Jewish apocalyptic book 2 Esdras (also known as 4 Ezra), thought to have been written in the late-first or second century CE, we see immortality associated with a joyous resurrection (2:45), with "spacious liberty" and enjoyment (7:96), and with the end of sorrows (8:54). An associated dualism between the two worlds can be seen clearly here, but immortality is characterized as more natural to us:

> And so the entrances of this world were made narrow and sorrowful and toilsome; they are few and evil, full of dangers and involved in great hardships.
> [13]But the entrances of the greater world are broad and safe, and really yield the fruit of immortality. (2 Esdras 7:13-14)

Hardship, danger, and sorrow are products of the world, but not of God. They are products of a fallen world, while God's way is "broad and safe" and yields the joy and peace of eternal life. This broad and safe way back to God has resonances of Isaiah's broad highway (Isa. 35:8, 10), which we will cite in relation to universalism in the last chapter.

Eternal Life in Jesus' Teaching

The following vignette, wherein Jesus answers directly how to "have eternal life," appears in all three synoptic gospels:

> And behold, a lawyer stood up to put him to the test, saying, 'Teacher, what shall I do to inherit eternal life?' [Jesus] said to him, 'What is written in the law? How do you read?' And he answered, 'You shall love the Lord your God with all your heart, and with all your soul, and with all your strength, and with all your mind; and your neighbor as yourself.' And

[Jesus] said to him, 'You have answered right; *do this, and you will live.*' (Luke 10:25-28, my italics)[99]

Jesus' wording here ("do this, and you will live") suggests that eternal life is able to be experienced here and now, so that we need not wait for death nor physical resurrection to "have" it. We need only recover *awareness* of it, which begins with cultivating love in ourselves, a happy practice, and ends with the full certainty of transcendent knowledge and oneness. We have put ourselves in a position where we must exert effort and accept help to experience what is normal and natural for us as creations of God.

In the passage, Jesus is telling his questioner that love is the basis and essential message of the commandments. He states quite clearly that the way to eternal life is through *total love* involving the whole of our being ("all your heart, ... all your soul, ... all your strength, and ... all your mind"). This love is total in another way as well because it is meant to generalize, to be applied universally to everyone without regard to worldly status or merit. Thus do we learn to think and feel like God — fully and joyously and non-judgmentally, with one's entire being, and universally for all beings, maximally in every way, no degrees, no limits, and nothing at all held back. This is the ultimate goal, but time is kind as we gradually work our way back to our original eternal awareness.

To love this wholly, this universally, and this completely is within our capacity. Our heart is big enough. It is the mind that must expand to meet the heart and integrate with it. We limit the mind and darken the heart by believing they are limited by embodiment and the problems and situations inherent in the world. In truth, the divine image and nature is limited by nothing. Only thus is it possible that our joy be unlimited.

Jesus also teaches immortality by expressing it in terms of deathlessness. He speaks of "some standing here" who "will not taste death" before they see the kingdom of God come "with power" (Mark 9:1).[100] They will not subjectively *experience* death because

---

[99] My italics. Para. Mt. 22:34-40; Mk. 12:28-34.
[100] See also parallels Matt. 16:28 and Luke 9:27.

they will be subjectively experiencing the kingdom of God instead, and death has no bearing on the eternal mind with which they will come to identify. Note that there is no waiting for a general resurrection here; deathlessness comes to each individually as they become fully aware. This is why some will see the kingdom to enter it, while others will not. Once every individual being has this knowledge and awareness, then the resurrection is complete.

Jesus uses the expression "eternal life" over a dozen times in the Gospel of John. He says: "Very truly, I tell you, whoever believes has eternal life" (John 6:47), making it seem that all we need to do is believe we have it, and it will be ours. This would support the idea that, ontologically, *it is already ours*. The problem, then, would be that we have denied who we are and therefore refuse to believe in our eternal nature. And this is why we do not allow our hearts to love naturally.

Other sayings affirm that eternal life comes with simple "belief" in "the Son": "He who believes in the Son has eternal life" (John 3:36). We tend to assume that this means believing in Jesus, based on later theology about him, but we shall see that it expands to include *our own* sonship/daughterhood to God, which is by definition eternal and immortal. Just as Jesus' *sonship* reflects our own, so does Jesus' *eternal life* reflect our own. As he assured his students: "This is indeed the will of my Father, that all who see the Son and believe in him may have eternal life" (John 6:40). Eternal life lies in our identification (which may be a re-identification) with the Son. We will expound on this in the next chapter and in the final chapter.

Immortality in Paul

Like Jesus, Paul most often uses the phrase "eternal life" to express the idea of immortality. He associates "righteousness" with eternal life and differentiates believers' reception of it from the previous age when "sin reigned in death" (Ro. 5:21). Paul carries this theme forward in Romans 5:14 and 6:22-23, saying, "the wages of sin is death" and contrasting this with "the free gift" of "eternal life."

Paul's declaration, "the free gift of God is eternal life" sounds like an ontological statement. In the restorative view of deification, God has given this gift of eternal life once, at the moment of creation, but we lost knowledge of it in the fall. Note that we did not lose the actual gift itself, the life-in-itself, which cannot be rescinded, and as a true gift would not be rescinded, but only awareness of it.

When Paul says in the same verse that "The wages of sin is death" (Ro. 6:23), he is speaking of the consequence of the fall, which was itself a willful denial of this eternal life. Death is therefore not the result of a judgment from God, but a self-imposed belief cut from whole cloth, the ultimate limitation in a world beset by them.

Jesus had by his resurrection already exposed the illusory nature of death, which had entered our minds as a result of the fall. By identifying solely as physical creatures in the world, and not gods, death seemed inevitable, and we came to expect it. But a simple shift of mind, a reidentification as gods, returns awareness of God and all he has given, affirming that death is an illusion. It has an appearance only, but no impact whatsoever on our true eternal self. One might even say that death was made to delude us into thinking our eternal self does not exist.

We seem at the present time to have two natures. However, only one can be real and true. Therefore, one of these natures must inevitably subsume the other:

> For this perishable nature must put on the imperishable, and this mortal nature must put on immortality. [54]When the perishable puts on the imperishable, and the mortal puts on immortality, then shall come to pass the saying that is written: 'Death is swallowed up in victory.' (1 Cor. 15:53-54)

The "perishable nature" must be replaced with the "imperishable" nature, which again is a "nature," characteristic of our ontological being, yet which might be experienced as the product of a simple change of mind. It is by focusing or devoting the mind to one or the other that we give it reign over our lives: "To set the mind on the flesh is death, but to set the mind on the Spirit is life and peace" (Romans 8:6; cf. Ro. 8:13).

This simple change in thinking results ultimately in an actual exchange of natures. Paul contrasts these two natures elsewhere as the corruptible "flesh" versus the "eternal life" of the Spirit (Gal. 6:8). He contrasts "our outer nature" ("wasting away") with "our inner nature" ("being renewed every day") in 2 Cor. 4:16. Our "inner nature," already eternal, already like God, has been hidden from awareness by our hyperfocus on the "outer nature."

Conclusion

The phrase "eternal life" has long had qualitative as well as quantitative overtones. In the quantitative aspect, it means immortal life, life that persists forever, endures endlessly. But qualitatively and subjectively speaking it was a way of living blissfully, peacefully, and wholeheartedly in the timeless present, with no guilt from the past nor anxiety about the future, which distinguished it from worldly life which speeds from past to future, bypassing the present altogether. [101] This blissful and blessed way of life corresponds to our true life in timeless reality, which is how it acquired its association with immortality. What is this eternal life, with its associations with immortality, ease, and living timelessly and peacefully in the moment — except godhood?

In my opinion both Eastern and Western fathers felt the need to temper their language and to pull back from a true union of essence and nature due primarily to the opponents they faced while they were writing. Their perceived need to refute certain popular Gnostic ideas (such as the body's illusory nature) led them and their successors to play up the importance of the body. However, the Gnostics were correct that the mortal and corruptible could not

---

[101] Aristotle is the Greek philosopher most closely associated with this qualitative sense of eternal life.

logically be the original and eternal creation of God, while the patristics were correct that the body and world were not evil in themselves. They can be turned by the mind into blessed aids in recovering its original immortal nature. What were once hindrances then become helps. All this requires is a change in awareness. The body need not interfere with eternal life when it takes a secondary place in the mind.

In truth, either immortality was conferred on us at the moment of creation — a moment lost to us long ago in the primordial mist — or it is a property we acquire in the future. I share the premise of the patristics that it would not make sense for God to have held it out to us as a potentiality that can be taken away. Either it is fully given, as a *truly* free gift, or it is conditional. If it is truly and freely given by a timeless God, then it was in our possession *prior to* our current existence. That is, we are already immortal but do not realize. The conditionality is our acceptance or rejection of it.

If God did not set the condition for our continual enjoyment of immortality, then who did? The condition was set entirely by us. Our *experience* of eternal life is now in our hands. But the eternal life itself, this irreversible gift from God, remains forever sure, while we await only re-acceptance of reality. The fall from grace was a rejection and repudiation of our own original eternal life. But because we cannot lose it in actuality, we only lost awareness of it for a time.

We tend to imagine immortality as a continuation of human existence, but consider the possibility that life is either immortal or it is not. The kind of life we have and experience as physical existence is not, but the kind of life granted by God is. Therefore, to have immortality and eternal life is to find the kind of life God has given us and re-identify with it.

3

SONSHIP AND DEIFICATION

As with immortality, sonship was identified with deification from earliest Christian theology. To be a son or daughter of God was to be a god. Such transcendence does not preclude but rather fosters true closeness and familiarity with God and others. In this chapter, we begin by examining the patristic emphasis on the language of "adoptive" sonship, asking whether such language is necessary for a valid and comprehensive system of deification. In doing so, we will place Paul's adoptive sonship language in its proper context as a way of expressing the early grafting of Christians into the universal blessings promised Abraham's progeny rather than the ontological transformation he expresses elsewhere. Then, we will examine Jesus' use of *begotten* sonship as a mediating image for deification and finally examine the provenance of the idea in Hebrew literature.

Adoptive Sonship in the Patristics

We have mentioned, regarding the patristic interpretation of sonship, that Irenaeus, with great consequence for deification theology to come, emphasized the adoptive sonship language of Paul over the begotten model of John. Many interpreters, ancient and modern, seem to neglect Jesus' consistent use of the familial language of father and sons (mothers and daughters always a given), and how this indicates a very close and even ontological relationship. They also neglect his essential teachings that we must be begotten from above (Jn. 3:7), that we must be perfect like God is perfect (Mt. 5:48), and that we can know our sonship and likeness to God by loving universally with our entire being (Mt. 5:44). We are either like him, entirely and truthfully, or we are not.

Irenaeus favored Paul's adoptive sonship language to explain the transformative process of deification. This is evident in one of Irenaeus' versions of the exchange formula for deification:

> He who was the Son of God became the Son of man, that man, having been taken into the Word, and receiving the adoption, might become the son of God.[102]

Here Irenaeus adds sonship to the formula for deification that we saw before. The idea of "sonship" itself would seem to denote close, familial relationship between ourselves and God, but the addition of adoptive language maintains a sense of distance that has persisted in Christian theology since that time.

Irenaeus speaks of adoptive sonship 23 times in *Against Heresies*. He is interested in refuting Valentinian (Gnostic) dualism via use of such language, and in the process Irenaeus promotes an unfortunate notion of a substance exchange as deification rather than an idea exchange and a complete change of mind.[103] Whereas adoption would require a transformation from one substance or essence (humanness) to another (godhood), a return to begotten sonship requires only a simple yet comprehensive change of mind.

Let us remind at the outset that adoptive language plays an invaluable role in the Bible. Abraham adopts the slave Eliazer in Genesis 15. Jacob adopts Ephraim and Manasseh in Genesis 48. Pharoah's daughter adopts Moses in Exodus 4. God himself adopts David's son Solomon in 2 Samuel 7:12-15. It is suggested that Joseph adopted the infant Jesus in the gospels. There is much holiness and tremendous love imbued in the very concept.

We shall see that Paul's use of the concept has mistakenly been attributed to deification and sonship, when in truth it refers to early Christians' being grafted onto the blessings originally given to Abraham's descendants. Irenaeus employs such language for

---

[102] Irenaeus, *Against Heresies* 3.19.1, (*ANF* 1:448).
[103] See Guthrie 2014 for more on Irenaeus' use of adoptive language.

polemical reasons. He held great influence on later patristics, including those who insisted that only Christ is the preexistent Son. His way of presenting deification prompts Russell to say: "The recipients of adoption and deification have simply received the *name* of sons and gods."[104] It gives the mistaken impression that gods are neither gods nor sons, and that we were something entirely other than gods when we received the adoption. Western writer Tertullian seems to have followed Irenaeus in his interpretation of the gods of Psalm 82:6 as the "adopted" sons of God. Yet there is nothing in the original Psalm or in Jesus' restatement in John 10 that requires this.

Origen, conversely, states that human beings have a "natural desire to become acquainted with the truth of God and the causes of things."[105] This natural desire arises naturally from the depth of our being, yet it is rediscovered via the reasoned way the mind operates in its search for truth, tracing all things back to their origins and causes. Being a natural desire, it arises naturally from the repressed memory of our original state of being. Even though we do not consciously remember our perfect original creation, hints and traces of its fullness and magnificence remain forever available to us due to its eternal nature. Origen himself employs adoptive language for a different reason than Irenaeus: to describe our transformation *back* into minds. Rather than a nominal godhood, one in name only, this is a true return to a true godhood of truly transcendent beings.

For Athanasius, as for the Alexandrians before him, our growth in virtue here on earth leads to a growing realization of sonship and godhood. But Athanasius like Irenaeus stressed adoptive sonship language because his opponents the Arians believed in a more natural sonship. As he wrote with some venom: "Thus hearing that men are called sons, they thought themselves equal to the True Son by nature."[106] An intermediary is needed for us to enter the family of God, despite our having been created in the divine image and called gods and sons and the very glory of God:

---

[104] Russell 2004: 171, my emphasis.
[105] Origen, *On First Principles*, 2.11.1, (*ANF* 4:297).
[106] Athanasius, *Contra Arianos* III: 25.17. *NPNF* 403.

> For though we have been made after the Image[107] and called both image and glory of God, yet not on our own account still, but for that Image and true Glory of God inhabiting us, which is His Word, who was for us afterwards made flesh, have we this grace of our designation.[108]

All of this is related to the Christological argument Athanasius was making against the Arians. For Christ to be promoted to one in essence with the Father, human beings in general had to be demoted to adopted sons and daughters, sons by grace and not by nature.

As regards the Cappadocians, who were more closely aligned with Origen's line of thought, Gregory of Nazianzus in his *Orations* and poetry writes enthusiastically of the soul's "kinship" and "affinity" with the divine nature.[109] Gregory of Nyssa also contains descriptions of a more personal and natural relationship, yet he pulls back lest God's utter transcendence be lost. Ultimately, even these blessed theologians stress with Athanasius that there must be some distinction between human and divine nature, and also between human and Christic nature.[110]

As Russell describes it, Cyril of Alexandria in the 400s reverts to a teaching of Jesus as "a true Son" and ourselves as adopted sons.[111] The growing emphasis on participation language in reference to deification, which began with Origen, may narrow the gulf between God and humankind, but it does not close it entirely in the minds of most of these early patristics.

There is an encroaching closeness in the philosophical theology of Pseudo-Dionysius the Areopagite (writing between 485 and 528 CE), who used the metaphor of lovers' ecstasy to describe the loving relationship between God and the soul. Seeing Christ as spouse or bridegroom harkens back to Origen's commentary on the *Song of Songs*, which Harnack calls the source of all Christian

---

[107] Original editor's note: Aug. *de Trin.* vii. fin.
[108] Athanasius Against the Arians III.25.10. *NPNF* 399.
[109] See McGuckin 2007: 101.
[110] See Russell 2004: 232-33.
[111] *Commentary On John* 1.9.91bc. Translated by P. E. Pusey (1874/1885).

monasticism and mysticism. Maximus the Confessor (580-662) also strongly emphasized the loving relationship between Father and (adopted) sons thus positing a closer, more intimate relationship while still retaining the distance necessitated by God's utter transcendence (as in nearly all the patristics' thinking).[112]

Early Western father Hilary of Poitiers (310-367) had, prior to Athanasius, refuted Arius' argument that the Son was subordinate to the Father, thereby emphasizing the equality and transcendence of both. He did this to uphold the deification exchange formula, because of which Jesus had to be divine to make humans divine.[113] Thus, although on the one hand he upholds the idea that Son and Father share one essence (my ontological argument), on the other hand, he leans towards the physical exchange theory of deification that Athanasius would soon use in his own arguments against the Arians.

Continuing in the Western tradition, Augustine (354-430) does not fully dispel this tension between closeness and distance, intimacy and transcendence. He writes with passion and personalism, such as for instance when he says: "We must fly to our beloved *patria* ... our way is to become like God."[114] Yet he, too, draws back: "If we have been made sons of God, we have also been made gods: but this is the effect of grace adopting, not of nature generating."[115] We will seek to explain as we continue how this is a false dichotomy between being gods by nature or grace because we are graced first and foremost by the nature of our original sinless and perfect creation.

Thomas Aquinas (1225-1274) picks up the tradition of adoptive sonship, equating it with the godlikeness promised by deification.[116] With Thomas, as with Augustine, there is a growing natural closeness in this process: "The adopted child becomes

---

[112] *See* Russell 2004: 265.
[113] *See* Sidaway 2019: 117-19.
[114] Augustine, *De Civ. Dei* 9.17, CSEL 40(1).434. 21-4, cited in Russell 2004: 330. Plotinus' influence on Augustine is evident here.
[115] Augustine, *Enar. In Ps.* 49.2, CCL 38.575. 5-576; trans. Cleveland Cose, NPNF, modified by Russell, cited in Russell 2004: 331.
[116] *See* Townsend 2015: 223.

destined to receive, to partake of, and to manifest God's glory, just like God's natural Son."[117] If it is "just like," then would it not be the same in terms of origin and nature?

Thomas arrives at a somewhat compromise solution that "by the work of adoption the likeness of natural sonship is communicated to men."[118] And so, we might say from our fully restorative view, the adoption is one back to natural sonship. It is only from our earthly point of view, which is limited not by nature but by choice, that it seems as if we are being adopted into a new category of being. But from the eternal point of view, of which we are fully capable, we are simply returning to what we always were. If we are natural sons and daughters of God, then the adoption step (from the eternal viewpoint) is unnecessary — except that it might become a mediating image by which one *experiences* one's deification back to natural sonship.

To be a son or daughter of God is not merely to take on a new human title. Rather, it is to inhabit an entirely new being or, as John expresses it, a new kind of "life": perfectly loved and loving. It is to receive the immense "power to become children of God, [13]who were born, not of blood or of the will of the flesh or of the will of man, but of God" (Jn. 1:12-13) — that is, *begotten*, thus truly and eternally so. The doctrine of begotten sonship and deification rests on powerful experience, ready and able to transform our belief into knowledge.

The problem with depending on such language to explain deification is that it presupposes a different kind of essence to begin with, thus requiring a (for most, physical) transformation as regards our deification. Thus, God would have had to create beings *unlike* himself in the first place, so that he could then adopt them into his family and way of being. It draws out the process, draining the idea of sonship of its inherent connaturality, and confuses the issue. The problem must fall on us, not on God. It is better to conclude that we are naturally like our Father, who created us in his own image, and

---

[117] Townsend 2015: 229.
[118] Aquinas, *Summa Theologiae* 3.23.1. Second and Revised Edition, 1920. Translated by Fathers of the English Dominican Province. Online Edition Copyright 2017 by Kevin Knight/newadvent.org.

that any differences we believe we see are only temporary and nonessential.

Adoptive Sonship in Paul's Teaching

For all the stress that Irenaeus and later patristics lay upon adoptive sonship language, it has been derived largely from a misreading of Paul. Paul uses adoption language regarding sonship in only two instances: Romans 8:15 and Galatians 4:5, with a third instance in the Pauline Ephesians, and in each case the author's purpose is not to explain ontological sonship. Rather, Paul employed adoptive language and Roman inheritance law specifically to proclaim that Gentiles have access to the same blessings God promised to Abraham's descendants. Furthermore, the context of these passages, considered carefully, instead affirms the idea of natural and ontological or begotten sonship in Paul's thinking.

Galatians 4:5

Let us examine the Galatians passage first:

But when the fullness of time had come, God sent his Son, born of a woman, born under the law, [5]in order to redeem those who were under the law, so that we might receive adoption as children. (Gal. 4:4-5)

In the passages using adoptive language, Paul is speaking specifically about Christians being adopted into the blessings of the Judaic law through the universalism of Jesus' Sonship. In using the "adoption" language in Gal. 4:5 Paul refers only indirectly to ontological sonship itself, for his point here is to express the idea that Christians receive all the promises made to Abraham, which promises *include* a sense of sonship to God and countless descendants.

The context affirms this interpretation. Just before this passage speaking of Christians being adopted into Abraham's blessings by faith, Paul writes about how Jesus' message of faith replaces and improves upon the law as a way toward sonship. The first step is simply to *believe* that "you are all children of God through faith" (Gal. 3:24). Again, we are sons of God simply by believing we are, which itself bespeaks a natural, begotten sonship. The problem, then, is that we do not believe this. Paul explains how this type of belief about ourselves generalizes to others so that surface distinctions are erased: "There is no longer Jew or Greek, there is no longer slave or free, there is no longer male and female; for all of you are one in Christ Jesus. [29]And if you belong to Christ, then you are Abraham's offspring, heirs according to the promise" (Gal. 3:28-29). The point Paul is making with the adoptive language is that those who belong to Christ are grafted onto Abraham's family tree.

Note that not only are believers saved by Christ, they are *identified* with him; they have "clothed [themselves] in Christ," (v. 27) having immersed themselves in his eternal way of being, thus to become, truly, one with him. Paul is saying here that the newfound faith taught by Jesus is a means of thinking of oneself as a child of God just as the law had been in the past, albeit more closely, simply, directly, and experientially. His theme here is how Christians have become heirs to God's promise to Abraham specifically that he would have many blessed sons, as many as there are stars in the firmament (Gen. 26:4). It is here that Paul applies the adoptive language, not to the sonship itself. Christians are to consider themselves among Abraham's countless adopted children. Paul is speaking about how Judaism has effectively become universalized beyond Judaism with Jesus, so that those once outside the law are now heirs to its blessings.

In these earliest stages of Christian theology, Paul is wrestling with the question whether Christians should see their religion as an offshoot of Judaism or an entirely new thing. He comes down on the side of the former view, saying that Christians are adopted as children of the promise (i.e., Jews) rather than outsiders. Paul is using adoptive language in Galatians to make a social theological argument rather than an ontological argument. Our "adoption" as children of Abraham makes us heirs to the blessings promised to his descendants.

Paul's ontological arguments about sonship in Galatians are distinct from this adoptive language. It is through "the Spirit of his Son" that both adopted and natural children recognize their Father, which causes them to exclaim: "Abba! Father!" (Gal. 4:6). Such a spontaneous recognition signifies familiarity, which indicates both natural and adopted have known him, simply by virtue of having been created by him, but we have since forgotten him. In this moment of familial recognition with God is where we realize that we are truly children of God (4:7). Nor do we need to become anything different to develop into this sonship. We are like him, ontologically sharing one being with him, although each of us have our own individual experience of this being.

Romans 8:15

The Romans passage with adoptive language employs largely the same formula and language of the Galatians passage. It reads as follows:

> For all who are led by the Spirit of God are children of God. [15]For you did not receive a spirit of slavery to fall back into fear, but you have received a spirit of adoption. When we cry, 'Abba! Father!' [16]it is that very Spirit bearing witness with our spirit that we are children of God, [17]and if children, then heirs, heirs of God and joint heirs with Christ — if, in fact, we suffer with him so that we may also be glorified with him. (Romans 8:14-17)

As with the Galatians passage, Paul's language of "adoption" is incidental to the sense of natural sonship that underlies it. The adoption is once again of Christians into the blessings given to

Abraham.[119] Verse 15 contains the adoption language: "you have received a spirit of adoption," which here Paul contrasts with "a spirit of slavery to fall back into fear." Later in this letter, Paul lists the blessings promised to Israel as "the adoption, the glory, the covenants, the giving of the law, the worship, and the promises" (Rom 9:4). It is for these blessings specifically that Paul speaks of the adoption of Christians into the family of Abraham.

Paul uses identical language as Galatians to describe those who receive the spirit of sonship, whose hearts cry out, "Abba! Father!" (v. 15), again a cry of familiarity and recognition. As in Galatians, Paul says that this comes from the Spirit of God "bearing witness *with our spirit* that we *are* children of God" (v. 16, my emphasis). So, here again we have the Holy Spirit sparking and bolstering a spirit already natural to us, convincing us ultimately that we "are" indeed *already* "children of God." Ontologically, our naturally existing spirit seals the deal, confirming the Holy Spirit's conviction that we "are" children of God because our inner spirit (with mind and heart) *is* the child of God. And so, here in this passage despite the adoptive language, Paul is indicating instead a natural, begotten sonship.

Then Paul delivers the familiar argument: "and if children, then heirs, heirs of God and joint heirs with Christ — if, in fact, we suffer with him so that we may also be glorified with him" (v. 17). This idea that we will "be glorified with him" seems to indicate that we will have our own glory much like Christ's. The ontological question is: Does this mean that we share the same essential being that he and we received from the Father?

Contextually, we find that Paul is speaking as in Galatians about how Christians are freed from "the law of sin and death" through "the law of the spirit of life in Christ Jesus" (Romans 8:1). His point hinges on the Jewish law. This reinforces the idea that when Paul speaks of Christians' adoption as children of God, both here and in Galatians, he is referencing specifically Christians' *freedom from the law* yet their rightful share in the benefits derived therefrom. He

---

[119] This is similar to how Paul uses the grafting of the wild shoot of Christianity into the olive tree representing Israel, in Romans 11:16-24.

is speaking of a newly universalized Judaism (his traditional religion) in Christianity. This opening paragraph of Romans chapter 8 goes on to contrast the "flesh" with the "spirit," with the culminating statement: "To set the mind on the flesh is death, but to set the mind on the Spirit is life and peace" (v. 6). True sonship is a matter of setting the mind on the proper identification.

The context immediately following the highlighted passage includes this statement of glorious hope:

> I consider that the sufferings of this present time are not worth comparing with the glory about to be revealed to us. [19]For the creation waits with eager longing for the revealing of the children of God; [20]for the creation was subjected to futility, not of its own will but by the will of the one who subjected it, in hope. (Romans 8:18-20)

The glory that awaits us, but which soon will "be revealed to us" is so great that it makes any present suffering miniscule in comparison. To attempt to find such happiness in this world is a futile endeavor. However, we will eventually uncover it within ourselves. Thus, the solution comes through the "revealing" of our sonship, which wording suggests we already have it. Our sonship is our underlying but forgotten reality, established by God. We suffer and yearn all the more because we had it before and then lost it. Only if we once knew it does the creation itself yearn "with eager longing for the revealing of the children of God" (Ro. 8:19). In fact, the cosmos has been orchestrated so that "all things work together" (v. 28) toward this revelation of our sonship and glorification, and therefore our deification. It is a natural longing for a natural, predestined and even preexistent sonship (v. 29), and so there is no reference in this ontological section of the text to adoptive language.

Ephesians 1:5

The final instance of adoption language in the Pauline corpus is from the Letter to the Ephesians, which is commonly thought by scholars to have been written by an anonymous follower of Paul. That said, it does have a deeply Pauline spirit, and evidences Paul's influence.

> Blessed be the God and Father of our Lord Jesus Christ, who has blessed us in Christ with every spiritual blessing in the heavenly places, [4]just as he chose us in Christ before the foundation of the world to be holy and blameless before him in love. [5]He destined us for adoption as his children through Jesus Christ, according to the good pleasure of his will, [6]to the praise of his glorious grace that he freely bestowed on us in the Beloved. (Ephesians 1:3-6)

In parallel to the Romans passage, verse 5 associates adoption with predestination and quite possibly preexistence, which means it is not speaking of adoption in a strict sense but rather recognition of some preexisting relationship with God. If we are predestined to be children of God, and/or if we preexisted as children of God, then the relationship already exists in the Mind of God even if we have forgotten it. If the relationship preexists, then so must the being that God knows and loves, which we have relegated to just a part of our being, and furthermore to the unconscious mind.

Our sonship is preexisting and therefore unconditional, ontological, founded in timeless being, and unchanging. Again, we will examine this controversial issue of preexistence (along with predestination) more closely in chapter 7. For now, we note that, as with the passage in Romans, a predestination based on preexistence is an argument for a natural and universally restored sonship. The idea is that, if we existed prior to coming to the world, then our true state of being cannot be this current worldly existence, but instead the way we were originally created by God.

And so, we gather quite a bit of ontological information from these few passages, and none of it has anything to do with adoption into sonship, but rather with a preexisting sonship that we can remember, realize again, and claim as our personal transcendent reality. In fact, examining the context of this Ephesians passage, we next find the statement that the overall purpose of the universe is to gather all things (back) into one universally shared, comprehensive state of being. As in Romans, it is "a plan for the fullness of time, to gather up all things in him, things in heaven and things on earth" (Ephesians 1:10).

As we go a little further into the context, we find that the author of Ephesians, whether Paul or one of his students, is concerned about the same ongoing conflict between Judaism and Christianity we had seen in Galatians and Romans (see Ephesians 2:11-22, which begins with "So then, remember that at one time you Gentiles by birth..."). Earliest (Apostolic) Christianity was trying to navigate its way through Judaism while transforming it in some essential ways. Jesus had a unique way of interpreting his given religion, so much so that he often provoked anxiety among its traditional adherents and teachers. Paul and the Pauline writer of Ephesians attempted to explain and rationalize the apparent newness of these ideas in traditional, scriptural, and rhetorical terms. As Michael Peppard concludes in his study of adoptive language in Paul versus begotten sonship language in John:

> James C. Walters is right to argue that Paul's adoption metaphor functions well in the cultural context of Greco-Roman household practices, and especially laws of inheritance. In the two places where Paul explains adoption as the means of Christian divine sonship he has already introduced inheritance as the chief concern. In both contexts 'there was controversy regarding the status of Gentile believers vis-à-vis Jewish believers. So adoption functions for Paul as a metaphor that gives nuance to what he wishes to communicate about inheritance.'[120]

---

[120] Peppard 2011:95, citing James C. Walters, "Paul, Adoption, and Inheritance," in *Paul in the Greco-Roman World: A Handbook* (ed. J. Paul Sampley; Harrisburg, PA: Trinity Press International, 2003), 42-76.

Peppard's analysis of Paul's adoptive sonship language versus John's begotten sonship concludes that adoption is "one of the images Paul uses to try to unite Jews and gentiles in Christ at the end of days."

That the patristics applied such adoptive language to their deification teaching is perhaps understandable considering their dependence on Paul for the bulk of their theology. However, we have pointed out some of the ontological aspects underlying these passages containing adoptive language, which we will now compare with Jesus' teaching and John's "begotten sonship" language.

Begotten Sonship in Jesus' and John's Teaching

Throughout the synoptic gospels, Jesus consistently encouraged people to think of themselves as children of God and of God as their spiritual Father, as with this example:

> And call no one your father on earth, for you have one Father — the one in heaven. (Mt. 23:9)

Earthly existence was almost beside the point. The focus is squarely on our inner, spiritual being. Our true Source is spiritual, not physical nor even genetic, which means that our true self is the inner one, not the embodied one we normally think of. The physical world of appearances in Jesus' teaching is almost incidental to the spiritual reality God knows — *almost* incidental because, seen rightly, even that which was meant to hide the truth holds something of the truth.

Jesus encourages his audience to think of God as "your Father in Heaven" numerous times.[121] Not once does he employ adoptive language to describe this relationship. In fact, we shall see that throughout John's gospel he employs "begotten" sonship language in regard to human beings. In the synoptic gospels, he attempts to draw his listeners into a very close, personal, even intimate relationship with their ever-present spiritual Father who will see and

---

[121] Matt. 5:16, 45; 6:1, 6; 7:11 and parallels.

hear them "in secret,"[122] whereby they may depend on him for all their needs[123] and for all manner of "good gifts."[124] Their Father is so close and knows them so well that he will speak *through* them.[125] Their heavenly Father cares for all life, even that of a sparrow.[126] Although he knows not of bodies, every hair on our heads is accounted for. [127] The point is he knows us, even in his transcendence, much better than we know ourselves. He cares for us, much more than we care for ourselves. And he seeks only our true happiness. Jesus accomplishes the astounding task of combining God's utter transcendence with his utter closeness to us.

Jesus makes the connection between sonship and deification (being like God) crystal clear in one of his core teachings from the Sermon on the Mount:

> You have heard that it was said, 'You shall love your neighbor and hate your enemy.' ⁴⁴But I say to you, Love your enemies and pray for those who persecute you, ⁴⁵so that you may be sons of your Father who is in heaven; for he makes his sun rise on the evil and on the good, and sends rain on the just and on the unjust. ⁴⁶For if you love those who love you, what reward do you have? Do not even the tax-collectors do the same? ⁴⁷And if you greet only your brothers and sisters, what more are you doing than others? Do not even the Gentiles do the same? ⁴⁸You, therefore, must be perfect, as your heavenly Father is perfect.
> (Matt. 5:43-48)[128]

Jesus describes here how thinking and loving universally like God will allow his listeners to experience a new *identity* as "sons of your Father who is in heaven." This new identity as divine beings

---

[122] Matt. 6:4, 6, 18.
[123] Matt. 6:8.
[124] Matt. 7:11.
[125] Matt. 10:20.
[126] Matt. 10:29.
[127] Matt. 10:30.
[128] Para. Luke 7:27-36.

comes with a mere change of mind, yet it begets a complete change in reality. Note that the categories "just" and "unjust" and even "good" and "evil" as we know them are dissolved, which tells us that our human distinctions in these regards have nothing to do with God, Creator of our spiritual reality. In his reality, all is "just" and all is "good" because of who he is and because of what his creation is to him. What is proposed here in the centerpiece of Jesus' great sermon is that if human beings become like God from the inside, by loving universally and indiscriminately, they will realize that such godhood is natural to them. This is the essence of Jesus' message, momentous in every way, and therefore often missed because it seemed too outlandish.

Let us note here that the perfection mandate which concludes and summarizes the teaching in Mt. 5:48 — "You, therefore, must be perfect as your heavenly Father is perfect" — is itself an indicator of deification. To become perfect *as God is perfect* necessitates the transcendence of ordinary human nature for a new, Godly nature. And to be capable of such perfection is to possess it already not only in potential, but as the basis of our very being. And note well that Jesus does not limit sonship to himself in his teaching; this would be the product of later theologizing. Sonship belongs to all of us. It is who we really are, in an eternal sense. Once we fully realize we *are* daughters and "sons of God," as we saw in the last chapter, we will realize we "cannot die any more" (Luke 20:36).

This teaching that loving like God makes us children of God is reminiscent of Jesus' core teaching about the "greatest commandment," otherwise known as the "double love command" (Mt. 22:36-40) where Jesus sums up the commandments in one with two parts: love God with your entire inner being ("all your heart, all your soul, all your mind") and love others as yourselves. Not only do we love completely and universally by this standard, but we *become* love, like God. Identifying with love, we return to our eternal selves as created.

God gave us the power and capacity to love, but he also gave us a mind to decide for ourselves if we want such love or not. Most theologians call this "free will," but it is more a freedom of thought and decision than actual volition because our will is not truly free unless we are willing and loving naturally and universally with God. God allows his creations to decide for themselves whether to accept love and the peace, joy, and beauty that accompany it, and so of course he wants them to choose love, which is their joy as it is his, but he holds the ultimate respect for his beloved children as having free minds and hearts of their own.

Loving indiscriminately leads to deification through its universality, its integrative vision of total equality, and its removal of the human categories unjust, "enemy," and even "evil" from our minds. To love this way, this universally, is precisely to "be sons of your Father who is in heaven." Stephen Finlan, in his refreshing summation of Jesus' deification teaching, sees conditionality in this passage, saying "Sonship with God is made *conditional* upon forgiving one's enemies (Matt 5:44-45),"[129] but I would contend that it is not our sonship itself, but only our *awareness* of sonship with God that is conditional. (The same is true of forgiving and being forgiven by God in Mt. 6:14-15, whereby our forgiveness of others allows us to *realize* we are *already* forgiven by God.) We could not love this way, to the same extent as God, without having been created to do so. Moreover, the very concept of sonship evokes genetic — or more precisely, ontological and begotten — relationship. And, indeed, the thrust of the teaching is that God is entirely *unconditional* in his bestowal of love and sonship, goodness and justice — i.e., he gives them fully and freely to everyone — and therefore so should his children be.

Staying for now with the synoptics, Jesus' "Parable of the Prodigal Son" from the Gospel of Luke also indicates a natural sonship. The prodigal takes his inheritance early and leaves his loving father and his family, squandering his fortune on worldly pleasures. When he grows tired and remorseful about his decision, he slinks home, feeling guilty and preparing to be reprimanded:

> And he arose and came to his father. But while he was yet at a distance, his father saw him and had compassion, and ran

---

[129] Finlan 2011: 28.

and embraced him and kissed him. ²¹ And the son said to him, 'Father, I have sinned against heaven and before you; I am no longer worthy to be called your son.' ²² But the father said to his servants, 'Bring quickly the best robe, and put it on him; and put a ring on his hand, and shoes on his feet; ²³ and bring the fatted calf and kill it, and let us eat and make merry; ²⁴ for this my son was dead, and is alive again; he was lost, and is found.' And they began to make merry. (Luke 15:20-24)

The father in the parable does not heed his son's protestations of guilt. Rather, the mere sight of his son setting for home elicits spontaneous joy and excitement in the father, for "my son was dead, and is alive again, he was lost, and is found" (v. 24). Seeing the love in his father's face, the son realizes that his guilt was needless, his presumed sins, which once tortured his conscience, utterly swept away. The *relationship* with his family (and his former identity) was everything. Although he had long forgotten it, his sonship remains intact, for whereas he was ready to deny it if need be (v. 21), he discovers something he had always known, but had forgotten — that sonship is a *permanent* relationship and identity. All this occurred during the son's mere *approach* to his father.

The parable counters the notion that we must earn our sonship, as with the adoption model favored by the patristics. Our sonship is already ours, even though we had not valued it as highly as we should have and thereby lost awareness of it. But God himself will remind us, with the love in his countenance, and with joy and thanksgiving, once we draw near to him.

Begotten Sonship in John

The Gospel of John emphasizes the begottenness of sonship — both Jesus' and our own. Begottenness is a direct emanation from God so that the beings begotten by God are forever part of him. They are created, not out of nothing, but out of God himself. The church councils concluded that Jesus was begotten by God, but they failed to extend this to human beings generally, despite the abundant evidence in John. English translations of the past have not captured this essence of begottenness in John's Gospel and Letters. Nearly every one of them translates "begotten" as "born" throughout. Thus, wherever the Gospel and Letters of John speak of our having been "born of God," we should keep in mind they mean having been "begotten of God." Jesus' role was to impart knowledge of a specifically "begotten" sonship to those who believed:

> But to all who received him, who believed in his name, he gave power to become children of God, [13]who were begotten (*genesthai*), not of blood or of the will of the flesh or of the will of man, but of God. (Jn. 1:12-13) [130]

The children of God realize they are "begotten" (*genesthai*) of God, made out of his substance, thus forever part of him. The context clarifies this means they are not made out of flesh and blood, nor of their own will as human beings. It is such a separate reality that only the mind that comes directly from God can truly believe it. But we already have the testimony in ourselves (1 Jn. 5:10), that is, the *reality* in ourselves: that we were begotten from God directly. Neither blood nor flesh, nor the will of the flesh tell us who we really are because we are begotten of God.

Jesus refers directly to our having been "begotten from above" in his statement to Nicodemus:

> Very truly, I tell you, no one can see the kingdom of God without being begotten (*gennethe*) from above. (Jn. 3:3)

There is nothing we can do to change our birthright, as Nicodemus argues, so how can we possibly be born again? Nicodemus' question is not quite on point, so Jesus explains directly:

---

[130] The *Weymouth New Testament* (1912) is one of the only English versions that uses "begotten" in its translation of Jn. 1:13: "who were begotten as such not by human descent, nor through an impulse of their own nature, nor through the will of a human father, but from God." In the following Johannine passages, I have replaced the NRSV's translation of "born" with "begotten" as appropriate.

> Very truly, I tell you, no one can enter the kingdom of God without being born of water and Spirit. ⁶What is born of the flesh is flesh, and what is born of the Spirit is spirit. ⁷Do not be astonished that I said to you, 'You must be born [begotten] from above.' (Jn. 3:5-7)

The reply is direct: What we know as "flesh" and "spirit" have two different, even opposing, origins. This is hard to believe, which is why it is never quite grasped by human beings. Nicodemus' confusion is our own. But the spirit within us already understands its own begottenness. Jesus' follow-up that the wind blows where it wants suggests the presence of a spirit that already has agency:

> The wind blows where it chooses, and you hear the sound of it, but you do not know where it comes from or where it goes. So it is with everyone who is born of the Spirit. (Jn. 3:8)

Jesus speaks of a natural yet transcendent way of being which is "begotten of the Spirit," an elaboration of "being begotten from above" earlier in the passage. To be begotten of the Spirit is to live as spirit ourselves, insofar as we can, with similar boundary-crossing qualities.

To be "born from above" is to be "begotten by God" in the same way that theologians believed Jesus was: a true Son, "begotten, not made, one in being with the Father."[131] Here, he is telling Nicodemus that we, too, must think of ourselves in this way in order to see and enter the kingdom,[132] basically as spiritual emanations of God himself. Such spiritualization of our being continues in John 4:23-24 where Jesus states that because God is spirit, we ourselves must be spirits to worship him, that is, we must

---

[131] This phrase is from the Apostle's Creed, repeated often in Sunday services.
[132] Peppard 2011: 103 also sees a distinction in John regarding how the kingdom is entered, saying: "The result of the begetting is the ability to 'see the kingdom of God' and 'enter into' it [Jn. 3:3], which is distinct from other NT authors' concepts of 'inheriting' and 'entering' the kingdom of God."

know ourselves as spirit to know him as he is. Contrary to popular opinion, God does not seek nor desire praise or adulation; we praise him by manifesting our God-created spiritual nature and by seeing the same in others. All of this is what it means to be begotten children of God. And recall: it all begins with being able to believe in greatness and privileged to love.

Michael Peppard claims that John's prologue regarding the Word and Light has been misinterpreted for most of Christianity's existence:

> According to John, Jesus Christ is absolutely unique — but his uniqueness is not his begottenness.[133]

In other words, Jesus is not ontologically distinct from us in John's Gospel, nor distinct as a son of God, but rather, he is distinct for other reasons. He was "sent" for a particular mission, and came willingly, to reveal our own begottenness. Regarding the verse: "we beheld its glory — glory as of a unique [one/kind] from a father full of grace and truth" (Jn. 1:14), Peppard's linguistic analysis reveals that "the word 'son' has been added to translations" not long after the Greek was translated into Latin.[134] That the Word/Light is rejected by his own in Jn. 1:12-13 may have reference both to ethnic lineage (Jesus not accepted by his fellow Jews) and to ontology (Jesus as Word/Light not accepted by those who were *also* begotten as Word/Light). Peppard concludes that "there is no divine begetting expressed in the Prologue, except that of Christians in v. 13," and this is true "[e]ven if one admits that the word "son" must be supplied in verses 14 and 18."[135]

Moreover, Jesus says many times in John's Gospel that he seeks to share *his own* relationship with God, which is the subjective sense of closeness, including his glory and his joy, as if this sharing were something that we could make real in our personal experience simply by coming increasingly to believe in it. Jesus did not call

---

[133] Peppard 2011: 106.
[134] Peppard 2011: 107.
[135] Peppard 2011: 107.

attention to himself alone as the only begotten Son of God; this was the product of later theology. In John 20:17, Jesus emphasizes our brotherhood and sameness with him: "But go to my brothers and say to them, 'I am ascending to my Father and your Father, to my God and your God.'"

John's "begotten" language continues into his First Letter, which is basically a treatise on what it means to be a begotten child of God:

> See what love the Father has given us, that we should be called children of God; and that is what we are. The reason the world does not know us is that it did not know him.
> [2]Beloved, we are God's children now; what we will be has not yet been revealed. What we do know is this: when he is revealed, we will be like him, for we will see him as he is. (1 Jn. 3:1-2)

As John says in verse 1, it was a supremely loving thing for God to have created us as his children. It was the greatest gift and grace we could ever receive, yet it was given with our life *as* our life. And note that we "are" (present tense) "God's children now," *already* transcendent, *already* like our Father. The full revelation of this transcendent reality awaits us in the future simply because, as human beings, we cannot fathom its difference from our existential reality. But by the time we see God as he is, "we will be like him."

And so, our sonship is both present and future, present because ontologically true, true on the level of being, and future because we live currently in denial of this truth. Once they are known as simply the denial of who we really are, both sin and evil will be things of the past:

> Those who have been born [begotten] of God do not sin, because God's seed abides in them; they cannot sin, because they have been born of God. (1 Jn. 3:9)

The part of us begotten by God "cannot sin" and therefore remains pure. This God-created part is, like God, fully identified with love ("God is love" in 1 Jn. 4:8, 16). John refers to our begottenness and Jesus' in the same terms: "We know that those who are born [begotten] of God do not sin, but the one who was born [begotten] of God protects them, and the evil one does not touch them" (1 Jn. 5:18). We shall see that this evil part is our own responsibility, originally our doing, not God's or anyone else's, but, fortunately for us, it cannot exist at the moment that we are realizing and experiencing our begottenness from God. Note also the parallelism between our having been begotten by God and Jesus' having been begotten by God, and how they are expressed in identical language. The difference is that Jesus was first fully to realize it within himself and about us.

Those begotten of God cannot fall away from their Source because their reality remains forever established within his Mind. What is more, their righteousness is self-evident and comes directly from God: "If you know that he is righteous, you may be sure that *everyone who does right is born of him*" (1 Jn. 2:29, my italics). This applies not only to Christian believers, but also to anyone who acts with righteousness toward others, thus affirming a natural theology in Christianity (which we will explore in chapter 8). And doing right is summed up by another natural act, loving, because when we love, we are coming from God, begotten by God, who is love. In short, we are being true to our God-given reality, identity, and relationship.

> Beloved, let us love one another, because love is from God; everyone who loves is born [begotten] of God and knows God. [8]Whoever does not love does not know God, for God is love. (1 Jn. 4:7-8)

It is a tremendous thing to have been begotten by God. Because he is love, we too must be love. It is within us to be and to share the very essence of God, and the glory and joy and fearlessness, the peace and goodness, that results therefrom, simply because of our capacity to love. And we will recognize that every hint of love, goodness, joy and peace anyone finds or sees or practices in this world comes from him and reinforces our connaturality with him and all beings.

Because it is our ontological nature to love, when we are not loving, we are behaving unnaturally and incongruently, causing ourselves conflict and turmoil rather than peace and joy, and we and the world will suffer thereby. However, when we love, we fulfill the commandments (1 Jn. 5:3) and overcome the self-destructive tendency in the world to distance and alienate ourselves from others (5:4).

Sonship in the Hebrew Bible and Apocrypha

Working backwards now to Jesus' possible influences, we will see that the phrase "sons of God" has a rich history in the Hebrew Bible and intertestamental literature. Sonship was associated early on with the king (2 Sam. 7:14) and the messiah figure(s) expected to come to redeem Israel and save the world (Isa. 9:6). The words Jesus heard at his baptism were similar to those from a Psalm:

> I will tell of the decree of the Lord:
> He said to me, 'You are my son;
> today I have begotten you.' (Ps. 2:7)

The phrase "son of God" comes to apply not only to kings and messianic figures, but also collectively to the entire nation itself:

> 'Thus says the Lord: Israel is my firstborn son.' (Exodus 4:22)

> 'When Israel was a child, I loved him,
> and out of Egypt I called my son.' (Hosea 11:1)

These statements express an early sense of collective sonship, and there are also hints that this incorporation will be universalized to Gentiles and indeed to all the world at some point in the future, wherein all souls participate together as one, as we will examine further in the last chapter of this book. The Book of Job opens with a heavenly council composed of "sons of God" (Job 1:6; 2:1), who are purely spiritual beings and consultants of God in shaping and running the world. Sonship had always carried with it a sense of obligation as well as benefit. The people of Israel should act in ways true to their sonship (Deut. 14:1; Mal. 1:6; 2:10), just as God will be true to them, even should they go astray (Jer. 31:9). They should strive with their entire being to "live up to" their sonship, this very high status and identity which raises human beings beyond their usual self-conceptions.[136]

The intertestamental books written between the Old and New Testaments stress the potential for any righteous person, such as the follower of Wisdom, to be "reckoned among the sons of God," saying that "his lot is amongst the holy ones" (Wisd. 5:5).[137] This latter phrase continues the association of sonship with angels and purely spiritual beings. The Book of Jubilees contains a comprehensive passage expressing the nature of our return to sonship from God's perspective:

> And after this they will turn to me in all uprightness and with all [their] heart [...] and I will create in them a holy spirit, and I will cleanse them so that they shall not turn away from me from that day unto eternity. And their souls will cleave to me and to all my commandments [...] and I will be their Father and they shall be my sons. And they shall all be called sons of the living God, and *every angel and every spirit shall know, yea, they shall know that these are my sons*, and that I am their Father in uprightness and righteousness, and that I love them. (Jubilees 1: 14, 21, 23–25, my emphasis)

Such bonding love between God and his children is both a natural one and a supernatural one, to the point where the supernatural

---

[136] Maurer, Joshua and Amy Peeler (2011). "Sonship in the Bible," *St. Andrews Encyclopedia of Theology* (online; retrieved 12/25/2023).
[137] NRSVUE: *New Revised Standard Updated Edition*.

becomes the natural for those who realize their true nature. It is for this simple change of mind, from being strangers to God to thinking of ourselves as sons and daughters, that the commandments and covenants were given both in codified form and as inscribed in our very being. Note that the Holy Spirit is said to be part of our inner being from the beginning of our earthly sojourn, indicating natural theology. Note also the complete universalism of the passage so that "every angel and every spirit" will realize their sonship.

Conclusion

Although Paul employed adoptive language to describe how Christians can share in the blessings promised to Abraham and Israel, he does this while teaching a natural sonship between humans and God, and a real transcendent closeness. For instance: "the creation waits with eager longing for the revealing of the sons of God" (Romans 8:19). Such a "revealing" of sonship is the bringing of a naturally preexisting but hidden truth to light.

And what does it mean that the entire creation eagerly awaits "the glorious liberty of the children of God" (8:21)? Does this not mean that we return to an intended transcendent freedom and that there is within ourselves a most natural state of sonship and closeness to God already, awaiting our realization? As Jesus had said, "If the Son makes you free, you will be free indeed" (Jn. 8:36). Nothing impedes our freedom like our own mistaken and limiting assumptions about God and God's creation.

We have found that Paul employs the language of adoptive sonship in only a few places, and in these instances he is emphasizing other things than cosmology, soteriology, ontology, or even anthropology. Instead, he is speaking about how earliest Christians would be adopted as Abraham's heirs into the promises and blessings of the mother religion. Thus, we cannot claim it as necessary language in explaining the true process of deification or our own ontological structure. A better place to study Paul's mechanics on human ontology (or spiritual being) is in his teaching about the "inner man," the spiritual being already within us.

The real question, for us as it was for the patristics before us, is what kind of being we begin with, for it is this that determines with certainty what kind of gods and children of God we will be. If we began as embodied corporeal creatures, then quite a transformation lies ahead of us to get to godhood. Yet, even then, we are for many patristics too far from real godhood (like God's own) to attain it in full. If, on the other hand, we began as full-fledged gods who fell from godhood, then a simple yet comprehensive change of mind is all creation longs for. And to think this transformation is grounded in our natural abilities to believe and to love. It all emerges from the deepest, most interior recesses.

That is not to say that it does not involve learning, study, much practice, great patience, an ear for reason, self-discipline, and the courage to go against the grain at times. But, because there is a naturalness to it, it also comes by intuition, simply by natural striving for authenticity and genuineness. It is this organicity that leads to real freedom: freedom of mind and heart to live as natural as humanly *and divinely* possible.

Christian orthodoxy has consistently hyperfocused on the eternal sonship of Jesus to the extent that it neglected our own eternal sonship. Yet, much of what it says about Jesus' eternal sonship does, in retrospect, apply to our own. For instance, we are all begotten of God. We all came forth from the Father and are returning to the Father (Jn. 16:28). And because we were begotten by God, we were graced by nature with life in ourselves as God has life in himself (Jn. 5:26). This life remains a viable reality within us, within our mind, but it cannot truly manifest itself without our openness to it. If, in this world, we must span two natures, then ultimately we have one too many. In the end we will need to choose, or accept the happy realization that the choice has been made for us.

We will speak about a tendency in the world, which comes from an unconscious propensity since the fall, towards distancing and dissociating from transcendence, which is the reverberating echo of having denied our godhood. Because it leads away from truth, it is a drift toward emptiness, nothingness, and thus futility (Ro. 8:20). The part of our mind that has assumed control holds us to a certain way of thinking about our human nature, which is to constrict ourselves to smaller and more meaningless spheres of humanness, to accept limitation even unto death for ourselves and to perceive the same in others. God's way is infinitely more expansive and thus more freeing.

The misappropriation of adoptive language to restrict belief in a more natural and begotten sonship may stem from this unconscious repression of our true nature. We unconsciously fear our true selves as beings of God because they extend so far beyond our current circumscribed comfort zone. Limitlessness scares us, infinity terrifies us, and true freedom horrifies us: they all threaten our precarious sense of tight control over reality. We prefer to hide in the nooks and crannies of self-imposed limitation and restriction. Even death, at times we fear, would be preferable. But we don't really fear transcendence; in fact, we love it more than anything because it is our true natural begotten state.

4

THE NATURE OF GOD

Having seen that human beings are called children of God created in the divine image and likeness, and that this God-begotten being is immortal and transcendent of all we know, we turn next to the nature of God himself for an indication of who we really are and where we come from as gods. The New Testament teaches that God is utterly transcendent of the world, and yet he is intimately familiar with *us*. We must hold these two seeming opposite poles in tension, his complete transcendence and his total love, until we discover their harmonization in *our* transcendence.

Divine Simplicity

Divine simplicity is the principle, common to Christian theology going back to its earliest centuries, that each of God's attributes (goodness, truth, beauty, justice, equality, love) is identical with God's being. He is in no way separate from his qualities; they are one with him and he with them. Unlike physical organisms, God is not composed of parts, or ingredients. If he is loving, then he is *all* love; he is love itself. Likewise, if he is just, he is justice itself and in no way unjust.

Divine simplicity upholds the purity and transcendence of God, and the idea that God in all his aspects is perfectly consistent and integrated. None of his attributes or qualities conflict with another, and none ever falls away from him. He cannot lose any of his virtues because he is fully identified with them. His simplicity is thus part of his changelessness. As it is written, "For I the Lord do not change" (Malachi 3:6). Our thoughts about him may change and indeed must evolve, but he does not.

In Christian theology, this idea that God is "simple, uncompounded Being" without diverse parts goes back at least as far as Irenaeus in the second century. As he puts it:

> God is not as men are. For the Father of all is at a vast
> distance from those affections and passions which operate
> among men. He is a *simple, uncompounded* Being, without
> diverse members, and altogether like, and equal to Himself,
> since he is wholly understanding, and wholly spirit,
> and wholly thought, and wholly intelligence,
> and wholly reason ... wholly light, and the whole source of
> all that is good.[138]

Human beings will think of God in many ways before arriving at the conclusion that he is "simple, uncompounded Being." This is wholly true of God, as Irenaeus states, but very few of the fathers reckoned that it must also be true of ourselves if we were begotten of God.

Divine simplicity proved an essential part of Western theology for Augustine, Anselm, and Aquinas. Anselm, for instance, says of God: "Life and wisdom and the other [attributes], then, are not parts of You, but all are one and each one of them is wholly what You are and what all the others are."[139] God's characteristic love is identical with his characteristic beauty and goodness and truth. Although we see them as parts, or distinct attributes, they are integrated and interconnected as aspects of one integrated Being. The same is true of ourselves in relation to God: We are each parts of a greater whole of divine beings, yet also whole gods individually within ourselves, each with a mind free to think and feel as it wills. Augustine argues in *On the Trinity* that, as the three persons of the

---

[138] Irenaeus, *Against Heresies,* 2.13.3, (*ANF* 1:374), my italics.
[139] Anselm, *Proslogion* 18. S. N. Deane, trans. (Chicago: The Open Court Publishing Company, 1903, reprinted 1926.)

Trinity are one, so do our mind, emotion, and reason form an internal trinity, unified and congruent in their perfect state.[140]

The idea of divine simplicity stems from the premise that God is one, a motif central to the Hebrew Bible. God is one not only in number and integration but also in the purity of his will and his single-minded love. The Book of Deuteronomy emphasizes the theme: "the Lord is our God, the Lord is one" (Deut. 6:4). Jesus includes God's creation in this oneness when he prays "that they may all be one. As you, Father, are in me and I am in you, may they also be in us" (John 17:21). His creations began as one and remain one with their Source and their fellow creations. They are part of God's oneness, which means each is essential and integral to it. Hence, the call for human beings to simplify, to integrate mind, heart and behavior, and to love increasingly perfectly until they realize their godhood.

The fewer words, the better to capture the divine essence. This difficult, overly complicated world is a result of the complexity of a mind that has fallen and branched far from the divine simplicity at its heart. We have lost ourselves in the complications we ourselves have wrought. We human beings are inconsistent and in conflict *with ourselves*, which is where the division started and why we cannot understand God or our fellow beings. We can be loving sometimes but spiteful other times, at peace only in moments, happy rarely if at all but not consistently. But God is locked into love with its accompanying peace and joy. He cannot *not* love, or he would not be God; it is his singular nature, and most natural for him.

A most important implication of divine simplicity has to do with how God creates, and therefore with the true nature of human beings. Anselm says of God: "you are of so simple a nature, that of you nothing can be born other than what you are."[141] This idea is foundational for a fully restorative deification. Because of his

---

[140] Augustine, *On the Trinity*, 12.4.4. A. W. Haddan, trans. *Nicene and Post-Nicene Fathers*, First Series, Vol. 3. Edited by Philip Schaff. (Buffalo, NY: Christian Literature Publishing Co., 1887.)

[141] Anselm, *Proslogion* XXIII. S. N. Deane, trans.

simplicity and perfection, God can only have created beings like himself.

God as Being

When Moses encounters God on Mount Sinai, he "sees" him in the burning bush which "was blazing, yet it was not consumed" (Exod. 4:2). When Moses asks what name he should give this God who appeared to him in supernatural vision, God introduces himself to Moses as "I AM THAT I AM" (Exodus 3:14, KJV). This divine self-statement and most holy name signifies that God's transcendence is a different, more pure kind of being than anything in the world. God is being itself, and being *in himself*, meaning that his being is not contingent or dependent on anything else. And yet, it is from this utterly transcendent Uncreated Being that all life and every other being has sprung.

Jesus uses a similar expression to describe *his own* sense of higher being. Abraham was by Jesus' time a legendary figure from the distant past, but Jesus still could say: "Very truly, I tell you, before Abraham was, I am" (John 5:58). Echoing Exodus 3:14, he signifies that his own true nature, like God's, transcends the world and time itself. In fact, his true being *precedes* the world, and this renders him ever-present.

"Being" is a term for God that highlights his divine simplicity. He is pure being without form or parts. He has no name to match his comprehensiveness: only "I am." His holy name is one with his being. He simply is what he is. No words are adequate. Even Being, the Uncreated Creator, Universal Mind, Father, Spirit and Love — although the best descriptors we have — fail to capture the true Divine Essence. It must be experienced and lived to be known.

With "I am that I am," we are no longer in the human world, nor even in the realm of time and space. These are not worldly terms with worldly referents. "I am" indicates that God lives in an eternal and timeless present. We, on the other hand, think of ourselves as strung along in time and confined to a restrictive space, dependent on appearances, and bound to a past which fatalistically determines our future, bypassing the present, transcendent, eternal and timeless moment altogether. This is why it is so difficult — some say impossible — for the human mind to comprehend God. Thankfully, as we will continue to find, we also have a divine mind so fully capable of knowing him that it *already* knows him.

God is *pure being* unfettered by form. Any kind of form (or body) would only serve to limit God. Having being in himself, independent of form, God is unaffected by time, space, or any kind of constraint, including death, the ultimate limit. With God there are no orders of being, no distinctions among beings except Creator and created. His creations are truly one with him and therefore the same in essence. There is only one true essence: pure being.

"*Being*" is best reserved for God's type of eternal life, while "*existence*" signifies embodied life on earth. Despite all the anthropomorphisms with which he is portrayed in parts of the Bible, such characterizations are simply ways of expressing the inexpressible. [142] God as pure being transcends all such human characteristics, as well as the human fund of knowledge. As God states in the Book of Isaiah:

> For my thoughts are not your thoughts,
>   nor are your ways my ways, says the Lord.
> [9] For as the heavens are higher than the earth,
>   so are my ways higher than your ways
>   and my thoughts than your thoughts. (Isa. 55:8-9)

God is utterly transcendent of the human mind. But this does not mean that he is transcendent of *our* mind, which contains, alongside the human part, the divine *Imago Dei* and the mind of Christ. It is only the human part, the creaturely and limited part, that God transcends; the divine part is where we connect and remain as one.

---

[142] Litwa (2012: 50) comments: "the central Jewish deity (Yahweh) is almost always conceived of anthropomorphically as a person. (This is generally true for the Greeks as well.)."

Being is the super-reality: the formless and ideal reality beyond and behind all seeming realities. It is life itself and life-in-itself. Even without a form, having no form at all, no physical structure, no earthly tent, we would live. Because of the formless reality of being, we are in God and God is in us. Form is ultimately more a psychological limit than an actual one. We can see beyond it quite easily if we want to. It is this formless aspect of being that is also spoken of as "spirit," which descriptor of God we examine next.

God as Spirit

> God is spirit, and those who worship him
> must worship in spirit and truth. (John 4:24)

With these words — "God is spirit" — Jesus relegates any anthropomorphisms about God (as having bodily features or human characteristics) to the realm of symbolism. God is a different reality than humans understand, which is why we must learn to think of *ourselves* entirely differently — as spirits (i.e., "in spirit and truth") — if we want to know him. To say that God is spirit is a way of saying God is pure being, all mind and heart, entirely unlimited by form or time or space. To say that we must worship him in spirit and truth is to say that we must know ourselves likewise if we are going to know him at all.

We must be like him if we want truly to know him, and to know him is to adore him. The Greek word used for "worship" in most English translations of John 4:24 (*proskunountas*) has connotations of prostration and respect but also means simply to "kiss," to adore, which our heart does naturally whenever it loves. We cannot know God through a mind shaped by limitation and constriction, yet we can come to know God while we are still human. That is *why* we are human for the time being: to see and love beyond our humanness.

As with the wind, we know spirit only through its effects. Human eyes cannot see it, for it is formless, but heart and mind can feel and know it. While we can learn *about* it through reason and revelation, we can *know* spirit only through firsthand lived experience. As Jesus teaches, in many different ways with a plethora of images, the closer we come to our own spiritual nature, the closer we come to knowing God. Where once material reality seemed everything to us, and spiritual reality a secondary thought, now spiritual reality becomes increasingly primary to reveal its presence in literally everything.

Spirit is not a substance, and so it should not be thought of as a lighter, airier atomic element, like the "ether" of ancient philosophers. Spirit is the broad category of invisible, non-physical realities including those of mind and heart. Mind is a reality unto itself, invisible to the physical eye, but we know it subjectively through its experience and its effects. We know it in the same way we know spirit: just by *being* it, experiencing it, and seeing its effects. "No one has ever seen God" (Jn. 1:18). Yet we may know him with a certainty that extends beyond physical perception, and this is imaged in theology as a vision of the mind, but it transports its experiencer beyond embodied perception into knowledge.

If God is mind and we are mind, there is nothing between us, no form to separate us, no physical outlines to make us seem different and alienated, wondering what the other is thinking and feeling. All boundaries are crossable which is why, with God, all things are possible. Even now, because of the interconnection of mind, we can gladden others from wherever we happen to be just by thinking well about them.

God as Father

We have been examining the main descriptors of God in Christianity. "Being" and "spirit" verge on philosophical ways of expressing God's utter transcendence of the world, denoting that he abides in an altogether different reality than the one we know as humans. We have seen that Jesus upholds God's transcendence by referring to him as spirit and thus teaching that he is a different kind of being than humans tend to realize. At the same time, however, Jesus portrays God in most *intimate* terms to emphasize the closeness, the heart, of this transcendent being. Both aspects appear together in Jesus' oft-used phrase "Father in heaven," which holds the transcendence of "in heaven" in delicate balance with the intimacy of the familial term, "Father." [143]

We have seen regarding sonship that Jesus speaks continually to his audience about "your Father in heaven." He wants his students to raise their perception of themselves to children of God, the highest level of transcendent being. He goes so far as to ask his listeners not to call anyone their father on earth because "you have one Father — the one in heaven" (Mt. 23:9). Jesus was trying to convince them that they originated from a different reality than the world. He encourages them to think of themselves more like gods and less like human beings. The greater and more real part of ourselves "comes from heaven" and "is above all" (Jn. 3:31). God as Father is also Creator of transcendent beings like himself.

In addition to these transcendent aspects, God as "Father" has aspects of earthly protector and provider. The Father watches over his creations, *not* for the supposed wrongs they are doing, but to protect them, to keep them safe in his heart.[144] He is tolerant beyond our present capability to understand. He is a giver of gifts and of "heavenly rewards." Jesus speaks of an immediate sense of "reward" people will receive simply by sitting with this transcendent but loving God "in secret."[145] He thus points us inside ourselves to find and experience for ourselves our own intimate relationship with God. We will discover that such interior change transforms our relationships in the world as well.

Jesus teaches people that, if they learn to love and appreciate other beings, they can expect to be like their Father in heaven, who loves all beings equally and perfectly.[146] They are in fact the "children" or "offspring" of this utterly transcendent God. Father-

---

[143] See, for example, Mt. 5:16, 5:45, 7:11, 12:50 and parallels.
[144] See, for ex., Mt. 10:29-31.
[145] Mt. 6:1-6.
[146] Mt. 5:48.

son language is meant to suggest sameness and equality between them. As Jesus said, "whatever the Father does, the Son does likewise" (Jn. 5:19). Both parties love with their entire beings, and through loving, create. Moreover: "The Father loves the Son and has placed all things in his hands" (Jn. 3:35). The Father shares *everything*, down to his own subjective state of mind and heart, thus godhood, with his children.

Calling God our Father and ourselves his children signifies that we are like him. We do what the Father does because we share the same mind. His transcendence does not make us different from him, but rather the same. In other words, if we are his children, we must likewise be transcendent. Even now we must be transcendent, before we consciously realize it. Not only do we have the potential to live far beyond the world (or any world), but the purest part of our mind must already be there. If it is God's will that we be with him and like him, and if his will is inviolate and must always come to pass, then we must still be with and like God in the most real sense.

God as Love

We have seen that Jesus encouraged his students to love universally so that they could be like God, therefore sons/daughters of God,[147] and therefore (by the association between sons and gods in Psalm 82), gods. When Jesus was asked for his opinion on the greatest commandment, he replied with the "double love command": Love God with your entire being and your neighbor as yourself.[148] We have seen also that Jesus taught that cultivating such total love is the way to realize eternal life.[149]

Love, clearly, stands at the heart of Jesus' teaching. And this is because it is the way to be like God. We are capable of identifying

---

[147] See Mt. 5:43-48; para. Luke 6:35-36.
[148] Mt. 22:34-40; Mk. 12: 28-34; Luke 10: 25-37.
[149] Matthew 22:34-40; Mark 12:28-34; Luke 10: 25-28.

with love just as God is identified with love. The First Letter of John sums up Jesus' teaching in the clearest way: "God is love."

> Beloved, let us love one another, because love is from God; everyone who loves is born of God and knows God. [8]Whoever does not love does not know God, for God is love. (1 Jn. 4:7-8)

God *is* love, and is in fact fully identified with love. He loves with his complete being, which means that love stands behind everything he does. It is his one motive for everything he creates, all he does and all he thinks. It also means that he never leaves that which he loves. He remains with them and they with him because of his great love for them and their great love which matches his. They are inseparable. They "abide in" him and he in them, eternally.

> God is love, and those who abide in love abide in God, and God abides in them. (1 Jn. 4:16)

Furthermore, the statement "God is love" signifies that we already know God's essence, and we share it already, simply because of our natural capacity to love. It is within our ability to love, as God loves, and so here is yet another overlap with God. The only difference is that we find it difficult if not impossible to love perfectly like God. We do not yet identify ourselves completely with love. Because we love only in part, we know only in part.

Love is transcendent of the ways of the world, which runs instead on the self-interest of alienated, conflicted selves competing for survival and status. Love wants only to share its happiness, to equalize, to know others as itself. Acting on love rather than self-interest would transform the world so that it begins ever so slightly to resemble heaven. In a very real sense, this is the end of the old world and the dawn of a loving new one to replace it. Love is the most powerful thought and emotion we have at our disposal.

We have been born into a world where love seems a precious, rare, even fleeting commodity. But this is because we are not ourselves. In God's reality, love is everywhere and everything, and it is steadfast, standing firm forever, remaining with each of his beloved creations because it is their truth. Love is God's essence and his true nature, and so it must be theirs and ours as well.

Conclusion

Theologians and philosophers are adept at complicating even such a pure idea as divine simplicity. Each limb grows in their minds countless more branches and offshoots, until we are smothered by the categories and intricacies of "simplicity." It seems a better practice would be to keep this idea in particular as simple as possible, to describe it with as few words and concepts as possible, and experience it ourselves if we are to understand both God and ourselves via this principle.

Because of divine simplicity, everything that God created shares his essence. Being does not define him; he defines being. He can create only perfect limitless beings like himself because that is who he is and what he knows. His thoughts are always and forever perfect and limitless and they remain one with him. Therefore, we, his children, created in his divine image, must also share his perfection, his limitlessness, and all his attributes. We, like he, are also one, one with God who is one with his attributes. God himself is our true essence, and so God himself is the measure of our progress towards a fully restored deification.

There is a delicate tension in Jesus' teaching about God. On the one hand, God is defined by love, so also, love is defined by God. On the other hand, he is spirit. On the one hand, he is very close to us, while on the other hand, he is so far beyond the world that we cannot fathom him. Jesus paints a picture of our true and eternal relationship with universal and cosmic being, but this entails transcendence of everything we have learned in the world about who we are, in order to find ourselves sitting and loving with him already in the heavenly places.

To say that God is pure being is to say that *all* being is God. To say that God is love is to say that all love among beings shares his essence (John's argument). Therefore, God is not so distant as appearances might show. We already have being, but this seems limited by temporary existence. We already love, yet not enough for total joy and knowledge. We *can* be perfect as God is perfect — and in fact we are in all but our thinking. The problem is that we have imagined limits around ourselves and our love that do not exist in reality.

If God as pure being has no direct relationship with *human* nature, then we must ourselves be *more than human*. We have the capacity for divine being and transcendent relationship and this was once our reality. We must conclude that we, like God, have and are pure being, an ontologically coequal nature with God, a truly divine and timeless nature despite, alongside, and in some ways underlying our anthropological and human nature because we were created for direct and real relationship with God and his beings.

This other nature is the only way to understand and relate to him. It is through this divine nature that we know God directly by firsthand experience and love him with all our being. He is pure subjectivity and so are we, but this subjectivity includes all things. He cannot be perceived by the human eye, nor understood by the human mind, but he can be seen and known by the mind he created, felt and loved in the heart he gave us, and thus known immanently yet transcendentally in our own essential being.

God is pure being, he is spirit, he is love. And so are we if we are his image and children. We too are pure beings, with life in ourselves. We are goodness and truth and justice and light as well. It does not always seem this way in the world with its limits and imperfections, its coldness and carelessness. But God's reality is very different from the world's, and so, in truth, is ours.

5

CREATION AND DEIFICATION

We have just begun to lay out the centrality and ubiquity of deification in Christian theology, but certain questions arise from what we have learned. If human beings are potentially gods, doesn't this necessitate a rethinking of the entire concept of being human? Also, what happens to the boundary between humanity and divinity, and that specifically between us and God? We will find that the patristics often had to contort their positions to avoid Gnostic objections and other diverging trends of thought.

Christian Negative Attitudes Towards the World

The idea of deification sheds new light on early Christian negative attitudes towards the world. Although God was believed by ancient Christians to have created the world, they believed at the same time that the world had fallen into different hands since. The world they lived in was therefore controlled by some nefarious force other than God, indicated for example in Jesus' having told his disciples: "the ruler of the world is coming. He has no power over me" (John 14:30-31).

If God is not the ruler of this world, then who or what is? The context of Jesus' statement is that death is approaching in the person of worldly authorities hunting him down for some of his seemingly radical religious ideas. And so, the ruler of the world, elsewhere called the devil, in John 14 seems here to be death itself, working in lockstep with the worldly authorities. The ambiguity seems to be deliberate. The devil here boils down to a generalized idea of imperfect and mortal creation, i.e., interference with original

Jesus proclaims that those with the *least* power in this world (most notably children) are greatest in the kingdom of heaven.[150] Those who seek to exalt themselves on earth are actually denigrating their own true value. They are, despite their self-satisfaction, on the road to self-destruction. But the values of the world are entirely reversed in the kingdom. All that we had forged for ourselves, by a will apart from God's, had been misguided, hurtful, and the opposite of how we truly are. In fact, we have worked it to be the opposite of God's reality, in the process losing our true heart, seat of our true values, along with our capacity to properly assess worth — our own or anyone else's.

It is for this reason that Jesus says his followers were mistaken to argue who would sit at his right (the seat of secondary power) or at his left in heaven:

> You know that the rulers of the Gentiles lord it over them,
> and their great men exercise authority over them.
> [26]It shall not be so among you;
> but whoever would be great among you
> must be your servant.... (Mt. 20:25-26)

Jesus envisions a reality in which all are perfect equals, naturally respectful and conscientious, cooperating rather than competing, serving rather than lording it over others, realizing that our true reality is intertwined with theirs, that their destiny is ours as well. Hierarchies such as we find in this bureaucratic world do not exist in heaven. It is the absolute dignity of each person that will eventually become the basis for a new world with a new way of thinking. Such new thinking about heaven would evoke experience of oneness with the world. To be willing to take the second place as the world judges such things is to uphold the primacy of God's reality which is wholly equal because glorious in every aspect.

---

[150] See also John Dominic Crossan, *In Parables: The Challenge of the Historical Jesus* (Eagle Books, 1992).

Hell is a state of mind where conflicting interests hide our natural equality, where everything good is fractioned by some degree of negation, where superficial differences are mistaken for inequality, where shadowy illusion replaces the brilliant clarity of truth, and where self-constriction replaces self-expansion. The world we see is marked by competition, conquest, enslavement, estrangement, alienation, abuse, trauma, marginalization, ostracism, hatred, envy, covetousness, larceny, misunderstanding, impulsivity, murder, and hopelessness — to name a few. Even if only partially so, such a world is not meant for humans let alone for gods. What is the source of all this trouble and turmoil that the world must struggle through? It is the part of our unconscious mind that *chose* turmoil, behind a cloak of plausible deniability, a mask of innocence, intending it for others only to have it splash back on ourselves. This is the part that we must now learn to examine honestly and judge against (in ourselves, not in others). Questioning our assumptions and discovering our values ultimately leads us to decide again for our godhood. Our godhood is the deeper part of our unconscious mind, covered over and zealously guarded against by the chaotic, restless, and unwittingly self-destructive part (also unconscious, yet appearing to be in total control) that normally rudders our little boat.

Humankind is restless, to the point of desperation, to recover its original equilibrium. Yet, this is not consciously realized. It strives to do so, but in haphazard, uncalibrated ways, not knowing what it does or how, thus reeling from one unstable extreme to the other in all it does, then covering over the cause, projecting it onto others, and making it increasingly worse for itself and for all others. Because ontological deification is true, we cannot fully acclimate to such carelessness, such recklessness, and such self-produced difficulty. We secretly long to be saved from *ourselves* and such a perilous and convoluted mindset.

The world is not evil, in and of itself. Nor is the body, nor any externality. But neither are they our true home. They are, as always, only what we make of them by our power of interpretation. We are the judges of such things. If there is evil in the world, or simply fecklessness, this comes from us. If there is *any* meaning in the universe, it is we who detected it. We are cosmic deciders of our own experience and its significance. We introduced careless thoughts, systematized them, and imprisoned ourselves in them. We could not have done this had we remembered our true selves and the immense love we held in reserve.

The realization of our own divinity is what will ultimately save us: "For whatever is begotten of God overcomes the world" (1 John 5:4). Once we begin to accept the part of us that is indeed "born of God," begotten, exactly like God — we begin to transcend yet at the same time embrace the world in a loving way. We have buried this perfect reality deep within ourselves. Gradually, by degrees and stages, we are meant to relearn and remember our true selves, while in inverse proportion, the world and its trouble fades from its former foremost position in our mind.

The General View of Creation

Most patristics, while they believed in a restoration of some kind, did not believe in a restoration to full godhood. This is because their views of creation do not *begin* with full godhood. We were not created as mature and completed gods in their estimation, despite having been created in the divine image *and* likeness, and despite God obviously creating what he knows, but rather, we were created as limited and immature creatures with only the *potential* to, after a prolonged process and much trouble, become gods.

Theophilus of Antioch (120-183 CE) wrote that Adam in the Genesis creation accounts was created, not as a full-fledged god but instead immature and undeveloped like an infant. As such, he was rebellious in spirit or at least strong-willed, needing firm guidance and development, which view steered the discussion away from a fully restorative model of deification:[151]

---

[151] *See* Kharlamov 2006: 76-78.

> Neither, then, immortal nor yet mortal did He make him, but, as we have said above, capable of both; so that if he should incline to the things of immortality, keeping the commandment of God, he should receive as reward from Him immortality, and [man] should become God.[152]

According to Theophilus, as we saw in chapter 2, God created us on the razor's edge between immortality and mortality. But what kind of hybrid being would this be? And what does this say about God, who would have so precariously perched his children between life and death and created beings in opposition to him and to themselves? Was *God* of two minds when he created us?

Irenaeus (130–202) shared his contemporary's idea that God created beings in need of development, immature and even infantile human beings with only the potential for godhood. Modern scholars note that this explanation seemed necessary to him to oppose the growing popularity of Gnosticism, not only the Valentinian idea of a plurality of Gods[153] but also the Gnostic notion of three static classes of human beings.[154] These were the *pneumatic* (from Gk. *pneuma*, "spirit" or "breath"), the *psychics* (lower mind-based), and the *somatics* (from Gk. "soma" or "body-oriented"). A caste system with predetermined fates and levels of elitism might have easily arisen from such a notion, and this would have led to misperception of those deemed inferior in the world. The problem was that these were seen as static categories rather than as stages of increasing spiritualization all humans must undergo. The goal is to rise from the somatic or hylic state of total embodiment, first to the psychic state (believing oneself increasingly to be a mind), then ultimately to the deified state of pure pneumatic or spiritual being.

Marchant remarks that Theophilus' and Irenaeus' view persists to the present day:

---

[152] Theophilus of Antioch. "To Autolycus 2: 27." Ante-Nicene Fathers. Ed. Alexander Roberts. Vol. 2. New York: C. Scribner's Sons, 1905. 2:105.
[153] *See* Mosser 2005: 46.
[154] *See* Marchant 2011: 8.

> Orthodox theology, therefore, rather than viewing man's original created state as a condition of static immortality, understands man's created nature to occupy a middle position between mortality and immortality and capable of dynamically attaining to either through the exercise of free choice.[155]

This does appear to be our human situation. However, it seems impossible that an eternal and sure-minded, let alone loving, God would *create* beings who live in uncertainty between mortality and immortality. Because of their supposed need of development, Irenaeus insists on a slow and tortuous process of human development into godhood:

> Now it was necessary that man should in the first instance be created; and having been created, should receive growth; and having received growth, should be strengthened; and having been strengthened, should abound; and having abounded, should recover [from the disease of sin]; and having recovered, should be glorified; and being glorified, should see the Lord.[156]

The stages here are: 1.) creation, 2.) growth, 3.) strengthening, 4.) abounding, 5.) recovery from the disease of sin, 6.) glorification, 7.) a vision of God. Immortality comes only after this elongated process, and each stage must be complete before the next can occur. This is perhaps an apt description of a human being's progress toward deification, but none of the problems and pitfalls needing development or recapitulation should be attributed to God. There are too many unnecessary steps between creation and perfection for this process to have come from God.

Our divine creation, therefore, our begottenness directly from God, must have occurred prior to our human birth. This is the solution Origen proposed, that there must have been preceding

---

[155] Marchant 2011: 8.
[156] Irenaeus, *Against Heresies*, 4.38.3-4. (*ANF* 1:522).

steps to our having found ourselves with a dual nature, which must have been our doing, not God's. The responsibility for this precarious state must lie in our own free decision. This is an explanation that Augustine and others shared in many of their writings, as we shall see, before the idea became forbidden even to discuss in the fourth and fifth centuries.

While deification stands at the end of this process, Irenaeus diminishes the original creation by stating that humans need first to be "taken into the Word," and then receive "adoption" before they can "become the son of God." We can see this in another version of his exchange formula:

> For it was for this end that the Word of God was made man, and He who was the Son of God became the Son of man, that man, having been taken into the Word, and receiving the adoption, might become the son of God.[157]

Irenaeus qualifies sonship with adoptive language simply because of his insistence that we were created *human* first, only later to be given both sonship and godhood. We are thus humans foremost, sons and gods only second. Irenaeus asserts that "we have not been made gods from the beginning, but at first merely men, then at length gods."[158]

While this may seem reasonable on the surface, it is fraught with philosophical quandaries. According to this argument, Adam and Eve were created incomplete because they could not possibly bear full godhood as infants. Like Theophilus of Antioch, Irenaeus presupposes that Adam and Eve were born as innocent naïfs in the woods, who impatiently grasped at godhood before even becoming fully human first. Rather than wait patiently for their development into mature humans and then gods, these early proto-human/proto-gods attempted to snatch the prize early, as Augustine would likewise theorize in his interpretation of the fall of Adam and Eve in

---

[157] Irenaeus, *Against Heresies,* 3.19.1. (*ANF* 1:448).
[158] Irenaeus, *Against Heresies,* 4.38.3-4. (*ANF* 1:522).

the Garden. We were meant to be gods, but we rushed it and thus interrupted the entire prolonged process.

Irenaeus must posit a God who created us into a state of limitation, imperfection and incompletion — to the point where we could not possibly accept the weight of the magnitude of godhood in the beginning:

> God had power at the beginning to grant perfection to man; but as the latter was only recently created, he could not possibly have received it, or even if he had received it, could he have contained it, or containing it, could he have retained it. It was for this reason that the Son of God, although He was perfect, passed through the state of infancy in common with the rest of mankind, partaking of it thus not for His own benefit, but for that of the infantile stage of man's existence, in order that man might be able to receive Him. There was nothing, therefore, impossible to and deficient in God, [implied in the fact] that man was not an uncreated being; but this merely applied to him who was lately created, [namely] man.[159]

Irenaeus speculates that humankind was too immature to receive full godhood. They did not have the capacity to bear its magnitude, being newly created. The problem with this argument is not what it says about human beings but what it says about God. For God to have created imperfect or incomplete beings, we would need to assume a God with at least some imperfect, incomplete, and timebound thoughts. To the contrary, a perfect God with perfect thoughts could by simple logic create *only* perfect beings like himself because that would be all he knows.

Our immaturity must come from elsewhere than God. While it was important for many patristics that our innocence remained intact, even with our exponentially multiplying mistake, we must accept responsibility for the condition (and conditioning) we find ourselves in. We have misused our otherwise blessed capacity for

---

[159] Irenaeus, *Against Heresies*, 4.38.2, (*ANF* 1:522).

free thought and feeling, by deciding to eschew the original reality in favor of a different, necessarily limited, self.

Irenaeus insists that it was good for us to have been created in the process of development:

> For we cast blame upon Him, because we have not been made gods from the beginning, but at first merely men, then at length gods; although God has adopted this course out of His pure benevolence, that no one may impute to Him invidiousness or grudgingness.[160]

To be sure, God is purely benevolent, purest good, but this is not, as Irenaeus states, so that people may not impute anything to him, let alone "invidiousness" (sparking resentment and anger) or "grudgingness." God has no such human foibles, and such things *never* cross his most holy Mind. He is therefore *infinitely* patient, neither quick to anger nor prone to fear. His goodness and ours comes from who and what he is.

Irenaeus was genuinely striving to preserve the Old Testament God in the face of the Valentinians who could not reconcile some of the acts and motives of the OT God with the NT God of love, and so the OT God took on characteristics of a supposed intermediary, the Demiurge, creator of the physical world which allowed the Cosmic Father to remain transcendent. In the next section I will argue that this Demiurge can be no other than ourselves, as a collective entity, in our creative (or in this case miscreative) aspect as gods from before the beginning of the world.

For Irenaeus, the gift of immortality is "the gratuitous bestowal of eternal existence upon them by God."[161] By this he means that it is a "gratuitous" gift, not a necessary product of the original creation. It would be given only after our creation as human beings, and then only after an eons-long process, requiring "their continuing in being throughout a long course of ages" before they

---

[160] Irenaeus, *Against Heresies*, 4.38.4, (ANF 1:523).
[161] Irenaeus, *Against Heresies*, 4.38.2, (ANF 1:522).

would finally "receive a faculty of the Uncreated."[162] As Mosser describes Irenaeus' thinking: "Human beings come to share in properties that are not natural to their created human nature."[163] Deification in this view depends on a long, slow changeover from pre-constricted human nature to a much more expansive supernatural nature. But, why would God create the constriction if expansion was his intent all along? Would he not have created perfect beings from the beginning?

Irenaeus sees the restoration as ultimately resulting in a greater state than Adam enjoyed in his Paradise, because we will attain an incorruptibility Adam did not have due to our adoption into divine sonship.[164] For Irenaeus, humans made divine remain lesser gods than God the Father.[165] By this, again, he meant to preclude entirely the Valentinian plurality of Gods.[166] Yet, at the same time, it renders God to be the author of imperfection, who birthed his beloved children into immediate existential dilemma.

Moreover, because of a common philosophical premise of the day, for Irenaeus, God's creations must always be inferior to him simply because they come after in time:

> But created things must be inferior to Him who created them, from the very fact of their later origin; for it was not possible for things recently created to have been uncreated. But inasmuch as they are not uncreated, for this very reason do they come short of the perfect. Because, as these things are of later date, so are they infantile; so are they unaccustomed to, and unexercised in, perfect discipline.[167]

Irenaeus accepted premises we would no longer consider today, such as that only an Uncreated Being like the Father could be perfect,

---

[162] Irenaeus, *Against Heresies,* 4.38.2, (*ANF* 1:522).
[163] Mosser 2005: 49.
[164] See Irenaeus *Against Heresies,* 3.18.7, (*ANF* 1:448); Mosser 2005: 44.
[165] See Irenaeus *Against Heresies,* 3.6.3, (*ANF* 1:419).
[166] See Mosser 2005: 46.
[167] Irenaeus *Against Heresies* 4.38.1, (*ANF* 1:522).

and that therefore we, his creations, must have been designed imperfect — and thus, to him, necessarily "infantile." This is despite the fact that, for example, Jesus encouraged his students to "be perfect, as God is perfect" (Mt. 5:48).[168] We must therefore have a capacity for perfection, and the ability to recognize the complete reality, within ourselves.

Because created beings have a beginning, they were thought to be changeable, therefore imperfect. But what if they began in timelessness, like their Creator? In that case, we cannot speak of either beginnings or endings, only an endless present-infinity. Thus, having a beginning does not necessarily imply inferiority in all things, *only* in terms of uncreatedness, not necessarily in any other aspect. Their createdness might well be the *only* difference between them and their Creator. Otherwise, they may forever, from the beginningless beginning, share the same basic infinite nature.

The more reasonable explanation of deification is that we were given perfect godhood from the beginning but let it slip through our hands. It is not that we could not contain or retain it, because that would mean that God set us up for failure, having created us with the prize in sight but no capacity to hold or enjoy it. It is rather that we were given it in full originally but willingly gave it up in favor of a necessarily inferior mode of being. We know God himself would not do such a thing, but why would gods do such a thing? Would gods throw a tantrum like a toddler might? Perhaps if they, accustomed in timelessness to having everything, being complete, wanted something that their Source could not grant them, for instance, something that rendered them unequal, or that had the potential to diminish any one of them in any way, including themselves and their completion.

---

[168] My modification.

The Double Creation

Although the Bible begins with God as designer and creator of the physical world, we have seen that by Jesus' time (c. 4 BCE-30 CE, possibly later) there is a strong sense that the world is controlled by evil or ungodlike forces. God cannot have created this evil, mortal and corruptible side of creation, and so something must have intervened between God's original creation (proclaimed "good" by God in every aspect in Genesis) and the world we now see. What exactly intervened, to turn Paradise into turmoil, is not clearly spelled out, but it is salient that the Genesis myths gloss over Paradise and seem more interested in explaining why creation fell from this blessed state, and particularly why humans find themselves to be, even to this day, mortal and corruptible, subject to time and random chance.

By the time of the intertestamental literature, within a couple hundred years before Jesus, the idea of a double creation arises as a way of reconciling the goodness of God with the evil detected in the world:

> 'For an evil heart has grown up in us, which has alienated us from God, and has brought us into corruption and the ways of death, and has shown us the paths of perdition and removed us far from life — and that not merely for a few but for almost all who have been created.'
>
> [49] He answered me and said, 'Listen to me, Ezra, and I will instruct you, and will admonish you once more. [50] For this reason *the Most High has made not one world but two.*' (2 Esdras 7:48-50, my emphasis)[169]

The idea that God created two worlds is needed to account for the two very different natures we find in the world and in ourselves. We will examine these opposing natures in more detail in the next section, but for now simply emphasize that the "evil heart" which

---

[169] 2 Esdras in the KJV and NRSV is also known as 4 Ezra, from the Vulgate.

sprang up to cause alienation, death, and perdition cannot have been created by God. Nor can the world it produces. Yet, there does exist, in addition to God's perfect creation, *another* world and system that seems opposed to God's creation in significant ways. It is this latter creation, the one we perceive around us, that is the imposter, the false idol, attached to the false self that made it.

Esdras (also known as Ezra) questions whether the mind is made out of the same substance as visible things. "O earth, what have you brought forth, if the mind is made out of the dust like the other created things?" (2 Esdras 7:62). He cannot imagine that the mind in all its richness will succumb to dust like all material things. The author laments in the next verses that the mind has grown self-aware of its problematic duality and its body's eventual death. These together form the basic problem of existence, or existential crisis. Two very different states of being coexist uneasily in our minds, and the tension between them is the underlying cause of all conflict. All conflict grows from self-conflict.

We have seen that Jesus taught that our true life and worth lies elsewhere than the world. We have seen that he views "the world" and "life" as opposites in Mt. 16:26, indicating that they are different realities altogether. His parable about the seed scattered in the field and on the path is another example: "the cares of the world and the lure of wealth choke the Word, and it yields nothing" (Mt. 13:22).[170] The world and its cares attract but distract us from the preexistent Word within us ("sewn into the heart" in Mt. 13:19), which is to say, our godhood. Elsewhere in the NT, the double creation is signified by the stark duality in the human being between the outer and inner person, the mind of flesh versus that of spirit.

Origen, in unfolding this idea of a double creation, must first make clear that God can indeed create purely cognitive or spiritual beings. Just as Christ, the Logos or Word of God (in John 1:1) and Holy Spirit were created by God as bodiless beings, so also was every rational mind in every human being:

---

[170] My capitalization of "Word."

> All souls and all rational natures ... are incorporeal; but although incorporeal, they were nevertheless created, because all things were made by God through Christ....[171]

These first creations (Gk., *logika*) are called "souls" or "rational natures." Origen also calls them "minds" and "spirits." Some ancient scholars call them "intelligences" or "understandings." Others call them "luminous beings." These are the original incorporeal and unembodied creations of God, and in Origen's understanding, they are our true selves. They are purely spiritual beings like "Christ" and "the Word" (or Logos) which in Origen's treatment preceded all things but helped to create all things with God or for God. In that case, Christ and the Word's imprimatur and imprint remain with each one of its creations, another strong indication of a divine imprint within our inner being.

Origen's view of a double creation was in fact prompted by such scriptural questions as where the creation of the Word, said to have created all subsequent things in John 1, itself came into being in the Genesis accounts of creation, and why the earth and heaven are created in Gen. 1:1 but the "firmament" and "dry land" appear only several creation days later in Gen. 1:6-10.[172] The idea is reinforced by his interpretation of Psalms 118: 6-8 and 129: 4-6, particularly where God "created" the soul and then "fashioned" the body.[173] Origen, like many of the early fathers, including early Augustine, sought to uphold the idea of the perfect fairness of God via this idea of a double creation. The fairness and justice of God underlies his view of a precosmic, primordial, preexistent creation:

> When He in the beginning created those beings which He desired to create, i.e., rational natures.... He created all

---

[171] Origen, *De Principiis,* 1.7.1, (*ANF* 4:262).
[172] Martens 2016: 525 also points out that Origen may have derived this particular distinction from Philo, the Hellenistic Jewish philosopher who lived at the time of Jesus, who also held to a doctrine of double creation.
[173] Scully 2011: 125-126.

whom He made equal and alike, because there was in Himself no reason for producing variety and diversity.[174]

If God gives all to all, or maximally to each, holding nothing back, then he gives equally all to all. The diversity we see among beings in the world is therefore nothing to God. What God knows as creation is entirely spiritual, composed entirely of equal beings, bodiless minds. Thus, our inner life of mind and heart is primary, having been created first and foremost. Such priority is not really related to time, as Tripolitis explains:

> Although Origen speaks of the *logika* as being created, they were not created in time. Creation with respect to them means that they had a beginning, but not a temporal one.[175]

This original creation of minds or intelligences is located specifically outside of time, within God's entirely different, timeless reality. God is not entirely tied to human history in Origen's expansive vision.

Origen writes that this invisible creation is our inner being, which is the divine image in which we were created:

> But what is created *in God's image* is our inner man, which is invisible, incorporeal, incorruptible and immortal.[176]

The divine image, our "inner man," is already a god, signified by its being "incorporeal, incorruptible, and immortal," characteristics of godhood as we see again and again in the patristics. This "inner man" is for Origen related to the "inner nature" of which Paul speaks in Romans 8:18-22 and 2 Cor. 4:16.

> Even though our outer nature is wasting away, our inner nature is being renewed day by day…. ¹⁸for what can be seen

---

[174] Origen, *De Principiis*, 2.9.6 (*ANF* 4:292).
[175] Tripolitis 1978: 94.
[176] Origen, *Hom. Gen.* 1.13, cited in Jacobsen 2008: 220.

is temporary, but what cannot be seen is eternal. (2 Cor. 4:16,18)

Regarding these passages, Origen writes: "The hope is that of being delivered from this corporeal and corruptible state."[177] The body, just by nature of its material composition, is corruptible, sadly, subject to decay like everything else in the perceptible world. Perhaps more significantly, but for this heap of dust and clay, and where and how it happens to land in the fatalistic wheel of existence, we might know ourselves as equals. We need to be delivered, not so much from the body itself as from full cognitive identification with it, so that we do not confuse its mortal and corruptible nature as representing in any way our permanent, innermost godly reality.

The inner, purely spiritual human must then have been created prior to its embodiment. Origen sees in Genesis 1:1 ("In the beginning, God created the heavens and the earth") a *different* heaven and earth from that which appears several verses later on the second day (where God makes a different "heaven" (the dome of the firmament or the sky) in Gen. 1:6) and the third day when a different "earth" ("the dry land" called "the Earth" in Gen. 1:9-10) is finally formed. The first creation of heaven and earth in 1:1 is spiritual, the second several verses (and days) later is material, physical, and necessarily limited by its dependence on form. Because of this, Origen says of Gen. 1:1:

> For it is certain that the firmament is not spoken of, nor the dry land, but that heaven and earth from which this present heaven and earth which we now see afterwards [in Gen. 1:6-10] borrowed their names.[178]

The original creation was for Origen a "rational mind," capable of knowledge, justice, and the general "capacity to bring

---

[177] Origen, *Com Rom.* 7.4 ed. Von T. Heither, *Fontes Christiani*, Herder, Frieburg 1990-1996, Vol. 2/4, 50, 20-21, cited in Jacobsen 2008: 221.
[178] Origen, *De Principiis,* 1.9.1, (*ANF* 4:267).

about every good."[179] This last phrase suggests a creative capacity for the original mind, and highlights its original loving and unified state with the rest of creation. Elowsky sees in this double creation a similarity to the Platonic view of "two realities, or worlds, running simultaneously, side by side, or, one on top of the other."[180] Thus, the true creation preexists on one track, while we experience the fallen creation on the other track. We can choose to experience either, depending on which we most *want* to experience and hold in mind at any given moment.

The minds or intelligent beings that resulted from the first creation, the true creation, are also symbolized as light (Gen. 1:4-5). God created light per Genesis on the first day of creation prior to its physical sources in the sun and stars: "God said, 'Let there be light'; and there was light" (Gen. 1:3). Yet, it wasn't until the fourth day of creation that physical sources of perceptible light (the sun and stars) were made (Gen. 1:14-19), reinforcing that the original creation of light was unencumbered by form. The Gospel of John will later bolster this understanding, wherein this original light is "the life" of "all people" (Jn. 1:4). Paul also speaks of a celestial or "light body" (1 Cor. 15:44) similar to the "inner man" with which Origen had linked the original spiritual creation. This light is emblematic of our true creation, preexistent of the world or the body or any form at all. It is all content, all substance, all inner being, all mind and heart, this light of life that appeared before the sun and stars in a timeless reality.

For Origen, the first creation of spiritual minds did not take on embodiment until they fell, which fall therefore also took place prior to the material creation. The fall, which we will examine in more detail in the next chapter, resulted from a "cooling off" of their original fiery ardor, their loving state of pure spiritual being and the unified state that results from this. Origen locates our true heaven, both origin and destination of humankind, not geographically, but rather in our mind. In fact, he calls it "our mind" and "our spiritual man" or person:

---

[179] Martens 2013: 528.
[180] Elowsky 2011: 154.

And, therefore, that first heaven indeed, which we said is spiritual, is our mind, which is also itself spirit, that is, our spiritual man which sees and perceives God. But that corporeal heaven, which is called the firmament, is our outer man which looks at things in a corporeal way.[181]

The two creations, one spiritual and one material, present us with two different ways of knowing. The original spiritual creation or "inner man" truly knows, while the "outer man" perceives and is limited to externalities. Each, therefore, has its own mind, which we refer to as the higher mind and lower mind respectively. The former is identified with the creation of the original "heaven" in Gen. 1:1.

Martens pieces together what information we might glean about Origen's lost *Commentaries on Genesis* from references made to it in other places:

> Origen describes the Edenic paradise in a fragment from his *Commentarii in Genesim* as "some divine place" … unsuitable for corporeal inhabitants. In fact, he repeatedly insisted that the garden in Eden was not to be literally understood as an actual, perceptible place here on earth. In the passage already cited above from *De principiis*, he thought it a 'silly' … idea that God planted a paradise in Eden, with actual trees, and then proceeded to walk around in it.[182]

The original creation of minds and spiritual beings did not require a "place," a physical location, as there was nothing physical about it. Therefore, the original Paradise was a state of pure mind and heart, of universals and ideals vast enough for gods to inhabit, rather than an earthly location.

Origen's reason for proposing a double creation was to reconcile and harmonize two often opposing but necessary principles, those being the perfectly fair justice of God and the God-

---

[181] Origen, *Homilies on Genesis and Exodus*. 1.2. Ronald E. Heine, trans. (Washington, DC: The Catholic University of America Press, 1981).
[182] Martens 2016: 526.

given freedom of the human will. It helps to explain the apparent inequalities of existence without attributing these to God. These two principles taken together lead to a cosmology or creation account in which preexistence plays an important part.[183] The real action takes place before the world ever came into being, but it set the conditions under which we now exist. This preexistent reality includes both the original creation of pure and perfect minds by God and their fall from perfection into lesser ideas of being. The second creation occurred when these lesser *ideas* of being crystallized into lesser *forms* of being. In our daily existence we deal with the difficulties and limitations brought about by these forms, the aftermath of the fall, the second creation, while at the same time striving to return to the original splendor our heart desires above all else.

As for God's reason for creating the spiritual creation in the first place, Origen teaches that God had no other reason for creating these rational natures except "on account of Himself, i.e., His own goodness." He wanted simply to share his joy, which meant that his creation had to share his way of being. God created beings who were entirely "equal and alike" with "neither any variation nor change, nor want of power."[184] Without form or anything physical to limit them, they were equal in power, being, and the capacity for joy. It was out of "His own goodness" that God created them with the same or very similar nature. But not even this goodness is foisted on them. They can decide whether to remain good, but, as Givens notes, "neither are they inherently evil. They are rational and, therefore, free."[185] Our freedom of mind, we glean from the scriptures and from existence itself, is sacrosanct in God's eyes.

Hilary of Poitiers and Gregory of Elvira follow Origen in postulating a double creation of humankind. They observe Origen's distinction between the spirit and body. Hilary, like Origen, understood the dual creation to correspond to the inner and outer man taught by Paul. The spirit or inner man was created first, in the image of God, while the physical, earthly outer man is secondary. It

---

[183] See chapter 7 for a fuller exposition of preexistence.
[184] Origen, *De Principiis* 2.9.6 (*ANF* 4:292).
[185] Givens 2010: 93.

is this distinction that renders humankind to be a composite being with two natures. Despite their different origins, rather than seeing these dual natures as oppositional (as in Platonic philosophy and Paul), Hilary views them as initially harmonious (as with Stoic philosophy), destined to return to congruence and thus be saved together.[186]

Hilary takes a recapitulative view that we were truly and physically present in Adam when he sinned, but we were *also* truly present with and in Christ when he assumed humanity, when he was resurrected, and when he was glorified. [187] Most Christian theologians from that time period could not conceive of an original creation composed entirely of mind, and so they hypothesized a physical union with Jesus. But the outcome was similar: This physical union was all spiritual in its outcome, including a *present* glorification and resurrection, one that we might experience even now. However, this attempted synthesis is not the best explanation because, for one thing, there is nothing divinely simple about a composite being with two natures.

Gregory of Nyssa and Augustine also saw human beings as primarily rational creatures, but not to the point that they were originally disembodied minds or purely spiritual beings. Augustine seemed to agree with the idea of a double creation in his earlier writings, such as *de Genesi ad litteram*, ("Genesis Understood Literally"), wherein, following Plotinus, he sees two "moments" of creation, the first of which consists of the "causal reasons" of all things that will ever be, like pure ideals, while the second consists of their physical manifestations.[188] However, later in his *City of God* he replaced these preexistent causal reasons with his doctrine of inherited original sin. [189] This idea of original sin was revived a thousand years later by Western Reformed tradition and took hold to become the current general Christian viewpoint. We will examine later how a fully restorative deification replaces the presumed total

---

[186] Scully 2011: 128-129.
[187] See Hilary, See *De Trinitate* 11.49; Scully 2011: 129.
[188] O'Meara 1984: 55.
[189] Couenhoven 2005: 362.

debasement of Augustinian original sin with the pure and natural blessedness of original godhood.

The Dual Nature of Human Beings

It is difficult to go through life with a double nature. It produces deep struggle and identity confusion within our mind. So distressing is this inner conflict that we made it unconscious to ourselves, but that means that we now deal with it only obliquely and ineffectively. Each nature is insistent in its own way, and each maintains that it is our one true nature. One presses us more insistently, while the other, in timeless eternity, patiently waits and responds. One side of this split nature has a life of its own, given by God, the other, while depending on this original creation for its rudimentary life, takes on a distorted semblance of the former.

The idea of a double creation is indicated by the stark dual nature that fills the pages of the New Testament. Paul expresses this double nature personally as a struggle between his "inmost self" and his ordinary creaturely nature:

> For I delight in the law of God in my inmost self, [23]but I see in my members another law at war with the law of my mind, making me captive to the law of sin that dwells in my members. (Romans 7:22-23)

The split here is between the mind and the physical self. The "inmost self" already "delight(s) in the law of God." It lives in a different reality, even now, and it is our divine nature. The outward self, on the other hand, is the physical self we most often think we are. It lives in a world of external forms and limitations amid the multitude of problems thereof, most of them, like the world system in which they are couched, obviously self-made. Paul exclaims he longs to be rescued from this outer self and its embodiment he refers to as "this body of death" in the next verse (Ro. 7:24). He expresses the distinction as one of "mind" versus "flesh" in verse 25: "So then, with my mind I am a slave to the law of God, but with my flesh I am a slave to the law of sin" (Ro. 7:25). The mind is not required to think of itself as a self-limiting body nor be controlled by anything unless it allows it, but we tend to live our lives as if that is our only choice.

Paul refers to a similar distinction in Second Corinthians between our "outer nature" and our "inner nature":

> So we do not lose heart. Even though our outer nature is wasting away, our inner nature is being renewed day by day. (2 Cor. 4:16)

The outer nature is already "wasting away," which is reflected in the corruptible, degenerative world in which it abides. Meanwhile, the inner nature reflects the eternity in which it abides. It is being "renewed" each day and indeed every moment because it is timeless and unchanging. Such a distinction between our inner and outer natures reinforces the idea of a double creation in which two very different realities are occurring at the same time.

We therefore cannot speak of human beings as having a single human nature, because they are equipped with two. There has been much confusion about this even among patristics, and this confusion became enshrined in dogma before it was fully sorted out. We must specify which we mean when we talk about "human nature." Normally, we think of human nature in simple anthropological terms, but scriptural revelation presents us with an entirely other side, the ontological side, the inmost part composed of pure being, the one God created to be perfect and eternal like himself.

Paul speaks of our embodiment as a "slight momentary affliction" compared to the "eternal weight of glory beyond all measure" that we can expect as creations of God (2 Cor. 4: 17). Thus, we look not to temporal bodily perception to show us our true selves and nature, but rather we look to the eternal yet internal nature that the body cannot perceive (as we saw in 2 Cor. 4: 18). Over time and with practice we can train ourselves to apprehend universals and intelligible realities which human eyes cannot ordinarily see. Paul seems to be expressing here a process of deification via a renewed perception brought about by a spiritualization of our thoughts.

Ephesians likewise encourages us to concern ourselves with "the inner being" (Eph. 3:16), where Christ dwells in our heart and our heart is "grounded in love" (3:17), which are, of course, inner realities. "The Spirit" works to "strengthen" or reinforce the inner being with the "love" and "fullness of God" (3:18-19). The inner self is here the focal point of the religion, and that which is truly salvific in it.

We tend to think of it the other way around — characteristic of our fallen attempt to reverse God's reality — that God focuses on the outer self and its behavior. Against this practice, Jesus counseled: "first cleanse the inside of the cup and of the plate, that the outside may also be cleaned" (Matthew 23:24), which indicates that the purification of the outside *depends* on the purification of the inside. Proper morality depends on having the mindset, qualities, virtues and values of a god. But these are internal realities that human beings do not generally perceive. Thus, we need to refocus away from outward appearance — *even if* it is the outside that we want to see purified.

Jesus was speaking of our bifurcated but temporary condition when he stated that: "Every kingdom divided against itself is laid waste, and no city or house divided against itself will stand" (Mt. 12:25). For Jesus, as we have seen, it was deceitful to "outwardly appear righteous to men," while we are "full of hypocrisy and iniquity" inside ourselves (Matthew 23:28). We saw how he likened this bifurcated way of being to a condition of walking around like "whitewashed tombs, which outwardly appear beautiful, but within are full of dead men's bones" (Mt. 23:27). Such a fundamental opposition supports the idea that God is concerned with the state of our mind and heart rather than anything having to do with "appearance," form, or perception. God is God of the inner being, consorting with heart and mind rather than outward appearances.

We did not create our true nature as minds and gods, which is fixed and permanent, but we can choose whether we will accept and experience this reality. We retain the divine image, but we have a choice as to whether to assent to the likeness (most patristics would agree). If we do not accept our likeness to God, we are left with only a self-constructed self with unfortunate self-destructive tendencies that blunders through a world drifting into nothingness, a temporary and confused self unwittingly perpetuating the division by which it was born. The more tightly it tries to control everything around itself to maintain its autonomy from the inner self, the more desperate it becomes if one piece falls out of place, exposing the emptiness and irrationality at its core.

Paul teaches that we can "set" our minds on either of these two selves, and each self is an immersion into a different reality, its own world, which would bolster the idea of a double creation. Ultimately, we choose between God's reality or the world we have made to replace it. Paul says:

> For this reason the mind that is set on the flesh is hostile to God; it does not submit to God's law — indeed it cannot... (Romans 8:7)

At their core they are two fundamentally opposed realities. But note that it is not the flesh itself that is "hostile to God," or opposite of God, but rather "the mind that is set on the flesh." The flesh itself is neutral, neither good nor bad. It is an appearance, whatever the mind makes of it, and can be used either for ascent or descent, whichever way we set our mind. By default, if we punch our ticket here on earth, that is, if we are here at all, then we have set our minds on flesh. Yet, it may be revealed to us at any time that we have a different possibility for living, even here in the world.

The mind identified with the flesh is "hostile to God" because God did not make it that way. Where God created only life, the mind set on flesh sees death. Thus, Paul says: "To set the mind on the flesh is death, but to set the mind on the Spirit is life and peace" (Ro. 8:6). 1 Peter 3:4 urges us to "let your adornment be the inner self" with its "lasting beauty," its "gentle and quiet spirit," and its preciousness "in God's sight." This inner self is the self God sees, the beautiful self

God created in timeless majesty, the divine self and nature God shares with us out of his own goodness.

Jesus presents the duality as a similarly stark contrast: "It is the spirit that gives life, the flesh is of no avail; the words that I have spoken to you are spirit and life" (John 6:63). He indicates that this dichotomy stems from two very different realities with different sources in the human being: "What is born of the flesh is flesh, and what is born [begotten] of the Spirit is spirit" (Jn. 3:6). Ontology stands at the heart of these sayings; these are two opposed ways of being. The upshot is that we find ourselves in an untenable situation, caught between two conflicting realities within each person. But one of these realities, having been created by God, has priority over the other:

> He who comes from above is above all; he who is of the earth belongs to the earth, and of the earth he speaks; he who comes from heaven is above all. (John 3:31)

What both orthodox and Gnostic theology failed to understand was that Jesus is not speaking of two different types or classes of people here, but of two different natures (or possibilities of self) within each individual mind. Such sayings are helpful in determining how to differentiate or judge between the two natures within our own person, which are known through experience. We should see the following statement of Jesus in the same way:

> [O]ut of the abundance of the heart the mouth speaks. [35] The good man out of his good treasure brings forth good, and the evil man out of his evil treasure brings forth evil. (Mt. 12:34-35)

Again, these are not two groups or classes of people so much as they are two natures within each self (like Paul's "inner man" and "outer man"). From the human standpoint, because of our bifurcated nature, no one being is fully good, and none is fully evil. Everyone begins this leg of the journey with composite beings, natures, and values. Even Jesus had his human moments[190] along with his divine.

God, himself forever one and divinely simple, did not create dual beings in conflict with themselves. What we were originally given by God is purest godhood, which was once and is still the kernel and truth of reality, thus the whole of reality, while our denial and distortion of this original being is the negative pole marked by degrees of void and emptiness from the original truth. Augustine asks: "What, after all, is anything we call evil except the privation of good?"[191] Evil is not a thing in and of itself. It is rather the absence or void of the pure good that *should* be there (or that *is* there but goes unseen and unappreciated), because God himself placed it there. Thus, it is a vacuum that pulls downward toward spiraling emptiness and denial.

Jesus defined the good more specifically to be love. Evil, therefore, can more specifically be defined as the absence or privation of love, as with Origen's cooling off of the original loving minds. The attributes of God are purely positive, always miraculously adding more to the fullness, each reflecting and representing the same whole reality, and so the negative pole is the denial and absence of wholeness as well. It is incompletion, always in process of becoming, striving but never quite arriving.

Augustine states that we have accepted an idol, a caricature, instead of the true God-given self. Yet, "an idol cannot do justice to the depth of 'your inner self.'"[192] The idol, for Augustine, is the false outer self that we have made and substituted for the one God created. Plato in his *Phaedrus* had depicted the bipartite aspect of human beings as a result of humans having attached their chariots to one good winged steed and one wicked one, making it difficult for the charioteer (the deciding mind) to control them. Whereas as gods

---

[190] For instance, his vented anger at the Temple moneychangers (Mk. 11:15-18; para. Mt. 21:12-13) and his cry on the cross: "My God, my God, why have you forsaken me?" (Mk. 15:34; para. Mt. 27:46).
[191] Augustine, *The Enchiridion*, Ch. 11, trans. Albert C. Outler (1955).
[192] Augustine, *The Enchiridion*, Ch. 11, trans. Albert C. Outler (1955); in Puchniak 2006: 127.

we had two good winged horses pulling in the same direction, now we experience one good (tending toward eternity) and one evil (tending toward the void).[193] This metaphor of an actively bipartite self pulling in opposite directions seems to correspond with the New Testament teaching regarding duality we have been studying.

We need to retake the reins and responsibility not only for what we do, but also for what we think and feel. We are meant to think the highest thoughts, with God, and to experience the deepest, most fulfilling and bonding emotions, just as he does. We retain the capacity to do so, and the practice of this and its resultant joy allows us to remember who we really are in God. And, because we are one, as we shall see, our responsibility and our journey is not only for ourselves, although it is an inner process, but for all others as well.

Conclusion

Most patristics accept human nature as our true, God-created nature. But appearances can be deceiving, and myths and folktales, however speckled with revelation, can be confusing, even for great early scholars such as those we have been studying. As we will see next, the fall is a delusory state, a state of delusion and dissociation, mistaken assumptions and faulty premises, whereby we believe what is not true and deny what is. This is the normative state of the world, the insanity and emptiness at its hollow core.

If the world is not our true home, and the body is but an "earthly tent" (2 Cor. 5:1), a temporary dwelling, and the mind set on flesh is "hostile to God" (Ro. 8:7), then how can we assume that human nature is our true nature graced and granted by God? Would it not be the temporal world of appearances that is alien, the divine inner person actually closer and more familiar to our hearts and minds although it seems, for now, farthest away?

Early church father Irenaeus went a long way towards systematizing deification. There is beautiful symbolism and

---

[193] Plato, *Phaedrus* 246a-b; in Forger 2018: 231.

symmetry in his idea of Jesus being a recapitulative parallel figure to Adam, saving the world by correcting Adam's disobedience at each step of his own existence with his own obedience to God, so that human beings who fell with Adam might rise and ascend with Jesus to their originally intended godhood. Such an idea makes Jesus both truly human and at the same time a true god to follow.

However, Irenaeus' conclusion that God must have created human beings as immature, naively innocent beings is ultimately unsatisfying. It is unsatisfying, not only for what it says about God's creation, but for what it says about God. This notion of imperfect creation, along with his emphasis on the language of Pauline "adoptive" sonship rather than Johannine begotten or natural divine sonship, has held too great a sway over later theologians.

Theophilus of Antioch, the probable originator of Irenaeus' idea, was prevented from seeing Adam as immortal because that would suggest equality with God, and, on the other hand, "if he were mortal, God would be responsible for his death."[194] The only solution from his viewpoint was to land somewhere in the middle. God could have made us immortal but chose not to do so. No one ever stopped to ask: Is this what a most loving Father would do, how a loving Source would create? It would be chaos from the outset, like giving toddlers the run of the house; surely they would hurt themselves.

It is true that we must be careful not to attribute death and mortality, things so unlike him, to God. God is the God of life, and death is not a reality for him. It is inconceivable to the eternal mind. And his own eternity is imprinted in every one of his thoughts, which would include each of his most holy creations. Thus, the only conclusion we can reach is that God created us immortal and perfect like himself.

Adam (as representative of ourselves) blazed his own trail of future death by desiring a way of being necessarily lesser than the godhood he had been given. He had been given life, eternal and incorruptible, life in himself which could never be rescinded. Therefore, the death he found at the end of the trail, though tragic, turns out to be an illusory death, but one that haunts and recurs,

---

[194] Kharlamov 2006: 77-78.

until he finally finds the path that leads back to the life he originally walked naturally alongside God. He does not at first realize that he himself is responsible for his lostness. His hiding was not from God, but from himself.

Like Adam, we do have free choice — but not regarding what type of being we will *be* (i.e., gods), only regarding what type of being we will *experience*. Most patristics agree we have power over our likeness to God, but not to having been created in his image. And the result of our choosing presents us with either actual immortality or the illusion of mortality depending on the identity, reality, and experience we choose.

It was also important for the early Christian writers to hold that our godhood was a free gift from God, a blessing provided by grace and not produced by ourselves — i.e., that it was not a *self-deification* but a gift from God. To emphasize that salvation in the form of deification was a gift of God, Irenaeus, along with Augustine and most patristics after them, concluded that our deification is acquired only in the distant future (usually not until the general resurrection at the end of time). In this view, we start off as humans, to become gods only later — much later, as it turns out.

The fully restorative view of deification likewise sees our godhood as a free gift from God, not a self-deification. The difference is that it sees God as having granted us a complete and established godhood from the moment of our creation. What Irenaeus calls maturation, then, is instead rehabilitation and restoration, a climb back to wholeness after a terrible fall. In the fully restorative view, our rehabilitation is the restoration of a state of mind and being we already had and already have, but no longer realize. The revelation of this original gift of godhood is the second grace, an additional grace, added for our salvation via our reidentification with the divine image within our mind.

This perfect being, with Its purely divine nature, is not only still accessible to us, it is forever who we are, in spite of all the changes we experience along the way back. The idea that human beings were created in the image and likeness of God means that they already have what they are searching for — *they already are what they will forever be* — but they have driven the part of the mind that knows this from awareness. What we call consciousness is therefore *lack* of awareness, and just the tip of the iceberg, as what is now unconscious to us holds so much more than we believe we can receive.

6

THE FALL OF GODS

If God is perfect, then all his thoughts are perfect, which means his creation is perfect, reflecting him and transparent to him in every way. Perfection is not something we attain for ourselves; it is something we are granted by a perfect Creator. It is pure grace, a free gift. We do not need to strive for it so much as simply accept it. It is, at root, only our refusal of the grace of our own God-given perfection that stands in our way.

The Fall of Gods

Examining the world clearly and fairly, we must admit that it is not perfect. Yet, the world is said to be God's creation, and a perfect God's creation *must* be perfect, or else this perfect God would be capable of imperfect thoughts. So, what went wrong? From where did all the problems come?

Obviously, if creation was perfect to begin with, then in the interim there must have been a fall, a descent or defection from perfection into imperfection, simply because we find ourselves now in an imperfect world. If the perfect God's thoughts are eternal, his will unbreakable, then the perfect world God created for perfect beings must still exist, but it is hidden from our sight and experience. What we ordinarily see as the world and what we experience therein is not therefore God's true creation. But God has arranged it so that we can, if we wish, uncover the fullness of perfect creation even here amidst the fallen and broken world.

How do gods become something less than gods? In the strictest sense, they cannot. Once a god, always a god. Godhood is an eternal and changeless state of being, like God's. But in another sense, only a god *can* make itself seem to be less than a god. There is no other power in the cosmos that can so diminish a god — except itself.

Thus, it is only we who must be responsible for our fall from godhood and its resultant condition. Although in the creation tales Adam blames Eve (Gen. 3:12), and in doing so blames God ("the woman *you* gave ... me"), and Eve blames the serpent (Gen. 3:13), we must admit that it is by our own doing (or way of thinking) that we exist in a fallen world. Here, then, is where repentance, recapitulation, and a reversal of direction comes in.

That is to say, as gods to begin with, we ourselves are responsible for the fallen world in which we find ourselves, including the apparent corruptibility and mortality that shades everything in it. Death and corruptibility, we have seen, were viewed as major results of the fall based on Gen. 2:16 and 3:19 as well as Psalm 82:1, 6-7 and Jesus' re-statement of this in John 10:34-35. Paul carries this theme forward in Romans 5:14 and 6:22-23 ("the wages of sin is death" which is opposed to "the free gift" of "eternal life").

We tend to speak of the Gnostics as having reacted against a Judaic view of positive material creation, but this is an oversimplification. The narrative in Genesis 2-3, traditionally referred to as the "J" story of creation, is already questioning how creation came to incorporate the many problems inherent in it. These include pain even in childbirth (Gen. 3:16), "enmity" or conflict (Gen. 3:15), toil and struggle to survive (3:17), difficulty and complexity (3:18), and the ultimate limit, death (3:19). The perfect paradise that came before is given short shrift, perhaps because it is not translatable in human terms, except that we glean from the accounts that the original beings had direct communication with God, and they needed nothing because their desires were satisfied. This "creation story" is an attempt to explain, not so much creation itself, but rather how creation became corrupted, subject to decay and eventual disintegration, and how it became mortal, or subject to death. As such, the "J" version of creation is more a narrative of the fall from godhood than a creation story per se. Although they are clearly myths, not meant to be taken literally, containing more than a hint of irony and sardonic wit, there are certain insights and revelations that may come from reading them.

Eastern fathers are generally careful to insist that God is not responsible for Adam's punishment and banishment from Eden. These are, rather, inherent and natural consequences of a fall away from union with God and from love itself. According to Basil of Caesarea, for instance, Adam fell from a state of loving oneness with God. This caused him to become "insolent through satiety" and to prefer physical pleasure over spiritual joy. "And immediately he was outside paradise and outside that blessed way of life, becoming evil not from necessity but from thoughtlessness." [195] Basil thus concluded that it was "thoughtlessness" and not a truly wicked intention by which Adam stumbled into evil and out of paradise. Such a way of thinking reinforces the idea that God does not seek to punish Adam and his progeny, but rather only to guide them back where they belong. For many patristics, the physical creation was meant for just this: as a means to return to original spiritual bliss.

Thoughtlessness and impulsivity must be involved because there is no good reason why gods would choose to abdicate their godhood and abandon their power, their total peace, and their heart's greatest desire. It cannot therefore have been a decision grounded in reason nor stability. The consequences are far too tragic, the benefits far too fleeting to rationalize with any comparatively miniscule advantage. It seems likely that the desired gain was a different form of control, no longer grounded in the eternal values of God, so we relinquished our true power and minimized any happiness therefrom. We had it within our power to maintain the joy we were given, and the vastness in all we knew, but we let it slide in favor of — what? The satisfaction of having sabotaged ourselves, in a futile and desperate effort to sabotage God? As we have stated, there is only one way for gods to fall — and that is downward on the ladder of being. In order no longer to be

---

[195] St Basil The Great, *On the Human Condition*, p. 74. Translation and Introduction by Nonna Verna Harrison. St. Vladimir's Seminary Press: Crestwood, NY, 2005.

itself, a god would have had to become a lesser being, a more limited being, something a god in its right mind would never willfully choose.

All of this leads us to conclude that the fall was a tragic mistake, not well considered, and therefore the product of a raging fit, an irrational tantrum rather than a well-conceived decision. But that does not mean we were created that way, as per Irenaeus; this was our impulsive decision, our miscreation. There *was* an element of naivete and even infantile and overreactive thinking in this, particularly in our having been so careless of the consequences. Should we blame God for having given us entirely free minds, or should we rather blame ourselves for misusing such a gracious gift? It was uncharacteristic of both God's perfection and our own perfect creation.

Augustine found in the early chapters of Genesis indications that we were intended to be gods from the start, but were seduced into a different kind of godhood, a pipe dream of wayward autonomy that does not actually exist. He argued that Adam and Eve, representing all humans, tried to self-deify (or rush deification) rather than accept their true deification from God. Such a scheme could only backfire as evidenced by the outcome that they became mere mortals and utterly forgot their original path to godhood. As Augustine put it:

> We wished to be God ourselves when we fell away from him, after listening to the Seducer saying, "You will be like gods." Then we abandoned the true God, by whose creative help we should have become gods, but by participating in him, not by deserting him.[196]

Thus, Adam had already fallen into ignorance and self-deception by the time he accepted or even considered seriously the serpent's dubious and redundant offer in Genesis 2-3. The "crafty" (Gen. 3:1) serpent, then, was an unconscious projection of Adam's already

---

[196] Augustine, *City of God* 22.30. Translated by Marcus Dods. From *Nicene and Post-Nicene Fathers*, First Series, Vol. 2. Edited by Philip Schaff. (Buffalo, NY: Christian Literature Publishing Co., 1887.)

active guilt. When Adam grasped for this illusion of autonomy, he took something less than he already had and was. He wanted autonomy in a way unnatural to him which left him disempowered, alienated, vulnerable, guilt-ridden, paranoid, and estranged not only from God but from Eve and even from himself. Having buried his true godhood out of a mixture of recklessness and guilt, he began to fear his true being and everything like it (i.e., God), thus ensuring that it would be virtually impossible to gather it back without transcendent help. When a god decides to hide, it hides exceedingly well, covering its tracks almost perfectly.

The aftermath of this fall into lovelessness is played out in all aspects of the world. We have seen that the earliest Christians had such negative attitudes toward the world that they considered it to be ruled over by death and the devil. Genesis 2:16 tells us that death is introduced into perception by the fall, via ingesting the "fruit" of "the tree of the knowledge of good and evil." This could be confusing because it is not "knowledge" that brings death, or the illusion thereof, but rather the disavowal of knowledge of God's way of life which led us to invent the lower-order faculty of perception to replace it. We lost knowledge (or hid it away) when we gained perception. They are two different ways of "knowing" and of living.

From a fully restorative vantage point, there is no true mortality but only the illusion or perception of death. Perception is indicated in the "J" story by the consequence that "the eyes of both were opened, and they knew they were naked" (Gen. 3:7), which announces this new ability of physical perception resulting in a semblance of newfound autonomy marked by alienation. They got their autonomy, but with it came a slew of negative unintended consequences, all because their self-alienation induces fear (Gen. 3:11). Their guilt, which triggered their attempt to hide from God, was made exponentially worse by the fear of outlandish punishment they now expected from the distorted view of their loving Creator it produced. The fall was cemented in their perception as soon as they "hid themselves from the presence of the Lord" (Gen. 3:8). The cover-up was worse than the crime because it perpetuated the problem without their even realizing. Pride and anger would have been containable and soon laughed off as ludicrously overwrought had we original gods not taken it too far.

The Fall for Origen

Origen's theory removes the fall from having happened at a moment in time, and relocates it to the realm of timeless eternity. For him the fall occurred among our unembodied minds prior to mortal existence. Before the world, and its constant, measured turning from day to night, there was no way nor need for minds to measure time. The fall happened outside of time, thus we might say before time, but it brought time, death, and every other limit into existence. All of this was eventually reflected in our embodiment in the world. We might appropriate Anselm's statement here that "I fell before my mother conceived me."[197] We were not so much born into fallenness as into its aftereffects.

Origen states that some of the minds God created, originally hot with the ardor of love, "cooled" as they distanced themselves from love. These cooled minds then coalesced in denser form and hardened into various types of embodiment, and a world coalesced around them to house them. Origen explains the origin of the fiery loving minds of God:

> For in sacred language God is called a fire, as when Scripture says, Our God is a consuming fire [Heb. 12:29]. ... As God, then, is a fire, and the angels a flame of fire, and all the saints are fervent in spirit, so, on the contrary, those who have fallen away from the love of God are undoubtedly said to have cooled in their affection for Him, and to have become cold. For the Lord also says, that, because iniquity has abounded, the love of many will grow cold.... [T]he love of many is said to wax cold; we have to inquire whether perhaps

---

[197] Anselm, *Proslogium* Ch. 17 (1926 reprint ed.), translated by S. N. Deane. Chicago: Open Court Publishing Company.

the name soul, which in Greek is termed ψυχή, be so termed from growing cold out of a better and more divine condition, and be thence derived, because it seems to have cooled from that natural and divine warmth, and therefore has been placed in its present position, and called by its present name.[198]

We were spiritual and cognitive beings to begin with, who took on form or concretized as our original loving nature cooled. Thus, at root, lack of love was the "sin" that led to the fallen world we see around us.

Origen argues that the diversity of material creation stems from the creation's original "freedom of will." For whereas God created souls to be "equal and alike because there was in Himself no reason for producing variety and diversity," the creation fell from this perfect equality into diverse creatures that now spend eons ascending and descending the ladder of being.[199] Diversity among creatures ("different vessels, or souls, or understandings") is produced by "the freedom of the individual will." Origen valiantly upholds the idea of God's fair justice, equally applied to all, and how God gives to each one "according to his merits." There is remarkable hidden organization within the world because all the beings in the world of perception are moving up and down the ladder of being according to their "merits." The general trend is upward, but there are some who lose touch and descend further. Each is ultimately "advancing through each stage to a better condition" until at last they "reach even to that which is invisible and eternal," and all of this goes "according to their own actions and endeavors."[200] There is a greater and more intricate plan in motion than we normally can detect, and our experience of it depends on us.

Origen's theology upholds, along with God's justice, the dignity of creation, particularly the mind. With such freedom comes accountability and responsibility for human beings. Origen writes: "it

---

[198] Origen, *De Principiis*, 2.8.3 (*ANF* 4:287-288).

[199] Origen, *De Principiis* 2.9.6 (*ANF* 4:292).

[200] Origen, *De Principiis* 1.6.3 (*ANF* 4:261).

lies within ourselves and in our own action to possess either happiness or holiness, or by sloth and negligence to fall from happiness into wickedness and ruin."[201] We can have either complete happiness, or self-deception leading to ruin. Our powerful mind will grant us our wish, so we should learn to choose reasonably and responsibly. For Origen, this process of increasing good judgment during our existence(s) on earth is preliminary to the last judgment. We will undergo many bouts of self-judgment before the last judgment.[202]

Because we were naturally spiritual beings, there is a certain preexistent guilt that comes merely with bodily existence:

> There were certain causes of prior existence, in consequence of which the souls, before birth in the body, contracted a certain amount of guilt.[203]

A preexistent source of guilt had to be postulated in order to explain the innate diversity. And so, the body is not the cause of guilt; the causes are preexistent. The causes of the differences we see are hidden to us. Although they are quite diverse, and some seem impossible, all the problems we bring with us are resolved in similar fashion: by hastening the realization of godhood.

For Origen, the individuality of the soul can reflect divinity in its own particular ways.

> This individual soul is indicative of the intended function of all souls, i.e., to reveal the divine mystery in unique ways, insofar as the meaning of this mystery is deposited within them, as theandric (God-human) potentiality, to be drawn out and revealed through co-operation with God.[204]

---

[201] Origen, *De Principiis*, 1.5.5 (*ANF* 4:260).
[202] See chapter 10 for more on such judgment and eschatology in general.
[203] Origen, *De Principiis*, 3.3.5 (*ANF* 4:337).
[204] Origen, *De Principiis*, 2.9.2-8 (*ANF* 4:290).

This inner divinity is evoked in the way best for each through their increasing cooperation with God, which allows them to rise on the ladder of being, in Origen's version from angel to archangel and ultimately back to the original minds of God. How far we must rise depends on how far we have let ourselves fall away from love. In this sense, the fall and return is individualized for each being.[205]

The reason we were able to fall away from God at all is that God declined to impose his will upon us, even if it is for our own good. We have discussed that this respect for freedom of the mind appears to be a sacrosanct principle for God as regards his creation. We have been given complete freedom of mind to decide for our own greatest happiness. God trusts us, implicitly and completely, infinitely more than we trust ourselves.

A Note on Dissociation

It is a well-documented psychological truth that the human mind can build solid walls within itself, invisible and unconscious yet experienced as very real, then hide parts of *itself* behind these walls. That is, the mind can successfully forget significant parts of itself even while they remain operational in the human psyche. Such a process is known to occur for instance in preverbal children who have suffered significant trauma, which reaffirms the unconscious nature of this process of forgetting and splitting. The child does not consciously choose to divide its mind in order to escape, for instance, the effects of abuse and trauma; the mind does it for the child, a kind of natural protective mechanism built into the mind, which springs into action when needed. Psychology calls this the unconscious process of *dissociation*.

There are different types of dissociation, ranging from *amnesia*, a temporary forgetting of details of one's life, up to and including one's previous identity, to *Dissociative Identity Disorder* (formerly called Multiple Personality Disorder), wherein whole new

---

[205] See Origen, *De Principiis*, 1.8.1; Koutcheau's Text, 67; in Givens 2010: 94.

identities and personalities emerge from the mind. Fascinatingly, these new identities and personality fragments each have their own ways of thinking and styles of speaking and even handwriting. It is as if one lone mind can itself produce any number of possible identities. The mind, in itself, is an amazing thing.

I say all this simply to note that the unconscious process of dissociation is a real, known phenomenon with real effects in the world. A fully restorative deification proposes that human beings are born dissociated from their own spiritual truth. We arrive on this planet pre-dissociated, so to speak, and this stands in the way of seeing ourselves as gods *as if it meant to do so*. We already are gods, by virtue of our creation by God in his image. The only problem is that we have rejected this truth and dissociated it from our conscious minds. Thus, we have no *conscious* memory of it.

In this fallen world in which we now exist, all its norms and traditions, its institutions and systems, reflect the fallen mind, the traumatized mind that seeks desperately to hide from God, itself, and all it loves. We see everything through a distorted lens, although this now seems natural to us. The mind can acclimate to nearly anything if it decides to do so. But, as with *Post-Traumatic Stress Disorder* (PTSD), there are numerous triggers sparking even unconscious memory of our past rash and ludicrous decision, our tragic fall from blessed perfection, and the utter devastation and general aimlessness that ensued.

If we really did fall all the way from the heights of godhood, then the fall, even if initially desired, must have proven a highly traumatic event for the innocent children of God, whether naïve or not. It was a long, hard fall, the prototype of every tragedy and trauma we suffer on earth, and ultimately the cause of all of them. We have done ourselves a greater disservice by having forgotten all of this by covering it over. Yet, we relive it indirectly, without realizing, so vestiges of the initial trauma crop up in a variety of distorted ways. The fall from original godhood into the vicissitudes and limitations of imperfect existence was an immense change, a radical change that resulted in a bevy of unintended negative consequences. Because the cause of this has been long ago buried deep within our minds, the resolution also escapes us.

The Undescended Soul

There is a philosophical concept that may help to further explain some of the theological concepts we are presenting, particularly those referring to the double creation, our double nature, preexistence, predestination, and apokatastasis. The Neoplatonist philosopher Plotinus (204-270 CE), a peer of Origen, much admired by Augustine and other patristics, taught about "the undescended soul," which is the higher part of the mind that did not fall with the lower part, but remains forever in heaven with God. This higher mind or soul remains utterly transcendent in heaven even while we play out our existence on earth.

Before we discuss Plotinus' concept of the undescended soul, let us note that there is some provenance for such an idea in Christian scripture. We have mentioned that Jesus spoke of two selves in John 3:31. One self "comes from above" and is "above all," while the other "belongs to the earth, and of the earth he speaks." The self that is "above all" "comes from heaven," directly begotten from God. This indicates that the transcendent self *remains* in heaven, "above all," even while we exist on earth.

When Jesus presents us with life, meaning eternal life, he is presenting us with something preexistent as well as postexistent (or pertaining to an afterlife). Such eternal life does not depend on our physical creaturehood for its being. Being preexistent, it already exists everywhere except in our conscious mind where it might benefit us. Being postexistent, it already resides in heaven, and will forever in a timeless way. We could rejoin it at any point in time, and in fact, we are continually invited to do so.

I see further evidence of this unfallen soul in Jesus' teaching that each person on earth has a corresponding angel in heaven which is always contemplating the Father:

> See that you do not despise one of these little ones; for I tell you that in heaven their angels always behold the face of my Father who is in heaven. (Matthew 18:10)

Each person has a direct connection to heaven through their higher angel that sits already in the presence of God. There is a sense of a "guardian angel" here, one for each soul, which represents them in heaven while they exist on earth. This helper angel is conceptualized as being outside oneself at first, until the realization dawns, when we are ready, that it is one with our own higher selves. Indeed, Jesus states elsewhere that our resurrected beings are "like angels in heaven" (Mt. 22:30). Augustine had also described our post-resurrection life as being equal to the angels.[206] Origen saw rising souls as advancing through angelic ways of being back to their original spiritual reality. These angels are in many cases our own higher minds already protecting and helping us, even just by contemplating the essence of God for the good of all.

There are other indications in the Bible of the spiritual part of ourselves remaining at home in heaven. We will be pointing them out as we go, but let us here mention Ephesians 2:6, which states that God has already "raised us up with him and seated us with him in the heavenly places in Christ Jesus." We have already been raised and ascended with Jesus. We are therefore in heaven now, but we have yet to realize this. Where is heaven if not in our higher minds? It is not a location on earth, nor in the sky except insofar as the sky symbolizes our higher mind. Heaven is already wide open to us, but we have denied our own greatest joy. Otherwise, we could glimpse its loveliness everywhere, even here through the things of earth.

M. David Litwa describes the seeds of the unfallen soul in Platonic philosophy: "In the *Timaeus*, each soul has a consort star to which the soul returns, provided it has been good (*Tim* 41-42)."[207] This directly recalls to mind Jesus' saying about "their angels in heaven" (Mt. 18:10). John Dillon likewise sees the concept as in part "a development of Plato's suggestion, at the end of the *Timaeus* (90a

---

[206] See Fokin 2014: 219.
[207] Litwa 2012: 145.

ff.) of the highest part of the human soul as a sort of guardian *daimon*."[208] The concept goes back to Plato's idea of the "genius" or "guardian angel" in each person but Plotinus expands it well beyond this. Narbonne sees in Plotinus' theory of the undescended soul a reply to Plato's question: "how could a plant be without roots and be without contact with that in which it is rooted[?]"[209] If the soul (or mind) emanates from God, then it remains firmly rooted in God, and indeed one with God, its Source. Its true life remains there, in the transcendent and spiritual world of mind, even if part of it would fall into a prodigal sojourn.

Plotinus begins his explanation of the unfallen soul a bit hesitantly, realizing its difference from how his fellow Platonic philosophers saw the soul:

> Since I should be bold enough to speak more clearly what seems to me to be true contrary to the opinions of others, even our human soul has not entirely sunk, but there is some aspect of it forever in the intelligible world.[210]

The higher self retains its original state and remains in what we call heaven, "the intelligible world" of pure minds and spirits. Plotinus arrived at this conclusion by first questioning whether our transcendence and therefore our true happiness comes from within or outside ourselves:

> But are we to picture this kind of life as something foreign imported into his nature?

Obviously, from wherever we believe this original happy self comes, and with whatever externalities we might associate it, happiness

---

[208] Dillon 2020: 181. "In Plotinus, we have his doctrine of the 'undescended' status of the highest part of the soul, which he conceives of as remaining 'above', in the intelligible realm. Such passages as *Enn.* IV 8 [6], 8, V 1 [10], 10 or III 4 [15],3 come to mind -- though in the last passage the doctrine gets mixed up with that of the 'guardian daemon' (if that is indeed a mix-up!)."
[209] Narbonne 2011: 61.
[210] Plotinus, *Enneads*, IV, 8, 8, 1-3, cited in Rist 1967: 410.

itself is always a subjective, internally realized experience. He answers that it must come from *within* each being:

> No: there exists no single human being that does not either potentially or effectively possess this thing which we hold to constitute happiness.[211]

Everyone has this second self, source of its true happiness, but few realize it. Plotinus contends that, because all people have the potential for happiness, therefore all people must deep within themselves possess the "second self" that makes for happiness.[212] Happiness is reasoned and experienced to be assimilation and identification with this higher self, which is really our original self, but which from the human perspective *seems* like an alternate self. Whether we think of its primacy in terms of time or, better, priority, this "second self" of Plotinus is in terms of time the "first self," the "higher and original self" of Christianity, created in the divine image and fit to be called "son of God" and "god."

In Christian terms, what we have been calling the original creation of God did not fall with the rest of our mind. It remains one with God and therefore unaffected by the changes and troubles of embodiment in the world. It allows us to see these lesser, temporary things (including body and lower mind) — however essential they may be in the world — as secondary to our true life in God and therefore resolvable. Thus, this unfallen self helps us like our personal angel and guide while we wander lost amid the weeds.

Plotinus believed it was the larger part of us that fell, and indeed this fall seems all-consuming in our human experience. However, in terms of priority, power, and potential for happiness, the second self (which Plotinus acknowledges is actually first) is infinitely greater. In my opinion, it is only a most miniscule fragment of the mind that descended from its original state of happiness and finds itself lost amid the difficulties and complexities of this world. It is small and incomplete, but is magnified because we have set it in

---

[211] Plotinus, *Enneads*, IV.4.4.
[212] Plotinus, *Enneads*, IV.4.4, 9ff; see Rist 1967: 419-420.

our minds and central to our vision. Yet, it is with this very small part of a much greater reality that we have decided entirely to assimilate and identify. It is not a perfect fit; it is much too constrictive and limiting for our higher mind. We wear the outer self like clothing, to use Plotinus' analogy, as we make our way through the world of externals. To identify with the higher mind is to be cognizant of this even while we exist on earth. It is much like Paul's saying that the body is an earthly tent and our true reality is much more glorious, to the point we, in our constricted state, cannot currently imagine.

The small part of the mind of which we are conscious was split off from the greater (original) mind, so as to become what seems to be its own entity. Yet, this fallen self remains entirely dependent on the original being for its own existence. This is why it must delude and deceive to maintain our allegiance. Having no life of its own, or life-in-itself, as does the original creation of God, it is as dependent on us gods for its semblance of life as we are on God (which Plotinus calls the One) for life in ourselves.

Even in our current condition, says Plotinus, "our soul, too, is a divine thing, belonging to another order than sense."[213] The higher part remains one with God, the Supreme One, which forever remains unified even while the soul experiences its splitting off, its split between this higher phase joined with God and the other divided among bodies:

> The entity, therefore, described as 'consisting of the undivided soul and of the soul divided among bodies,' contains a soul which is at once above and below, attached to the Supreme and yet reaching down to this sphere, like a radius from a centre.[214]

The higher soul maintains its original integrated nature, which means we always have access to it:

---

[213] Plotinus, *Enneads*, 5.1.10.
[214] Plotinus, *Enneads*, 4.1.1.

> Thus it is that, entering this realm, it possesses still the vision inherent to that superior phase in virtue of which it unchangingly maintains its integral nature.[215]

The Soul retains its original "integral nature" even while part of it is consumed with the machinations of the world. To assimilate to it is to realize it already exists within ourselves — as ourselves. Our practice of experiencing it allows it increasingly to be itself within existence. To identify with it is to know our higher selves, God, and all there is to know, implicitly but with full certainty.

Plotinus was one of the first philosophers to appreciate the self's multiple levels of consciousness, which makes him one of the first depth psychologists. He makes the point that we are not always aware of everything going on inside even our lower mind. Automatic and autonomic processes are occurring all the time. Narbonne notes Plotinus' "justly famous ... theory of the self's multiple levels of consciousness," saying: "According to this theory, the soul is not always aware of what is occurring within itself, both on the side of the Intellect (hence, it is not yet aware of participating in it), and on the side of the body and its desires."[216] In this, Plotinus was describing daily dissociation, autonomic processes, and other unconscious processes before they acquired their psychological names. For instance, we are *thinking* all the time, and yet, we are not always consciously aware that the mind is constantly thinking.

Russell describes how according to Plotinus the lower part of the mind (the *psyche*) attaches itself to the body, which attachment splits it off from the higher part of the mind (or *nous*). The task of the *psyche* or lower part becomes to re-identify with the *nous*, the higher part of the mind.[217] As Rist puts it, to do so is to reclaim our "second self," our "soul above."[218]

The undescended soul is our treasure awaiting us in heaven, and it is the spiritual identity that already has this treasure because

---

[215] Plotinus, *Enneads*, 4.1.1.
[216] Narbonne 2011: 62.
[217] Russell 2009: 115-116.
[218] Rist 1967: 418.

it *is* this treasure. Thus, we ourselves already have this treasure in heaven (Mk. 10:21), even if we are not aware of this fact, just as we are already seated in the heavenly places. The things and thoughts of the world block the idea from our mind, but they will not do so forever. The mind, set free of the limitation and complexity it has heaped upon itself, will, like the river, find and follow its natural course.

This concept of the undescended soul helps us understand how there may be a power "at work *within us*" that yet comes from far beyond who we thought we were: "far more abundantly than all that we ask or think" (Ephesians 3:20). Who we *think* we are is quite circumscribed and limited, which limits *all* our thoughts, including all our expectations, for the very reason that we chose not to remember the transcendence of our own inner being, which had been our reality since "before the foundation of the world" (Eph. 1:4). What makes salvation and godhood more certain and unearned than to learn that our soul is *already* where it is forever going to be?

Conclusion

If God created us as eternal minds, then we remain eternal minds to this day. God's creation does not change in nature and essence. This is because God created us, not out of nothing (*ex nihilo*), as many theologians after Augustine believed, but rather, out of himself (*ex se*), out of his own essence and nature. The physical world is by comparison a kaleidoscopic illusion meant to hide this fact from our minds, so that our eternal minds almost forgot entirely what they truly are and from whence they came.

The ontological implications seem clear, but they are all too often neglected or distorted. If we were created to be like him, and if we do not know this now, it is because we are *not ourselves*. Some kind of amnesia or dissociation has cast a shadow over our minds, a shadow in which "we," this conscious part, tried to hide. We fell from the transcendent heights of divinity into an alien world, to which we are now attempting to adapt as if it were our primary reality.

By seeing the fall as secondary to God's original creation and noting the bifurcated self or dual nature that results, a case can also be made that the fall is not real to God, nor even to the divine part of ourselves, but *only* to the *fallen* part of the mind. It is a lived experience for the small part of our mind which undergoes it, having no effect on our changeless God or on our own eternal being (our unfallen soul). It is like a dream that seems very real for a time, but fades quickly with the waking day.

If God's will is that we remain in heaven with him, and his will is inviolate and cannot be broken, then from his perspective we *must* still be there. Only a small part of our minds has fallen, but the greater part, the structural part so to speak, remains as it ever was: transcendent, pure, and even entirely self-aware. We may experience this higher nature at any time, which experience carries the surprise revelation: we already have it.

Although they came to conclude that Jesus must be both human and divine — human so that he could reach and save humankind, divine so that humankind could reach God — the patristics did not quite see the full significance of *humankind* itself as possessing a composite being: part human, but the greater part divine. Some came close, but most tended eventually to hyperfocus on speculative Christology to the exclusion of human anthropology let alone ontology. Yet, what they found regarding Christology has tremendous application to ourselves. Like Jesus, we have a composite being while we live on earth, and so we have access to either side of this being, eternal or temporal, even while we are here.

The idea that we have a higher self awaiting us in heaven accords with the Platonic idea that knowledge of the inner self is more a remembrance of eternal truths than an acquisition of newfound information. The same is true of happiness; we must have known it before to recognize it. As with Augustine, we long for what we have known. Our quest for God is a quest for return, not only to God, but to the gloriously joyful selves he created.

Mind and body exist independently as separate realities. They are fundamentally unable to be integrated. The patristics were much more prone to see the soul (mind, intellect) as attached forever to the body, so that for some of them even the soul died when the body died. Few reckoned with the fact that only one side of this dual nature can actually be real. The other is an imposter, a false idol as Augustine puts it.

In truth, God gave us only one true nature — exactly like his — but the fall added degrees of negation and thus nothingness to it. There is only one true nature, and everything else is ultimately self-delusion. Because we decided to forget and forego this true nature, or not to remember it, we had to create a substitute identity in its place. This replacement nature is not our true nature, but it is a decision-beholden reality with which we must reckon, made more difficult by our having willfully forgotten that it was our decision.

It was not inevitable that we would fall. It must rather have been a recklessly crossed but clearly defined boundary. We must not have been in our right minds when it happened, simply because the consequences were too severe for the hardly viable benefits gained. Hence, it must have been a sudden, impulsive, and emotional decision, a raging tantrum of sorts wherein reason was suspended in impulse and remained suspended, and in this sense the product of a childlike naivete. Ultimately, we can chalk it up to innocence in the sense that we were already not ourselves, and likely not fully cognizant of the full ramifications of our decision to forget Self and Source, at the time we made it.

7

PREEXISTENCE OF SOULS

This chapter presents a controversial topic related to a fully restorative deification: the idea of preexistence of souls (or minds). This is the idea that souls or minds were created before the body as timeless, eternal realities. They precede the body in both time and priority, meaning they have a separate reality of their own. The subject is controversial in large part because it has been so greatly misunderstood. Many early theologians (like Origen and early Augustine) had employed the idea as a reasoned solution to valid philosophical and theological problems.

In Origen and the Patristics

We have discussed Origen's account of the double creation, whereby God first created eternal minds, before the physical creation come about. For him, mind and body were two separate realities, with mind having primacy and priority, not only in time, but also in terms of ontological order. Origen taught that "the necessity of logical reasoning compels us to understand that rational natures were indeed created at the beginning," and that only afterward the "material substance" of human bodies "appears to have been formed for them, or after them."[219] The mind (or soul) was first; this was God's original creation. The physical and mortal part of our existence was produced and organized for our benefit in the aftermath, as a consequence of the fall of this spiritual mind.

---

[219] Origen, *De Principiis*, 2.2.2. ANF 4:270.

To recap, Origen points out that the first words of Genesis 1:1 ("In the beginning God created the heavens and the earth") cannot signify a temporal beginning because time had not yet been made.

> And, therefore, that first heaven indeed, which we said is spiritual, is our mind.[220]

The mind was created outside of time, in the same timeless reality that God enjoys. Therefore, when Genesis goes on to describe the creation of the heavens or firmament *again* in 1:6-8, it must be referring to the appearance of a later physical reality.

We have seen that Origen deemed the body to be an insufficient container for the divine image of Gen. 1:26-27, and reasoned that this image must instead reside within the mind.[221] "For what is made 'in the image' is not made from matter."[222] The mind was a separate reality, a primary reality, a more objective reality, and an eternal reality. In every way, it had priority over the physical reality. He asks some fundamental philosophical questions: "How does a bodily nature investigate the processes of the various arts, and contemplate the reasons of things? How, also, is it able to perceive and understand divine truths, which are manifestly incorporeal?"[223] His reasoning begins with the idea that God is incorporeal and eternal, deduced from Jesus' statement in John that "God is spirit" (Jn. 4:24).[224] If God is truly spirit, or bodiless, then so must his image be.

Origen proposed the issue of preexistence for many reasons. It also helped to resolve some difficult theological questions, such as why in Gen. 25 God favored Jacob over his twin Esau from before their birth and before either could gain or lose any merit. His questioning led him to postulate that Jacob and Esau must have built up merit or demerit in God's eyes *prior* to their arrival in the womb.

---

[220] Origen, *Homiliae in Genesim* 1,2 (28,4-16 D.), cited in Martens 2013: 526.
[221] See Martens 2013: 528.
[222] Origen, *Dialogue with Heraclitus*, cited in Martens 528.
[223] Origen, *De Principiis*, 1.1.7 ANF 4:244.
[224] See Origen, *De Principiis*, 1.1.1 (*ANF* 4:242).

In doing so, he was attempting to uphold the principles of the equal justice of God along with the freedom of the individual soul to decide its course. He asks: "can it be said that there is no unrighteousness with God when the elder serves the younger and is hated (by God) before he has done anything worthy of slavery or of hatred?"[225] Paul himself had argued similarly regarding Jacob and Esau that, although on the surface the story would indicate it, there could be no injustice on God's part (Ro. 9:14: "What then are we to say? Is there injustice on God's part? By no means!").

Origen contends that this story reinforces the idea of preexistence of minds because God could not favor Jacob over his earlier born (thus rightful heir) twin brother unless some preexistent cause gave good reason to do so. He understood God to be entirely fair with his children and to love them equally. Taking the story at face value, Origen asks whether this was simply foreknowledge on God's part, or did it mean that Jacob and Esau did something to merit their fates prior to embodiment? The fact that they are born into different circumstances must have had nothing to do with God, but rather with Jacob and Esau themselves prior to their manifestation on earth.

Origen saw further evidence of the preexistence of souls in Ephesians 1:4 ("he chose us in Christ before the foundation of the world to be holy and blameless before him in love"), which would seem to indicate the preexistence of our mind before its descent into a body. If we were knowable by God "before the foundation of the world," then our essence and being must have preexisted the world. We will elaborate on this later. He also referenced Jeremiah 1:5 ("Before I formed you in the womb I knew you"), which prompts him to ask in regard to the prophet:

> How could his soul and its images be formed along with his body, who, before he was created in the womb, is said to be known to God, and was sanctified by Him before his birth?[226]

---

[225] Origen, *Commentary on John*. II, 25.
[226] Origen, *De Principiis*, 1.7.4. (*ANF* 4:263-264).

The mind (or soul) must exist independently of the body for preexistence to be possible. Because of the mind's priority, the body must be the epiphenomenon, the contingent reality, which glimmers but fades like the flower in the field. The body will not always be necessary for us. It can, however, be useful as a temporary instructive mechanism, a way for us to (re)learn about our spiritual reality. For Origen, this great restoration occurs specifically when Christ has fulfilled his mission to deliver the kingdom, purified, deified, and whole, back to God:

> Christ is said to deliver up the kingdom; and thus it appears that then also the need of bodies will cease. And if it ceases, bodily matter returns to nothing, as formerly also it did not exist.[227]

The body will no longer be necessary once godhood is experienced consistently. The emerging god will gradually slough off its limitations, up to and including its apparent mortality, until its original bearing is restored.

> Now, if all things may exist without bodies, there will undoubtedly be no bodily substance, seeing there will be no use for it.[228]

Regarding the other patristics, historian Philip Schaff points out that Augustine argues for preexistence in his early *De libero arbitrio*.[229] Terryl L. Givens, in his book-length study of preexistence, *When Souls Had Wings*, notes that Augustine "openly embraced Plato's argument for preexistence in his *Soliloquies* (c. 386-387)," where he also taught a Platonic kind of recollection (necessitating preexistence) in regard to our capacity to discern truth from falsity in matters of morality.[230] Augustine also "clearly favored ... a fall

---

[227] Origen, *De Principiis*, 2.3.3. (*ANF* 4:272).
[228] Origen, *De Principiis*, 2.3.2. (*ANF* 4:271).
[229] Schaff 1867: 831.
[230] Givens 2010: 111.

from preexistence" in his *On Free Choice of the Will* (c. 395) and in *Two Books on Genesis against the Manichees* and his unfinished *The Literal Meaning of Genesis*.[231] Augustine writes regarding the origin of the soul that he deemed it "permissible to consider and discuss these matters", specifically whether the soul was preexistent or created individually with the body.[232]

In his autobiographical *Confessions* (c. 397-398), Augustine asks earnestly: "Where was I before I was in the womb?"[233] Related queries, similar to those we have seen in Plotinus, arise: "But where and when had I any experience of happiness, that I should remember it and love it and long for it?"[234] He states plainly the cause of his struggle: "Obviously we have [this memory of happiness] in some way, but I do not know how."[235] He comes to a resolution, citing the woman in Jesus' parable who lost a coin: "She would not have found it if she had not remembered it. For when it was found, how should she have known whether it was what she sought … ?"[236] Preexistence is the obvious solution to all these queries. The soul has experienced this specific happiness before, but does not remember until it decides once again to know itself as created.

It was the Pelagian controversy brewing toward the end of his life that steered Augustine away from his otherwise consistently favorable views on the preexistence of the soul. Where his opponent Pelagius championed a definitive freedom of the human will, Augustine, who had previously emphasized the same freedom, felt Pelagius was downplaying the need for grace, and therefore countered this with a doctrine of original sin, "inherited depravity," "unmerited guilt," and "unmerited unavoidable condemnation," as Givens puts it.[237] Despite this, the idea of preexistence of the soul remained open for Augustine until the end of his life, despite certain

---

[231] Givens 2010: 111.
[232] Augustine, *On Free Choice of the Will*, 3.21; cited in Givens 2010: 111.
[233] Augustine, *Confessions* 1.6-7, trans. F. J. Sheed (Indianapolis, IN: Hackett, 1993), 7-9; cited in Givens 2010: 112.
[234] Augustine, *Confessions* 10.20-21; Givens 2010: 112.
[235] Augustine, *Confessions* 10.20; cited in Givens 2010: 113.
[236] Augustine, *Confessions* 10.18; cited in Givens 2010: 112.
[237] Givens 2010: 113.

narrowly focused passages in his later *The City of God* (c. 427) and *Retractions* (c. 427). Givens concludes:

> But in this late work, Augustine only condemns Origen's theory of the *reason* behind the world's creation; he condemns neither Origen's theory of preexistence in particular nor pre-mortal existence in general. In spite of general assumptions that Augustine moved beyond his flirtation with preexistence in his later years, the evidence suggests that Augustine was unwilling fully to relinquish the best hope for reconciling guilt, accountability, and God's justice.[238]

The idea of preexistence and its explanatory power deserved a better fate:

> The aftermath of the Augustinian episode is, in the case of preexistence at least, a sacrifice of dogged rational inquiry for mystery and plain dictate. At the same time, the powerful undercurrent that persists in Augustine's own studied ambiguity is a tacit signal that the problem is far from resolved.[239]

Gregory of Nyssa, Nemesius, and Cyril of Alexandria shared Origen's belief that the soul was created before the body.[240] Other Christian theologians who advocated for a preexistent soul include Clement of Alexandria, Basil of Caesarea, Gregory of Nazianzus, Synesius, Arnobius, and Prudentius. We will next examine the scriptural basis for this view in the New Testament and the Hebrew Bible and intertestamental literature.

Those who did not accept this teaching about the preexistence of souls or minds generally chose from one of two other options. They believed either in *creationism* of the soul, the view that

---

[238] Givens 2010: 118. My emphasis.
[239] Givens 2010: 119.
[240] Schaff 1867: 831.

each soul is created by God along with the body, each time being a new event, or they believed in *traducianism* of the soul, the idea that the soul is transmitted naturally along with the body. Both options have the disadvantage of tying soul inextricably to the body, an eternal reality to a temporal one. Creationism places God in time and deemphasizes his timelessness, while both views confuse soul with body, and fail to cede priority to the soul.

In the decades and centuries after Origen, some of his adherents (including Evagrius and, more indirectly, Didymus the Blind) were thought to have taken his ideas a little too far in the eyes of some of the more political religious authorities of the day. During the first Origenist crisis in the late 300s, Theophilus of Alexandria, who had formerly supported Origen's ideas, did a quick reversal to condemn Origen's incorporeal, non-anthropomorphic view of God which he himself had once espoused. Such a sudden reversal under suspicious circumstances and a fiat from the emperor smacks of political and worldly motives. The powers that be demanded and forced a consensus.

Even though it is difficult for many to understand, it is no crime to think of God as pure spirit, mind and heart. Similarly, it is no crime to think of God anthropomorphically, although it is technically incorrect. Many metaphorical statements in the Bible do the same, such as those which speak of the power of God's Hand, or the glory and transcendence of his Face. These have true meaning, but not anthropomorphically in regard to God, not literally in a perceptual or physical sense. After all, Jesus states directly that "God is spirit" — all mind and heart — and therefore, Origen stands closer to Jesus' true revelation about God than do his critics who insisted on interpreting such anthropomorphisms literally.

The second Origenist crisis occurred in the sixth century CE during the reign of Justinian I. It again dealt with groups who had been influenced by Origen rather than Origen's own writings. It ended in 553 CE with the Second Council of Constantinople. An anathema was issued against Origen and all his writings were commanded to be burned. Fortunately for us and for posterity, a portion of the great theologian's voluminous corpus has survived.

Most modern theologians and historians acknowledge the tremendous merit of Origen's early Christian theology even if they disagree on certain points. And many point out the pettiness of his detractors; Harnack comes down especially hard:

> The belittlers and enemies of this man were vain and ambitious obscurantists, hero-levelling fellows ... — Methodius, Eustathius, Apollinaris, and Theophilus....[241]

Benjamin Winter points out that Origen's later critics like Methodius "grossly misunderstood" his conception of the body. He contends that most of the problems involved interpolations and opinions of Origen's followers rather than his own concepts.[242] He points out that: "The criticisms of Origen's doctrine on the body almost invariably involve the resurrection."[243] That is, his opponents' interest was to uphold the idea of a physical resurrection along with a physical creation. Winter describes Origen's true purpose in teaching preexistence:

> [I]n the face of deterministic allegations, Origen attempted to safeguard the freedom of rational entities by positing a precosmic fall in which each creature 'took a free and distinct decision to what extent [they] wanted to participate' in the turning.[244]

Origen advocates for the God-given freedom of individual minds while also affirming God's equitable justice with his teaching of preexistence and a primordial fall. Each mind determines whether it will fall and how far it will fall down the ladder of being, and determines how much progress it will make as it works its way back. However many eons it takes in time, God, being timeless, can wait them out without waiting at all.

---

[241] Harnack, *History of Dogma*, Vol. 3, Ch. 1, p. 130, note 31.
[242] Winter 2013: 12.
[243] Winter 2013: 12.
[244] Winter 2013: 11.

meant to elicit the same kind of transcendent preexistent being he himself exemplified. This transcendent vantage point ends up giving us a more objective and fair view of the world as well as of ourselves.

The Hebrew prophets had spoken about having been "sent" by God to fulfill certain divine functions. Isaiah states: "the Lord God has sent me and his spirit" (Isa. 48:16). We have seen that Jeremiah spoke of having a sense of sentness before his birth:

> Before I formed you in the womb I knew you
> and before you were born I consecrated you;
> I appointed you a prophet to the nations. (Jer. 1:5)

Not only was Jeremiah sent, he was known before he ever took on bodily form. Likewise, John the Baptist is spoken of as having preexisted and been *sent* "that he might give testimony to the light" (Jn. 1:7). It would seem that Jesus is not the only one to have been sent from heaven, or descended willingly to help humankind, therefore to have preexisted. Perhaps because of God's perfect love, justice, and equitability, the "sentness" of John and the prophets is a revelation all will one day share. Perhaps belief in Jesus' sentness is a step toward believing in our own preexistence. The identification is made in many places:

> Truly, truly, I say to you,
> he who receives any one whom I send receives me;
> and he who receives me receives him who sent me.
> (John 13:20)

As he does in Matthew 25, Jesus identifies with those he sends into the world. They do the same work because they share the same essential being. Note that this identification goes both ways: Jesus identifies with us, even as we identify with him. If we share even his sense of sentness, then we also share his preexistent self-knowledge and therefore his essential being.

A belief in preexistence helps greatly to understand deification from God's timeless perspective. Whether this operates on the basis of reincarnation as commonly understood, metempsychosis, or transmigration of the soul is an open matter. Jesus may have hinted about such a concept when he said: "and if you are willing to accept it, he [John the Baptist] is Elijah who is to come" (Mt. 11:14). Jesus' statement, "if you are willing to accept it," indicates that he knew this teaching would be a difficult one for his audience to accept, even to comprehend. His religion at the time was just then starting to believe in an afterlife for the soul. But while John the Baptist may or may not be the literal re-embodiment of the Elijah of old, he is said to be the "Elijah who is to come," meaning the transcendent spirit of Elijah, the one who never died, who was swept up into heaven in a chariot of fire.

Preexistence and Predestination in Paul

Paul offers some startling statements about preexistence, and these are most often linked with his teaching about predestination, which has been almost completely misunderstood. This familiar passage from Paul's Letter to the Romans contains both ideas — preexistence and predestination — in equal measure:

> For those whom he foreknew he also predestined to be conformed to the image of his Son, in order that he might be the firstborn within a large family. (Romans 8:29)

Note first that Paul connects Jesus' predestination with our own. He speaks of "those" (plural) whom God foreknew, all of us, as being predestined to share his transcendent sonship so that, all together, we would know ourselves as essential parts of the same "large family." This means that we are equally predestined and, if so, equally preexistent.

As far as God's foreknowledge, what God knows is sure, knowable to all, and his reality is timeless, and so, what he knows has already occurred and continues in heaven. So sure is it to happen that it has already happened, except in our perception. It is because of God's timelessness and the power of his thoughts that his foreknowledge is also predestination, and it applies equally to all his supernatural beings or creations, to the "large family" destined to be conformed to the likeness of his Son.

We have seen that sonship to God is a mediating image for godhood. It tells us that we come from God and will return to God. Paul speaks clearly in Romans 8 of a predestination that does not belong to Jesus alone, but to "a large family" consisting of similar divinized beings. Each and any of us might participate and *will* participate because we are predestined to do so.

The idea of predestination has been tainted by the assumption that predestination must be dual, whereby one is bound for one of two eternal destinations, heaven or hell, paradise or punishment, and there is little one can do to change the outcome. This is one assumption of theologian John Calvin (1509-1564 CE), originator of Presbyterianism, who popularized the idea of dual predestination. The assumption behind such dual predestination is that because God is omniscient, he foreknows the fate of each individual soul, specifically whether they will end up in heaven or hell (for Calvin, not eternal torment but annihilation), and this fate cannot be changed, not even by God. Such a deterministic view would deny the power of our free and powerful minds to change everything, even move mountains. Our freedom of mind to decide our own course would seem (from scripture and even just from present life experience) to be sacrosanct in God's eyes, such is his patience and respect for every mind he created.

God as infinite love only draws, attracts, and persuades. In this world that means he (through his Spirit) also reasons with us so that we might understand:

> Come now, let us reason together, says the LORD: though your sins are like scarlet, they shall be as white as snow; though they are red like crimson, they shall become like wool. (Isaiah 1:18, ESV)

Such will be the final verdict for all the predestined souls of God. For we have seen that God cannot think in terms of punishment (via 1 John) and that certainly would apply to annihilation as well. He will save every last scrap of what can be saved, and what can be saved is every perfect being he created. And he rests sure in his present knowledge of this (which to us, whiling away in time, is foreknowledge).

A singular view of predestination seems more appropriate to a God identified completely with love. Under this singular view, everyone would eventually undergo a process like that of this Pauline formula for deification, found in the very next verse:

> And those whom he predestined he also called; and those whom he called he also justified; and those whom he justified he also glorified. (Romans 8:30)

Note that the entire process is spoken of in the past tense, as if it has already happened, which it has in God's Mind. The call of God has gone out to all who are predestined for glory, which is every creation of God. Because all are predestined — and it can be no other way with God — all are therefore called. The Pauline formula for deification *begins* with being predestined, which is beyond our control, a gift from God, a product of our foundational creation by God. It is completely unearned and quite different from our current human nature. But each hears and answers the call in one's own time and in one's own particular way.

The next step follows. It is simply by having been predestined and recognizing the call that we are justified. Justification is an inner realization, an acknowledgment of the legitimacy of our calling. All its associations with morality and righteousness or "rightness of mind" come from identifying with the right being, our true divine being. Our predestination, our call from God, and our justification all are, from a strictly human viewpoint, beyond our control. We were made that way. The last step in Paul's formula is glorification, deification, which is a return to the predestined state. As such, the *deification* and salvation of all beings is guaranteed and universal.

The fact that we are "predestined" and therefore "called," "justified," and "glorified" suggests an inherent knowledge or memory of our blessed origin and thus our destination.

There are other examples of our having been predestined to return to a state of preexistent being in Pauline literature. We have seen that God "chose us in him before the foundation of the world, that we should be holy and blameless before him" (Ephesians 1:4). We were chosen before the world began, which points all the way back to preexistence. The next verse explains that "He destined us in love to be his sons through Jesus Christ, according to the purpose of his will" (Eph. 1:5), another indicator of the overlap between preexistence and predestination. If we were foreknown by God prior to even "the foundation of the world," then we were obviously *knowable* before the existence of a body, another indication we were minds, then, before we were bodies. Such foreknowledge on God's part is not simply from omniscience, as if God stands apart from his knowledge. His thoughts, and therefore his creations, assume the same nature and reality as he. God is one with his thoughts and therefore one with us. What we fail to understand is how infallible the will of God really is — how certain, how inevitable, how unbreakable. It is the total love behind it that makes it so. God's kind of love *must* come true, in *exactly* the way he intends.

Colossians 3:10 asserts that we are given a "new self, which is being renewed in knowledge according to the image of its creator." This "new self," like the second self of Plotinus, initially *seems* new to us, and yet it is being *"renewed"* because it is more truly a preexisting innate being. Such original being is renewed through refamiliarization and gradual remembrance. This view is reinforced by Paul's having said that the whole of creation waits with eager longing for *us* to realize the children of God we really are (Ro. 8:19). Such longing indicates that we already know the thing for which we yearn, from the deepest and most transcendent, preexistent and predestined, part of ourselves. In fact, we have been called and justified and glorified because of it, but we do not realize this either.

Augustine says:

> This human nature of ours was predestined to be raised to so great, so lofty, so exalted a position, that it would be impossible to raise it higher.[247]

This, then, is how we should think of ourselves and those around us. I would add that it is because we preexist in glory and transcendence that we are predestined for glory and transcendence. And it is because we are predestined for glory that our oneness is, despite appearances, a true interlocking oneness, an essential oneness, so that *every* fragmented mind that wandered away from its fullness and purity must and will eventually find its way back — ultimately to realize it is *already there*. One might even say the wholeness and oneness of God himself depends on it, yet we must keep in mind that it cannot be put at risk because in reality it, like God, is changeless.

Preexistence and predestination are two sides of the same coin in the sense that if we know where we come from, we will know where we are going (and vice versa). One might even say that the two *must* go together, for they coincide if one believes that to end up as gods, we must have begun as gods. If we are predestined, we must have preexisted this mortal coil. The intervening time, however long and drawn out it appears, is nothing but a blip in timeless eternity. In this sense, we are striving to become what we always have been and forever will be — and are even now.

In the Hebrew Bible and Apocrypha

In this section we will find that there are suggestions of preexistence in the Old Testament in spite of its overall earthy perception of human beings. Some of these are found in the prophets, such as in Jeremiah 1:5 cited previously: "Before I formed you in the womb I knew you." God's foreknowledge is itself a form of preexistence. If God knew us before we were born, this means we

---

[247] Augustine, *De Praedest. Sanct.* xv; cited in Aquinas, *Summae*, 3.24.2.

existed as ideas in the Mind of God before we were born. Foreknowledge *is* preexistence if God's thoughts take on immediate reality because, as some theologians (like Aquinas) believed, God is "pure act." His thoughts *are* reality, and being timeless like he, possess *immediate* reality, and these thought-realities, born of his ever-present, eternal way of thinking, are the divine beings which populate his never-ending kingdom.

If God knew us *before* we were "formed in the womb," then what he knew was not yet a body, meaning God knew us as mind and spirit prior to embodiment. This is explained further by the idea that "the Lord does not see as mortals see; they look on the outward appearance, but the Lord looks on the heart" (1 Sam. 16:7). These are early intimations, or revelations, that God knows us through our inner being (mind and heart), rather than through our body or physical existence. The anthropomorphic personifications of God prevalent in the Hebrew Bible are simply ways of expressing parts of God's transcendent reality, so that our divine mind and human spirit might be evoked to recognize themselves.

Zechariah 12:1 states that God "formed the human spirit within," which "human spirit" is spoken of as separate and distinct from the bodily and physical creation, suggesting a double creation. The Psalmist likewise specifies that it was God who "formed my inward parts" (Ps. 139:13), that is, the mind and heart, which are spirit. The same Psalm addresses God and his cosmic "book of life":

> Your eyes beheld my unformed substance.
> In your book were written
>   all the days that were formed for me,
>   when none of them as yet existed. (Ps. 139:16)

This "unformed substance" that God beheld and saw to completion is the inner being, the mind and soul, that has priority in God's reality. This inward part — this "human spirit" — is the part that our spiritual Source knows as us. It is in this same light that we most truly know ourselves and God:

> The human spirit is the lamp of the Lord,
> searching every inmost part. (Proverbs 20:27)

Here again we find a very active "human spirit" that seeks and therefore already knows and loves God. This "human spirit" is the self God knows, our true self that we long to know again. Preconnected with God, yet present within ourselves, it allows us to understand God, the one true Origin, where we come from:

> But truly it is the spirit in a mortal,
> the breath of the Almighty, that makes for understanding.
> (Job 32:8)

Again, the spirit we already have understands perfectly. The "breath of the Almighty" is as close to us as our own breath. God shares his own breath, his own spirit, his own life, nature, and being. This is the same spirit he breathed into us at the moment of our creation (Gen. 2:7). This spirit is our true being, begotten of God.

The Book of Job declares that, before the "bases" of the world were sunk, its foundations laid, there was a point "when the morning stars sang together and the heavenly beings shouted for joy" (Job 38:7). Here is a snapshot of the prevailing emotion in our premortal existence, as well as what is to come.

Hamerton-Kelly's book-length treatment of preexistence points out that preexistence is present in both Judaism's Wisdom and apocalyptic traditions, specifically in the divine figures of Wisdom herself and the eschatological Son of Man.[248] The follower of Wisdom, divine consort of God and humans, lives even on earth in a reality of spirit,[249] a truer reality than physical existence.

The apocryphal Book of Wisdom contains a direct statement of preexistence:

> As a child I was naturally gifted,
> and a good soul fell to my lot;

---

[248] Hamerton-Kelly 1973: 22.
[249] Wisd. 1:13, 16, 2:23, 5:23.

²⁰ or rather, being good, I entered an undefiled body. (Wisd. 8:19-20)

Here, the author speaks of having, prior to his existence, chosen a suitable body to inhabit. He attributes this to fate first but then corrects himself. Fate was not involved so much as a preexistent decision. And of course, Wisdom herself was personified as a preexistent being, divine consort and companion of God from before the world existed and bearer of preexistent wisdom to human beings. Givens explains how the idea of preexistent beings spread quickly and influenced earliest Christianity:

> In one line of Jewish thought, this figure of Wisdom will metamorphose into the Torah as a preexistent entity, the agent and blueprint of creation, embodiment of eternal wisdom. Among Alexandrian Jews, as is apparent in the writings of Philo, Wisdom merges with the Logos, the classical Greek term for the divine intelligence that orders the cosmos.[250]

The Torah as blueprint for creation and Word as agent are thus preexistent as Wisdom was preexistent. The Gospel of John nominally associates such preexistence with the preexistent Logos of Platonic cosmology ("In the beginning was the Word [Logos]" (Jn. 1:1)). Eventually, Israel herself is known to have been preexistent, which idea may have influenced Paul's exposition of the preexistence of early Christians.

Additionally, in both the Jewish and Christian apocalyptic literature, the whole of creation exists in the mind of God before it appears in perception.[251] Therefore, the entirety of creation is

---

[250] Givens 2010: 51.
[251] Hamerton-Kelly 1973: 18: "There is also in apocalypticism the idea of things pre-existing in the mind of God. The idea that everything takes place according to God's plan is central to the apocalyptic outlook (1 En. 9:3, 39: 11, Ass. Mos. 1:12-14, 12:4). The whole creation exists in the mind of God before it takes place (1 Q.S. 3:15-17, 1 Q.H. 1:19-20). This idea is similar to Philo's concept of the noetic world,

preexistent and independent of the world we see. This puts us in the mind of Plato's Forms or Ideals or Aquinas' "universals," eternal realities that underlie this world of particularized realities. The mind is becoming known to be a separate reality.

The apocalyptic Son of Man also "exists before his manifestation,"[252] as is suggested by the bulk of the related sayings referring to his waiting in heaven for his "coming"[253] or his "day."[254] It also means that even his physical manifestation, meant for human consumption, is not so much the real him as is his heavenly reality.

Hamerton-Kelly explains how the future manifests in the present in the apocalyptic literature:

> In the eschatological hope the future could be treated as if it were present. When this idea of *the present future* is combined with the idea of heavenly entities, the result is that the entities to be revealed in the future pre-exist now in heaven. This is the fundamental structure of apocalyptic thought.[255]

That which will be already awaits us, eagerly, in heaven. It yearns for us as we yearn for it. Yet, all this can be realized here and now in "the present future." Apocalypticism presents us with the future in the present, thereby transforming our sense of time, leaving us with only the present spiritual experience of our preexistent being that comes from outside of time, where past and future no longer apply.

Other Jewish apocalypses contain direct statements of preexistence:

... and provides an important point of contact between apocalypticism and Jewish Platonism. We have called this idea 'ideal' pre-existence, as Harnack suggested."
[252] Hamerton-Kelly 1973: 46.
[253] Luke 12:8ff, par., 12:40 par.
[254] Luke 17:23-4 par., 17:26-7 par., 17:28-30.
[255] Hamerton-Kelly 1973: 17. My italics.

> All souls are prepared to eternity before the foundation of the world. (Slavonic Book of Enoch 23:5)[256]

Souls are preexistent, which means the reality we perceive as the world around us is secondary. In the apocryphal book, Jubilees, written in the second century CE, Moses is portrayed as saying that God created the spirits of all human beings on the very first day of creation.[257] They preexist in heaven and then manifest on earth at their appointed times. In the Apocalypse of Abraham, written between 70-150 CE, Abraham sees a vision of all the preexistent souls of human beings past and future.[258] The Talmud also contains a story whereby the head of the human embryo contains a light that can see from one end of the world to the other, but this knowledge is forgotten at birth.[259]

Philo of Alexandria (20 BCE-50 CE), the Middle Platonic Jewish Philosopher beloved by many patristics, taught that the divine being within us yearns to be free from bodily limitation and to return to our spiritual heaven. The mind has its own existence independent of the body, so that it need no longer remain imprisoned and limited by it but can escape it altogether for moments at a time. The mind exists independently of the body and takes priority over it. The body is healed by the mind's reordering of the levels of existence, reclaiming its primacy.

Regarding early Christian extracanonical literature, the Gospel of Thomas is thought to have been written or compiled in the late first or early second century CE, not long after John's Gospel,

---

[256] Translated from the Slavonic by W. R. Morfill, M.A. Further corrected and HTML edited by Adam Jerome, 2002. (Retrieved 12/12/2022.) Although discovered whole only in Slavonic translation in the Middle Ages, Coptic fragments and Origen's reference to it in *On First Principles* 1.3.3 suggest a first-century date.

[257] *Jubilees* II.2, trans. O. S. Wintermute, in Charlesworth, *Old Testament*, 2:55; cited in Givens 2010: 48.

[258] *Apocalypse of Abraham* XXI.7- XXII.5; Givens 2010: 48.

[259] The William Davidson Talmud, Niddah 30b (sefaria.org), retrieved 12/12/2022. The pertinent part reads: "And a fetus is taught the entire Torah while in the womb.... And once the fetus emerges into the airspace of the world, an angel comes and slaps it on its mouth, causing it to forget the entire Torah."

and is considered the Fifth Gospel by some. It is a collection of sayings by Jesus that most often match the sayings found in the four canonical gospels, with a few unique proto-Gnostic sayings. Human preexistence is expressed clearly in saying 19:

> 'Blessed is the one who came into being before coming into being.' (GThom log. 19)[260]

M. David Litwa comments that "Jesus, who speaks this verse, is almost certainly not merely blessing himself but is referring to others."[261] He points out that in the Gospel of Thomas, "The human 'image,' ... as several interpreters have argued, refers to the preexistent divine self."[262] Litwa writes that in Thomas, human beings, like Jesus, "preexisted as luminous beings living in union with God."[263] Our preexistent beings come from "the light" (log. 50), which is equated with "the kingdom" (log. 49). This preexistent light represents our true preexistent divine self. Until we re-identify with this original luminous self, we will be in conflict. "The suffering that the elect will bear is caused by the contrast of their present sarkic [fleshly] state with their preexistent divine state."[264]

We have seen that preexistence is a fairly common concept from the intertestamental period onward. It grew in popularity from the time of the canonization of the Hebrew Bible[265] through the time of Jesus and increased in popularity in the succeeding centuries, appearing in many Hebrew and Christian apocryphal books. The budding branches of Gnosticism were equally taken with it. Origen in the next century was the Christian theologian who most logically integrated this nearly ubiquitous idea into his theological system.

---

[260] Litwa 2015: 432.
[261] Litwa 2015: 432.
[262] Litwa 2015: 439.
[263] Litwa 2015: 432.
[264] Litwa 2015: 439.
[265] The dating is uncertain but ranges from c. 140 BCE to the second century CE.

Plato and Preexistence

Origen's ideas about preexistence parallel in some ways Plato's, and so it was once assumed that he had derived his ideas from Greek philosophy. But according to the extant writings, we can see that his thinking about the issue was circumscribed by scripture. His questions were evoked by scripture and his thought system steeped in it. He knew Platonism well, having been trained as a philosopher himself (as had many of the patristics), but he did not appeal to Greek philosophy to any great extent in his argument. He is in effect the architect of a Christian theological system that rivals Plato's philosophical system, but which stands on its own as a Biblically grounded system.

Let us briefly note Plato's idea of the preexistence of minds, which was a fundamental aspect of his philosophy. For Plato, knowledge of any kind is remembered rather than acquired. The fact that human beings can recognize any point of knowledge as true presupposes that they once possessed this knowledge in an unremembered past, prior to their physical existence. Human beings had knowledge before they ever became human, and our quest for knowledge and truth is but a relearning of what we once knew as preexistent spiritual beings (and still know deep in our unconscious minds).

In Plato's *Phaedo*, for instance, Socrates says:

> Now if we had acquired that knowledge before we were born, and were born with it, we knew before we were born and at the moment of birth not only the equal and the greater and the less, but all things such as these? For our present argument is no more concerned with the equal than with the beautiful itself and the good and the just and the holy, and, in short, with all those things which we stamp with the thing itself that is in our dialectic process of questions and

answers; so that we must necessarily have acquired knowledge of all these before our birth.[266]

We already possess knowledge of all these ideals (equality, beauty, the good, justice, holiness, etc.) corresponding to the eternal attributes of God, because we acquired such knowledge "before our birth." Here on earth, we are born with it, but only in embryo, unconsciously, pre-dissociated, because such knowledge is reacquired through remembrance or recollection (*anamnesis*). Thus, we are relearning it rather than learning it fresh. Our embodiment required forgetfulness of our original state (amnesia or dissociation), and so knowledge of our true state requires the opposite process, gradual and gentle remembrance or recollection.

Plato reasoned that if the soul is immortal *after* temporal existence, then it must have been immortal *before* — and indeed it is immortal now.[267] Lenz points out how the Eastern patristics intended to differentiate themselves from Plato (not to mention the Gnostics) by teaching that immortality was a "gift" we earn through existence rather than an essential part of God's creation.[268] Besides the fact that a gift is not generally "earned," we might ask *to whom* is God giving this "gift"? Would not our preexistent being *also* have been a gift graced to us by God? Would it not have been the ultimate unearned gift — a gift inclusive of everything, in fact? After all, no further gifts are possible without our first having been gifted life, a being to receive them.

Plato's own ideas about preexistence are often traced back to two major sources: Orphism and Pythagoreanism. Orphism, which derives its name from the mythological Greek god Orpheus who entered the underworld to rescue his beloved Eurydice, is represented in Givens' presentation by the philosopher Empedocles (c. 495-435 BCE), who believed that the soul (or mind) ascended back

---

[266] Plato, *Phaedo* 75b. *Plato in Twelve Volumes*, Vol. 1 translated by Harold North Fowler; Introduction by W.R.M. Lamb. Cambridge, MA, Harvard University Press; London, William Heinemann Ltd. 1966.
[267] See for instance Plato, *Timaeus* 37C-38B.
[268] Lenz 2007: 53.

to its blissful origin "through successive stages tied to rites, knowledge acquisition, and spiritual refinement."[269] Pythagoreanism traces back to the mathematician-philosopher Pythagoras, who, incidentally, may have derived some of his ideas from his knowledge of Zoroaster, original founder of ancient Persian Zoroastrianism, quite possibly the first philosopher in the Western world and the first monotheist (and influence on Moses).

An old adage states that all philosophy is but a series of footnotes to Plato. Plato represented the culmination of a centuries-long methodical quest for philosophical knowledge. His discursive thinking and intuition on these subjects sparked other questions down through the ages, as Givens describes:

> [I]t will become for Augustine the question: how can we hunger and search for a God unless we have already known and loved him? For Descartes, it will be a problem to be solved by invoking innate ideas, the only alternative he can see to giving over the field of human knowledge entirely to the vagaries and inadequacies of sensory experience or inventions of the mind. Kant will reconstitute modern philosophy in navigating the same dilemma.[270]

Preexistence has also been used traditionally to explain the problem of evil in the world, how a benevolent God seems to have allowed for the darkness, as well as to seek to elucidate why some people suffer in existence and others seem not to. The problem with the idea of preexistence was that it was too different from the ordinary human way of looking at things. It means at its base that the world is not our true home, origin or destination. Most later patristics refused it out of hand, and it became forbidden even to discuss, but both before and after that point, reason and intuition persuaded many thinkers, Christian or otherwise, to look in its direction as a way to synthesize apparently divergent theological currents.

---

[269] Givens 2009: 24.
[270] Givens 2009: 28.

Conclusion

Jesus was preexistent. John the Baptist was preexistent. Jeremiah was preexistent, as was the author of the Book of Wisdom. Could it be that all God's children are preexistent, but most do not realize it? Before Abraham existed on earth, Jesus had eternal being. Even in his earthly existence, Jesus identifies with timeless being rather than physical existence. He tells his disciples that he is going back to the place from which he came and, more importantly, that they know where he is going and how to get there. He could not have described this transcendent destination sufficiently to them in words nor in discursive thought. It must be experienced to be known. We must live within it, participate in it, before we know it for certain. Even so, his disciples *already* knew this transcendent reality because they are "not of the world." Yet there was nothing extraordinary about them, nothing they knew that we cannot know about ourselves.

The only way to *know* we are "not of the world" is to raise our thoughts far above the world, thus to find out how familiar it feels to us. This will allow us to identify with mind and spirit, shifting our self-reference away from the body, not because it is evil but because it is constrictive. All the practices of Christianity — acquiring the virtues, the sacraments, prayer and fasting, love and forgiveness — are meant to detach us from smallish and worldly ways of thinking *and being*. They are meant to show and convince us that neither world nor body are our true home. They are not even our true starting point.

Seeing this, we can see all things differently. We can foreknow as God foreknew. We can know right now where we are going and how to get there. If we are already there, we need not speculate. Something within us knows already. If we could accept it, we are, even now, more *there* than we are *here*. But for now, our preexistent mind lives on the periphery of our awareness, where we have relegated it. It is still there, and the true "us" there with it, for it is more truly us than the selves we construct from patchwork while in this whirlwind of a world.

Only preexistence of minds or souls accounts for the goodness, love, perfection, and fairness of God while at the same time upholding the sacrosanct freedom of the minds he created. Givens expresses how surprising it is that this idea of preexistence was so vociferously opposed in later Christianity, forcing the idea underground, particularly when logic stood on its side. He states rightly that "the arguments adduced in opposing the doctrine were almost invariably logically inferior to those invoked in its support."[271] He notes that "particular moments of historical crisis, like the Pelagian controversy, the Gnostic menace, the Origenist debates, all combined to render the dangers inherent in preexistence weightier than its virtues."[272] We in the modern world are not so self-constricted, yet we seem to have a reflexive fear of even considering preexistence because of an unconscious fear of the transcendent power of our mind — i.e., our long-forgotten godhood.

We gain conviction and fearlessness of our transcendent nature by contemplating our preexistence with God. The fact that we may relate with such a Source means that we are not truly "of the world" or bound to the world. The world is no longer the measure of our reality; nor does our worldly reality determine our fate and destiny. Heaven and godhood grow closer and more clear when we understand that God graced us with his own kind of being *before* the foundations of the world were laid.

Divine foreknowledge is foreknowledge only to us. To God, everything occurs in a timeless present, an eternal moment that endures without time. For God (and for ourselves as gods), the future is a present reality. There is no need for a past when there is no judgment and no guilt to hang on it, and there is no need for a future when all is perfect and complete and there is no death to anticipate. Thus are we graced to live our lives as gods in total bliss and timeless certainty.

---

[271] Givens 2009: 7.
[272] Givens 2009: 7.

8

THE HOLY SPIRIT AND NATURAL THEOLOGY

A fully restorative deification makes of natural theology a natural ally. The divine being God created is still our "inmost self," and so, although we live in unconscious denial of our godhood, it has continuing influence just by being there. Every human has a spirit that is subject to natural theology. It is from this natural spiritual inner being that the creation's yearning for a full return to godhood comes.

Natural Theology

A fully restorative model of deification fits neatly with the idea of natural theology. Natural theology is organic theology, a theology that arises from natural origins. Its revelations may come from somewhere elsewhere than scripture or philosophy, such as from intuition, play, relationship, nature or meditation.

If human beings derived originally from God, then there must remain something naturally Godlike about them. The fall has not swallowed up their godhood, but only hidden it. Moments of realization of this natural godhood can break through at any time. This means we have a natural propensity toward spirituality which may or may not involve religion as the world knows it; it can come from natural remembrance and recollection of aspects of the intelligible or spiritual reality that is always there.

There are strong statements of natural theology in the Pauline letters. Paul writes that one's religion is private and individualistic, "a matter of the heart":

> Rather, a person is a Jew who is one inwardly, and real circumcision is a matter of the heart — it is spiritual and not literal. Such a person receives praise not from others but from God. (Romans 2:29)

Paul argues that the real significance of religious ritual and practice is what happens in our inner being. It awakens our own natural spirit, and this experience may be had without ritual or ceremony. Ultimately it is entirely internal, having little to do with the business of religion as the world knows it.

Paul's vision and revelation on the road to Damascus changed him immediately from a devout Jew, beholden to his religion's ancient laws and practices, to more of a natural mystic. Suddenly, he realized that the heart of religion was "spiritual and not literal." Despite doctrinal hardening that even the New Testament authors engaged in, there is a sense in each of religion as a natural, internal and individualized process. Indeed, this is likely why Paul spun off so many images in his letters, to express for different people and groups with diverse backgrounds various valid ways of envisioning their internalized spirituality.

Paul writes that people need not be aware of the religious law to follow it because they follow it "instinctively" and are therefore "a law to themselves":

> When Gentiles, who do not possess the law, do instinctively what the law requires, these, though not having the law, are a law to themselves. (Romans 2:14)

Those who follow the law "instinctively" without knowing the law are "a law to themselves." The idea that God has written his spiritual law on our hearts allows for natural religion for those who were not beholden to the codified or written law. They follow it naturally, intuitively, even unconsciously. The law itself arose from natural origins, collectively to strengthen early human society and individually to elicit gratitude to God and respect for our fellow humans. The parameters of religion, and goodness, even godhood are all within our mind already. Religion does not teach us the spiritual law so much as it reminds us of what already exists by nature — divine nature — within ourselves. Ultimately, the revelation brought about by spiritual experience is not reducible to human terms and concepts. The way to transcendent reality can be elicited and explained, but the transcendent reality itself is *known* only through firsthand experience. The law and everything else in religion is meant to lead us back to this natural, original experience.

We have spoken of two main tendencies in the world, one which seeks to "suppress the truth" (Ro. 1:18), the other to expose by revelation the divine nature in all creation. As Paul puts it:

> For what can be known about God is plain to them, because God has shown it to them. [20]Ever since the creation of the world his eternal power and divine nature, invisible though they are, have been understood and seen through the things he has made. (Ro. 1:19-20)

Try as it might, the world cannot hide the "divine nature" within its forms. Something deep within us can see past the forms into the depths. The "divine nature" in us seeks itself in everything, each aspect of creation, including ourselves and all we see.

Thomas Aquinas taught that human reason even without influence of religion could know and act upon certain religious truths. He writes that "all acts of virtue are prescribed by the natural law: since each one's reason naturally dictates to him to act virtuously."[273] For Aquinas, people act virtuously through natural reason. It is not just the right thing to treat others well, but it is the natural thing as well. Many know this somehow, to treat others as they would like to be treated, without knowing how they know it. It

---

[273] Thomas Aquinas, *Summa Theologica*, "Question 94, Article 3." Translated by The Fathers of the English Dominican Province (Second and Revised ed.), 1920.

is intuitively or implicitly known. He writes about the core precept of the natural law as being "that good is to be done and promoted, and evil is to be avoided. All other precepts of the natural law are based on this."[274] Human beings thus have a natural propensity to the good and, at the same time, a natural resistance to evil. The desires to live and to procreate are counted by Thomas among those basic (natural) human values on which all positive human values are based. He also writes that, on a societal level, "Human law is positive law: the natural law applied by governments to societies."[275] As with Paul, the codified law is basically good when applied equally and fairly, but it is also limiting and constrictive and does not account for individual difference and circumstance. Its real purpose therefore is to lead beyond itself to our spiritualization. As with Jesus, the natural yet divine emotion of love, applied universally, fulfills the law perfectly.

Part of the spiritual curriculum for some might be finding God in rare moments of tranquility, joy, camaraderie, or mesmerizing natural beauty. Just to consider another person with selfless love is enough to spark a god's awareness in each party. The interconnection is already there for us; we simply need to find it. Traces and intimations are available daily, but like dreams they are quickly covered over by the usual preoccupations in daily life. But these hints and traces are the confident whisper of the Spirit, appealing to both mind and heart, asking our consent to reveal the grace and graciousness of God in literally everything, including ourselves and all we love.

This having been said, we must remember that the natural world includes evidence not only of God and the original souls, but also of the fall of these souls. And so, there is both Godlikeness and its opposite, constriction and carelessness and the privation of good, in nature, in the world and in ourselves, and we should expect to see both until falsity falls like scales or lifts like veils from our eyes, leaving only the truth for us to see and appreciate. Examples of this

---

[274] Thomas Aquinas. *Summa Theologica*, "Question 94, Article 2." Translated by The Fathers of the English Dominican Province (Second and Revised ed.), 1920.
[275] Thomas Aquinas, *Summa Theologica*, "Question 94, Article 3." Translated by The Fathers of the English Dominican Province (Second and Revised ed.), 1920.

carelessness can be found in the viciousness and randomness of survival of the fittest as well as in the apparent mortality and corruptibility of all earthly creatures. Yet, this sad but seemingly necessary aspect of the world is not our true nature; our true instincts run far deeper than that, for they come all the way from our inmost being and divine nature.

The Holy Spirit in the Hebrew Bible

Natural religion of various kinds peppers the Hebrew Bible and apocrypha. The idea of "the Holy Spirit" arose from a natural, personal experience of the "presence" of God, as the Psalmist writes:

> Cast me not from thy presence,
> and take not thy holy Spirit from me. (Psalms 51:11)

Here in the world, the Holy Spirit represents the presence of God, whose divine nature far transcends the world. The Psalms continually stress the joy of this transcendent yet personal presence.[276] The Holy Spirit is the internal presence of God, allowing us to learn from God through its mediation. It is a joy to learn from because each lesson brings a little more freedom, along with the encompassing peace of understanding.

Is the Holy Spirit already within us, or does it enter us from outside? Consider that it was already at work in the world when the Spirit of God swept over the roiling waters of chaos in the second verse of Genesis. It cannot at first be too direct, because it does not seek to frighten and, like God, respects the freedom of the mind. Thus, it eases us gradually and often indirectly into this very different reality with which we have lost familiarity.

The Book of Proverbs speaks of a similar spirit it calls "the human spirit":

---

[276] See Ps. 16:11 and 21:6.

> The human spirit is the lamp of the Lord,
> searching every inmost part. (Prov. 20:27)

The "human spirit" is, again, one we already have — but may not yet know. It is familiar with our mind intimately, knowing "every inmost part" including those we have dissociated from awareness. This natural, God-given "human spirit" connects us already with transcendence, whatever our theology (or lack thereof) may be. The human spirit is our true self, the inner god, already divine by nature and having a pre-established connection with our true Source and fully aware of its (and our) continual, timeless presence.

> Truly it is the spirit in a mortal, the breath of the Almighty, that makes for understanding. (Job 32:8)

A "mortal" is not a mere "mortal" if it has a spirit directly from God. The spirit inside ourselves possesses a perfect and eternal nature like its Source.

God spoke to Elijah in "a still small voice" (1 Kgs 19:12 RSV), which is how the spirit speaks, gently yet authoritatively, spontaneously and intuitively yet well-reasoned, and always in a way we can best understand. The Spirit is not pushy, and is in fact unobtrusive, to the point where it often seems like a partially dissociated aspect of our own mind that appears when we need or want it. As such, once we attend to it, it helps to confirm reason and draw conclusions from new premises that we ourselves, through our lenses of presupposition, had not considered.

Even the core idea of Judaic covenantal law is given a strong natural element by the OT Prophet Jeremiah:

> But this is the covenant that I will make with the house of Israel after those days, says the Lord: I will put my law within them, and I will write it on their hearts; and I will be their God, and they shall be my people. (Jeremiah 31:33)

This last covenant will be a spiritual covenant, whereby the law emanates from inside individuals because it is written "on their hearts." This is a more direct, personal, and spiritual agreement than had previously been known, less a formal, legalistic covenant and more an unspoken understanding based on spiritual similarity. This affirms that the externalities of religion are meant to elicit the inner law, the natural religion, and the perfectly natural way of being, which Jesus will sum up as "love."

Intertestamental literature finds the Holy Spirit associated with "the spirit of Wisdom" (Wisd. 7:7), a personalized feminine aspect of God named Sophia (Greek for "Wisdom"). Jesus declares himself and John the Baptist to be adherents of this divine Wisdom, pointing out that, in spite of the different teaching and life styles between him and the Baptist, "Wisdom is justified in all her children."[277] Jesus did not follow the same restrictive lifestyle as the Baptist, but still they are both adherents. The Holy Spirit eventually became part of the Trinity (along with the Father and the Son) in Christian theology. An earlier version of the Trinity was "God the Father, his Word (Logos) and his Wisdom (Sophia)" for both Theophilus of Antioch and Irenaeus. The Word became identified with the Son in the later version, while Wisdom became associated with the Holy Spirit.

We have mentioned the Holy Spirit's role in arranging the chaos or "formless void" that preexisted the world:

> In the beginning when God created the heavens and the earth, ²the earth was a formless void and darkness covered the face of the deep, while a wind from God swept over the face of the waters. (Gen. 1:1-2)

This chaos or void of formless matter preexisted the world, and so something had to preexist the chaos because a privation

---

[277] Jesus speaking in Luke 7:33-35: "For John the Baptist has come eating no bread and drinking no wine, and you say, 'He has a demon'; ³⁴the Son of Man has come eating and drinking, and you say, 'Look, a glutton and a drunkard, a friend of tax-collectors and sinners!' ³⁵Nevertheless, Wisdom is vindicated by all her children."

presupposes a previous fullness. Scholars have wondered through the Christian centuries why matter, even if chaotic, seems to preexist God's creation. Our preexistent participation in its development needs to be taken into account.

The fact that "earth was a formless void" indicates that matter was still just a thought in the mind struggling to find its organizing principle when the Holy Spirit was created, while the fact that "darkness covered the face of the deep" suggests that the dissociation had already begun. This primordial "wind from God," alternately translated "the Spirit of God,"[278] rearranges and calms a preexistent chaos before humankind arrives upon the scene. It works with the chaos we ourselves have made in order ultimately to spark the ancient memory of our luminous original creation.

This Holy Spirit was created to counter the downward pull that prevents us from rising to and fully accepting our own spiritual nature. It is the Holy Spirit that both keeps human beings from falling into nothingness and helps them in their upward ascent, their transcendence of a confusing and constricting material reality and, ultimately, their realization of godhood. As such it is a transitional figure whose presence within us guarantees our salvation while it reminds of our own spiritual being.

In Jesus' Teaching

We turn now to the New Testament, where the Holy Spirit is said to have been instrumental in Jesus' incarnation, his transition from godhood to humankind (Mt. 1:18-20). We see the Holy Spirit at work already preluding the infancy narratives about Jesus, where the parents of John the Baptist, Zachariah and Elizabeth, would each be filled with the Holy Spirit[279] and so would John their son, of whom it

---

[278] "The Spirit of God" is given as an alternative interpretation to "a wind from God" in the NRSV. The Hebrew *ruach* means spirit, breath, and wind. Spirit was associated with wind because, although invisible to the human eye, its effects can be seen.

[279] Luke 1:41 re: Elizabeth and Luke 1:67 regarding Zachariah.

was said that "even before his birth he will be filled with the Holy Spirit" (Luke 1:15). This idea that John was filled with the Holy Spirit before birth (his own and Jesus') has been used as an argument for the soul's preexistence. It also gives indication that the Holy Spirit was in operation before Jesus' birth. As an adult, the Baptist states that while he baptizes with water, the one coming after him (signifying Jesus) would "baptize you with the Holy Spirit and fire" (Mt. 3:11). Jesus is understood as the one who becomes instrumental to the dispensation or sparking of this universal Spirit in individuals. But the Holy Spirit preceded Jesus into the world and helped instruct him about God.

At Jesus' baptism, "the Holy Spirit descended upon him in bodily form like a dove. And a voice came from heaven: 'You are my Son, the Beloved; with you I am well pleased'" (Luke 3:22), signifying that it was at this moment of baptism that Jesus became convinced of his own divine sonship. After this initial blissful experience, the Spirit led him into the wilderness where he struggled through temptation (Luke 4:1). The Holy Spirit had a revelatory function, an instructive function, and a protective function. It functions as a revealer of truth in Luke 10:21, and it has a purifying function in Luke 11:2.[280] It is said to be the happiest gift given by the Father (Luke 11:13). It would give Jesus' students spontaneous inspiration as needed (Luke 12:12).

It would remind his disciples of Jesus' teaching after he left their sight, suggesting that Jesus himself received his teaching from the Holy Spirit:

> But the Advocate, the Holy Spirit, whom the Father will send in my name, will teach you everything, and remind you of all that I have said to you. (Jn. 14:26)

The Holy Spirit is called here "the Advocate," "the Helper," like a defense attorney who argues on our behalf against the overzealous prosecutor and judge. The Holy Spirit is also a mentor, "wonderful counselor" (Jn. 16:13), and trusted advisor, a confidant and guide,

---

[280] The alternate reading prays: "Send your Holy Spirit to cleanse us."

working intimately with human beings, teaching them "everything." Jesus told his disciples they could not yet "bear" the revelation of the Spirit (John 16:12). It was thus an advanced teaching that even his closest disciples could not yet understand. Yet it would lead them inevitably to "all the truth" (Jn. 14:26). Thus, the Holy Spirit is called by Jesus "the Spirit of truth" in both Jn. 15:26 and here:

> This is the Spirit of truth, whom the world cannot receive, because it neither sees him nor knows him. You know him, because he abides with you, and he will be in you. (Jn. 14:17)

Although ever-present and inhabiting many beings at once, or more precisely every being at once, the Holy Spirit goes unrecognized by the world. Thus, it *appears* to be sent at different times to different individuals. However, Jesus tells his disciples they will recognize the Holy Spirit and in fact already know him from within, just as they will know the kingdom of God from within. It will not only remind of his teaching but will build upon it after Jesus is no longer physically present (Jn. 16:12-13).

The First Letter of John reaffirms the close, personal instruction we receive from the Spirit based on the experiential truth that "he abides in us" (1 John 3:24). And it is the Spirit, as "the anointing" ("christening") we have received from Jesus (1 Jn. 2:27), that "teaches you about everything, and is true, and is no lie, just as it has taught you, abide in him" (1 Jn. 2:27). As it is written, God said, "I will pour out my Spirit upon all flesh" (Acts 2:17, citing Joel 2:28). God has sent everyone in the world a Spirit to help them understand everything, first and foremost that we ourselves are spiritual beings and therefore so close to him that we are one.

In Pauline Literature

Paul insists that the presence and leading of the Spirit of God leads to sonship:

> [A]ll who are led by the Spirit of God are sons of God. (Romans 8:14)

Sonship and spiritualization go hand in hand. To know that the Holy Spirit is working in our mind and in our lives is to awaken and elicit our own inner spirit so that "it is that very Spirit bearing witness with our spirit that we are children of God" (Ro. 8:16). "Our spirit" is a spirit we already have, obviously, and so Paul is referencing a sonship we already have by virtue of this innate spirit.

The Holy Spirit is also a bearer of God's love to us:

> God's love has been poured into our hearts through the Holy Spirit that has been given to us. (Romans 5:5)

Recall that love in Jesus' teaching is a means to deification because it sparks the realization of sonship and makes us like God. Both he and Paul teach that love fulfills and therefore supersedes the codified law. This is why Paul speaks strongly against "the old written code" in favor of "the new life of the Spirit":

> But now we are discharged from the law, dead to that which held us captive, so that we are slaves not under the old written code but in the new life of the Spirit. (Romans 7:6)

Not only is the codified law unnecessary to those who walk in the Spirit and those who love, but the law held us "captive," that is, it did not allow us to be our true and natural selves. The love poured into us by the Holy Spirit is its own law, but it is no longer external to us; it arises from within. It is in fact a new way of thinking, feeling, and being. It has been written in our mind and implanted in our heart so that we can follow it naturally. Using equally strong language, Paul states: "For the law of the Spirit of life in Christ Jesus has set you free from the law of sin and of death" (Romans 8:2).

From the clarity of this new paradigm, the old law can become an impediment for individuals rather than a benefit as originally intended. Every law removes a portion of freedom, and so, we should carefully consider which laws are truly necessary. When it grows into a hydra-headed monster and the quibbling of lawyers and bureaucrats sets in, the natural guidance of the inner spirit and love is hindered, which is pointed out numerous times in both the gospels and Paul's letters. See especially Mt. 12:1-2 where Jesus and his disciples were accused of breaking the law by plucking grain on the Sabbath.[281] Jesus tells his accusers that human beings are "lord(s) of the Sabbath." That is, the importance of each person takes precedence over the law. Also, when admonished for healing on the Sabbath in Mt. 12:9-13, Jesus' stance is that, as long as the will of God is being done, and those in need are helped, no regulation should stand in the way.[282] Religion is evolving into a more natural, organic process here before our eyes, by becoming internalized and based on a divinely loving common sense.

We have noted that the Spirit grants a conviction of immortality just by its presence. Indeed, God "will give life to your mortal bodies also through his Spirit that dwells in you" (Ro. 8:11). Even while the body is mortal, the Spirit gives us life because: "you are not in the flesh; you are in the Spirit, since the Spirit of God dwells in you" (Romans 8:9). We are no longer at that point merely physical creatures. The Spirit's presence elicits our human spirit, which, though immortal, rules the body and our perceptual faculties.

It is through the Holy Spirit that we, while existing on earth, "may understand the gifts bestowed on us by God" (Ro. 2:11). These gifts include all the qualities that characterize God — his love, his gentleness, his justice, his fairness, his peace and joy and beauty, his holiness — as well as full relationship with him. The Eastern fathers would speak of these qualities as the "energies" or attributes of God,[283] while the Western were more prone to note the sameness of essence that sharing these qualities would necessarily imply. A real relationship with God requires likeness to him. The presence of

---

[281] The "Son of Man" or "Son of the Human" here is the transcendent part of each human being. Para. Mk. 2:23-28; Luke 6:1-5.
[282] Para. Mk. 3:1-6, and Luke 6:6-11.
[283] Particularly Maximus, on whom Palamas depended in his defense of the monks of Mount Athos.

the Spirit allows us to understand all these aspects of God in daily experience, objective and subjective, reenlivening the sacred qualities we had let gather dust due to disuse. Paul teaches that we might know the essence of God when he says that "the Spirit searches everything, even the depths of God" (1 Cor. 2:10). I take this to mean that the Spirit allows us to know and to experience the subjective essence of God for ourselves and *as* ourselves.

In his First Letter to the Corinthians, Paul speaks about the personalization of the Spirit, conforming itself in some ways to our human spirit as it works in individual lives. Besides the gifts it gives to all equally in terms of knowing the attributes and essence of God, the Spirit provides different "gifts" to each according to the learning and teaching styles that work best for them. "To each is given the manifestation of the Spirit for the common good" (1 Cor. 12:7). Paul's examples are instructive as to how the early church operated. Some speak wisdom and knowledge (v. 8), some are bolstered in their faith, some receive "gifts of healing" (v. 9), some work "miracles," some "prophecy" (v. 10), and so on. The Holy Spirit works with different individuals in personalized ways "for the common good." These differences are temporary. "For in the one Spirit we were all baptized into one body — Jews or Greeks, slaves or free — and we were all made to drink of one Spirit" (1 Cor. 12:13). Despite the diversity of gifts it fosters, the sense of unity promoted by the Spirit's presence reveals the equality and oneness of God's creation.

Again, the Spirit is meant to transform us (back) into divine beings:

> And all of us, with unveiled faces, seeing the glory of the Lord as though reflected in a mirror, are being transformed into the same image from one degree of glory to another; for this comes from the Lord, the Spirit. (2 Corinthians 3.18)

Paul suggests that our spiritualization by the presence of the Spirit is a process that occurs gradually, in stages, "from one degree of glory to another," until we are fully glorified, deified. These stages coincide with the veils being lifted one by one from before our eyes, reinforcing that something we already have (and are) is being gradually revealed to us, and the image of the "mirror" confirms this interpretation.

The Pauline Letter to the Ephesians speaks of "the promised Holy Spirit" as being "the guarantee of our inheritance until we acquire possession of it" (1:13-14), that is, the holder of our spiritual and immortal identity until we are ready for it. The Holy Spirit is both a reflection and example of our own spiritual nature and a guide back to it. And, being already within us, it has been dispersed liberally and fully among all beings, so that we might recognize it in others as we uncover it from within ourselves.

Conclusion

Perhaps the epitome of natural theology is Jesus' teaching referred to as the Golden Rule:

> In everything do to others as you would have them do to you; for this is the law and the prophets. (Mt. 7:12)[284]

This simple statement sums up "the law and the prophets," i.e., the entire religion, without mention of religious language. Moreover, it sums up "everything," all situations, by stating that in each it is best to treat others with the respect and care we ourselves desire. It encourages natural love and respect for one's fellow beings by seeing them as legitimate beings like ourselves. It is the idea that we are all in this together and, in spite of surface differences and diverse abilities and opinions, we are *essentially* the same.

It may seem strange that the entire religion — two religions in fact — can be summed up succinctly without religious language. There is no reference to God in it, yet the underlying assumption is that our fundamental equality as human beings should encourage us to treat others with dignity and respect, even honor and love. The

---

[284] Para. Luke 6:31.

world need not be aware of the underlying foundational reality of spirit to fulfill the cosmic law naturally. Eventually, the people will overcome the world to the extent they can do naturally what the law requires, because this is the way they are most themselves and therefore happiest.

The Holy Spirit *is* natural theology. It was at work long before Jesus elaborated upon it as a divine guide from the Wisdom tradition and worked to impart it. Most patristics believed it worked through the scribes of the Hebrew Bible as well as through other non-Christians (such as the Greek philosophers Plato, Aristotle, and Plotinus). If it worked through them, no doubt it works through many more who knew next to nothing of Christian theologizing. It is up to us to discern it in them as creations of God.

If godhood is part of us by virtue of the divine image in which we were created, then it will remain with us forever. If we were once gods and now cannot believe it, the truth will eventually overcome our unbelief. This will come naturally, although religion can hasten the process by adding understanding. It may take eons for every single being to accept the greatness held out to them by the "still, small voice" of the Spirit, even though its message is so spectacularly simple and universally beneficial.

Almost anything can spark awareness of our spiritual reality, whether this be a moment of tranquility, of ecstasy, or of closeness. The Spirit speaks spontaneously, in the moment, and we hear it more clearly as we give it space. It functions through our intuition and capacity for reason to lead us to "the whole truth," the great, grand picture, using every available means to do so. If the Holy Spirit and the inner human spirit with which it works are already in us, then technically speaking they and all their ideas need to be *recognized* rather than *received*. The Spirit itself "comes" or appears to us whenever we are ready to recognize the truth behind illusion.

9

DEIFICATION AND SALVATION

We have emphasized with the patristics that salvation is a gift from God. However, whereas most patristics viewed it as *the* gift of God, the only gift, the primary gift, in the fully restorative view, salvation is a secondary gift. The first gift was our foundational creation as gods, perfect and eternal beings, granted us prior to our arrival on earth. We rejected this gift prior to our arrival on earth in the fall from godhood. The second gift is meant to restore the primary gift to full awareness. Thus, salvation is the full restoration of what God has already given us: our godhood, perfection, eternal life, total love, and the opportunity for complete and total happiness.

Beyond the Cross

St. Paul wrote in his First Letter to the Corinthians about how his previous message to them was more basic than the advanced teaching he is now bringing them:

> When I came to you, brothers and sisters, I did not come proclaiming the mystery of God to you in lofty words or wisdom. [2]For I decided to know nothing among you except Jesus Christ, and him crucified. ... [6]Yet among the mature we do speak wisdom, though it is not a wisdom of this age or of the rulers of this age, who are doomed to perish. [7]But we speak God's wisdom, secret and hidden, which God decreed before the ages for our glory. (1 Cor. 2:1-2, 6-7)

Paul tells his audience that, in his former zeal to spread the message of Jesus, he had presented only the most basic message: "Christ, and him crucified" (1 Cor. 2:2). However, he continues, "among the mature we do speak wisdom," which he specifies as an ageless wisdom, actually prior to the world itself, and one that he had been reluctant to announce before. This advanced teaching is described as "God's wisdom, secret and hidden, which God decreed *before the ages for our glory*" (verses 6-7).[285] Here we have a secret knowledge that involves a predestined glorification whereby God wanted to share *his* glory with us before time ever started rolling.

God seeks to share everything he has with us, up to and including *himself*. What is "God's own wisdom," "secret and hidden," *except* the essence of God? Paul confirms this interpretation when he states that this knowledge and experience is "revealed to us through the Spirit," which searches "even the depths of God" (1 Cor. 2:10). What are these "depths" except his inner essence and subjectivity?

Paul is in this passage going well beyond the crucifixion as redemptive sacrifice focus of much recent Christianity, telling the Corinthians that the crucifixion message was only the most basic introductory message of Christian salvation, their entry-point perhaps but far from their finishing-point. The overarching idea was not to remain human beings who believe certain things, but instead, to come to believe in *themselves* as transcendent beings. Coming to know themselves as godlike beings, Paul asserts, "they are themselves subject to no one else's scrutiny" (1 Cor. 2:15), even *divine* judgment. Indeed, they actually "have the mind of Christ" (2:16). Christ is the model of their own godhood.

The crucifixion was not a focal point of Jesus' teaching, for he barely mentions it. Jesus taught consistently that salvation was a matter of forgiveness and love, and entering the kingdom of God. Forgiveness of others comes from the realization that we have been projecting guilt onto them, thus forgetting the total mercy of God for both them and ourselves. Love is the natural divine emotion. The emphasis on the crucifixion as especially salvific is a more modern

---

[285] My emphasis.

development within the past few hundred years. For the first millennium-and-a-half of Christian history, the crucifixion was not especially salvific except as part of Jesus' overall life. It was not so much Jesus' death that saved humankind from death as his resurrection. Deification (expressed as glorification) was the actual salvation, its culminating stage after purification and illumination (or sanctification). Anything else of importance was related to that. Crucifixion was a symbol of Jesus' selfless love, but the resurrection was where Jesus triumphantly exhibited his divinity. And, as we have seen with the exchange formula, the incarnation was of greatest significance because of its association with our own deification.

Harnack traces "the theology of sacrifice or propitiation based on the death of Christ" back to Origen and his reading of Ro. 3:25 and like passages, and states that in this Origen was "following the precedent set by the Gnostics," who insisted on some kind of salvific act. This "vicarious suffering of punishment, was adopted by Athanasius who combined it with the other ideas that God's veracity required the threat of death to be carried out, and that death accordingly was accepted by Christ on behalf of all, and by him was destroyed." [286] Both Cappadocians Nazianzus and Nyssa doubted, with good reason, the necessity of Christ's death as a sacrifice to appease God. Better is Origen's idea that Christ is the one who saves the world by presenting the kingdom, healed and whole, back to the Father — however long this takes respecting the complete freedom of mind God graced us with.

As Ledwith puts it:

> [G]iven the Ancient Near Eastern background of sacrifice as a basic religious practice, it was only natural that an attempt to grasp the significance of Christ's death in these terms would be fundamental to the early Christian understanding.[287]

Indeed, Paul in Romans 3:25 is using the sacrifice analogy, as he does frequently with other analogies, to point up that the righteousness

---

[286] Harnack, *History of Dogma*, Vol. III, Appendix to Ch. VI, Section 1, 307-308.
[287] Ledwith 1977: 148-149.

derived from faith in Jesus has superseded that of the law. Paul's preoccupation is to reinterpret the significance of the law more than to uphold the sacrificial view of the cross.

The ubiquity of the sacrificial culture in early humankind would seem to affirm the idea that humans are born with existential guilt. This guilt is free-floating in that it has no solid cause — we do not know clearly what the sin is — except existence itself, and perhaps a vague sense of not fulfilling our potential. It manifests often as anxiety, depression, or neurosis; it can lead to somatic illness. The mind usually resorts to projection, the unconscious process of blaming others for our own thoughts, which Jesus himself seems to confirm when he speaks about the human propensity to judge others for what we ourselves are doing or thinking. The only way to truly deal with the problem of guilt, then, is to develop a nonjudgmental attitude towards others, i.e., to forgive.

The practice of sacrifice eventually proved only temporarily effective and thus was relegated to the prehistory of most religions in part because it was ineffective and needed to be continually repeated. The guilt always returned, now worse, often in a different form. Perhaps this is why Israel's ancient prophets, centuries before Jesus, had already taken sacrifice off the table:

> What to me is the multitude of your sacrifices?
> says the Lord;
> I have had enough of burnt offerings…. (Isaiah 1:11)

Supplication, sacrifice and subordination are not necessary to have relationship with God. The prophet Micah voices the kind of inner attitude with which we should replace sacrifice:

> [W]hat does the Lord require of you
> but to do justice, and to love kindness,
>   and to walk humbly with your God? (Micah 6:8)

Paul's emphasis on the crucifixion as the basic message was shaped in part by the fact that neither early Jewish-Christians nor those trained in classical philosophy could accept a crucified messiah. In Judaism, such an ignoble death had long been associated with a divine curse (see Deut. 21:23).[288] This is why Paul called the crucifixion "a stumbling block to the Jews" (1 Cor. 1:23). It was just as repulsive to Greek philosophy that God would require such barbarity. We can see that Paul used his rhetorical skill to transform this curse into a blessing, as here: "Christ redeemed us from the curse of the law by becoming a curse for us — for it is written, 'Cursed is everyone who hangs on a tree'" (Gal. 3:13). Note that the redemption here as in Romans is from "the curse of the law," which, like sacrifice, is the attempted solution of a bygone era.

One of the many ways in which Paul sought to redeem sacrifice was by employing the older justification/juridical model which harkened back to the early Israelite covenants that referenced the sacrificial cult, whereby God was perceived as a distant even fearsome overseer — a tribal judge rather than a Father. But Paul expressed salvation in a multitude of other ways as well, including via images of sonship, corporate sonship, a collective spirit, sharing the divine image and likeness, a love relationship with God, participation, putting on immortality, at-one-ment in its original sense of oneness, spiritualization, Christification, and glorification — each of these emblematic of our own deification. These many means of salvation by deification save God from having to think of his beloved children from within the self-imposed strictures of human forensic categories and hapless ancient sacrificial attempts at propitiation.

Jesus would himself affirm that showing mercy is a proper replacement for the old practice of sacrifice:

> But go and learn what *this* means: 'I desire mercy and not sacrifice.' For I did not come to call the righteous, but sinners, to repentance. (Mt. 9:13, NKJV)

Forgiveness is the key to salvation because it allows us to love again. Often our hardest grudges are held for those we most love. Sacrifice,

---

[288] See also Justin Martyr, *Dialogue with Trypho*, 89-91.

like holding grievances, does nothing but perpetuate the unfulfilled and deprived mindset of the world. If we place forgiveness instead on the altar, this substitutes for all thoughts of sacrifice. The only way to forgive all things is to transcend the world's ways of thinking entirely, thus to see "the other" with entirely new eyes as essentially like ourselves. Repentance means giving up worldly ways of thinking, including forensically "religious" ones that deny both the closeness of God to *all* his children and the full transcendence afforded us by our divine birthright.

Jesus taught of our relationship with God in intimate relational terms, not in terms of justification and righteousness. In fact, in Jesus' teaching, the "righteous" or self-satisfied were not yet ready for true salvation. The prostitutes and tax collectors would get there before the doctors of the law, being more open to the experience of salvation because they were shut out from the traditional, institutionalized versions. We would do well to humbly admit our lostness as to both what reality is and what we are meant to be saved from. We are saved specifically from the self that binds us to such misinterpretations.

Jesus' teaching about salvation revolved around love, forgiveness, and the glad tidings of the kingdom, whereby the sick would be healed (Luke 9:1-2), love would abound (Jn. 14:21), and sins would be forgiven (Mt. 6:14-15). There is next to nothing in Jesus' teaching about salvation by the cross, and what is there seems like later interpolation. This is evidenced by the fact that, when Jesus did bring up his impending death, just days before it was to occur, even his disciples "understood nothing about all these things; in fact, what he said was hidden from them, and they did not grasp what was said" (Luke 18:34). Obviously, then, salvation by crucifixion was not a key teaching of Jesus himself and sprang into existence only after his death, in large part to mollify those who could not see past it.

Jesus had been willing to lay his body down for his friends out of love (Jn. 15:13). He showed through the cross but more specifically the empty tomb that death is nothing compared to the reality of the divine nature. Jesus demonstrated to his students in this extreme way that a god cannot die — no matter what the world does or what it perceives.

His disciples asked Jesus who among them would be the greatest in the kingdom of heaven. Jesus answered: "the Son of Man came not to be served but to serve, and to give his life a ransom for many" (Mt. 20:28). Again we see an inverse relationship between greatness in the world and greatness in God's reality. Jesus is making a point here specifically about the importance of service to enter into the kingdom. The Son of Man, a divine messianic figure with which Jesus is identified here, does not come to be served or praised, but instead to devote his life to serving and saving others. He does this through his "life," not through his death.

Origen attempted to construct a ransom theory of salvation out of this passage, but it did not catch on. Jesus' death as a ransom for Satan mistakenly places Satan on par with God in terms of power, leading to dualism rather than reinforcing monotheism. Moreover, God does not see things in worldly terms as we do, and this goes double for legal or contractual terms. Even if the world is primarily the devil's possession, that has no effect on God's reality nor on his children's ontological or inner being. Much better is Origen's position, similar to Irenaeus' recapitulation, that Jesus reconciles the world to God by deifying its inhabitants, in order to present the regathered spiritual kingdom back to God as whole and holy, so that God might again be "all in all."

Rather than focus primarily on the cross, Irenaeus' recapitulative view of salvation indicated that Jesus' sharing of human feelings (including anxiety and sorrow over the death of his friends) throughout his life was itself redemptive. He saw Jesus as Savior in a holistic way, through his overall life. The cross was important in this recapitulatory sense as a way of overcoming specifically death for humankind.[289] Jesus represents the new spiritual man, who succeeds where Adam failed — in every aspect of his life, not only in his apparent death — and from all these redemptive actions reclaims his and our original divinity. For salvific purposes, the cross is outshone by the incarnation which for most

---

[289] Finch 2006b: 116.

patristics sparked our deification, as well as by the light of the empty tomb, the resurrection, sparking the remembrance of our own eternal life. It is stated that Jesus rose from the dead and raised others with him so that "they might live in the spirit like God" (1 Peter 4:6). His rising reflects our own deathlessness, showcasing that death is a mere appearance and that deified life is immortal.

The crucifixion was never, for the first fifteen hundred years of Christendom, the *sine qua non* of salvation that the past few hundred years have made it out to be. It was for the East a sacred mystery, its significance and solemnity inexpressible in human terms, and, although the West was on the one hand more inclined to see relationship with God as a legal formality, it was also more prone to view our final relationship with God to be one of essential closeness based on shared essence and being.

The Simplicity of Belief

Salvation is far simpler yet more complete than we tend to think. A change of mind is all that is needed, but this simple change of mind changes everything. It is simple, but that is not to suggest that it is "easy" in human experience. Jesus' initial message was simply this:

> The time is fulfilled, and the kingdom of God has come near; repent, and believe in the good news. (Mk. 1:15)

A new age has arrived, the happy one promised by the prophets, and it all begins to dawn simply by believing in the possibility of a very different reality: "the kingdom of God." Starting with belief in it, the reality of God will reveal itself to us through firsthand experience. It will be a very different experience than that to which human beings have grown accustomed, as we might suspect due to its original association with apocalyptic thought. To "repent" is to change one's life and entire perspective, thus to stop resisting what our higher mind knows as true, and to allow the natural heart to run and embrace the world and God at the same time.

Jesus brings the reality of God *and ourselves* near so we can better believe it. Belief in Jesus means believing in his sonship, which means believing in our own very close relationship with God. To believe in *his* sonship is to believe in our own. This is what he meant when he said that the person who believes in him "has passed from death to life" (John 5:24). In this the person recognizes their own divinity and immortality, by realizing they, like him, are likewise eternal mind and spirit rather than body. What begins with simple belief in Jesus ends with full conviction of our own godhood.

Thus, belief is much more than the memorization of rote statements and creeds. Nor does belief require a suspension of reason; in fact, reason helps solidify belief and convert it to knowledge. When Jesus talks about belief, he is highlighting the *power* of mind to overcome the world. "All things can be done for the one who believes" (Mk. 9:23). Conformity of belief was never his goal; instead, he emphasized how it changed everything. This idea is seen clearly in Jesus' healings, wherein it was the person's belief or faith which, coupled with a sense of forgiveness, healed their minds and bodies. He speaks of belief as giving power to prayer: "So I tell you, whatever you ask for in prayer, believe that you have received [or, are receiving] it, and it will be yours" (Mk. 11:24). Note that the receiving occurs in the present, within the prayer itself.

Jesus stated that those who learned from him would become his "friends" and coworkers. Their belief in him led to learning from him, and this led to union with him. Jesus had learned from the Holy Spirit, just as we learn from him and our own inner spirit, specifically this: "He who believes in the Son of God has the testimony *in himself*" (1 John 5:10, my italics). What we are to believe in, supported and enhanced by reason, is already within us awaiting our recognition and appreciation.

Jesus taught the transformative powers of belief, mercy, understanding, and love. We would do well to have implicit faith in others like he had in us, and like we do in him, and believe in them and ourselves as much as we believe in God. We are all together

God's glory, his achievement and his companions. In the end, eternal life depends on our belief in it because, if it was given to us "from the beginning" and "from before the foundation of the world," then we already have it but do not believe we do. We remain in a state of self-deception. We have placed ourselves into an unnatural position where we must come to believe in what the mind knows forever, and must now decide for what is forever rightly ours.

Original Sin Revisited

Original sin is a theory, a speculative theology, that is more Augustinian than it is scriptural. Since it was rediscovered by the Western Reformers, it has come unfortunately to emphasize humankind's utter depravity and helplessness in the face of our fallen nature. Almost nothing was left of the original divine nature, our creation in the divine image, and what *was* left was severely debilitated. We needed, more than ever, what I would call an additional grace, a secondary salvific grace to restore the original created grace.

Augustine's impetus for developing the doctrine was to ward off the challenges of the Donatists and of Pelagius (c. 354-418), an Irish theologian who emphasized free will in salvation and denied inherited sin. A person, born innocent in Pelagius' system, could freely choose to do good, such as follow the law or enter a monastery or treat others well, without need of a secondary grace to do so. Augustine takes an extreme position to counter, giving the impression that humankind was so impaired by inherited sin (originally from Adam) that they could not decide for goodness without divine grace, unearned and dispersed somewhat randomly. Perhaps influenced by his former Manichaeism, Augustine tied the transmission of original sin to the act of conception and sexual desire. The doctrine languished for a thousand years until Luther and

Calvin made use of it in their own theological systems, so that it became accepted Christian doctrine in the modern West.[290]

Augustine wrote at length and in many places, yet not entirely systematically, about original sin. It is an inherited sin, a collective sin distinct from personal sin, which traces all the way back to our unconscious participation in Adam's sin, thus to some limited form of preexistence whereby all subsequent souls were originally materially present in Adam. Couenhoven's 2005 article, "St. Augustine's Doctrine of Original Sin," contains a detailed discussion of Augustine's teaching and its development in his works. To sum up:

> In his theological controversies with the Donatists, Augustine had argued that saving faith in Jesus Christ was available through the Catholic church alone, and, in particular, through the sacrament of baptism. If there are paths to salvation independent of Christ, into whose death we are baptized, then Christ died in vain. This belief led Augustine to be committed to the idea that all human beings, of whatever age, are sinners who need Christ, and thus to infant baptism.[291]

Thus, Augustine had his ecclesiastical reasons for developing the idea of original sin. Orthodoxy was coalescing, and alternate views of salvation were deemed too threatening to tolerate. Anselm, too, had his reasons for supporting such a view centuries later, and these had to do with the restoration of honor to God. Christ restores this honor and thus does humankind avoid punishment. Several hundred years later, Calvin focused on justification and punishment, influencing the Western view to the present day.

We may extract from the idea of original sin the idea of a collective mistake, a mistake in which all of humankind participated

---

[290] Anselm in the Middle Ages did contribute to the idea but, as we shall see, he held a more restorative view that original sin was nothing more than the absence of the original state of perfect justice that humankind had with Adam.

[291] Couenhoven 2005: 361, citing Augustine, *Grace and Free Choice*, 2.29.34; *Nature and Grace*, 9.10; *Unfinished Work in Answer to Julian*, II.146.

(otherwise they would have remained gods). Thus, they are born into human existence with an inherent (not inherited) guilt, which in itself is their real immediate problem because they do not remember the act or thought that produced the guilt, which occurred before they ever arrived. But this does not mean that they are totally degraded, as Augustine sometimes seemed to imply, but rather that they are almost entirely dissociated. The real problem with original sin is that its popular conception came to stress human degradation to such an extent that it crowded out the divine nature with which we began, i.e., our having been created in the image and likeness of God.

Another major problem posed by original sin is that the substitution theory that Jesus died for humankind's sin, contorted from Anselm's view about restoring honor to God, actually made God look like a monster [292], a bureaucratic drone without even human feeling. He was to be feared above all else. How, then, could we possibly cling to him for our salvation? This view has probably done more to steer the modern mind away from God and from personal responsibility than anything ever has. It is all the more insidious because based on a fabrication now commonly believed, one that was never shared by even its originators.

Much of Augustine's underlying theology is understandable, based as it is on maintaining God's goodness:

> Augustine also has a theodical reason for his belief in original sin: it would simply be unjust for God to allow infants to suffer deformities, disease, mistreatment, and death, unless they were already sinners. Augustine is confident that bodies not corrupted by sin would not undergo any of the evils just mentioned. Of course, Christ died, but this was because he took on the "likeness of sinful flesh" in order to renew it. In

---

[292] Ledwith 1977: 151 explains it thusly: "Anselm fully recognized that God's personal honour could never be augmented or decreased by human action. Sin can therefore never disturb God's honour in itself, but only the created order that depends on it."

all other cases, these evils are the penalty of sin, and thus a sign of sin.[293]

Augustine proposed original sin for the same reason Origen (and the earlier Augustine) proposed the idea of preexistent minds: to explain apparent inherent injustices in the world. God cannot be the author of unequal treatment. Both explanations sought to preserve God's honor and truth, his fairness and sense of justice. But the idea of original sin in its extreme versions negates the eternal splendor of original creation, whereas preexistence depends on it.

Three scriptural passages are generally cited as support for the idea of original sin: Genesis 3, Psalm 51:5, and Romans 5:12-21. For Augustine, Adam in Genesis 3 fell into a state of disordered desire and ignorance, a fallen "second" nature, which vitiated and defective state was a punishment unto itself. The vitiated state passed on to Adam's progeny is thus the problem we must deal with, as is the guilt that accompanies it. Any supposed sin other than this, including concupiscence, is purely speculative. The real problem is our diminished identity, for which we experience existential guilt because we were created for so much more.

Augustine also cites Psalm 51:5, which he believed to have been written by King David, as reinforcing his idea of original or inherited sin:

> 'For, behold, in iniquities I was conceived.' Was David born of adultery; being born of Jesse, a righteous man, and his own wife? What is it that he saith himself to have been in iniquity conceived, except that iniquity is drawn from Adam? Even the very bond of death, with iniquity itself is engrained? No man is born without bringing punishment, bringing desert of punishment. A Prophet saith also in another place, 'No one is clean in Thy sight, not even an infant, whose life is of one day upon earth' [Job 14:5, LXX].[294]

---

[293] Couenhoven 2005: 361, citing Augustine, *Grace and Free Choice*,.2.20.22; *Contra Julian*, I.6.24; *Unfinished Work in Answer to Julian*, I.39.
[294] Augustine, *Expositions on the Book of Psalms*, Psalm LI.10, *NPNF* 1.8: 192.

The verse from Job at the end is simply saying what Paul would later say: that the body and world are not our true home. The "punishment" in having selected such a lesser identity is inherent in that lesser identity, thus self-inflicted. It cannot be attributed to God because God does not think in terms of punishment, but only in terms of love. John's argument is that: "There is no fear in love, but perfect love casts out fear; for fear has to do with punishment, and whoever fears has not reached perfection in love. [19]We love because he first loved us" (1 Jn. 4:18-19). God, being perfect and total love, therefore neither fears nor punishes.

Augustine employs Psalm 51:5 as support for original sin: "Indeed, I was born guilty, a sinner when my mother conceived me," but this verse's supposed connection to a sexually *inherited* version of original sin is nebulous and quickly resolved in the Psalm, which reads in the very next verse:

> You desire truth in the inward being; therefore teach me wisdom in my secret heart. (Ps. 51:6)

This speaks clearly of an interior locus and impetus for salvation through the acquisition of sacred knowledge, which advanced knowledge, as we have seen with Paul, is knowledge of our own Godlike state of being. This interior and self-willed salvation is further enhanced by the following verses:

> Create in me a clean heart, O God,
>   and put a new and right spirit within me.
> [11] Do not cast me away from your presence,
>   and do not take your holy spirit from me.
> [12] Restore to me the joy of your salvation,
>   and sustain in me a willing spirit. (Ps. 51:10-12)

The Psalmist quickly posits to showing that humankind is not entirely nor even fundamentally depraved. If we have a deep-seated inner yearning for a clean heart and a willing spirit, then there is something within us that strives for goodness from beneath the layers of guilt and the self-deception that sparked them. In fact, the yearning and asking itself is goodness in action, purifying and sanctifying, arising from a goodness that must already lie within, beneath conscious awareness and beyond debasement.

The Psalmist's 'sin' is his/her felt distance from God, nothing more but nothing less, which is fully resolved (as one would think) by a sense of God's "presence" and "holy spirit." All of this is meant to "restore" to us "the joy of your salvation," which restoration confirms it was something we formerly enjoyed but lost. Altogether, if verse 5 speaks of original or existential sin, it is one that is easily resolvable by an interior openness to the presence of God which is always and therefore already there but goes unnoticed. A better explanation for the innate guilt of Ps. 51:5 is offered by Origen's teaching of preexistent but perfect minds that have fallen into limitation before they ever arrived on earth. Their guilt arises, simply but profoundly, from not being themselves. But the original sin does not leave them helpless. Their hope lies in their original identity contained in the divine image, always just a belief away.

The same can be said for the other primary text Augustine used to explain the effects of original sin, Romans 5:15: "the many died through the one man's trespass." Augustine led the Reformers to believe that the tragic effects of original sin destroyed the holy willpower of human beings to the point that they became utterly depraved and could not help but sin. Hence the crying need for grace. The context of this verse is much more hopeful, however, speaking of a grace already given, the "free gift" (and "grace") of righteousness (5:17), which we have seen is associated with eternal life. Paul's optimism leads him to exclaim that "where sin increased, grace abounded all the more" (5:20). We might parallel this, and answer the Augustine-influenced extreme pessimism about human nature, by stating similarly that despite the depravity and evil sometimes found in human nature, by virtue of the original grace of creation plus the secondary grace of its restoration, grace abounds all the more.

Let us not forget, too, that human nature is bipartite, including (for a time) *both* the depraved part *and* the divine part, and we can decide to operate from either at any time. The question regarding original sin or blessedness is which of these two has priority. Which is the real us? The Bible consistently recognizes both sides, the two divergent natures of the human being. Because of the great disparity conceived between the transcendence of the gods and lowly human nature, the Psalmist asks:

> [W]hat are human beings that you are mindful of them,
>   mortals that you care for them?
> [5] Yet you have made them a little lower than God,
>   and crowned them with glory and honor. (Ps. 8:4-5)

Verse 4 suggests that God and human beings are two such very different natures that they would seem to have no overlap. And yet, verse 5 asserts that, because of their creation by God, human beings have been "crowned" with "glory and honor," i.e., things associated with godhood, and that they are, even now, only "a little lower than God."

If we have fallen into sin and distance from God, we cannot lose heart because we were graced beforehand with the infinitely greater reality of godhood. Because our godhood was given as a free gift from God, it must still be there, like a gift discarded because its worth was initially overlooked, along with the close relationship this would indicate. We tried to get rid of it, and we nearly succeeded, but we cannot lose what God has given. Nor can we hide from our true selves forever. We cannot lose our perfectly good, divine, original being, however depraved and helpless the secondary nature we added to the mix. The very reason we might at some points be called "miserable sinners" is just because of the magnitude from where we came. We fell from the majesty of full divinity, the highest order and status of being, which is what grants our misery and debasement all the more poignancy.

Moreover, if, as Augustine avers, evil is but a privation of the good, a void that has the appearance of being but no being in itself, then the degradation can never be the truth of our being, but only a degree of privation from such truth. And we can see in the world that what we see as evil is most often a loveless reaction to this void of love in the world, which reaction cyclically perpetuates the lack of love. It is because of this withholding of love that sin continues to affect the world with a barely hidden guilt. There is no inheritance about it, and no need to deny the plenary nature of God's grace to resolve it.

Generally speaking, the Eastern Orthodox churches reject Augustine's idea of generational sin because we as individual minds are responsible for our own participation in the fall. Ezekiel 18:20, which states that a son is not guilty of the sins of his father, shows that the idea of generational sin was archaic even in this great prophet's time (c. 600 BCE). Ezekiel asserts forcefully: "A child shall not suffer for the iniquity of a parent, nor a parent suffer for the iniquity of a child; the righteousness of the righteous shall be his own, and the wickedness of the wicked shall be his own." Rather than inherited sin, Ezekiel emphasizes personal responsibility. The restorative view might detect a universal experience of guilt, but this is baked into our mistaken identification with limited creaturely being.

Paul's declaration that "all have sinned" (Romans 5:12) and therefore all are subject to death can be taken as a statement of universal responsibility for our current fallen condition rather than a generational impartation. The sin had been an exchange of immortality for mortality, which hurts God only indirectly — because it hurts us. He did not set this condition of mortality for us; nor do we remember setting it. If we are truly responsible for this, it must have been a decision *we* made *before* we limited and forgot ourselves, consistent with Paul's suggestions and Origen's statements about preexistence. Some patristics (Augustine included) seek to explain this by saying that we were part of Adam when he sinned, but even this would involve some sort of preexistence. It is better to say that Adam is symbolic of our own preexistent decision, so that we no longer project the responsibility elsewhere.

We wanted an autonomy separate from the one God had already given us. That is why we are experiencing this now. We wanted something other than the godhood we had already been given. We must have known it would necessarily be something lesser than full godhood, so we would be severely limited but at least we would have the type of autonomy we thought we wanted. Modern Eastern theologian Panayiotis Nellas writes:

> [A]utonomy is the source and the content of sin, since it constitutes a counterfeit of the truth about man … and his restriction to the biological level of existence.[295]

For Nellas, the idea of sin as a misplaced attempt at autonomy produced our self-imposed limitations as biological creatures. The counterfeit self we made is a false idol that we adore because we made it, but it is born of a wayward desire. Again, a mere change of mind would right all things. We are not limited unless we have somehow, somewhere along the line chosen to be.

In chapters 17 and 18 of his *Proslogion*, Anselm of Canterbury (1033-1109) similarly recasts the question of original sin as a rejection of our original perfection. Anselm writes first of the bleak effects of the fall on our original spiritual senses:

> Still you are hidden, O Lord, from my soul in your light and your blessedness; and therefore my soul still walks in its darkness and wretchedness. For it looks, and does not see your beauty. It hearkens, and does not hear your harmony. It smells, and does not perceive your fragrance. It tastes, and does not recognize your sweetness. It touches, and does not feel your pleasantness. For you have these attributes in yourself, Lord God, after your ineffable manner, who hast given them to objects created by you, after their sensible

---

[295] Nellas 1987: 93.

manner; but the sinful senses of my soul have grown rigid and dull, and have been obstructed by their long listlessness. [296]

Again, we cannot accuse God of hiding from us; we only made it seem that way by hiding from God, thus forgetting both God and our own true nature. But the point of the passage is that our distancing from our true selves has dulled our normal spiritual senses, which include a sense of the infinite and of closeness, even union, with God and others. As Kerr puts it, for Anselm: "original sin is not being the creatures we were intended to be."[297] It is this denial of our original state of being that causes us to seek the lesser things of the world and deludes us into thinking they are ends in themselves. For Anselm as for most patristics, sin is overcome by the restoration of our original perfect being which shares the joy and other attributes of God. All of this is consistent with a fully restorative, ontologically based deification, a deification by grace *and* by nature.

Anselm speaks eloquently of what sounds like a firsthand despair at the fleeting nature of our foretastes of godhood while we exist in this world:

> I tried to rise to the light of God, and I have fallen back into my darkness. Nay, not only have I fallen into it, but I feel that I am enveloped in it. I fell before my mother conceived me. Truly, in darkness I was conceived, and in the cover of darkness I was born. Truly, in him we all fell, in whom we all sinned. In him we all lost, who kept easily, and wickedly lost to himself and to us that which when we wish to seek it, we do not know; when we seek it, we do not find; when we find, it is not that which we seek.[298]

To acknowledge our apparent fallen nature does not imply that human nature is utterly depraved. Humankind forever has access to

---

[296] Anselm, *Proslogium* 17 (1903; 1926 reprint ed.), translated by S. N. Deane. Chicago: Open Court Publishing Company.
[297] Kerr 2007: 181.
[298] Anselm, *Proslogium* 18 (1903; 1926 reprint ed.).

love, its greatest joy and most natural state, but it does not see its true worth. The fullness of eternal life just cannot be consistently experienced here in the world, and this is temporarily distressing to our heart and mind. But it can be learned and made known, eventually to be fully and consistently experienced, and this is cause for celebration.

> If, then, the heart of man will scarce contain his joy over his own so great good, how shall it contain so many and so great joys? And doubtless, seeing that every one loves another so far as he rejoices in the other's good, and as, in that perfect felicity, each one should love God beyond compare, more than himself and all the others with him; so he will rejoice beyond reckoning in the felicity of God, more than in his own and that of all the others with him.[299]

Salvation is a reassertion of the original joy of creation and its Creator. Kerr remarks: "In redemptive grace, God simply gives us again the gifts to be the creatures that we are, gives to us again our created nature as that means through which we shall enter into God's own perfect *beatitude.*"[300] It is not a *re*-creation, which would be unnecessary because of the perfection of the first, but an additional gift, a new grace added to the eternal abundance, which helps us to remember and thus restore the original grace: the entirely joyous and loving free gift of creation.

We are corrupted, but only partially so, when we are not ourselves. We can live that way for a while, perhaps eons, but eventually we will find it intolerable to continue with such dissonance, cognitive and emotional, even if unconscious. Although powerful, or perhaps because of its concentrated power, our godhood is in this sense a delicate thing; it cannot rest where it cannot freely be itself. "Foxes have holes, and birds of the air have nests; but the Son of Man has nowhere to lay his head" (Mt. 8:20).[301]

---

[299] Anselm, *Proslogium* 25 (1903; 1926 reprint ed.).
[300] Kerr 2007: 183.
[301] Para. Luke 9:28.

Conversely, nothing unlike it within our minds can withstand it but disappears as it enters. The denial of our godhood is the root of all our problems. A god has no problems.

Most simply put, sin is the choice we made to throw limits on love. Adam did not make it for us; we made it for ourselves, as shown by our current experience of the effects. Both the problem and its inbuilt punishment is a dissociative condition because we, like our Creator, *are* love when we are most truly ourselves. Being love is our most natural way of being and our essence, as it is God's. It is where we are most at home and joyously carefree yet as creative as God. We think we have been hurt by love, but our hurt and the world's comes from denying love. We are not hiding from God because of any specific act, but rather to deny our true selves and motivation, which hurts mainly us, but by extension those around us. The original sin was a denial of the original grace, a distancing from both God and our eternal selves. To forget the one, we had to forget the other. We also lost our joy and peace in the process, and our naturalness.

Our depravity was great because our original love was so much greater. We had to go to extremes to deny such original magnitude, such sweepingly powerful and foundational feeling. Yet, because of who and what God forever is, we remain forever what and who he created us to be.

Although Eastern scholars tend to fault Augustine for the West's recent over-emphasis on sin and justification in Christian salvation, Augustine is most often as nuanced as are they. He joins the Eastern fathers in linking justification to the first stage towards deification via the mediating image of sonship:

> Now He who justifies, Himself deifies, because by justifying He makes sons of God.[302]

Augustine equates justification with deification and being made sons of God, signifying that the purpose of the justification was, like purification for the Eastern patristics, ultimately for

---

[302] Augustine, *Enar. in Ps.* 49. 1.2, as translated in Bonner, 'Augustine's Conception,' 384. For the context see *NPNF01* 8.178.

deification. For him, justification was purification in that it provided the condition for reestablished relationship, but in this he and later Western theologians deemphasized sanctification on the way to deification. With his Eastern counterparts, Augustine sees sonship as being given only *after* creation, not with creation, but with the adoption, brought about by justification as a legal process. A fully restorative view argues instead for an original and natural sonship, a begotten closeness, and thus a true godhood from the beginning, so that deification is more a re-deification than a starting over again from scratch, and more a remembrance than a transformation. There is no need in this view to suppose a deficient creation. It is a return to our original identity as perfect creations of a perfect God.

The fall was tragic and hard, because we fell far from our eternally blessed origin. From that point on, a secondary gift was needed, and this is everything Augustine and the patristics say it is: a true gift, free and unearned, but it is an additional gift meant to return awareness of the original gift. The fully restorative view saves God from thinking in juridical and legal terms, such as justification has become, in regard to his beloved children. Justification is simply right-mindedness, a return to sonship and godhood by ridding our minds of everything unworthy of it.

It is ironic that the Western Reformers themselves (Luther, Calvin, Wesley, et. al.) never questioned deification as the culmination of salvation. Their only difference was in the process. They accepted the Greek patristics as readily as the Latin. For instance, Ollerton remarks that "consistent with the Patristic writers, Calvin never questions whether we will experience deification but what kind of deification it will be. Indeed, in his commentary on 2 Peter 1:4 Calvin sees deification as both the goal of the Gospel and the greatest possible blessing."[303] Calvin writes:

> And he then shews the excellency of the promises, that they make us partakers of the divine nature, than which nothing

---

[303] Ollerton 2011: 5. Regarding Calvin and deification, see also Billings 2005 and Mosser 2002. Regarding the Finnish school which discovered deification in Luther, see Mannermaa 1995: "Theosis as a Subject of Finnish Luther Research."

can be conceived better. For we must consider from whence it is that God raises us up to such a height of honor. We know how abject is the condition of our nature; that God, then, should make himself ours, so that all his things should in a manner become our things, the greatness of his grace cannot be sufficiently conceived by our minds. Therefore this consideration alone ought to be abundantly sufficient to make us to renounce the world and to carry us aloft to heaven. Let us then mark, that the end of the gospel is, to render us eventually conformable to God, and, if we may so speak, to deify us.[304]

Calvin, like Augustine, saw justification as the first step of the process culminating in deification, but Calvin took a particularly apophatic approach, following the Eastern patristics. He also shares their propensity to interpret "nature" to mean "quality" rather than truly "nature." At any rate, justification was for most patristics including Augustine and Calvin only a preparatory step toward salvation by deification. And so, to have made it the gist of the entire Christian message for the last few centuries has undercut the trajectory of the full arc of salvation, reducing the whole to its preparatory step.

It is important that we acknowledge, with Augustine and other theologians, the depraved and distorted part of human nature. We are not inclined solely to good, for we have a bipartite nature. However, for the same reason, we are not inclined solely to evil. The good in us is so much greater than the evil that the evil is only degrees of privation from the good, having no being in itself, but entirely dependent on the good for its sense and semblance of being. (Hence why Adam and Eve had to be deceived to accept it.) And so, the point of acknowledging this deprived side is not to remain there amid the depravity, and wallow in our infirmity, but instead to rise to the glorious original being that God created. This is exactly why deification is necessary: to bridge the gap between the

---

[304] Calvin, John. *Commentary on Second Peter*. "2 Peter 1:1-4" in *Commentaries on the Catholic Epistles*. John Owen, ed. and trans. Grand Rapids, MI: Christian Classics Ethereal Library. [http://www.ccel.org]

Existential Guilt and Its Concealment

The problem of existential guilt, as stated in 1 John 3:20, is that "our hearts condemn us." Existential guilt is the guilt we are born with, a guilt inherent to existence. It does not come from God, and must therefore come from ourselves prior to human existence. It is not erased by even the tightest of behavioral controls; the solution, like the problem, must arise from within, where the underlying motivation for behavior lies.

Although we don't remember the fall or what preceded it, the guilt persists as a free-floating guilt, an existential guilt without any specific object. It seems to be part of existence itself, part of our human nature, which shows that there is a lot going on beneath the surface. Such guilt without an apparent crime becomes what theologians in the twentieth century called existential guilt, a guilt inherent in human existence.[305] Because it is a free-floating guilt without specified object, the automatic executive functioning of our mind attempts to deal with it with such unconscious tools as denial, repression, and projection. These are basically the egoic defense mechanisms postulated by the depth psychology of Sigmund Freud, but while he attributed them to childhood and sexual roots in repressive Victorian culture, restorative deification sees them and the guilt that caused them as inborn because preexistent, continuing in this human existence rather than originating here.

There is nothing about sex in the creation/fall accounts in the Book of Genesis. In fact, sex was long viewed in Judaism as a healthy drive within a committed relationship. Nor is the serpent in the myth associated with Satan, also the product of later theologizing. Although there is no specific talk of "sin" or "guilt" in the Genesis accounts, a guilty conscience is implied in the defensiveness of Adam

---

[305] See esp. the works of Martin Heidegger, John MacQuarrie and Paul Tillich.

blaming both Eve and God in one fell swoop, saying, "The woman you gave me made me eat it" (Gen. 3:12),[306] in Eve blaming the serpent (3:13), and, especially, in both of their hiding among the trees from God (3:8).

Augustine writes that Adam and Eve were already "secretly corrupted" by an "evil will" *prior to* the act of eating the forbidden fruit. They already had a hidden motivation of "pride" and "the craving for undue exaltation." They must already had fallen, then, prior to their deception by the serpent, for they wanted to become ends unto themselves rather than truly exalted creations of God. In their "spontaneous" "falling away," they lost their "love of that higher and changeless good" and, as with Origen, their hot ardor cooled and they became "frigid and benighted."[307]

Adam and Eve "would not have believed the serpent spoke the truth" if their thinking had not already been impaired. This points to a preexistent decision as their fall, even for Adam, the very first human. He and Eve were already "wicked" by the time they ate from the "corrupt tree." Turning toward himself rather than God and the whole of creation, Adam's "being became more contracted," constricted, shrunken and diminished. But only the false idol he made of himself could have fallen away. Identifying with this fallen part, he almost became a "nonentity." His pride decreased and debased him, but his humility would have exalted him because "pious humility enables us to submit to what is above us; and nothing is more exalted above us than God." This contrast in motive between pride and humility is indeed the great difference between the two cities of which Augustine writes in his *City of God*.[308]

Augustine concludes that Adam had already begun his fall by the time he listened eagerly to the lies of the serpent:

> The devil, then, would not have ensnared man in the open and manifest sin of doing what God had forbidden, had man not already begun to live for himself. It was this that made

---

[306] My paraphrase.
[307] Augustine, *City of God*, Bk. 14, Ch. 13, *NPNF* V1-02: 273.
[308] Augustine, *City of God*, Bk. 14, Ch. 13, *NPNF* V1-02: 273.

him listen with pleasure to the words, 'Ye shall be as gods,' which they would much more readily have accomplished by obediently adhering to their supreme and true end than by proudly living to themselves.[309]

All of this is valid enough, and it is reinforced by the serpent's own words to the woman: "You will not die; ⁵for God knows that when you eat of it your eyes will be opened, and you will be like God, knowing good and evil" (Gen. 3:4-5). This is an obvious falsehood, being that Adam and Eve were already gods via Gen. 1:27, having been created in the divine image. They became subject to death by identifying with a lesser being, so that by the time their physical eyes were opened, the couple had already thought of themselves as different from God prior to their eating from the tree, as proven by their mere physical existence.

Augustine therefore supports greatly the idea of a preexistent fall, one that we must have chosen to forget before we ever arrived, thus likely arrived *to* forget. However, I must part ways with Augustine when he says definitively: "For created gods are gods not by virtue of what is in themselves, but by a participation of the true God."[310] Here Augustine verges on the constricted view of the East, that gods are not truly gods, but only by participation. For gods are indeed gods by virtue of what is inside themselves because the divine image is there. God himself is there, and all their love is there, and all the joy and peace they will ever have, held in store for them, so that it with their eternal happiness should be released to them when they are ready to receive it. This idea of the pre-corruption of Adam and Eve can be explained in a far simpler and more scriptural way, in my humble opinion. It comes from an idea that Augustine himself often entertained, that of the preexistence of the soul. And so, the fall is pre-human, pre-historic, and pre-temporal, its true cause lost in the mist, while we but try to deal with the aftermath.

While it is natural for the mind to want to rid itself of guilt, such constant unconscious projection of free-floating guilt is itself a

---

[309] Augustine, *City of God*, Bk. 14, Ch. 13, NPNF V1-02: 274.
[310] Augustine, City of God, Bk. 14, Ch. 13, NPNF V1-02: 274.

burden for us because, like sacrifice, it perpetuates the problem. Thus, Jesus taught people to reel it in and rethink it:

> Why do you see the speck that is in your brother's eye,
> but not notice the log that is in your own eye?
> Or how can you say to your brother,
> 'Let me take the speck out of your eye,'
> when there is the log in your own eye? (Matthew 7:3-4)

Jesus describes the unconscious psychological projection of guilt two thousand years before it was given the name. He saw within humans an inclination to search unconsciously and scrupulously for evidence of guilt in others because of *one's own* guilty conscience. We do it without knowing we are doing it. And this is precisely why our judgment of others results in a fear of self-punishment.

So, there is something to original guilt, but the doctrine of original sin as developed in recent centuries has led to unfortunate ways of thinking about ourselves and especially God. The idea of sin itself has been pumped up and emphasized to the point that it blocks our loving eternal embrace with God. It has strained and distanced the relationship and our sense of what the relationship should be.

What existential guilt tells us is that we are not entirely comfortable in our own skin. And this leads us to believe that perhaps we really are hiding from something — another entirely different way of being hidden *within ourselves*. Perhaps there is another way of being where anxiety does not flow from springs in the ground and where depression does not sweep in like winds from the north, or where the potential for conflict lies around every corner. Perhaps there really is a way of being that is truly relational and more emotionally close (even to God) than original sin has made it out to be.

The nearly worldwide sense of guilt in prehistoric humankind is the natural basis for those aspects of religion referred to as the sacrificial cult. The sacrificial cult in many ancient religions was meant to alleviate this deep-seated sense of pervasive guilt through a scapegoating system: projecting this guilt onto a creature (sometimes a goat) that was then either killed or released into the wilderness. Judaism passed through this stage early in its Mosaic development, although its sacrificial system did not entirely die out until the destruction of the Jerusalem Temple in 70 CE. That is, the guilt had been "dealt with" by being dissociated from the self and projected onto something else. Just so, our subconscious is forever trying to dissociate our personal store of existential guilt from the self, first by denial and repression, then, because this does not resolve it, via projection of this guilt onto others, all as a protection against looking within.

Having repressed it and made it unconscious, we fear it all the more. We fear *ourselves*. We fear real love, because love would return the interrelated self we have also, beneath even the layers of guilt, denied and made unconscious. We must learn that it is impossible to project guilt that is part and parcel of existence. The guilt of alienated existence must be worked through from within each self, within our confused and troubled and anxious mind. Only then can we say with Paul: "Happy is he who condemns not himself" (Romans 14:22, KJV).

Conclusion

What are we saved from when we are saved? The "sin" we are saved from is immersion in the wrong nature. Therefore, it is from ourselves that we are saved. It has nothing to do with God, and everything to do with us. We are the ones who introduced the sense of distance from God and from others simply by believing we live apart from them in physical existence. But this does not accord with the reality of God, which we know from deep within ourselves, and so existential guilt seems inherent in existence.

It is this misstep that produces a sense of distance from God, guilt and conflict, a point on which most patristics agree. And on the solution they agree as well: the miserableness of our existential situation can only be resolved by deification, sharing the nature of

God, his most gracious gift to us. Where they differed was in how closely we share the divine nature with God, and where we first acquire it.

If we acquire godhood only in the future, then we must have been created with a deficiency of godhood and therefore of love. But if we were created gods from the beginning, then we had it once in all its glorious fullness and then lost it. Which presupposition is more worthy of God, his love, his goodness, and his perfect thoughts? Did he create us in process and therefore incomplete, with all the difficulty and complexity not to mention random chance this implies, or did he create us to be perfect beings from the beginning, as his own perfect, timeless, and consistent nature would suggest?

The recent over-emphasis on "sin" and punishment in the Christian message has distorted the real message, making Christianity seem more mundane and yet more fearful than it really is. Since that time sin has become associated with everything from violations of social mores to dancing to worshiping God on the wrong day. Having forgotten that salvation is deification, we failed to realize that sin is a mindset to be overcome, a mindset that has grown estranged from everything around it and even from itself.

Still, sin and its deleterious effects on our nature should not be overemphasized to the point of overshadowing its simple and wonderful remedy, often just a verse or two away. The remedy transcends all else. "Love covers a multitude of sins" (1 Peter 4:8). To say that sin should replace love as the characteristic mark of human nature, or distract from love in any way, is to diminish and debase the perfect creation of God, the pre-deified inner being rooted in God, knowledge of which is the natural resolution to the self-distancing of sin.

God does not share our woeful perception of the world nor of ourselves. Perception itself is a lower-order reality from his vantage point. Adam and Eve's eyes having been opened to their own diminishment was something they did not share with God. Because of this, *sin is not a problem for God per se*. It is a problem for God only indirectly — because it is a problem for us. God does not think in terms of legalisms of any kind, nor of punishment, nor of rules and regulations, nor of inducing fear, nor of removing joy, and most certainly all of this nowhere in relation to his children. Nor does he know of limited being. He has no temper; he does not suffer fits of anger, wrath, or desperation due to our worldly actions. These are prime examples of the traditions and conditions of man wrongly projected onto God.

Jesus and Paul agreed that the law does not save. In fact, Paul laments it increases the burden of guilt. Jesus finds it insufficient because it dealt with surface behavior but not with the thoughts and feelings that underlie the behavior.[311] If sin is a matter of heart and mind, then so is salvation. The law does not save. Sacrifice does not save. Behavioral conditioning does not save. Nothing else truly saves except the restoration of the perfect deified mind and the perfection it knows all around.

As far as salvation was concerned in by far most of our beloved patristics, crucifixion was but a small aspect of a much greater picture, outshone by the light of the empty tomb, Jesus' incarnation, and by his transfiguration and ascension into heaven, which are more apt mediating images for realizing our divinity. There is no longer any need to interpret the crucifixion as if the archaic sacrificial cult were still valid. The true message of the cross is that death is unreal, and no matter how horrific it may appear to human perception, the entire world in which such a thing is possible is overcome by our accession to godhood.

Irenaeus had the right idea regarding salvation. He viewed Jesus as recapitulatory of Adam's waywardness every step of the way, not only in his selfless and loving act of going to the cross. Jesus' entire life was salvific. Truly effective, every little thing he did saved the world, which now awaits the simple realization. His mere arrival into our little world was salvific for *all*. Why? Because it restored to us our long-lost godhood, our peace, and all our misplaced happiness and trust.

Belief in Jesus is, at heart, belief in ourselves as well. There is no better praise of God. This is because Jesus taught us about *us*, the

---

[311] See Mt. 5:21-30, where in the examples given, the motivation is more significant than the act that follows.

divinity of God's entire creation, not only about himself. It is *our* mind which is powerful enough to move mountains and change the world. It is *our* mind that receives heavenly reward and rejoices with him in heaven. Even when he asks us to believe *in him*, he is asking us to believe in him *for our own sake*. He encourages us to cultivate and channel the power that already exists in our own mind, but which has been dissipated and wasted by our dealings with the world. Jesus believed in *us* infinitely more than we do in anyone, including God, him, and ourselves.

10

LIVING AS GODS IN THE WORLD

In this chapter we will explore some of the many types of experiences, processes and practices found in scripture and the patristics that help prepare us for the original and foundational experience of godhood. Whatever else it may be, deification is first and foremost a subjective experience of godhood. We can obtain the experience simply by taking the mediating images seriously. The experience comes briefly and transiently while we are embodied on earth, but these rare transcendent moments alter our earthly experience and how we think about it.

Experience of the Deified Self

The doctrine of deification is rooted in the individual's subjective experience and phenomenology. Even when the patristics focus on ritual and sacrament, it is the underlying subjective experience that is emphasized. Thus, baptism is only on the surface an immersion in water; in truth, it is immersion in a new reality: godhood. And the Eucharist is more than a sharing of bread; it represents our assimilation into godhood, a realization of the "Christ in us." Fasting and prayer were also practices intended to distance us from ordinary reality and induce the experience of an entirely different reality. However, these cannot be said to be *essential* steps if one may experience this new reality simply by asking for it:

> Ask, and it will be given to you; search, and you will find; knock, and the door will be opened for you. (Mt. 7:7)

It is not that God awaits our pleas so much as that what we ask for is already given but it cannot be uncovered and experienced until we open ourselves to it. Asking, like prayer, opens the mind to receive or experience what it has denied and dissociated.

Deification is received, not from outside ourselves, but from inside, where we have hidden it, deep below even our personal unconscious. Its mediating images (such as the divine image, sonship, glorification, and spiritualization) hold the power to elicit this inner godhood and transform ordinary human subjectivity into divine subjectivity. Jesus himself is a mediating divine image, and imitation of him and his way of being would also lead to deification. Seeing him as recapitulative of Adam's sin is eventually to see ourselves in the same light. The doctrinal aspects of deification grew out of the experience of deification, beginning with that of Jesus. They are like dry bones until our interest and application sparks the vitality in them.

Anselm laments that he cannot achieve the "felt experience" of his doctrine, permitted only by "full creaturely participation in the divine *esse*" or being.[312] The full experience awaits our full cognitive participation, but it will be an immersive experience for which our beliefs and doctrines could not fully prepare us. The true progression from doctrine to experience may be disorienting, as it seemed for Thomas Aquinas in his end-of-life experience.

A few months before his death, while still working on his magnum opus, *Summae Theologiae*, Thomas suddenly put his writing materials away. He told his friend that he could no longer write because of an experience he had, and he now believed all his former work to be "like straw."[313] Such is the great gulf between theology and experience. The experience clarifies the theology, but the theology can be useful to impart or evoke the experience. Even Thomas seems not to have enjoyed the full experiential effect of his grand and intricate theology, it seems, until this experience toward

---

[312] See Kerr 2007: 180.

[313] Foster, *Life of Aquinas,* 109–10. Aquinas a bit later had a vision whereby he heard Jesus tell him, "You have written well of me."

the end of his earthly existence. The experience, when it finally came, proved much more significant and transcendent than it was possible even for him to convey in words or conceptually. It is truly a grace from God, as we do not expect its magnitude, whether we think of it as first arriving at this late date or having been given to us before the foundation of the world.

St. Paul describes his own experience of being lifted into the "third heaven" which left him without words to describe it. He says, reluctantly and not wanting to boast, that he was "caught up into Paradise" and he "heard things that cannot be expressed in words, that no mortal is permitted to repeat" (2 Cor. 12:2-4).[314] For such brief transcendent moments, he experienced his superhuman, transcendent self. He was godlike, visiting the heavenly places.

Paul provides a framework for the experiences, stating that they reflect stages of increasing glorification:

> And all of us, with unveiled faces, seeing the glory of the Lord as though reflected in a mirror, are being transformed into the same image from one degree of glory to another; for this comes from the Lord, the Spirit. (2 Cor. 3:18)

Strictly speaking, a transformation in terms of substance is not necessary, only a progressive change of mind to be "transformed into the same" glorious being as that which we seek to know. Once the veils are removed, we find the divinity we seek within ourselves, so that we may recognize it in others, despite the presence of the body. This will generalize into a sense of oneness with God and all beings for brief, blessed transparent experiences. With "unveiled faces" (or honest minds without self-deception), we will ultimately behold "the glory of the Lord as though reflected in a mirror," meaning that we will know ourselves to be like God. In the end, as John writes, "when he appears, we will be like him" (1 Jn. 3:2).

The stages of increasing glorification represent levels of spiritual experience leading up to a full reidentification with godhood. Most people receive foretastes of the goal first —

---

[314] My wording.

significant introductory experiences that usually last only minutes, perhaps hours — but then must undergo the work of establishing the conditions for that experience to return. The dialectic process works from both sides: the negative way of purification removes obstacles to the understanding and experience, while the positive way of sanctification immerses us in the understanding and experience of the qualities of godhood and attributes of God. Both ways or steps involve self-reflection, study, meditation, prayer, and contemplation — but mainly just openness to new experience and knowledge.

It is generally believed that the Eastern patristics emphasized the negative or *apophatic* approaches, while the Western fathers advocated the positive or *cataphatic* methods. The negative approach reminds that the human mind cannot fully conceptualize the divine attributes (even our own divine attributes), while the positive approach immerses us in them. These seemingly opposite approaches work best together in an internal dialectic to deemphasize the limiting human nature within ourselves while at the same time enhancing the god within. Thus, while we might set out to contemplate God as beauty, we would at the same time remind ourselves that we have no human conception of what divine beauty really is. All our former conceptions were not only wrong but also quite limiting. John the Baptist said: "He must increase, but I must decrease" (Jn. 3:30). As our old nature and its narrow way of thinking is chipped away, we do not so much lose our self as gain a greater self; there is at the same time a gradual recollection of what is sacred and divine (but dissociated) in our mind.

Theologically, the apophatic or negative pattern runs, as Andrew Louth states, "through Gregory of Nyssa to Plotinus."[315] Dionysius the Areopagite sees it as an experiential transformation: comparing "those who pursue this path to sculptors, who bring beauty out of stone by cutting away" everything that hinders or conceals this beauty.[316] The *via negativa* is a pruning away at the egoic, grasping, acquisitive self until we are left with only the best

---

[315] Louth 2007: 42.
[316] Louth 2007: 42.

and most glorious within us. This chipping away can be thought of as the bracketing of everything within us that is *not* mind or spirit, keeping it of secondary concern. In this way we can look at *everything* more objectively, and how each part, even if seemingly unrelated to us in our former way of seeing, is essential to the greater whole.

Positive ways involve a sharing in the attributes and virtues of God, which suggests a sharing of essence and ontology. Positive practices include the cultivation of stillness through prayer, openness to the radical present, imitation, and contemplation of God and his virtues, which we will find are most natural to us and thus revelatory of our shared essence. The positive way of contemplation culminates in a vision of the essence of God under the principle that the mind becomes what it contemplates.

Christensen cites Clement of Alexandria's progressive process of assimilation to God:

> Being baptized, we are illuminated; illuminated, we become sons; being made sons, we are made perfect; being made perfect, we are made immortal.[317]

Like Irenaeus, Clement offers a progressive revelation powered by Platonic contemplation and vision. Baptism here is more than mere ritual; it is an illuminating experience of sonship, of perfection, and of immortality. At his baptism, Jesus saw the spirit descend like a dove and heard a voice from heaven saying, "This is my beloved son, with whom I am well pleased" (Mt. 3:17).[318] It is via this experience he may have fully realized his own divine nature.

Even so, we must wrestle with the lower part of the mind that resists its abdication and will fight to keep what it views as its control and autonomy, albeit severely limited in both. We must deal with both sides of our powerful mind, the part that longs for divinity and the part that resists it. Working on the resistance, which can be deceptive, simply by realizing its presence, we come to understand

---

[317] Clement of Alexandria, *The Instructor* I.6, cited in Christensen 2007: 25.
[318] Slightly altered from NRSV.

how not to hinder, but rather facilitate, the natural state of being that yearns honestly only to be itself.

As regards positive contemplation of the virtues, we are meant to see the "true" and the "excellent," the "lovely" and the "gracious," as listed by Paul in Philippians 4:8. These are the categories our heart longs to know again, which categories are inclusive of all God-created beings, and so they do not belong to the conflicted world and self we have chosen. As we learn to step back and not dictate reality but instead open to it, the strength of our desire for it will open an individualized way to it.

Differing beliefs are inconsequential in light of the experience God has in store for us. What matters most is that we get to the experience. Experience brings the certainty of knowledge, which is beyond belief. The Psalmist states: "*All* the paths of the Lord are steadfast love and faithfulness" (Psalms 25:10).[319] We are simply reacquainting ourselves with the core characteristics of God and of ourselves as well. All the divergent ways merge into what the prophet Isaiah called one broad "highway" to the Lord (Isa. 62:10), filled with individuals eternally attracted to the same ultimate goal of total freedom and eternal happiness for everyone — i.e., godhood.

It is an inner experience and reality to which we are returned. Augustine speaks of an interior ascent to an interior heaven even while he and his fellow experiencer, his mother Monica, are lifted through the ecstatic and unifying stages via study and prayer while stirring one another to ever greater heights of inspiration. He writes of timeless wisdom and being sparked by "a moment of concentration of the heart."[320] Our attention is scattered, but as we focus it on what the heart really wants, all things are possible and in fact are already done.

---

[319] My emphasis.
[320] Augustine, *Confessions* 9.10.24. Translated by J.G. Pilkington. From *Nicene and Post-Nicene Fathers*, First Series, Vol. 1. Edited by Philip Schaff. (Buffalo, NY: Christian Literature Publishing Co., 1887.)

Contemplation

The most frequent positive patristic approach to deification was contemplation of God and his divine attributes. Contemplation (Gk. *theoria*) is a way of assimilating to God by the principle that the mind *becomes* what it contemplates or beholds. It is a decidedly Platonic idea utilized heavily by Paul and the patristics that what we hold in mind determines what we will be, the mind being determinative of our reality (as in modern cognitive therapy). In the restorative view, the attributes of God are, like Platonic ideals, already fixtures in our higher mind. Consequently, immersion in divine things (by way of study, participation, reflection, practice, unitive ecstasy, and meditation) eventually restores our divinity to us. Early contemplation in the patristics had a highly visual element as it culminated in the vision of God, while more recently contemplation became associated with the highest form of prayer.

Paul speaks of Christ as "the image of God" (2 Cor. 4:4) for us to contemplate until we ourselves assimilate to that very image. Thus, Paul says, "Just as we have borne the image of the man of dust, we will also bear the image of the man of heaven" (1 Cor. 15:49). Whichever of these images we hold in our mind, we will become. We are being "clothed," enwrapped "with the new self, which is being renewed in knowledge according to the image of its creator" (Col. 3:10). Jesus is our model for imaging ourselves as gods or being "conformed to image of his Son" (Ro. 8:29).[321]

This "Son" is a Christian archetype, an image for our own sense of universal being to awaken, which, simply by letting it be itself, we grow into and become. It is one with God and with all beings. The collective Son is used similarly as the collective "Christ" in that we participate in both, as we shall see in the last chapter. As we find and fulfill our individual function on earth, we take on aspects of a universal being, composed of all individual minds, a collective soul in which all are meant to participate, somewhat similar to Carl Jung's collective unconscious, although it need not

---

[321] See also 1 Cor. 15:49; 2 Cor. 3:18; Col. 1:15. See also the discussion of image as archetype in Litwa 2015: 438.

always remain unconscious. This synthesis of beings would be the divine council of gods being, feeling, creating as one. While on earth, we need an image for this invisible reality that we can understand on a perceptual basis, while acknowledging that even this is necessarily a limited conception (as would any based on perception, words, or concepts).

Contemplation has acquired a secondary meaning over the centuries as wordless, non-conceptual prayer, the highest form of prayer which leads ultimately to direct contact with God. This is the kind of prayer Paul states that the Spirit facilitates with "sighs too deep for words" (Ro. 8:26). Eastern Orthodoxy follows a monastic tradition of "ceaseless prayer," which originated with Paul's admonition to "pray without ceasing" (1 Thessalonians 5:17), wherein prayer is a way of being. The Psalms counseled meditation on the law of God "day and night" (Ps. 1:2). Such ceaseless prayer need not be confined to monasteries; it goes on in our higher mind as we attend to our daily activities. Prayer is therefore a very individualized enterprise which yet joins together, or rather, points out where we are already joined. It is just us and God, while our oneness with the cosmos flows from that core connection.

The story of Jesus' interaction with his friends Mary and Martha in Luke 10:38-42 shows the priority of the contemplative life, the way of Mary, who "sat at the Lord's feet and listened to what he was saying," while her sister Martha was busily serving the bustling household. The point was to leave room, an empty space, for quiet contemplation, spending valuable time with our guiding light and its interconnection with all. In the Beatitudes, Jesus states: "Blessed are the pure in heart, for they shall see God" (Mt. 5:8). He makes it a practice to remove himself from the noise and distraction of the crowd every chance he gets (see Mark 1:35). He teaches a very interior, very personal type of prayer:

> But whenever you pray, go into your room and shut the door and pray to your Father who is in secret; and your Father who sees in secret will reward you. (Mt. 6:6)

In all these things, we are being pointed to the interior world of mind and heart, reflection and contemplation, stressing their great importance for direct relationship with God. The overarching message is: "Be still and know that I am God" (Psalms 46:10). It is our presumption that we know all things that prevents us from actually knowing all things.

Both of these forms of contemplation, one in its older, perceptual sense, the other in its newer sense as a way of prayer, are known to be deifying. In either sense, whether it is by studying and meditating on God until one becomes a god, or by ascending the stages of prayer in the presence of God ultimately to an inexpressible vision of God, contemplation leads to deification.

Irenaeus along with the Syrians Tatian and Theophilus of Antioch all pinpointed the importance of *theoria* or contemplation in obtaining immortality, incorruptibility, and eternal life. Most of the patristics who followed, both East and West, agreed. The vision of God is the last stage where perception, ever-variable, turns finally into eternal knowledge, ever-certain but inexpressible in words. Irenaeus writes:

> [T]he beholding of God is productive of immortality, but immortality renders one nigh unto God.[322]

The vision of God is one of mind rather than physical senses. It comes in a highly personalized, even private way and yet lifts us to the realm of universals and a joining with God.

Origen agrees, writing that Moses' face was glorified by being in the presence of God in the form of the burning bush. Being thus in the direct presence of God, Moses contemplated God, and, as Origen states, the mind "is made divine by what it contemplates."[323] Origen links this transformative vision with a godlike mind:

---

[322] Irenaeus. *Against Heresies.* 4.38.3-4 (*ANF* 1:522).
[323] Origen. "Commentary on John 32: 338-340." *Commentary on the Gospel According to John, Books 13-32*. Trans. Ronald E. Heine. Washington, D.C.: Catholic University of America, 1993. 406. Print.

> We must say that this is what is meant when it is said that the face of the one who contemplated God, conversed with him, and spent time with such a vision, was glorified. Consequently, the figurative meaning of the glorification of Moses' face is that his mind was made godlike. It is in this same sense that the Apostle said, 'But we all, beholding the glory of the Lord with unveiled face are transformed into the same image.'[324]

We cannot *see* the glory of God without *being* the glory of God. This is because by the time we see it, we have become it. In a fully restorative deification, this only *seems* to be a transformation, because it is instead simply a return to what we always were. Thus, we are delivered from the world of perception and particulars to an entirely cognized realm.

Gregory of Nyssa said of the knowledge of our own permanent and eternal nature that "to contemplate this good is to possess It."[325] Just to keep our eternal nature in mind is to begin to reassimilate to it. It happens by degrees, over time, as our awareness expands to meet its limitlessness.

Aquinas centuries later agrees: "Through the cognition of divine things, we may be totally deified."[326] He speaks of contemplation as a way to *see* and therefore *share* God's essence:

> It would seem that in the present state of life the contemplative life can reach to the vision of the Divine essence. For, as stated in Genesis 32:30, Jacob said: 'I have seen God face to face, and my soul has been saved.' Now the vision of God's face is the vision of the Divine essence. Therefore it would seem that in the present life one may

---

[324] Origen. "Commentary on John 32: 338-340." Commentary on the Gospel According to John, Books 13-32. Trans. Ronald E. Heine. Washington, D.C.: Catholic University of America, 1993. 406. Print.
[325] Gregory of Nyssa, *In. Eccl.* 1, PG 44:624, cited in Popov 2011: 75.
[326] Townsend 2015: 229.

come, by means of contemplation, to see God in His essence.[327]

Even in this "present life," "the contemplative life" allows us to see "the face of God," which is the divine "essence." Thomas calls this highest vision of God "the vision of the incomprehensible light in its essence."[328] This light is incomprehensible for human beings, but not for divine beings. As John 6:46 states, only the being who is from the Father can see the Father.[329] If we share the private experience, we must, therefore, share the divine essence.

For Gregory Palamas in his defense of the Hesychast monks who sought the radiance of Godlikeness through prayer, the fact that humans were created meant that they would always remain human. This is why, in contrast to Aquinas, he believed they would never assume the divine *ousia* or essence, the inner being and self-existence of God. They could only hope to participate in the divine energies, God's self-expression separate from his subjective self-existence. While this may be true of our human selves, it is not true of the selves God created out of his own glory.

Here on earth, we hold the power to consecrate and bless all things simply by contemplating them from our deified mind. This is because the deified mind sees *only* the good, the true, the beautiful, the equal, the just, and the eternal. It casts its own sublime light on whatever it graces with its vision.

> For everything created by God is good, and nothing is to be rejected if it is received with thanksgiving; ⁵for then it is consecrated by the word of God and prayer. (1 Timothy 4:4-5).

---

[327] Aquinas, *Summae Theologiae*, Second Part of the Second Part, Q. 180, Article 5, Objection 1. Translated by The Fathers of the English Dominican Province (Second and Revised ed.), 1920.

[328] Aquinas, *Summae Theologiae*, Second Part of the Second Part, Q. 180, Article 5, Objection 2. Translated by The Fathers of the English Dominican Province (Second and Revised ed.), 1920.

[329] "Not that anyone has seen the Father except the one who is from God; he has seen the Father." This refers to our begottenness and divine nature.

All things can become holy if we deem them such because all things ultimately come from God. Our vision generalizes onto all we see because our blessing returns to us as the world becomes sacralized along with us. It is then we realize that self and world are one. The world changes, objectively, simply by seeing it with new eyes. Everything is good, as long as we appreciate it, and anything might be helpful. The more we appreciate, the more we *see* to appreciate. A new world and reality comes with this new perception, which borders eternity and culminates in the vision of God. The more we accept into our holy vision, the holier it grows. Then we understand why from the very first primordial ray of his supernal light, God gazed upon his vastly arrayed eternal and spiritual, wholly loving creation and he "saw that it was good" (Genesis 1:1).

Selfless Yet Universal: Jesus' Example as a God

For Christian theologians from Paul onward, Jesus is the image of the deified human that we ourselves were meant to be. Thus, they spoke of imitating Christ and following his example to our own eternal truth. One way to our own godhood lies in following his basic process from humankind back to divinity. Again, Jesus does not seem to have viewed his sonship as unique to himself. His purpose was to *share* the power God had given him, the "power to become children of God" (John 1:12), which is the power to know ourselves as gods.

We have noted that Jesus speaks from his bipartite composite nature — sometimes as a human being, sometimes as a god — signifying that these two distinct ways of being alternated in his experience as they do in ours. As a human being, for example, he states: "I can do nothing on my own authority" (John 5:30). As a god, he says: "All things have been handed over to me by my Father" (Mt. 11:27) and "The Father and I are one" (John 10:30).

His humility and selflessness contrasts but does not conflict with the transcendent, cosmic elements. Thus, although he has no trouble placing himself on par with Moses (John 5:46-47), and even with God (Jn. 5:18), Jesus continually repeats that "I have not spoken on my own authority" (Jn. 12:49). Although he is transcendent, and one with God, remembering his preexistent glory, he speaks unassumingly and selflessly, pointing to God alone as the Source of his transcendence and his authority. What is the connection between these contrasting traits in one person? Paradoxically, it is the selflessness and transparency itself that makes him universal, "the true light that enlightens every man" (Jn. 1:9). Such an understanding helps explain Jesus' sayings regarding reversal of values such as "the least is the greatest."[330]

Jesus is universal also in the way he not only tolerates but lays claim to those with different religious beliefs, or to anyone who seeks their own spiritual reality: "I have other sheep that do not belong to this fold. I must bring them also, and they will listen to my voice. So there will be one flock, one shepherd" (Jn. 10.16). These mysterious "other" flocks include every spiritual seeker, everyone who is "of the truth."

Every one who is of the truth hears my voice. (John 18:37)

Jesus stands at the threshold of another reality, helping all who approach to cross to a much more expansive way of being and thus be translated into heaven. His tolerance of different paths and beliefs is also exhibited by his having told his disciples: "he that is not against us is for us" (Mark 9:40). Christianity was marked by diversity from the start, with many different people and groups interpreting Jesus in multiple ways. [331] His coterie was more like a very individualistic philosophical school in this way. Any similarity we glean between ourselves and others becomes a piece of this unified mosaic of equals in search of the truth. It was never meant to be constricted to just one approach, at least as far as Jesus is concerned.

Jesus spoke of himself as a mere instrument of God:

---

[330] Luke 9:48: "the least among all of you is the greatest."
[331] See, for instance, James D. G. Dunn, *Unity and Diversity in the New Testament*, SCM Press; 3rd edition (2006).

> He who believes in me, believes not in me but in him who sent me. (John 12:44)

Because of his selflessness, Jesus is fully transparent to God, thus a divine image for any human being seeking transcendence. We have noted that in John 10:31-36, Jesus encountered accusations that he was equating himself with God simply by having declared himself to be a "Son of God," thus identical to God in his particular time and culture. Yet, his purpose on earth was to convince those around him that they, too, were sons and daughters of God, to spark in them the same "power." Jesus did not seek praise from his human associates, but rather, he called them his friends:

> No longer do I call you servants, for the servant does not know what his master is doing; but I have called you friends, for all that I have heard from my Father I have made known to you. (John 15:15)

Once they know "all" he knows, Jesus states, they will know their transcendent equality as "friends" and siblings to him. Their own transcendent truth is the same truth. If they can share his degree of selflessness, they can share his transcendent Self.

His selflessness prompted Jesus to deny that he was the author of his own teaching: "My teaching is not mine, but his who sent me" (John 7:16). He receives it from God and broadcasts it like a relay station, directly from God to all beings without exception. The way not to let godhood inflate one's ego in the world (which would be both contradictory and counter-productive) is, first, to know where it comes from (i.e., God alone), and second, to know that we share it with *everyone* else.

Along these same lines, Jesus asserts that his followers will do even greater works than his (Jn. 14:12). He speaks of his followers as being equally transcendent as he because: "They are not of the world; even as I am not of the world" (John 17:16). Everyone has the capability and the proclivity to transcend the world entirely. Jesus is not possessive over his power as a god. Rather, comfortable in his power, using it only for the common good, he seeks to share it with all.

As Russian scholar Ivan Popov wrote: "In the soul that has likened itself to God, he abides really.... A human being who has imaged God in himself becomes, as it were, his living icon, a bearer of his Divine powers."[332] It is a high calling to which we are called because it is a high being we were created to be. Jesus became a living image for us: he imaged God in himself and became a god. The secret, even to Christianity, is that this is something any human being can do. The fact that Jesus identified completely with divinity even to the dissolution of his ego is precisely what makes him the first-born among many siblings in godhood. But the entire thrust of his teaching is that this godhood is *our* truth and *our* true nature. This idea goes against *all* our presumptions, but it doesn't go against our true nature. We cannot see it when we insist, simply for tradition's sake, that Jesus must be a different order of being from ourselves, or that we could never follow him to where he is.

We have been careful not to let Jesus' transcendently divine nature obscure the human Jesus, whose most cosmic act was to become an exemplar of our own divinity and that of all beings. Thus, he reaches us even thousands of years down the line. He is just as alive today as he ever was, just as gentle, and just as transcendent. Because he was human yet also a god, by way of example, humans can be gods, not in the sense of any material transfer, however rarefied we might imagine it, but instead because all humans share the same basic natures.

The Way of Love

Similar to becoming what we contemplate, we also become what we participate in, so that anyone who participates in the virtues

---

[332] Popov 2011: 69-70.

of God participates in God.³³³ This is due in part to the principle of divine simplicity, whereby God is one with his virtues, and his virtues are one in him. They are aspects of his fully integrated Being. To share these attributes is to share the same integration and therefore the very same essence of God. The attributes of God include goodness, beauty, truth, equality, justice, intelligence, and love.

We have examined Jesus' teaching that love is the "greatest commandment," containing all the others and in effect superseding them because it is the one upon which "*all* the law and the prophets," that is, all the scriptures, depend (Mt. 22:38-40).³³⁴ It is a divine quality we share with God consistent with our being sons and daughters of God (Mt. 5:44-45). Paul harmonizes with Jesus about the primacy of love in the religion when he points out that "Love does no wrong to a neighbor; therefore love is the fulfilling of the law" (Romans 13:10). Paul writes rhapsodically of love as essential to Christian identity in his First Letter to the Corinthians:

> If I speak in the tongues of mortals and of angels, but do not have love, I am a noisy gong or a clanging cymbal. ²And if I have prophetic powers, and understand all mysteries and all knowledge, and if I have all faith, so as to remove mountains, but do not have love, I am nothing. ³If I give away all my possessions, and if I hand over my body so that I may boast, but do not have love, I gain nothing.
>
> ⁴Love is patient; love is kind; love is not envious or boastful or arrogant ⁵or rude. It does not insist on its own way; it is not irritable or resentful; ⁶it does not rejoice in wrongdoing, but rejoices in the truth. (1 Cor. 13:1-6)

Love, for both Jesus and Paul, is the core of the Christian message. It is the entire reason for it, the truth behind it, and the destination all in one. It is Jesus' revelation to the world. It is a way of living in that "It does not insist on its own way" and is never

---

³³³ Vishnevskaya 2006a: 137, n42.
³³⁴ My emphasis. The Law and the Prophets, along with Wisdom, are the three major categories of the writings of the Hebrew Bible.

"arrogant or rude." And it is our way of knowing and enjoying the salvific experience of sonship and therefore godhood.

Peter sums up what early Christians needed to know: "Above all hold unfailing your love for one another, since love covers a multitude of sins" (1 Pet. 4:8). Love is the key and core doctrine of original Christianity, the prevailing motif, reason for salvation and deification, and so here is where the mind should concentrate its focus. It is God's essence, the religion's essence, and, if we would know the truth, it is truly our own essence as well.

John the Evangelist concurs, equating love of God with love of brother and sister, saying: "And this commandment we have from him, that he who loves God should love his brother also" (1 John 4:21). John further connects our love of other beings with the love of God, saying: "if we love one another, God abides in us and his love is perfected in us" (1 John 4:12). It is our own halting and imperfect attempt to love that allows us ultimately to remember God's perfect love. We need simply to trust mind and heart to function freely, to stand back and not limit its natural progress. Fear will dissipate because *our own love* has come to "reassure our hearts before him" (1 Jn. 3:19) that "we are of the truth" (3:19), particularly "whenever our hearts condemn us" (3:20). The way to godhood is through the perfecting of our own capacity to love.[335] It is this that will make us again like God. The salvific effect of love is shown clearly here:

> He who loves his brother abides in the light, and there is no cause for stumbling in him. (1 Jn. 2:10, NKJV)

Love removes all obstacles to godhood and all limits, replacing them with the shining truth of the original Godlike nature.

We love what we appreciate, and appreciate what we understand, which is why, if we truly intend to love, we should learn first to listen intently without judgment. Nor do we make demands on those we love. We love them most perfectly without wanting or needing anything from them except to love them, even from a distance if we must. We appreciate just their presence in our mind

---

[335] See esp. 1 Jn. 4:16-17.

and heart, which is their reality like ours. Their joy is also our joy and so, in a way, their being is our being. An experience of natural oneness ensues.

Pseudo-Dionysius the Areopagite writes of an ecstatic love that draws together and unites lover and beloved, ourselves and God. Dionysius' discussion of love is primarily limited to chapter 4 of his *Divine Names*, wherein he stresses that God's idyllic attributes, specifically goodness, beauty and love are found in all things. Each level and type of existence (even the inanimate) shares a natural and universal "yearning" toward its Creator and fellow creations. This is a vestige of the same ecstatic Self-giving with which God created us, a creative capacity we share with him. Moreover, in Dionysius' vision, up and down the ladder of existence, higher life forms yearn for the benefit of the lower forms, until all things are returned to their ecstatic loving oneness with their Creator.

Each party of this mutually bonding love goes out of itself to join with the other, yet in this finds its own self-fulfillment. The two meet and join in the middle to reveal an even greater level of conjoined divine being. This becomes a *perichoresis* or mutual indwelling. Therefore, one's individual capacity to love ultimately involves self-transcendence simultaneously with self-fulfillment, making the two one and therefore more like God. We are both individual beings entirely free in mind and spirit and infinitely expansive universal beings bound together by love.

For Maximus the Confessor, deification is a call back to "the original destiny of creation" through the exercise of love.[336] Love stands at the core of his theology, as this divine emotion leads to our deification. He writes:

> Nothing is more truly Godlike than divine love, nothing more mysterious, nothing more apt to raise up human beings to deification.[337]

---

[336] McGuckin 2007: 98.
[337] Maximus, *Epist.* 2 (PG 91:393 BC; *MC* 85), cited in Vishnevskaya 2007: 134.

Nothing is more true, except that even its mystery will be fully understood as it comes to seem natural to us, as if foreknown and predestined. Aquinas writes similarly:

> [I]nsofar as humans are made deiform by charity [i.e., love], they are *more than humans*, and their association is in heaven.[338]

Insofar as we are genuinely loving, then, we are gods. It really is that simple. It is the same with all the divine attributes. When we experience our love to be as constant as God's, and as universal as God's, it becomes a fixture in our mind and a habit in the world. But it is ultimately a revelation of our own true, transcendent and self-expansive universal identity. And thus it returns all the knowledge we once shared with God.

At its heart, Christianity is not about giving up things that we want and desire. It is more about bracketing what we *think* we want in order to allow desire to find its *true* satisfaction, its eternal fulfillment. One might call this a sublimation of our desires to a higher level, or simply a refocus upon their intended objects. But because such desire is a yearning for transcendence in union, it is a godly desire, not a fleeting human desire. The problem is not that we desire too much, but rather, far too little. Love is the divine emotion; thus, on earth we find it healing, salvific, and inducive of happiness. It is the most natural way to deification.

Conclusion

A fully restorative deification may entail both negative and positive ways to deification. The positive ways seek to immerse us in the attributes and assets of God and thus godhood. The negative ways remind us that we cannot grasp this immersion conceptually, but only through experience, which entails becoming these

---

[338] Aquinas, *Summae Theologiae* 1.12.5; cited in Townsend 2015: 212. My italics.

attributes. We must leave presuppositions and false premises at the door. The negative ways also promote a simpler, increasingly minimalistic way of life and thought via their chipping away at artifice. Through both approaches, we find and reinforce the godhood that already awaits within for us to come to ourselves.

Left to themselves the negative ways might devolve into an unnecessarily difficult asceticism wherein self-deprivation and flagellation becomes an end in itself, with no overarching purpose. At their best they remind us that the positive ways need to come from God, not from anything we constructed. Dionysius, Nyssa and others used them to highlight God's transcendence, but at the same time they highlight our own as well. For us to have real relationship with him, participation and union, we must be equally transcendent. This means we are in truth more than human, which means that we did not begin as human, but rather as spiritual beings not unlike God. It is our destiny, therefore, not to remain human beings forever but to come to know ourselves as gods. But all this means that our humanness has been blessed and sacralized because of the godhood stirring within.

Paul writes of a form of contemplation whereby we become divine beings like our archetype, Jesus Christ. Jesus' transcendent way of being is our own. Holding his image in mind, or what we know of him, we will increasingly resemble and grow into him. The process may begin with imitation, but it ends in authentic union by way of true participation. This is why Paul insists his listeners be careful what they keep in mind, because what they hold in mind is what they will become. In the mindscape of heaven, on the other hand, they already have and are eternal being, and so it is needless to even think of becoming or developing into anything, due to our *being* everything and therefore having no need of an image.

Jesus' way is simplest, yet it is perhaps most difficult for humans to do. Love divinizes literally everything because it literally is everything to a god. There is nothing left unloved anywhere, any time. Everything is known, appreciated, understood, and loved all at once and in one fell swoop. Love makes us like God and therefore it makes us divine beings, sons and daughters of God. If we can love with our whole being, we can know ourselves as beings of light. Our light extends out to all beings to help them, comfort them, shelter them, and lift them as we are lifted into the everlasting arms of our Source. And as John states: "if agapē abides in you, then God abides in you" (1 John 4:16). Our love and God's, our love and God, God and his love, are all one and the same.

God did not create limited, imperfect beings. He created beings exactly like himself, because this is what he knows. And so, of course we have the capacity to love like God loves. For him, there is no other way. For us, for now, it is a decision, made more difficult by our present fear of love because we sense its immense power, its ability to change everything in the twinkling of an eye. It is the power of God and his gods, which we had convinced ourselves was buried and forgotten. We fear God and our own godhood because we have rendered them "other," alien, different from us. We made ourselves strangers even to ourselves. This insistent barrier of multilayered fear and guilt without object must be hiding something infinitely great, even majestic. We seek to look past those preoccupying layers for the light that must shine still from behind them.

Love is a positive approach to deification, as are the many forms of contemplation, which are concerted efforts to share the attributes of God. A fully restorative deification specifies that we already share these attributes, so that as we contemplate them, study them and practice them, parts of our mind formerly consigned (by our fiat) to nothingness spring back to life. In a fully restorative deification, there is the added element of remembrance of the ultimate goal because it was also our origin.

Considering the seemingly impassable gulf between humankind and divinity, remembrance and recognition are more likely ways of achieving deification than attainment or appropriation, which would involve the establishment of something entirely new (godhood) in something innately different from it (alienated humankind). We must not be so different from God as we think we are. It was *our* thinking, not God's, that was the problem.

The key to living in this world as gods, Paul teaches, is to "deal with the world as though they had no dealings with it" (1 Corinthians

7:31). Those things we must do to navigate the world are now incidental to those things that brought us eternal life. They could not have prepared us for the fullness and splendor of godhood. Only our most worldless, selfless moments could truly prepare us because these selfless moments are not truly selfless. The self expands to meet the moment, revealing something of its transcendence and universality via our every notice of it in the world.

The world is a proving ground, not the final destination. We seek proof here of something that does not abound here, but we evoke it within the things of the world as we uncover the love within ourselves. God's creation is truly eternal and universal but it can be found within everything just as it is found within ourselves, often in the same moment, via love for all things, overspilling every container in which we had hidden it, which allows us to see clearly our eternal Self in all things.

11

THE END OF THE WORLD

Whenever we experience godhood in this world, the old world-self system is suspended in our mind. A new world or age (*aeon*), a new reality, dawns for us to match the rarefied beauty we encounter. With each such experience, the old world loses some of its grip on us. It seeks to control us but, as Paul declares: "The form of this world is passing away" (1 Corinthians 7:31), the old worn world *already* fading from our minds. As it fades, something new and revelatory yet surprisingly familiar emerges, complete in itself, to take its rightful place.

Realized Eschatology

Eschatology is the branch of theology that deals with matters pertaining to "the end of the world," including ideas about the afterlife, the general resurrection of the dead, the last judgment, the kingdom of God, the Son of Man, the Son of God, the throne of heaven, the book of life, the lake of fire, and the ultimate triumph of good over evil. While some of these apocalyptic images (like the New Jerusalem) have roots in the ancient Hebrew prophets, most of them (like the last judgment) were native to Zoroastrianism, an ancient Persian religion that influenced Judaism alongside Hellenism (or Greek culture) in the centuries prior to Jesus' birth and that therefore impacted Christianity as well through the Jewish and later Chrisitan apocalypses so popular in those centuries.

The concept of an afterlife (and hell) for individual human beings had been largely foreign to Judaism until a couple of centuries before Jesus. Recall that "Sheol" had meant the lifeless grave. The concept begins to flower with the very late OT apocalyptic Book of Daniel (c. 175 BCE):

> At that time Michael, the great prince, the protector of your people, shall arise. There shall be a time of anguish, such as has never occurred since nations first came into existence. But at that time your people shall be delivered, everyone who is found written in the book. ²Many of those who sleep in the dust of the earth shall awake, some to everlasting life, and some to shame and everlasting contempt. (Daniel 12:1-2)

Suddenly, in this very late book of the Hebrew Bible, we find a "book of life," a general resurrection, an afterlife, and a judgment resulting in heaven or hell, all of which would reappear in the Book of Revelation and dozens of other apocalypses written within the next several centuries. Not long thereafter, Jesus and Paul made their own contributions to the genre. Note that the "hell" here in its earliest use in the Book of Daniel is more "shame" and "contempt" from others than anything else. It is primarily regret at having wrongly decided. More worldly and psychological than it would ultimately become, hell is a state of mind and heart that results from not having fulfilled our higher purpose as realized gods.

Proto-apocalyptic passages can be found in post-exilic Hebrew prophets such as Isaiah, Jeremiah, Ezekiel, Zechariah, and Joel.[339] The major motif was that God would bring all his scattered people back together from the far ends of the earth. Isaiah envisioned a broad highway leading all the exiles back to their home (Isa. 35:8) from Assyrian and then Babylonian captivity. Zoroastrian influence was derived from these regions and from the expansive but tolerant policies of Cyrus the Great (d. 530 BCE), founder of the Achaemenid Persian Empire, who ended the Jews' Babylonian captivity and, with his immediate successors, respected the cultures and religions of the lands that he conquered throughout the Middle

---

[339] See especially Isaiah 24-27; 33; 34-35; Jeremiah 33:14-26.

East. Isaiah 45:1 refers to him as a messiah (a concept common to Zoroastrianism).

The Hebrew Prophet Jeremiah had foreseen a time when God would raise new shepherds from among his scattered people, who would lead all lost and scattered people back home, granting them a universal sense of oneness and family:

> Then I will gather the remnant of my flock ... ⁴I will set shepherds over them who will care for them, and they shall fear no more, nor be dismayed, neither shall any be missing, declares the Lord. (Jer. 23:3, 4, ESV)

In that happy day, because of the many good shepherds tending the common good, fear and dismay are gone. God and his inherent oneness will be known to all the ends of the earth:

> And the Lord will become king over all the earth; on that day the Lord will be one and his name one. (Zech. 14:9)

The universalism in this passage is evident, that all people ("all the earth") will ultimately know and appreciate "that day" the new reality dawns, and therefore the oneness of God and his creations will be known. "That day" is therefore a day of universal salvation, when goodness finally replaces its negation in *every* mind.

In the centuries just prior to Jesus, the ancient prophetic visions of Isaiah and Jeremiah mingled with Zoroastrian influence to produce a new genre, Jewish apocalyptic literature, which in addition to the Book of Daniel produced such writings as 3 Enoch (aka 2 Esdras; 4 Ezra), the Book of Jubilees, and pseudepigraphal apocalypses attributed to Abraham, Adam, Elijah, Moses, and other OT figures. Early Christianity became infatuated with such writings and interpolated Christian messaging into some of them, while Christian apocalypses (including the Book of Revelation and those attributed to Paul, Peter, Stephen, Thomas, and James, among others) sprang up in the succeeding centuries.[340]

Christian theologians have generally interpreted these stock images very literally, but many see them as symbols of internal realities. These latter engage in what is called "realized eschatology," wherein end-time events and future expectations are perceived as present experience of an idyllic future. We shall see that there is ample scriptural evidence to support this realized view. Jewish mysticism interpreted them in much the same way. The ancient apocalyptic dreamlike even hallucinatory images were meant to evoke in their hearers an experience of transcendent reality in the midst of their daily lives.

C.H. Dodd, an influential twentieth century historian of religion, postulated that the *eschaton* or world-ending event had already happened with Jesus' incarnation, death, resurrection, and ascension into heaven. From that time on, history has effectively ceased because its transcendent meaning has been fulfilled. The world has already ended; we now live in a new, post-apocalyptic era, "the Day of the Lord," whereby God's purpose, already realized, is just now being understood by human beings. Dodd writes:

> It is not as though the Creator had arbitrarily fixed a certain date as the 'zero hour' of his world, so that events which might conceivably have followed it are not permitted to happen. It is such that nothing more could happen in history,

---

[340] Jewish extracanonical apocalypses include 3 Enoch, the Apocalypse of Abraham, the Apocalypse of Adam, the Apocalypse of Moses, the Apocalypse of Sedrach, the Apocalypse of Zephaniah, the Apocalypse of Zerubbabel, the Aramaic Apocalypse, Gabriel's Revelation, the Genesis Apocryphon, the Greek Apocalypse of Baruch, the Greek Apocalypse of Daniel, the Greek Apocalypse of Ezra, Sefer Elijah, and the Syriac Apocalypse of Baruch.

Christian extracanonical apocalypses include the Apocalypse of Golias, the Apocalypse of Paul, the Apocalypse of Peter, the Apocalypse of Pseudo-Methodius, the Apocalypse of Samuel of Kalamoun, the Apocalypse of Stephen, the Apocalypse of Thomas, and the Coptic Apocalypse of Elijah. Gnostic Christian apocalypses include the Gnostic Apocalypse of Peter, the First Apocalypse of James, the Second Apocalypse of James, and the Coptic Apocalypse of Paul.

because the eternal meaning which gives reality to history is now exhausted. To conceive any further event on the plane of history would be like drawing a check on a closed account.[341]

From the point of view of a fully restorative deification the eschaton or world-ending event is a present reality that can and must happen at any moment because it *has* already happened. The eschaton is and always was a psychological reality that occurs to different individuals at different times. This realization of a radically present timeless reality can of course occur at any time:

> Take heed, watch; for you do not know when the time will come. It is like a man going on a journey, when he leaves home and puts his servants in charge, each with his work, and commands the doorkeeper to be on the watch. Watch therefore — for you do not know when the master of the house will come, in the evening, or at midnight, or at cockcrow, or in the morning — lest he come suddenly and find you asleep. And what I say to you I say to all: Watch. (Mark 13:33-37)

"The master of the house" who was away is the god within. The experience is so different from ordinary reality that it appears suddenly, or as Paul says, "in a moment in the twinkling of an eye" (1 Cor. 15:52). No matter how many times we have experienced it, it is always unexpected just because it is so different from ordinary reality. The immediacy of the kingdom breaking through lends credence to the idea that it is an unexpectedly powerful awareness.

Jesus tells his followers to: "be ready; for the Son of man is coming at an unexpected hour" (Luke 12:49). This Son of man, or "son of the human," is our own new identity breaking through. It is the progressed state of the human, the next generation human, the post-human. Because the apocalypse is now understood to occur

---

[341] Dodd, C. H. *The Apostolic Preaching and Its Developments, Three Lectures*, Chicago, New York, Willett, Clark & Company, 1937, 144.

individually and at different times, a staggered entrance into the kingdom, or realization of this reality is to be expected. We shall see in the next section that Jesus specifically tells his listeners not to look to the realm of perception, the external world, for the coming kingdom of God, stating they will find it instead "within" themselves (Luke 17:20-21). When we look to the world for the expected world-ending event, we are, in effect, seeking outside ourselves for an inner realization.

There are many realized eschatological overtones surrounding the idea of "eternal life" in Jesus' teaching.[342] Jesus says that the one who simply believes in one's own eternal life and sonship "does not come into judgment, but rather has passed from death to life" (John 5:24). Here both the last judgment and the resurrection itself are revealed to be present realities in that eternal life and a deathless state of mind can be known even now. We will delve into these topics in more detail in the following sections.

Note that eternal life begins in the present and changes one's outlook forever. If the world is no longer one's primary reality, then death suddenly becomes a non-factor, an illusion although it seems real to our limited perception. When Jesus says, "He who loves his life loses it, and he who hates his life in this world will keep it for eternal life" (John 12:25), he is expressing an inverse relationship between two different kinds of life and two different ways of being of which each of us is capable. This is why faith is needed, to make the leap from the life we know to the experience of a very different life.

Some of his parables contain more than a note of irony. Regarding the Great Supper (in Matthew 22:1-10 and parallels), Jesus asks his audience to imagine "a situation in which all the invited guests are absent from a banquet and all the uninvited ones are present." It will defy our expectations like that. This new kind of perception where the overlooked among us become great will obliterate our deep-seated conviction that we know what reality is, or how it is ordered. This can be duly humbling to our egos which try constantly to control and circumscribe our sense of reality, playing

---

[342] See Matt. 18:8; 25:46; Mark 3:29.

master of the house without wisdom, and as such it plays a great role in the *via negativa*, the removal of obstacles, primarily our former convictions about reality.

In the Gospel of John, Jesus presents the resurrection, expected at the end of time, as a present experience:

> Truly, truly, I say to you, the hour is coming, *and now is*, when the dead will hear the voice of the Son of God, and those who hear will live. (John 5:25, my emphasis)

Here again we see both a future element and a present element in the resurrection and end of the world or age. The hour is coming, it is close, but it also "now is." It will flower completely in the future, but it is already in full bloom here in the present, even if for most it is like a seed growing secretly (Mark 4:26-32). As with Paul, the world is already ending, and the true sense of life is springing up to replace it. Death has already been overcome via Jesus. This is consistent with Jesus' demonstration that death is not real, in both his raising of Lazarus and his own resurrection, and that it need not be experienced as such.

Even if we see the *eschaton*, or world-ending event, specifically as the return of Jesus, we will be like him when we see him in his transcendent state. The entire premise of his teaching is based on sharing the same type of transcendent being, that is, our deification. The fact that we can experience the future in the present indicates that the actual end of the physical world is far off in the future, so the presently experienced "end of the world" is more a change in interpretation and perception than a physical change. It is the end of one way of seeing the world and its systems in favor of another more suited to our inmost being.

Paul writes, "Behold, *now* is the acceptable time; behold, *now* is the day of salvation" (2 Cor. 6:2).[343] He speaks as if the expected end has *already* happened for those who have become part of Christ:

---

[343] My emphasis.

> Therefore if any one is in Christ, he is a new creation;
> the old has passed away, behold, the new has come.
> (2 Cor. 5:17)

Jesus inaugurated the end of history just because of his radical difference from the world. To follow him is to be led to this other philosophical and psychological as well as religious reality which, says Paul, is like a new creation, but of course it is the original perfect creation being restored.

Other evidence of a realized or present eschatology is found in Colossians 3:1, which states: "you have been raised with Christ." In Col. 3:2, believers are *already* made "alive together with Christ" and raised up with him. The resurrection is spoken of again in the present perfect tense, which would seem to confirm that the eschaton is more psychological than literal. This makes sense because, in all these instances we have cited, "the world" is spoken of as a malleable psychological reality that has become an oppressive web of systems, not so much a concrete reality. Once our psyche is changed, the world, product of our psyche, will follow suit.

Ephesians 2:4 continues the trend, stating that out of his "great love" for us, God has already "made us alive together with Christ" (v. 5) and, furthermore, has "raised us up with him and seated us with him in the heavenly places" (v. 6). For this author, the resurrection of Christ changed history and had lasting effectiveness. It is not only a future reality, nor one confined to him alone, but a present spiritual and cognitive reality that belongs to everyone.

Early Western father Hilary of Poitiers (c. 315-367 CE) was one of a few fathers who believed in both an individual and collective transformation as the end of the world.[344] Such an idea allows for a world-ending event (eschaton) that is psychological rather than physical and literal. It would come individually and spontaneously to

---

[344] See Sidaway 2019: 111-12: "Hilary of Poitiers (ca. 315-ca. 367) is often considered as a stepping stone to Ambrose, Augustine, and Leo rather than a theologian in his own right…. Hilary's ideas of individual, rather than collective, transformation at the eschaton have received little attention, yet I would argue are more original and hence relevant to any study of deification in the West."

each as they are ready to receive it. Hilary's idea allows "the end of the world" to come at different times for different individuals, yet ultimately the outcome is the same for all. Hilary believed that humans can be perfect like Christ and are indeed ultimately parts of Christ. Christ came to reveal the perfect personhood, which becomes the perfect godhood. Christ would eventually encompass the whole of humanity.

Interestingly, Hilary's ideas about the end time inadvertently circle back to the original Zoroastrian significance. In the *Gathas*, probably written by Zoroaster (Zarathustra) himself perhaps as early as 1500 BCE, the cosmic struggle is an internal one of the heart and moral conduct rather than a world-consuming drama. It was not until the 500s BCE that the evil spirit in Zoroastrianism develops a life of its own and good/evil becomes a true dualism, which influenced Judaism and helped shape Christianity with apocalyptic images and further dyads like good/evil and heaven/hell.

The Internal Kingdom

The kingdom of God is the subject of most of Jesus' parables. The kingdom has apocalyptic overtones, but it is most often addressed in everyday images. In Mark 4 alone Jesus likens the kingdom (or reality) of God to a farmer sowing seeds (vv. 3-9), to a lamp brought out from under a bushel basket (21-22), to scattered seed growing without cultivation (26-29), and to a small mustard seed that grows into a great plant (31-32). Jesus himself points out that the kingdom is difficult to describe in words (Luke 13:18), yet he attempts to describe it in natural images so that we understand it as a natural, even inherent reality.

Other parables show how the kingdom or reality of God grows like wheat in stages in our awareness (see Mark 4:26-29: "first the stalk, then the head, then the full grain in the head"). The kingdom is also said to be very "near" (Mt. 3:2, 10:7; Mark 1:15; Luke

10:9).[345] Although it generally develops gradually in stages in our awareness or from our limited viewpoint, its fullness could break through at any time because it is a complete reality unto itself.

The kingdom of God was traditionally associated with the end of the world, rooted in apocalyptic imagery, and yet Jesus makes it quite clear that the kingdom (or reality) of God and heaven is found inside us, *not outside us*:

> The kingdom of God is not coming with signs to be observed; nor will they say, 'Lo, here it is!' or 'There!' for behold, the kingdom of God is within you....
> And they will say to you, 'Lo, there!' or 'Lo, here!'
> Do not go, do not follow them. (Luke 17:20-21, 23, var.)

When Jesus says that "the kingdom of God is within you," he is locating the kingdom as a subjective reality, an internal reality like mind and heart. He is describing it as an ontological reality, a part of the structure of our inner being. Although a subjective reality experienced within, the kingdom is also objective in the sense that it is shared by all individuals, even if most are only dimly aware of its existence. Hence it is the "smallest of seeds" (Mt. 4:31), the smallest of thoughts, until it grows in the rich soil of experience and awareness to convince us of our natural Godlikeness.

I think it imperative to translate Luke 17 with the NRSV's variant reading, "the kingdom of God is *within* you," rather than the now standard *"among* you" of many translations because "within" is the reading that best accords with the surrounding context. Verse 20 clearly states that "The kingdom of God is not coming with things that can be observed," which clearly removes it from the realm of human perception, or indeed of any externality.

Biblical historian Stephen Finlan gives a vigorous defense of the *"within"* reading, noting a tendency among modern scholars to slant their interpretations away from the psychological and personal. He deems the standard *"among"* translation to be "a bland and misleading translation of *entos,"* which normally means "within,"

---

[345] See also Finlan 2011: 7.

and does so here in light of the passage's context. He lays out his hypothesis: "I suspect that the attempt to socialize, suffocate, and domesticate this saying arises from an anti-personalist and materialistic bias,"[346] noting the tendency among researchers to interpret this saying sociologically rather than psychologically or experientially, as regarding the inner depth of the individual. Finlan remarks:

> What is stunning about this passage is that Jesus says the kingdom is *already resident* within people. It may not yet be *realized*, but it is 'within' you.[347]

The kingdom or reality of God precedes us in the sense that it is already within our mind, but it has yet to be recognized. The usual social interpretation of the kingdom ties it too closely to the present world and its systems when its true significance is that it transcends the world yet is realized in each person, granting it great ontological significance as part of our inner being. Its sociological significance would be secondary to that.

We have noted the bevy of inward passages contained in the Gospel of Matthew such as Jesus' admonitions to give "in secret" (*krupto*) (6:4), to pray "in secret" (6:6), and to fast "in secret" (6:18). He railed against those who prayed openly in an effort to be seen and heard by others:

> And whenever you pray, do not be like the hypocrites; for they love to stand and pray in the synagogues and at the street corners, so that they may be seen by others. Truly I tell you, they have received their reward. (Mt. 6:5)

Religion was a very private matter. Jesus constantly directs us to look within ourselves, to examine our motives, honestly and authentically, to admit our mistakenness and move on, so that we might be honest and authentic with others (including God).

---

[346] Finlan 2011: 23.
[347] Finlan 2011: 24.

Finlan sums up the kind of attitude needed to begin to understand the ontological underpinnings of Jesus' teaching:

> The endeavor to explain Jesus sociologically and to deny the originality of his sayings is an attempt to stifle his, and their, revolutionary import. We must allow them to be as extraordinary as they seem.[348]

Finlan notes the tendency of translators to domesticate Jesus or try to explain away the life-changing psychological significance of his vision. To know that it is within ourselves subjectively, yet also within all others objectively, has greater social implications than humans have yet imagined. It means that *we ourselves* are the kingdom or reality of God, but do not realize it.

Hilary of Poitiers writes:

> [W]e, being conformed to the glory of His body, shall form the Kingdom of God.[349]

Ortiz calls this an "original and startling claim."[350] We enter the kingdom by *becoming* the kingdom, by accepting it as ourselves.

The part of ourselves that defines itself in any worldly sense or category cannot enter the kingdom of God because it stems from an entirely different identity. Our task is to refamiliarize ourselves with who we really are, in God's Mind, if we are no longer to fear it. If the coming of the kingdom of God means the world must end (because they are opposites), we find in Jesus' and Paul's teaching a very gentle and gradual ending of the world's hold on our mind while we are living in the world, an inner transformation that purifies and

---

[348] Finlan 2011: 22.
[349] Hilary, *On the Trinity* 11.39. Translated by E.W. Watson and L. Pullan. From *Nicene and Post-Nicene Fathers, Second Series*, Vol. 9. Edited by Philip Schaff and Henry Wace. (Buffalo, NY: Christian Literature Publishing Co., 1899.)
[350] Sidaway 2019: 126. See Hilary, *De trin.* 11.29.12 and *De trin.* 11.39.1.

sacralizes the external world, gradually over time, until every being of God recovers their own inner treasure.

The Last Judgment

Although Jesus employed apocalyptic language to emphasize the radicality of his teaching, he assures his audience that they can escape even the expected eschatological judgment *simply by not judging*:

> Do not judge, so that you may not be judged. For with the judgment you make you will be judged, and the measure you give will be the measure you get. (Mt. 7:1-2)

Judgment is here a product of our own minds and a condition set by ourselves. *We* set the standard for even *our own expected judgment*. That we do this unconsciously and indirectly via our judgment of others reinforces Jesus' statements about the unconscious projection of guilt. It is important to rid our minds of our presuppositions about everything, but especially judgment because these imagined slights harbor and reinforce the guilt, unconsciously and thus out of our control.

Jesus himself shuns the role of judge:

> I came not to judge the world, but to save the world. (John 12:47)

Perhaps more surprisingly, Jesus also states that *God the Father does not judge*:

> The Father judges no one but has given all judgment to the Son. (Jn. 5:22)

Paul seems to concur that God the Father does not judge, but only justifies, when he says:

> It is God who justifies; who is to condemn? (Romans 8:33-34)

God is not our judge. Nor does he condemn his own children. Rather, God is our *standard* of judgment. Our progress can be measured in how closely we approximate his way of thinking, which is entirely merciful because entirely loving. If all this is true, then what we imagined (and feared) about the last judgment must have been mistaken. God does not condemn. He does not and indeed cannot think in those terms. Neither does Jesus condemn; rather he "intercedes for us" (Ro. 8:34). The Holy Spirit is our Advocate, our Defense Attorney, our Comforter, our Wonderful Counselor. Neither does it condemn us. So, who is left to condemn? It can *only* be us.

Our fear of condemnation, then, comes only from ourselves. How can this be? We must be doing it unconsciously. Our own guilt and fear proves far too much for us to bear, and perhaps this is why we rendered it unconscious, covering it up so well we forgot the original crime and made it seem more fearful than it need be, and so an otherwise easily resolvable guilt was instead repressed and projected onto others. Eventually we learn that it is impossible to judge others and not judge ourselves in the process. The fact that it is in the same measure and degree reaffirms that our fear of judgment is directly proportional to how severely we judge others. Once we enter the hypercritical mindset where judgment seems natural, we cannot help but be critical of ourselves as well as others. Our underlying motive in all this is to avoid the transcendence which comes from realization of our and their transcendent spiritual nature and therefore total innocence, the vision of which awaits to meet our yearning.

Paul agrees that it is our own judgment of others that brings fear of judgment down upon ourselves.

> Do you imagine, whoever you are, that when you judge those who do such things and yet do them yourself, you will escape the judgment of God? (Romans 2:3)

"The judgment of God" is used here as a figure of speech derived from the apocalyptic genre of then-popular religious literature. Paul, like Jesus, taught about the dangers of unconscious projection:

> Therefore you have no excuse, whoever you are, when you judge others; for in passing judgment on another you condemn yourself, because you, the judge, are doing the very same things. (Romans 2:1)

We condemn others most harshly for those things that spark our own guilt, even if unconsciously. The focus should therefore shift to ourselves rather than others. Thus, Paul counsels:

> The faith that you have, keep between yourself and God; happy is he who has no reason to judge himself for what he approves. (Romans 14:22)

It is only as gods that we are fully capable of judging ourselves and coming to a fair verdict. God granted his beings total freedom to consider everything and decide what is right for themselves. We are each responsible for ourselves. But happy are we when we escape the critical and judgmental mindset altogether. Our hypercritical mindset will then no longer be projected even onto God, which projection had been the true cause of guilt and fear (such as when Adam and Eve hid in the garden). Losing ourselves, we lost sight of what makes God what he is.

The perceptible world cannot be the appropriate venue for judgment because we are taught not to "judge by appearances" (Jn. 7:24. Jesus teaches consistently that we cannot judge by external evidence because it does not tell us the motivation of the heart and mind. As Jesus said: "You judge according to the flesh; I judge no one" (John 8:15).

God's standards are infinitely greater than ours. God's standard is perfection. If, as most patristics insist, it is impossible for a human being to meet his level of consistency while existing in the world, then God must have created us superhuman, because only a god can meet God's standards. And that means we do not know ourselves or anyone else enough to judge, for any reason. Judgment is a human act, and yet humans cannot judge other humans with certainty because they have lost God's standard. Therefore, for spiritual progress, judgment must be internalized and applied to ourselves and our personal recovery of godhood.

Jesus indicates in his teaching that religion does indeed evolve. A large part of his audience is still, in his opinion, mistakenly using the standards of "ancient times" (Mt. 5:21). He empowers people to believe that they can judge their own state of mind according to how it affects their daily lives. And they can judge the world they helped construct by seeing it more objectively, and recognizing where it is lacking. If the love is lacking, they can provide it. When the unnecessary fear they have heaped upon it has all been swept away, the innocent world that was there all along rises along with their true Self. And with that, the exquisite gentleness of God returns.

The "last" judgment we will make is to reel in every last projection we have ever made. We learn as we go which thoughts we want to keep (along with their effects) and which thoughts (and their effects) we want to relinquish. It is in this way we, as sons and daughters of the human, sort the true from the false within our mind. It could not be more simple; it comes from being completely honest with ourselves and basically working with our higher mind and the gift of reason rather than against.

Resurrection

We have investigated whether the deified acquire immortality or whether they awaken gradually to the realization that they are already immortal. If, as we have seen, some bypass death and therefore judgment, then these deathless ones must already be resurrected. Jesus says this applies to "some standing here" (Mk. 9:1). So, we can safely say that it has already occurred for some. Furthermore, if the change happens simply with enhanced understanding, this reinforces the idea that resurrection is a realization of an immortality we already have, an ontological reality, rather than something we acquire anew.

We have seen earlier in this chapter that the New Testament speaks often about our "having been raised" up to the heavenly reality already, therefore lifted into experience of a supernatural kind, and so, because of this experience, we need neither await nor undergo death to know heaven. In such cases, a resurrection of the higher mind has already been realized during earthly existence.

Jesus approaches the topic of resurrection in some interesting ways. Consider this passage from the Gospel of Luke:

> And the fact that the dead are raised Moses himself showed, in the story about the bush, where he speaks of the Lord as the God of Abraham, the God of Isaac, and the God of Jacob. [38]Now he is God not of the dead, but of the living; for *to him all of them are alive.* (Luke 20:37-38, my emphasis)

Jesus says specifically that from God's perspective, the ancient patriarchs Abraham, Isaac, and Jacob are still alive. They are alive even now, before the presumed physical resurrection at the end of the world. The resurrection must have already occurred for them. This raises the question: Might this not be true of others as well?

If the resurrection occurs only at the end of the physical world, then Abraham, Isaac, and Jacob would not technically be "alive" right now, but would rather be in a state of suspended animation, somewhere between life and death. But Jesus states they are "alive" now, and in fact already "raised," which speaks against a general *physical* resurrection and indicates a more personalized spiritual resurrection which has nothing to do with the reanimation of the physical body.

Again, God knows a very different reality than we human beings see. All the beings he created are alive and remain alive because he willed it so. If his will is forever inviolate, as logically it must be if he is the author of all reality, then his living creations must still be alive from his holy perspective. They *cannot* die, as Jesus says regarding those who are resurrected:

> [T]hey cannot die any more,
> because they are equal to the angels
> and are sons of God,
> being sons of the resurrection. (Luke 20:36)

Death must therefore be an illusion that only human beings can perceive, and then only from *outside* the event itself. They are, even while walking about in the delicate flesh, in fact deathless beings. God's children, eternal like him, alive like him, "will not see death." The sons and daughters of God cannot conceive of death. The mind realizes its own eternity, its true state of being, so that physical death becomes for it an illusory transition instead of an inescapable reality.

After his crucifixion, Jesus was encountered alive by his disciples. It is significant that his close friends who had seen him in his resurrected body failed to recognize him at first. Mary Magdalene initially mistook him for a gardener (Jn. 20:15). The disciples did not recognize him while they were fishing (Jn. 21:4) or while he talked and walked with them on the road to Emmaus (Luke 24:13-35). He appeared different even to those who knew him best, which, along with the fact that he could appear and disappear at will,[351] suggests his risen body was a different *kind* of body than his earthly one, more like the transfigured body his disciples had witnessed or the "glory body" of Paul (1 Cor. 15:40) or even the "light body" of Thomas than an ordinary human body.

All of this leads us to believe that resurrection is more purely cognitive than corporeal. The cognitive is in fact the primary reality. The resurrection is the final realization and conviction of the deathlessness of mind and heart. Jesus' own deathlessness was realized well before death, and then he manifested in a special, apparently transfigured way three days after his crucifixion. This is indicated by his having said about his body:

---

[351] See esp. Luke 24:30-31 and Jn. 20:19.

> No one takes it from me, but I lay it down of my own accord. (John 10:18)

Jesus is, in a psychological sense, already resurrected before he lays down his body because he does it of his "own accord." So convinced is he of his deathlessness, that he does not conceive of death, even when physical death seems imminent. Neyrey comments about Jesus' attitude toward laying his body down:

> Jesus claims to be equal to God in having God's own power over death. Jesus, then, while not literally *deathless* himself, has full *power over death*.[352]

Jesus has, while still alive, bypassed death and is truly deathless simply by realizing the primacy of mind and spirit. He knew himself and God well enough to know that his eternal life would endure even if his physical body were destroyed.

Paul speaks of resurrection as resulting in a spiritual body as opposed to a physical one:

> There are both heavenly bodies and earthly bodies, but the glory of the heavenly is one thing, and that of the earthly is another.... [42]So it is with the resurrection of the dead. What is sown is perishable, what is raised is imperishable. [43]It is sown in dishonor, it is raised in glory. It is sown in weakness, it is raised in power. [44]It is sown a physical body, it is raised a spiritual body. If there is a physical body, there is also a spiritual body. (1 Corinthians 15:40, 42-44)

Paul sounds here to be talking about two very different bodies: the "glory body," which is spiritual and divine, versus the physical body, which is perishable, dishonorable, and weak. Because the spiritual is eternal, it is our true being. Paul speaks of it as a "body" to distinguish it as a being unto itself. Instead of a "body," then, it is more precisely a *being*, a spiritual and cognitive reality that is distinct

---
[352] Neyrey 1989: 661.

from physical existence. It is the product of an entirely different creation than we currently imagine ourselves to be.

Paul speaks of the difference in another way. The first Adam, as Paul calls him, is simply a bodily creature, a physical existent, but "the last Adam became a life-giving spirit" (1 Cor. 15:45). These are two parts of every human self: body and spirit. Spirit includes all our cognitive and emotional functioning. But which is first, or primary? Did the body precede the mind and the mind spring forth from the body, or should we say rather that the body, which *seems* first in our worldly experience, is actually secondary and contingent on the eternal mind and timeless spirit?

And so, when "the perishable puts on the imperishable, and the mortal puts on immortality" (1 Cor. 15:54), this does not signify a continuation of our earthly life, but rather the replacement of supposed mortal life with the conviction of another kind of life. This is what it means for the perishable to put on the imperishable, and for mortality to slip on immortality — to think of ourselves as the eternal being God gave us because *it is* the truth of what we are, thus to think of ourselves (and others) as mind and heart instead of only body.

Therefore, I must disagree with Origen on his assertion that it must be "a body which arises"[353] in the expected resurrection. Paul is speaking about an abstract reality — one that is *impossible* to communicate directly in ordinary words. While on earth, it is difficult to think of ourselves as bodiless beings; this is far beyond our current capacity for comprehension. This is why we need an "image" to latch onto. And so, Paul used the word "body" to describe what is not a physical or material body. A spiritual body is a contradiction in terms, seeing how distinct spirit and body are in New Testament teaching, not to mention Origen's own teaching, wherein mind has priority. And so, Paul proposes the idea of a spiritual body because humans need an image to conceive of bodiless beings, and it can be useful as a mediating image for our transition back into gods.

---

[353] Origen, *De Principiis*, 2.10.1. (*ANF* 4:293).

The Light of Revelation

The Book of Revelation, placed canonically at the end of the Christian Bible, is the most misunderstood in all Christian literature. Written by an exiled prophet named John, whose style is entirely different from the author of the Fourth Gospel and Letters of John, it presents us with an intense, even hallucinatory vision, of what is traditionally called the "end" of the world or age, but it is more a transition from one reality to another. A revelation is the sudden or surprising "unveiling" of a greater reality that already exists, but which had gone unseen, unnoticed, and uninhabited.

In the Book of Revelation we find such indelible images as a book of life, a lake of fire, a seven-headed dragon, a leviathan like serpent and a monstrous beast, and hosts of angels. The evil in the world is identified as largely the product of world empires, specifically the Roman empire which was persecuting early Christians at the time Revelation was written. We get a glimpse in chapter 4 into the throne room of God, a standard scene in apocalyptic literature, showing that God's reality exists on another bejeweled and sparkling plane. Meanwhile on earth, armies are gathering on both sides, good versus evil, for a final showdown.

After all this cosmic drama, and after "the first earth had passed away," the "New Jerusalem," an entire gleaming city, descends from heaven to represent "a new heaven and a new earth" (Rev. 21:1), a separate reality that returns the primordial creation of light. The light of this descending city comes from within, so that it "has no need of sun or moon to shine upon it, for the glory of God is its light" (Rev. 21:23). Its source of light is internal, not external. And with this majestic city, the natural features of Paradise also return in the Tree of Life and the original rivers from the Garden of Eden. As Origen taught, the end is a return to the beginning.

So great is this exchange of worlds or realities that *even the past is changed.* This is because a new "heritage" (Revelation 21:7) is received, a completely different *past* and tradition for a completely different reality. This idea that our heritage and starting point is pushed back beyond the current world supports the idea of a primordial transcendent identity as Children of the Father (Rev. 21:7).

"People will bring into it the glory and the honor of the nations" (Rev. 21:26). All that is glorious and honorable from what we ourselves have made will be preserved and spiritualized, the love and care with which we made it added to the original creation, so that the infinite light shines just a bit brighter. The Holy Spirit, too, adds its light to the original creation. The gates of this heavenly city will remain forever open for the multitude to enter at will (v. 25). The only caveat is that "nothing unclean will enter it" (v. 27). Only that which is worthy of God and our true selves will exist in this new reality which is always there waiting for us.

The New Testament is filled with images of light. Jesus teaches his disciples to think of *themselves* as divine light. He calls them "the light of the world" (Mt. 5:14) and encourages them to "let your light shine before others, so that they may see your good works and give glory to your Father in heaven" (Mt. 5:16). The Gospel of John states that the light Jesus shares with his followers is the true "life" of every person (Jn. 1:4). Suggestions of primordial being abound here and in Jesus' teaching where the body becomes transparent to the light of the true being within, which would be to the body's benefit:

> If then your whole body is full of light, having no part dark, it will be wholly bright, as when a lamp with its rays gives you light. (Luke 11:36)

If, rather than hiding our true luminous being even from ourselves, the mind were filled with this truth, then the body itself would spiritualize in our experience and become transparent to this light. The light suffuses the body and changes our perception by changing our mind. The mind is the true being with the true control mechanism, the ability to gather and interpret information, decide and will for itself, teach and heal, as well as create and feel emotion, which the body itself does not possess.

When at last we see ourselves as originally created, we "will shine like the sun" (Matt 13:43) and "stand without blemish" (Jude 24). Nothing will interfere with our true life, our light. Ezekiel's vision of God was one of "brightness all around," and this ancient prophet identifies this light as God's "likeness" and "glory" (Ezek. 1:27-28). In this he highlights our original creation in God's image and likeness (Gen. 1:27). Zechariah speaks of the "continuous day" of eternal light that would characterize this new end-time kingdom:

> On that day there shall not be either cold or frost. ⁷And there shall be continuous day (it is known to the Lord), not day and not night, for at evening time there shall be light. (Zech. 14:6-7)

The transfiguration of Jesus from the gospels is also bathed in light. The disciples Peter, James, and John were praying with Jesus when suddenly "the appearance of his face changed, and his clothes became dazzling white" (Luke 9:29). The disciples then saw Moses and Elijah standing with Jesus, each radiating glory and light (Luke 9:29-32). This occurs immediately after Jesus had told them, "But truly I tell you, there are some standing here who will not taste death before they see the kingdom of God" (Luke 9:27). Thus, the light of the transfiguration appears to be a glimpse into our own true eternal nature as the kingdom, which nature we share with the resurrected ancient prophets.

Jesus remembered the light and glory he enjoyed with God "*before* the world was made" (Jn. 17:5). He says that this newfound but primordial glory and light is ours as well (Jn. 17:22). This light is our true life, the eternal life that comes from our eternal Source (Jn. 1:4; 8:12).

In the proto-Gnostic Gospel of Thomas, a collection of Jesus' sayings that may antedate the gospels, Jesus tells his disciples they "come from the light":

> Jesus said, 'If they say to you, "From whom [or what] did you come?" say to them, "We came from the light, the place

where the light exists through itself alone, established [itself] and appeared in their image."'(GThom, log. 50][354]

As the image of the Father who is all light, we come from "the light," a vastly different place than the world. Note that "the light exists through itself alone," meaning both that this light has life in itself and that it has no need of body or image (as is affirmed in other sayings in Thomas)[355]. In saying 24, the disciples ask Jesus to show them the "place" where he is. Jesus points them to the light within themselves:

> There is light within a person of light, and it shines on the whole world. If it does not shine, it is dark. [log 24][356]

This light from which they came is a primordial reality vastly different from the world. The light has its own eternal being, as indicated by the fact that it "exists through itself alone." And God from the very beginning of his creative activity knew this light to be good, true, pure, holy, and beautiful — that is, glorious like him.

Conclusion

The arc from the Old Testament to the New is one of increasing spiritualization — of the law, of the world, of God himself. Not that God himself changes, but our conception of him evolves to meet us where we are. Thus, God appears as a human to those who think themselves human, but he appears increasingly spiritual as we ourselves spiritualize. As the idea of God developed over time, the trend in most religions was to see God as less human but more humane, less liable to changes in mood or mind, and increasingly transcendent. A further evolutionary step follows from this: If God,

---

[354] Litwa 2015: 432.
[355] See esp. *GThom*. sayings 83, 87.
[356] Blatz translation. *The Coptic Gospel of Thomas*, W. Schneemelcher, ed, *New Testament Apocrypha*, 1991.

our Creator, is utterly transcendent of all humans think and know, might not we be also, simply by virtue of having been created by such a being?

Jesus was born in a time and culture in which the idea of human beings having potential immortality was in the preceding centuries just beginning to filter in, as evidenced particularly in the Apocalyptic and Wisdom literature of the period. Jesus referred to both sets of images to relay his own insights and revelations about the transcendent reality behind this one we see every day. As a human being exhibiting his transcendent capacity, he was also through these images revealing our own.

The ancient religious code of law, prototype of modern societal law, although generally beneficial for humans at certain times, had the disadvantage of seeing both human beings and God himself bound to a physicalist and materialistic way of viewing the world. Jesus therefore stressed how the law and other elements of cultural tradition were meant, even in ancient times, to elicit internal, spiritual realities. Toward this end, he taught that the apocalyptic "kingdom of God" was an internal reality, hidden from the world, that would yet change the world completely in our perception. Most did not appreciate where he diverged from the apocalyptic genre while employing it to promote his own experience-based teaching.

Jesus tried to impart to his audience a way of escape from the ordinary ways of thinking that kept them bound to illusion. This included eschatological ideas about the need for judgment after death, or even for death itself:

> Very truly, I tell you, anyone who hears my word and believes him who sent me has eternal life, and does not come under judgement, but has passed from death to life. (Jn. 5:24)

The one who truly "believes" finds out he already "*has* eternal life" and has passed by death altogether. And with this powerful act of mind, the threat of judgment dissolves long before it reaches the

Court, allowing eternal life to replace the thought of death, God's reality to replace the one we shaped and fashioned out of nothing. Thus, Jesus alters the apocalyptic expectation along with the legal, all while stressing the internal and ontological realities behind and above it. Human beings are more important to God than the law; the divine and sacrosanct law was made for their benefit. As Jesus said: "The sabbath was made for humankind, and not humankind for the sabbath" (Mk. 2:27). Humans are gods even in the world and, once seen as such, will treat themselves and others accordingly.

We see abundant evidence in the Bible that the world-transforming event takes place individually as well as collectively, and in the present as well as the future. As such, the end of the world is an internal change, a change of mind, that shows us that mind has priority over environment as its causative factor. The world reflects our state of mind, partly inclined to darkness, evil, or lovelessness, and partly inclined to love, thus to the ultimate and universal good, to justice, to beauty and to joy. Each of these two parts is entirely devoted to its objective. Eventually, these two vastly different realities will be sorted, distinguished, and the difference between them made crystal clear. It is then that we will properly judge between the two at last — which one we want to be.

The world will spiritualize as we spiritualize. It will come to reflect our deification. As we uncover the fact that we ourselves are "gods walking about in the flesh," the world is glorified with us. A mere change of mind gives us new eyes to see it. The physical is no longer a solid barrier to what lies behind. Instead, the world grows transparent to the ultimate reality it formerly concealed.

One of Origen's guiding principles is that the end will be like the beginning. Although reality itself never changes, our *sense* and *awareness* of reality will return to the way God originally designed it. Inevitably reality as it truly is (and always was) will filter down into our limited awareness because God's will, being inviolate, is already done in heaven. The change will be in our acceptance of it, not in determining the reality itself.

We tend to fear that when the world ends, we will be left with nothing. But the world is as impermanent and changeable as the mindset that made it. We have mentioned that the world is inextricably fused with the self, which makes it hard to see beyond either. Whichever self we choose comes complete with its own context, its own immersive reality, an environment and even a cosmos appropriate to it. As gods, we stand always in the presence of gods. As humans, we can detect only their humanness (if that) and our own. An entirely different reality awaits only our change of mind, our belief in a new mindset. As we allow for a beautifully loving transcendent reality, we are graced to see it in the world even as the world's initial reason for being gradually dissolves.

12

APOKATASTASIS:

THE UNIVERSAL RESTORATION

Two of the great themes running throughout the Bible are those of the oneness of God and the idea (called *exitus-reditus* in theology) that all beings that emanate from God remain part of him and therefore will ultimately return to God. They are interlocking themes, together ensuring that all things are being restored to the original oneness they share with God, and he with us.

Universalism In the Bible

The Bible is a collection of 66 books, 39 in the Old Testament and 27 in the New, written by many different scribes, but we can see certain motifs running throughout. One is the idea that God is one, an idea central to monotheism. We have discussed how this idea of God's oneness gives us insight into his very nature both through the principle of divine simplicity (whereby God is one with his attributes and they are one in him) and through the principle that God creates by giving *himself* to his creations, making them beings like himself. After all, such perfection is all he knows, and it is all there is to know.

Another great theme of the Bible is known by theologians as "*exitus-reditus*," emanation and return, the idea that all things proceed from God and therefore will return to God. Both Origen and Aquinas based their theologies on it. This theme has application to the return of ancient Israel from captivity in Egypt (c. 1400 BCE), Assyria (720 BCE) and Babylon (c. 586 BCE), in the sense of a returning home from an unwanted and difficult exile or captivity, and to Jesus' parable of the prodigal son, who leaves home and family behind but returns to great welcome from his father. In an overarching sense, it applies to Adam and Eve's loss of the original paradisal way of being and its return at the expected end of time.

Exitus-reditus affirms that God is Alpha and Omega, first and last. God is our origin and our ultimate destination. Where we come from, everything is God, and where we are headed, God is all in all. All things remain rooted in him. Where are we in the meantime, then? We exist in a place where God seems largely absent. Who is in the wrong here — we, or God? We are in exile and long for our true home, and yet we must already be home if that is God's will. We must, then, be living a dream of a separate existence.

All of this is said by way of introduction to an even more controversial topic in Christian circles than preexistence. In the Book of Acts, Peter speaks of:

> *the time of universal restoration* that God announced long ago through his holy prophets. (Acts 3:21)[357]

The specification that it is a "restoration" signifies that all things are returning to a *prior* state of being. The fact that this great restoration is "universal" indicates that it involves everyone and all things. Together, "universal restoration" means that all things and all beings are bound to return to their original state, as God eternally knows them to be.

This universal restoration ("*apokatastasis*" in its original Greek) signifies, according to Origen and other patristics who took notice of it in scripture, the inevitable fulfillment of God's exceedingly merciful and unbreakable will for the salvation of all his children. It is God's will that *all* be saved and *none* should perish:

> The Lord is not slow about his promise, as some think of slowness, but is patient with you, not wanting any to perish, but *all* to come to repentance. (2 Pet. 3:9, my emphasis)

---

[357] My emphasis.

The Second Letter of Peter explains the apparent delay in the final restoration, which many believed imminent, as God "not wanting *any* to perish." Time exists for the very reason that "*all*" have ample opportunity to change their minds and (re)align them with God's will. It would seem, then, that time will exist for as long as it takes for all to be saved and none to perish. The *apokatastasis* will not be complete until "all" of God's beings return to him in their original blessed state. (Otherwise, it would not be universal, nor one.) God, in his infinite patience and blessed certainty, can wait them out. Actually, God does not wait. He lives in a timeless reality wherein his will is already done. All things that emanate from God remain one with God, rooted in God. We are, again, playing out a dream which lingers for a moment while we waken.

Seen as a whole, the Bible ends where it begins. In the Book of Revelation at the end of the Bible, speaking about the end times, the Tree of Life from the Book of Genesis returns with its abundant fruit, and now its leaves are healing for the nations (Revelation 22:2). With it comes a complete preexistent reality wherein no more is anything "accursed" (Rev. 22:3), but all is blessed, holy, and perfect. The original perfect creation is being restored to our minds and therefore to the world. This is the true object of "all things" according to Paul:

> We know that all things work together for good for those who love God, who are called according to his purpose.
> (Romans 8:28)

We have encountered this passage before in relation to sonship, to preexistence, and to predestination. But here we note the grand coordination involved in all of this: a working together of literally everything for the higher purpose of sonship (Ro. 8:29) and glorification (8:30). Darkness itself cooperates, unconsciously, even if just to show the contrast. Everyone and everything participates in the grand vision, whether or not it is recognized. And who are those who love God? *All* his children, his every creation, to the very depth of their being, and from before the very foundation of the world.

What we fail to recognize, besides the tremendous degree of orchestration continually going on around us, is how Jesus, although striving to remain in the confines of his own religion, ended up universalizing it. He was repulsed by its parochialism, its smug and self-satisfied traditionalism, how it was misused for personal puffery, and how its predictable multiplication of rules and laws overtook its original spirit. This happens with every religion and indeed with everything in the world; it is the countervailing force to the true freedom and equality of God. It is a byproduct of a religion needing to become a part of the world to survive.

The world tries to control even that about which it knows nothing. But because Jesus overcame the world, Paul writes that "God highly exalted him" and that "at the name of Jesus every knee should bend, in heaven and on earth and under the earth, [11] and every tongue should confess that Jesus Christ is Lord, to the glory of God the Father" (Phil 2:9–11). The universalism is very clear here, with "*every* knee" and "*every* tongue" both "on earth and *under* the earth" professing the one who fully transcended the world. They need not be conscious of Jesus' persona or his role in the universal salvation to benefit from it. The achievement is all the more striking because it truly saves *every*one, even those who came before him, not only going forward but retroactively as well.

Jesus himself proclaimed such universalism when he said that he had "other sheep" from other flocks for which he was responsible (Jn. 10:16). This suggests that some he would classify as adherents follow different beliefs and practices. Who is not against him is for him (Mk. 9:40). They need not parrot everything he says but only relay the gist and essence. His *identification* with all people, especially those neglected or disparaged by the world, also supports the idea of universalism (Mt. 25:40). He remains with them in the truest sense. He had taught that there is more rejoicing in heaven for the last straggler's return than there is even in heaven's natural state (Luke 15:7). And, quite clearly, he had declared: "When I am lifted up from the earth, I will draw *all people* to myself" (John 12:32).[358] How can these *not* be taken literally to mean every mind and every soul?

The Philippians passage cites these verses from the Book of Isaiah:

> Turn to me and be saved,
>   all the ends of the earth!
> For I am God, and there is no other.
> [23] By myself I have sworn,
>   from my mouth has gone forth in righteousness
>   a word that shall not return:
> 'To me every knee shall bow,
>   every tongue shall swear.' (Isa. 45:22-23)

Universalism was prophesied by the great prophet. It was the most holy plan all along, although appreciation of the full breadth of this vision was and is very rare. The grand design was more universal than anyone recognized because God himself was more universal and transcendent of ordinary thinking than anyone had recognized. He dwells far beyond *all* our thoughts and way of thinking, and yet, he dwells in our mind — alongside our true selves.

> Only in the Lord, it shall be said of me,
>   are righteousness and strength;
> all who were incensed against him
>   shall come to him and be ashamed.
> [25] In the Lord all the offspring of Israel
>   shall triumph and glory. (Isa. 45:24-25)

All the beings of God are the offspring of God. All those who consider the universal God their enemy will eventually realize that he is their one true friend. They will be "ashamed" to realize that they were projecting their own ideas onto their gracious Source, the One who, by whatever name they call him, gave them life and eternal

---

[358] My emphasis.

happiness and still offers them happiness, but such shame is only temporary. Once they realize, they naturally take responsibility for their own projections and misplaced assumptions, and will find themselves traveling the broad and safe highway back to God:

> A highway shall be there,
>   and it shall be called the Holy Way;
> the unclean shall not pass it by,
>   but it shall be for them;
>   no traveler, not even fools, shall go astray....
> ¹⁰ And the ransomed of the Lord shall return,
>   and come to Zion with singing;
> everlasting joy shall be upon their heads;
>   they shall obtain joy and gladness,
>   and sorrow and sighing shall flee away. (Isa. 35:8, 10)[359]

"No traveler, not even fools, shall go astray." Upon this broad highway travel *all* God's people, clean and unclean, pure and impure, learned and fool, Jew and Gentile, as they return to God and to their own eternal happiness. The vision is uncompromising, and uncompromisingly vast.

Apokatastasis has been feared as something foreign to God, when it is actually God who wills it. If indeed an all-powerful God does not want any to perish, then no one *will* perish and if God wants all to be saved, then all *will* be saved. All that is God's *must* return to God, or God would be missing the fullness and oneness which is characteristic of him — and we would be missing our loved ones.

Paul affirms that God "desires everyone to be saved and to come to the knowledge of truth" (1 Tim. 2:4). Who can withstand the most holy will of God, or any divine desire forever, let alone this one, seeing that it is meant for *them* as well? Who can refuse God's will, especially if it means complete joy for all beings forever, and even here on earth "a quiet and peaceable life in all godliness and dignity"

---

[359] NRSV variant translations used for verse 8 because these more literal interpretations better fit the context.

(v. 2)? Is this not the reality that our own deepest hearts crave, both for ourselves and for all we love?

Note that Paul specifies that Jesus is "himself human" (v. 5), although he has become the "mediator between God and humankind." Jesus strides the two realities, helping transition all beings from the lower to the higher, back into the one that truly belongs to us and remains forever etched in our heart. He chose to leave this earth to do just that, similar yet inverse to how he came into this world selflessly to begin his universal mission. In the same letter to Timothy, Paul states:

> [T]o this end we toil and struggle, because we have our hope set on the living God, who is the Savior of all people, especially of those who believe. (1 Tim. 4:10)

Note that it is not *only* those who believe who are saved, but rather, *"especially"* those who believe, for, in fact, "all people" will eventually be saved. Those who believe will have prepared themselves for comforting foretastes of visions and revelations *before* they lay their bodies down. God is precisely "the Savior of all people." Believing this, we truly believe. Jesus suggested the same when he said in Mt. 8.11: "I tell you, many will come from east and west and will eat with Abraham and Isaac and Jacob in the kingdom of heaven." The heavenly banquet is heavenly precisely because *all* will be there, purified, sanctified, and deified.

God's plan for us is universal and comprehensive, centering around his oneness. It is "a plan for the fullness of time, to unite all things in him, things in heaven and things on earth" (Eph. 1:10). Again and again, we read that *"all* things" will be included in this return to oneness and that we will yet see them harmonized, even in spite of diverse motivations, because of the eternal rootedness of all beings in God. When we are sure of this, we share the confidence of Jesus, who knew implicitly "that he had come from God and was going to God" (John 13:3).

Apokatastasis in Origen

Origen was one of the few early Christian theologians who had a truly universal vision. Regarding Peter's statement in Acts 3:21 about the *apokatastasis* or "universal restoration," Origen writes that God, working through the Holy Spirit and the Word, is "by the ineffable skill of His wisdom, transforming and restoring all things, in whatever manner they are made, to some useful aim, and to the common advantage of all."[360] Every being will eventually be restored to its original perfection because "all things" coordinate and contribute "to the common advantage of all." The fact that it involves everyone need not diminish its supreme value in our eyes, for it fulfills *our own* greatest desire.

Origen envisioned this grand coordination of all minds as a great restoration and reunion, fulfilling the overarching purpose or *telos* of creation. For Origen, even "the very variety of minds tends to one end of perfection," pursuing the same (often unconscious) goal as they all work together, and all this despite "the influence of different motives."[361] Origen calls it "the harassing influence of different motives and desires," which he contrasts with "the single and undivided goodness of their nature."[362] Even though they are in conflict with themselves and therefore others, these diverse beings are all moving to one ultimate and inevitable conclusion: that their true purpose is to uncover their original oneness with one another and with God.

Origen sees monumental significance[363] in Paul's statement that once death, the last hurdle, is vanquished, then all things will be subjected to Christ so that God is "all in all":

> When all things are subjected to him, then the Son himself will also be subjected to the one who put all things in

---

[360] Origen, *De Principiis*, 2.1.2. (*ANF* 4:268).
[361] Origen, *De Principiis*, 2.1.2. (*ANF* 4:268).
[362] Origen, *De Principiis*, 2.1.1. (*ANF* 4:267).
[363] See Origen, *Commentary on John*, Book 1, 120.

subjection under him, *so that God may be all in all.* (1 Cor. 15:28, my emphasis)

The fact that God will be "all in all" leaves no room for anything else. *Everything* in that case will be like God, everything "we feel or understand or think," which means the original transcendent creation is restored within every being. The relationship and even identification with God here is extraordinarily direct, no longer requiring mediation. Origen proposes God will suffuse our every thought and feeling, God will be within our every "mode and measure and ... movement."[364]

> I am of opinion that the expression, by which God is said to be 'all in all,' means that He is 'all' in each individual person. Now He will be 'all' in each individual in this way: when all which any rational understanding, cleansed from the dregs of every sort of vice, and with every cloud of wickedness completely swept away, can either feel, or understand, or think, will be wholly God; and when it will no longer behold or retain anything else than God, but when God will be the measure and standard of all its movements; and thus God will be 'all,' for there will no longer be any distinction of good and evil, seeing evil nowhere exists; for God is all things, and to Him no evil is near: nor will there be any longer a desire to eat from the tree of the knowledge of good and evil, on the part of him who is always in the possession of good, and to whom God is all.... He who alone is the one good God becomes to him 'all,' and that not in the case of a few individuals, or of a considerable number, but He Himself is 'all in all.'[365]

Origen connects this grand universal restoration, where "all" actually means "all," and where evil motives, vice, and death have been rendered meaningless because their privation has filled, with a

---

[364] Origen, *On First Principles* 3.6.3 (ANF 4:345); cited in Martens 532.
[365] Origen, *De Principiis*, 3.6.3 (*ANF* 4:345).

return to the original creation via his principle that the end will match the beginning:

> Seeing, then, that such is the end, when all enemies will be subdued to Christ, when death — the last enemy — shall be destroyed, and when the kingdom shall be delivered up by Christ (to whom all things are subject) to God the Father; let us, I say, from such an end as this, contemplate the beginnings of things. For the end is always like the beginning: as therefore there is one end of all things, so as there is one end of many things, so from one beginning arise many differences and varieties, which in their turn are restored, through God's goodness, through their subjection to Christ and their unity with the Holy Spirit, to one end which is like the beginning.[366]

This return to the original oneness and sameness of creation is the intricate and universal process of *apokatastasis*. God can be "all in all" only if "all" are restored. The question we must grapple with is: Does "all" literally mean "all" in 1 Cor. 15:28, or does it mean something else? Does the restoration involve "all things" as in Acts 3:21, and is it therefore truly "universal"?

He also cites Ephesians 4:13: "until all of us come to the unity of the faith and of the knowledge of the Son of God, to maturity, to the measure of the full stature of Christ." The prerequisite for reclaiming full knowledge is stringent: it is to attain the level and morality of Christ himself, even to the point of oneness with him. However, here again, this is something that will ultimately be achieved by "all." Through gradual identification with the original being of God, his thoughts, his values, and especially his love, "we all" come to share in the glorious reality given to us by God. And so: "speaking the truth in love, we must grow up in every way into him who is the head, into Christ" (Eph. 4:15). The believers in Christ become part of Christ, having not only individual being but also, all together, a collective being similar to the collective Son.

---

[366] Origen, *De Principiis*, 1.6.2 (*ANF* 4:260).

Origen reasons that the scriptural passages which seem to speak of punishment of sinners must be seen instead as discipline for the greater purpose of purification. Such discipline was not truly set in motion by God but was a natural consequence of our decision not to love, which produced a split in our mind which is projected onto others, even onto God. Such alienation from our true selves comes with the distorted autonomy we wanted and fell for. Our anguished struggle stems from not thinking and feeling in the way that deep within, even unconsciously, we know is right.

"Eternal punishment" is a misnomer, as Ramelli explains, because the aim of "*aionos* punishment" is therapeutic and pedagogical, as stressed by Clement, Origen, and Gregory of Nyssa. It is more a divestiture from illusion, which can be experienced with discomfort by those who are caught up in it. Such discipline can occur after physical existence, but can endure only temporarily, until its purpose is achieved. It may go on for eons and eons, but it will prove divestible once we sort the true from the false in our minds. In the end, all such self-discipline will be seen as universally beneficial, for our own good and the good of all beings. God is patient but persistent, and his Spirit stops at nothing in the working out of his will. This work is thus not confined to just this lifetime:

> For God deals with souls not merely with a view to the short space of our present life, included within sixty years or more, but with reference to a perpetual and never-ending period, exercising His providential care over souls that are immortal, even as He Himself is eternal and immortal. For He made the rational nature, which He formed in His own image and likeness, incorruptible; and therefore the soul, which is immortal, is not excluded by the shortness of the present life from the divine remedies and cures.[367]

Whereas Marcion and other proto-Gnostics early in Christian history were accusing the Old Testament God of acts of cruelty and injustice, Origen, believing with them that the God Jesus proclaimed

---

[367] Origen, *On First Principles* 3.1.13 (ANF04: 314).

would be incapable of any cruelty or injustice, yet wanting to salvage the revelatory nature of all scripture including the Old Testament, sought to reconcile these seeming opposites based on reason and coherent argument, and largely succeeded.

Origen did say that sinners experience distress and "must taste something bitter,"[368] but even these temporary consequences cannot be from God. Rather, they are built into the things — or better, the mindset — we made to detach from God and thus from ourselves. The bitterness is ultimately the remnant of lovelessness, of not being our true selves, the true original sin, which is yet entirely redeemable simply by opening to love. All the things we miscreated for obstruction can and will be turned to the common good and to our own best interests. (In the end, the two will be seen as one.) He points out that purification is needed but, again, the discipline is not everlasting:

> [T]here is punishment, but not everlasting. For when the body is punished the soul is gradually purified, and so is restored to its ancient rank. For all wicked men, and for daemons, too, shall be restored to their former rank.[369]

This last sentence is where later critics believed he went too far, by suggesting that even demons would be restored to their former rank as blessed angels. While there is controversy over whether Origen wrote the last sentence in the quotation, and at some points Origen expressly denies the idea, we will explore the merits of the statement in the next section.

Evagrius Ponticus (346-399) taught a similar process of universal restoration as had Origen, involving the return of minds (*noes*) to their source in the divine Mind. Later Origenists took this even farther, proposing the Christhood of individual minds, which

---

[368] Origen, *Homily 12 on Jeremiah* 183.
[369] Origen, *On First Principles* 1.4.6. This Greek fragment is included in Koetschau's rendering. There is a question whether Origen actually included all or part of this quotation in his original Greek text of *On First Principles*. In other places, he explicitly denies the restoration of demons.

caught the attention of the heresiologists, affecting Evagrius personally and condemning parts of Origen posthumously. It may seem quaint to modern ears that the *Christhood* of believers would garner such negative attention when the *godhood* of believers (i.e., deification) was accepted without question.

Apokatastasis was formally anathemized at the Council of Constantinople in 543. This meant that it had become forbidden even to discuss the issue, which is not the way to go if one desires a more rational approach to religion, particularly given the scriptural evidence we have cited. St. Augustine was a main opponent in his own time, going back and forth regarding preexistence, thinking at one point that it and universal restoration were errors that obviated the need for grace. But we have dealt with this criticism by pointing out that there is actually a more fundamental and unearned grace in the idea of an original spiritual creation than in the secondary grace of salvation. Augustine's argument against universal salvation is that it is contrary to the necessity of grace for salvation. Yet, would not the universal restoration of every original being, uncreated by us, be the very epitome of grace and unearned reward? A reward we already have but fail to realize would be *most* unearned.

The anathemas called preexistence "fabulous" and the restoration "monstrous." They spoke of "the danger of universalism." Is it not more monstrous to think that some are tortured forever, for ever-changing crimes of which most were entirely ignorant during their earthly lifetime? Is it not more arbitrary to ignore the question or force it out of existence than at least to consider it, particularly in light of the evidence and rationale we do have before us?

Origen emphasizes the universality of God, and thus his majestic grandeur. He reminds us that God does not belong solely to the parochial world systems that have appropriated him. Origen always defended orthodoxy as it was being established in his time, and indeed he *was* orthodoxy as Christianity's first truly systematic theologian. Orthodoxy would not be orthodoxy without him. He believed that universalism allows God's purpose and Jesus' salvation to be seen as universal and entirely effective. As Origen states: "John [the Baptist] converts many; the Lord converts, *not only many, but all*. For this is the work of the Lord: to convert *all* to God the Father."[370]

Origen believed God to be wholly good, the purest good, his sense of justice springing from his inimitable goodness, and thus God is fully intent on gathering *all* his minds back to himself. Even if it takes ages and eons to accomplish, which it probably will, it cannot be any other way.[371] Origen's argument was basically that God's will *must* prevail, and that if God wills all his children be restored to their happiness and his own, then this is what *must* finally occur. After all, Jesus had stated:

> So it is not the will of your Father in heaven that one of these little ones should be lost. (Matthew 18.14)

Universal salvation among human souls has been taught by Clement of Alexandria, Gregory Nazianzen, Gregory of Nyssa, Evagrius Ponticus, Duns Scotus Erigena, Didymus, Eusebius of Caesarea, Amalric of Bena, Gregory Thaumaturgus, St. Pamphilus, Methodius of Olympus, Marcellus of Ancyra, Diodore of Tarsus, and St. Macrina the Younger. Harnack had declared the Reformers themselves to have been universalists at heart.[372] As with preexistence, we must consider its possibility, particularly seeing as how well it fits scripture and reason, and considering the omnipotence of God's will and his unfailing goodness. This is the gist of the issue: Is God's will indomitable enough, his glory extensive enough, and his salvific design great and comprehensive enough to save *all* his fallen beings? If the answer is yes, then it is already being done, and in fact, from his perspective is already done.

Most patristics past and present would agree that it is right to hope and pray for the salvation of all beings and even to affirm that this is God's will. Some, like Gregory Nazianzen, leave it an open question as to whether this will include demons or fallen angels.

---

[370] Origen, *Homilies on Luke* 4; cited in Ramelli 2013.
[371] See Bauckham 1978: 48.
[372] Harnack, *History of Dogma*, III, 661.

Others, like Augustine, press for their persecution. It is understandable for us to desire the persecution of our persecutors, but we do not understand that we are convicting ourselves in the process. We are our own best tormentors — until we recognize what we do to ourselves.

Critics of universalism argue that it eliminates freedom — the freedom of those who might want to remain forever detached from their Source and their happiness. The fact is, only universalism upholds the true freedom of the individual will, surpassing every other doctrine in doing so. Thus, all are free to experience loveless partiality for as long as they think they want this, and free to work themselves back to what they most truly desire, for as long as this takes, but they cannot change their foundational eternal reality, nor even what they most desire, and so the possibility of waking to godhood will forever remain their unconscious aim. And any reality malevolently split off from God slopes toward weariness, chaos, void, and self-dissolution, i.e., nothingness, which is a secondary insurance that eventually all free minds will decide instead for joy, fullness, and the limitlessness of true freedom. The human mind has freedom in the Platonic sense of the ability to choose the good. But to choose evil is to grasp at air, because evil is the privation of good, and therefore it is not a real choice and is never free. No fully aware rational mind with the options clearly laid out would ever willfully choose self-destruction over full abundance, and nothing over everything.

Hell

If the *apokatastasis* or universal restoration is actually the will of God, then "hell" as commonly understood stands in need of major reinterpretation. Let us begin with the well-known fact that there is no hell in the Old Testament of the Bible. The word *Sheol* — which centuries of English translations (including the King James Version published in 1611) mistook for "hell" — meant simply "the grave," the receptacle of the dead, throughout the Hebrew Bible.

> Like sheep they are appointed for Sheol;
> death shall be their shepherd;
> straight to the grave they descend,
> and their form shall waste away;
> Sheol shall be their home. (Psalms 49:15)

Sheol, which may have a root meaning as "hollow," is throughout the Hebrew Bible solely the empty grave. Every creature on earth goes there, blindly, unwittingly, "dumbfounded to Sheol" (Ps. 31:17). The Psalms often parallel death and Sheol:

> The snares of death encompassed me,
> the pangs of Sheol laid hold on me;
> I suffered distress and anguish. (Ps. 116:3)[373]

The "distress and anguish" associated with Sheol began as the state of mind *anticipating* death and its nothingness. Thus, Sheol itself became a symbol of this intrapsychic torment centuries before it was re-imagined as a place of demonic torment. The anticipation and the torment that we normally associate with hell occur here within physical existence, not in Sheol itself. Rather than deal with them directly, we tend to dissociate these difficult feelings and questions from consciousness, with the unintended result that they seem to take on a life of their own outside ourselves. It was via such splitting that "hell" and "the devil" came about.

Ecclesiastes 9:10 states that nothing happens in Sheol. Nothing is there, "no work or thought." It had nothing to do with an afterlife. Sheol, or the grave, was an empty receptacle underground where absolutely nothing happened. Therefore, any distress caused by it is anticipatory and confined to earthly existence.

The desultory state of affairs is that everyone in the world *seems* destined for such nothingness. Not even the splendors and pleasures of the world can make up for the inevitable sorrow: "the

---

[373] See also Ps. 18:5: "the cords of Sheol entangled me, the snares of death confronted me." The Hebrew literary method parallelism equates the two terms.

nobility of Jerusalem and her multitude go down, her throng and he who exults in her" (Isaiah 5:14). All the forms, however splendid, in this world are transitory, as is every delight we take in the world. They become in this context symbols of the death, depression, and meaninglessness at the hollow core of this world, mocking us silently with their very existence. But there is a way to see them instead as indicative of a lost eternal magnificence and this will become clear to us.

All of the over 60 references to Sheol in the Hebrew Bible were mistranslated into English by the KJV with the German word "hell," (derived from "hel," a Germanic goddess of the underworld). Ideas about an afterlife were just beginning to dawn in the later books of the Hebrew Bible (such as Daniel and Zechariah). It was only later, in the intertestamental period (from approximately 200 BCE, when the Hebrew Bible was canonized, to c. 200 CE, when the 27 books of the New Testament were largely agreed upon), that the sense of an afterlife filtered into Judaism and from there into burgeoning Christianity.

Greek mythological influences, its dank underground caverns long-populated by personified gods and demons, are well known in the Judaism of this intertestamental period. The word "Hades" begins to take over for Sheol. Zoroastrian influence, with its dualistic conceptions of good/evil, heaven/hell, a final judgment and an end time, entered largely through Jewish apocalyptic writings popular during that time. The Wisdom writings were influenced somewhat by Hellenistic philosophy during this same period. Additionally, there had always been long-term influences from surrounding Middle Eastern mythologies (Babylonian and Canaanite, Sumerian and Egyptian) throughout the Hebrew Bible, although Judaism had up until this period stuck with a largely materialistic conception of the human being. This fortuitous assembly of ideas fed the rich soil from which young Christianity sprang.

With these foreign ideas the idea of an escape from the pit of death also rises, as here in the Book of Wisdom:

For thou hast power over life and death;

> thou dost lead men down to the gates of Hades and back again. (Wisdom 16:13)

Although dark and dank like Sheol, "Hades" contains escape hatches at least for some. In the fertile crescent of which Israel/Judah were a part, these escapes had in surrounding mythology occurred annually with the dying/rising cycles that follow the arid and growing seasons. The upshot is that, for the first time in Judaism, Sheol is survivable. Scribes were beginning to take seriously the idea of mind or spirit as a separate reality, a central feature of ancient Greek and Zoroastrian philosophy, and soon of nascent Christianity itself.

By New Testament times, "hell" and "the devil" have suddenly become common knowledge, suggesting that this foreign influence had a profound effect on the populace in the space of a couple of centuries. To understand the presence of hell and Satan swiftly appearing in the New Testament, we need to trace their roots back to the apocryphal apocalypses emerging in the centuries immediately preceding Jesus, which include 1 Enoch,[374] 2 Esdras (also known as 4 Ezra), the Book of Jubilees, and many other Jewish apocalypses. We learn from the Book of Jubilees that what we call demons were originally gods or sons of God who had descended to earth to help humans by teaching justice and righteousness, but they got waylaid by lust and human desires. Wray and Mobley point out how the authors of these pre-Christian apocalypses reinterpret the Old Testament stories and history to attribute "the more unsavory deeds of God to a malicious, evil being."[375] Thus, the devil grew in large part out of outdated warlike and unfeeling conceptions of God.

The first-century BCE Essenes at Qumran seem to have been heavily influenced by Persian dualism as their books exhibit a stark dualism in the human being who has access to two spirits, one good, one evil. Old combat tales from the Hebrew Bible are transformed into visions of cosmic combat and the eventual triumph of good over

---

[374] 1 Enoch contains an older part (the Book of the Watchers) written c. 300-200 BCE, and a Book of Parables dated c. 100 BCE.
[375] Wray and Mobley 2005: 103.

evil, truth over falsity, light over darkness.[376] In the first-century Life of Adam and Eve, Satan rebels by refusing to kneel before God's creation of Adam, saying, "I am prior in creation, before [Adam] was made, I was already made. He ought to worship me" (Life of Adam and Eve 12:3). Hence the seed of his enmity for humankind, and his tragic flaw, exaggerated pride. Over the centuries these bits and pieces coalesced and hardened into tradition. Satan, formerly an unnamed bureaucratic underling in the Book of Job (c. 600-400 BCE), had by the intertestamental period become the leader of a band of rebel angels or sons of God who now ruled not only the underworld, but the world itself.

Paul's letters barely mention Satan and never mention hell, indicating that such extreme imagery was not standard throughout early Christian teaching. Paul does remark that the devil has influenced some members of the Christian communities he founded to misconstrue his teaching against the law as a license for immorality.[377] But he does not seem to have believed in a hell of eternal torment, as for him death as annihilation denies afterlife for the ungodly. Luke mentions hell only once, in regard to the rich man who had failed to help the poor man, Lazarus.[378] The Gospel of John does not speak of hell at all although the theme of judgment is evident. As with Paul, then, John seems to see the choices as being either death or eternal life; nothing unlike God will survive. There was obviously a difference of opinion as regards the interpretation and importance of this particular apocalyptic symbol. In succeeding centuries, such Christian apocalypses as the Apocalypse of Peter, the Apocalypse of Paul, and the Apocalypse of the Virgin each would feature "a guided tour of hell" as hell took on increasing detail in the vivid imaginations of the people.[379]

There is a popular Christian tradition asserting that Jesus descended into hell immediately after his crucifixion to release souls

---

[376] Wray and Mobley 2005: 105-107. The evil spirit was called by many different names in almost as many different apocalypses, both Jewish and Christian.
[377] Wray and Mobley 2005: 128-130.
[378] Luke 16: 19-26; Wray and Mobley 2005: 152.
[379] Wray and Mobley 2005: 155.

that were trapped there. The spirits of the dead are by this time imagined to remain alive although perhaps in suspended animation underground until the apocalyptic resurrection. We see the budding of this tradition in Eph. 4:9, which states that Jesus "descended into the lower parts of the earth." Jesus holds the "keys of death and Hades" in Rev. 1:18. 1 Peter 4:6 states that Jesus "preached to the dead" (1 Peter 4:6) and "to the spirits in prison" (1 Peter 3:18). Hell, it seems, even this early in its development, has an escape hatch, a door that opens both ways. Why, then, would escape not be possible for all (eventually)?

The concept of the devil grew out of the same apocalyptic stew as that of hell, composed of characteristics of earlier, defeated gods and those from surrounding civilizations, as well as from earlier characterizations of the Hebrew God that were by the intertestamental period considered anachronistic or troubling. As such, both hell and the devil were used as catch-all categories for anything that was considered ungodly, including things as wide-ranging as human sacrifice, the making of weapons of war, cosmetics, and sexuality (all mentioned in 1 Enoch).

As an instance of how this stew drew on disparate elements, the serpent in the early chapters of Genesis is never called the devil, but became identified as such only in later theology. The devil or "the satan" (Heb., *hasatan*) started out as a low-level administrator for the divine council in the Book of Job, having no proper name, known only by his role as "the accuser" or "adversary" of human beings before God.

> One day the sons of God came to present themselves before the Lord, and the accuser (*hasatan*) also came among them. ⁷The Lord said to the accuser 'Where have you come from?' The accuser answered the Lord, 'From going to and fro on the earth, and from walking up and down on it.' (Job 1:6-7)

Thus, *hasatan* or the accuser started out as an overzealous self-appointed prosecutor roaming the earth to ferret out minor breaches of conduct among human beings in order to harass and test them. His peripheral association with the "sons of God" suggests that such frivolous prosecution is self-persecution. This accuser in Job plays a similar role as trickster figures in world mythology (such as the serpent in Genesis or Enki in nearby Canaanite mythology), dramatizing the self-deception involved in early humankind's rebellion from God and from their true selves.

Because "Satan" is not yet a proper name, we find "many different satans" in the preexilic Hebrew books.[380] As another case in point, let us investigate the development of the "Lucifer figure," a now common name for what eventually became the Satan figure. The first biblical use appears in Isa. 14:12 where it refers to a great king of the earth who in his original splendor was compared with the planet Venus, the beautiful morning "star" that remains visible at dawn:

> How you are fallen from heaven,
> O Day Star [*lucifer*], son of Dawn!
> How you are cut down to the ground,
> you who laid the nations low! (Isa. 14:12)

The earthly king being referenced here experienced a downfall after having destroyed his own land and killed his own people (Isa. 14:20). Again, as with "the satan," what eventually became a proper name is used originally as a descriptor. Moreover, the term "lucifer" is applied late in the New Testament to Jesus himself in the blessing of 2 Pet. 1:19: "until the day dawns and the morning star rises in your hearts." A god named Lucifer did exist in Greco-Roman culture, but we see from the New Testament that its personification as a common synonym for Satan was for Christians a much later (post-biblical) development.

The Hebrew Bible was canonized and translated into Greek just as the ideas of hell and the devil were beginning to flesh out. In the space of less than two hundred years, "the satan" and hell would grow from these humble beginnings into a full-fledged thought system. Thus, we find in the more apocalyptic gospels of Mark and

---

[380] Wray and Mobley 2005: 72.

Matthew Jesus casting out demons in order to heal people of psychic distress and to show that the faith of the person being healed was more powerful than Satan and his forces of evil, who were seen at that time as continually harassing humans and placing obstacles in their way.

By the time of the New Testament, the devil and hell already have some history behind them. When Jesus is led by the Spirit into the wilderness to prepare for his teaching role in each of the synoptic gospels, he is said to be confronted and questioned (somewhat accusatorially) by the devil.[381] Here it seems to be the personification of Jesus' own intrapsychic turmoil as he is tempted to consider what any deified being might have to wrestle with: whether to use this incredible power welling up in him for the common good or for his own personal gain. Just as the devil grew out of former gods, former conceptions of God, mythological figures, and historical figures, the devil is a repository of the secret motivations, suppressed thoughts and judgments, and past actions of which humans, on second thought, are not so proud. The underworld is the unconscious repository of all we would rather forget, thus inadvertently pieced together personally as well as collectively in a historical sense.

A major NT motif is that the devil acts as a stumbling block to the sons of God who are attempting to recover their sonship. Thus, Jesus says to Peter: "Get behind me, Satan! You are a stumbling block to me; for you are setting your mind not on divine things, but on human things" (Mk. 8: 33; Mt. 16:23). We have seen Satan acting as an obstacle in the Parable of the Sower,[382] wherein the devil works to combat the Word from growing in the hearts of human beings.

Judas is said to have been possessed by the devil to betray Jesus (Jn. 6:70). But this scheme backfired in a big way; the deceiver was himself deceived. In the Book of Revelation, likely written between 81-96 CE during the persecution of Roman Emperor Domitian, Satan and hell represent the Roman Empire. Thus, we see that the same stock images are used to represent many faceted

---

[381] Mk. 1:12-13; Mt. 4:1-11; Luke 4:1-13.
[382] Matthew 13:1–23, Mark 4:1–20, Luke 8:4–15 and the extra-canonical Gospel of Thomas (log. 9).

things. Satan and hell function as cosmic catch-all categories, repositories of ideas wherein anything feared ungodly was thrown.

However, Jesus teaches that the reign of this evil influence is bound not to last because: "Every kingdom divided against itself is laid waste" (Mt. 12:25). The devil is the intrapsychic division we have introduced into our minds. Because the demons that arose therefrom, like humans for most of history, are driven by self-interest, they cannot for long agree and cooperate. Born of intrapsychic conflict, they *must* turn on themselves. Moreover, the devil must deceive to gain our allegiance, so its power comes from humankind itself; its ability to keep us from divine self-knowledge is only ours to give. This is why it must deceive to have power over us, and so it is called "a liar and the father of lies" (Jn. 8:44).

"Hell" went on to become hugely popular in Medieval morality plays (the origin of modern theater). In 1314, Dante wrote his *Inferno*, the first third of *the Divine Comedy* with its rings of hell and satirically comical punishments, in Italian just as it was replacing Latin as the people's language. Likewise, John Milton wrote *Paradise Lost* in English in 1667, and Goethe penned *Faust* in German in 1790. Each of these masterworks of literature and others helped ingrain ideas about hell and Satan into the modern Western way of thinking. These imaginative fictional depictions added to the current popular patchwork conception of hell as a finished concept, so that by now, hell seems a long-established thing in our minds.

As regards the supposed fiery environment of hell, Clement of Alexandria and Origen had taught that the flames of hell referred, not to punishment, but to the ardor of God's love. Thus, it is a purifying but ultimately gentle personal fire, which would continue only as long as the mind needs refinement. Origen made clear that he believed the fire of purification to be an internal, individualized process:

> We find in the prophet Isaiah, that the fire with which each one is punished is described as his own; for he says, Walk in the light of your own fire, and in the flame which you have kindled [Isa. 50:10-11]. By these words it seems to be

indicated that every sinner kindles for himself the flame of his own fire, and is not plunged into some fire which has been already kindled by another, or was in existence before himself.[383]

The fire of hell is a personalized fire, coalescing over time from our own guilts and fears. Each of us must walk through the fire we ourselves have kindled and come to a final reckoning as to not only our actions but the thoughts and feelings that spurred them. Gregory of Nyssa similarly viewed the supposed fiery discipline to be akin to the refining of gold in a furnace.[384]

By the time of the New Testament, hell had become fully associated with Ezra's furnace of fire (Mt. 5:22) rather than just the cold underground. Sin or distance from God becomes associated with fire (Mark 9:43), and such fire had been associated with inner torment in the prophet Jeremiah: "there is in my heart as it were a burning fire" (Jer. 20:9). Such torment is expressed forcefully: "Why did I come forth from the womb to see toil and sorrow, and spend my days in shame?" (Jer. 20:18). The world itself, separated from God and from one's own purpose, is hell from this perspective. Yet, fire also holds an association with salvation. For example, John the Baptist says that, whereas he baptizes with water, Jesus will baptize people with "the Holy Spirit and fire" (Mt. 3:11).

Jesus mentions a couple of times a continually burning garbage dump outside Jerusalem called "Gehenna" or the "Valley of Hinnom." This seems to be a symbol of a way of life immersed in mental anguish, which becomes a recurrent living nightmare that is impossible to escape without heavenly assistance. Jesus cites Isaiah 66:22-24, which speaks of "dead bodies," thus annihilation, when he describes hell as a place "where their worm never dies, and the fire is never quenched" (Mark 9:48). So, again the torment is internal and does not continue forever, only while we are "conscious" of lesser ways of being than godhood. What is more terrifying and distressing than the prospect of a cycle of endless return to nothingness? Note

---

[383] Origen, *On First Principles* 2.10.4. ANF04.
[384] Gregory of Nyssa, "*De animâ et resurrectione*" (P.G., XLVI, cols. 100, 101).

that these are all present states: the distress, the anguish, the inner torment, the hopelessness — as is the escape (salvation) from all of it. They are states of mind, psychological states of subjective, internal experience, a too-neglected part of our theology and yet the basis for much of it. As with most internal processes, like deification, the biblical scribes, lacking a technical psychological jargon, used images and metaphors (poetic language) to describe them.

Jesus gives another positive spin to this fire imagery:

> For everyone will be salted with fire. ⁵⁰Salt is good; but if salt has lost its saltiness, how can you restore its saltiness? Have salt in yourselves; be at peace with one another. (Mk. 9:49-50, var.).

Here, the fire we are salted with is meant to restore our "saltiness" (or "saltness"), which seems to be both an inner essence and a state of mind we want to acquire, a calm tranquility that makes for peaceful relationships with others. It is a personal yet relational quality we appear to have once had, but lost somehow. The sense is that we are not truly ourselves when this hidden and inherent characteristic of "saltiness" — our essence — has dissipated from awareness. The "fire" here, with which beings are salted once they lose their inherent saltness, is a restorative one: purifying, sanctifying, and salvific.

His disciples asked Jesus about a Samaritan village that refused to accept them, "Lord, do you want us to bid fire come down from heaven and consume them?" (Luke 9:54). Jesus' reply was sharp:

> But he turned and rebuked them, and he said, 'You do not know that manner of spirit you are of; for the Son of man came not to destroy man's lives, but to save them.' (Luke 9:55)

Jesus is saying here that neither God nor he think in such retributive terms. We are following the wrong spirit when we think vengefully, coercively, or even carelessly about others, even if they themselves seem careless or disagreeable. God seeks to save, not destroy, because he comes always and forever from a place of love rather than discord.

Paul also employs the image of fire as a testing and refining phase through which the temporary is burned off and only the eternal and beautiful works of God — our true selves — will survive:

> [T]he work of each builder will become visible, for the Day will disclose it, because it will be revealed with fire, and the fire will test what sort of work each has done. [14]If what has been built on the foundation survives, the builder will receive a reward. [15]If the work is burned up, the builder will suffer loss; *the builder will be saved, but only as through fire.* (1 Cor. 3:13-15)[385]

Note well that Paul states that "the *builder* will be saved, but only as through fire." The fire does not burn up the inner person, the soul, the essential God-imaged being, but rather purifies by removing anything less. Again, this burning, as with the lake of fire, is an utter forgetting (and in that sense total annihilation) of all things that only reflected a lower reality, i.e., anything inconsistent with the love and truth of God.

We mentioned St. John's argument, expressed clearly in his first Letter, chapter 4, that God, being love, cannot think in terms of fear, and therefore cannot think in terms of punishment. This is by his will and his nature, which are one. Moreover, he created children out of this same nature; he did not make strangers, nor even potential strangers, and even if his children should make themselves out to be strangers, he would not share that judgment.

For most of the patristics, including Origen and Augustine, evil was merely the privation or absence of good, not a thing-in-itself. Thus, it had no substance or being of its own. Evil can only detract from the good, but it cannot overcome it nor stand independently without the good because it depends on that same good for its

---

[385] My emphasis.

existence. Like a parasite reliant on a host, it depends for its seeming existence on lost children of God who have stumbled out of the heaven of total love. Hence, its association with deceit and duplicity. The part of Augustine that viewed hell as an eternally established entity is inconsistent with this idea, whereas his insistence that evil is only the privation of good and the Alexandrian view of hell as a purgative process fit it well. Such ideas signify that no evil truly exists but was once good and will ultimately return to its truth.

Ramelli points out that the apocryphal Apocalypse of Peter (c. 100-150 CE) expresses the universal salvation of the damned in chapter 14. He also comments on a beautiful passage earlier in that same text, in chapters 3-4, when Peter, worrying about the supposed fate of sinners, says to Jesus:

> 'O my Lord, please permit me to quote your own words concerning these sinners, namely, 'Better if they had never been created.' Jesus immediately reminds him of God's mercy: 'O Peter, why do you say that not having been created would have been better for them? It is you who oppose God in this way! But you certainly do not have *more mercy than God has, who created* them.' If Peter pities the damned, but God is said to have even more mercy than Peter has, it is already possible to foresee an outcome of salvation. Immediately after this, Jesus, who is about to speak of the eschatological perspective, tells Peter, who is worrying about the damned, that 'there is nothing that perishes for God, nothing that is impossible for him' (4.5).[386]

The mercy of God, like his goodness and his love, is perfect, meaning it is total and complete. It is only because of the limitations we heaped upon ourselves that the mercy, goodness, and love of God seem infinitely greater than our own. And again, the passage ends suggesting that God does not see or know death, and so our self-imposed punishment is our own, of our own making or in this case, imagining, since "there is nothing that perishes for God."

---

[386] Ramelli 2009: 142.

Heaven

Heaven, like hell, is almost always symbolized as a place, but that place is almost always a symbol itself of a state of mind and being. Jesus teaches that we already know heaven because we came from there. We are familiar with its every aspect because, as Paul states: "our citizenship is in heaven" (Phil. 3:20). The abode of the gods in all its glory and transcendence is where we come from, where we belong, where we feel most comfortable and natural, and where we all will ultimately return. This is why heaven is so closely associated with the Paradise of Eden, our original home. Our heart is there, our longing for home comes from there.

> O Lord, I love the house in which you dwell,
>   and the place where your glory abides. (Ps. 26:8)

If we *love* heaven and *long* for heaven ("the house in which God dwells" and his "glory abides"), then we must already *know* heaven. To love it or long for it is necessarily to have known it. Something within our mind *does* know heaven, and our heart longs for it, but we do not consciously remember it, and so this knowledge and these longings come from elsewhere than our *human* selves.

This interpretation is reinforced by Jesus' many parables about the hiddenness of the kingdom, such as this one:

> The kingdom of heaven is like treasure hidden in a field, which someone found and hid; then in his joy he goes and sells all that he has and buys that field. (Mt. 13.44)

Although it remains for now a "hidden" treasure, we are the ones who hid it. This is how we know the great joy heaven would bring us, for we have known it before and its reality (if not its realization) remains with us. The joy is so great that it attracts us unconsciously long before we recover full cognitive awareness of it. Our burden is lightened with each step in its direction. It is not so much that we will find it, as it will find us. This will happen naturally as we realize increasingly that it is our total joy. The world is too tired to bring us such joy, too distractable to bring anything sustainable, too limited to bring us anything comprehensive. Jesus intended through his teaching to share *his own* true and lasting, complete and eternal joy:

> I have said these things to you so that *my* joy may be in you, and that your joy may be complete. (Jn. 15:11)[387]

Jesus repeats this thought in John 17.13: "But now I am coming to you, and I speak these things in the world so that they may have my joy made complete in themselves." He thus reiterates that he sees his purpose as being to share *his* joy with the world, which entails passing along the being he knows and has realized as well as the heaven which dwells within each.

Jesus teaches that heaven "has come near" and is "at hand" (Mt. 3:20). It is so near that "God, … out of [his] great love," has already "raised us up with him and made us sit with him in the heavenly places" (Eph. 2:4-6), according to which statement, surprisingly, we are already there, in heaven with God. It is as near as our realization of it; we need only change our way of thinking to appreciate it. We have seen that Jesus affirms to his disciples that each of them has a designated "dwelling-place" in heaven, and that they will meet him there and that they "know the way" (Jn. 14:2-4). Likening heaven to a great banquet, Jesus declares that "many" from both "east and west" will "come to eat with Abraham and Isaac and Jacob in the kingdom of heaven" (Mt. 8:11). Many will be surprised by the universalism of heaven and the multitude of divine beings that populate it. *Every* divine being that stumbled out of heaven will stumble back home, and every being of God is a divine being. What truly makes it heaven is that, miraculously, not one is missing.

Every being of God knows the way, having come from there, even while they are unaware. What else do we know without full awareness? Paul states that, from deep within, "we know that if the

---

[387] My emphasis.

earthly tent we live in is destroyed, we have a building from God, a house not made with hands, eternal in the heavens. ²For in this tent we groan, longing to be clothed with our heavenly dwelling" (2 Cor. 5:1-2). Again, these longings for "our heavenly dwelling" come from our natural self. We would not have the longings were they not natural, and had we not known and cherished their object already.

Heaven has not gone anywhere. It is still where it always was, and always will be. It is not far at all, nor situated above the sky although it does transcend the world, its way of thinking and feeling, and even the realm of perception. Heaven exists in the realm of knowledge, which we may share even here on earth. If this knowledge preexists in us, awaiting only our reclamation of it, then "we" never really left heaven. Only a small part of our mind, the remnant of which we are conscious, experiences the fall. It is that remnant that must be saved. It is the wheat that grows among the weeds (Mt. 13:30), the lost coin for which we search diligently (Luke 15:8-9). Although every last scrap of wickedness will be gone, every last one of God's creations will be saved and restored to its original perfection. The builder survives.

It was not God's will that we leave heaven. Therefore, we must still be there. The only way we could leave was to dissociate it from accessible memory, because in doing so we were going against the will of God, which is impossible. Having broken away from God, we were relegated to making and seeing only illusion.

Heaven requires a pure state of mind because heaven *is* a pure state of mind. Thus, it is an interior ascent we make to heaven. Paul describes an experience where he found himself being "caught up into the third heaven" or "Paradise," to the point that he did not know whether he was still in his body or not, and during this "vision" or "revelation," he "heard things that are not to be told, that no mortal is permitted to repeat" (2 Cor. 12:2-4). Words are simply inadequate to describe the vastness and harmony, the difference from human experience. He did not really go anywhere while he was experiencing this "heaven."

In his remarkable spiritual autobiography, *Confessions*, Augustine describes how he and his mother, Monica, while studying and contemplating together, rose by an interior ascent above the thought of corporeal, physical things in their minds and eventually beyond even their individual minds into the vast expanse of a cognitive heaven, "that region of unfailing plenty."[388] As Russell comments regarding this interior yet interrelational pilgrimage in Augustine: "heaven is not up in the sky. It is the totality of all holy souls, in whom God is enthroned." Such is heaven — the highest reality in every mind, where God is still enthroned, and we are in full accord with one another and with our Source.

1 Peter 1:4 states that our inheritance "is imperishable, undefiled, and unfading, kept in heaven for you." This is interesting wording, that this permanent and pristine "inheritance" (our godhood) is "kept in heaven for you." It suggests that when we find our godhood — our imperishability and holiness, our true likeness to God — we will find that we are already in heaven. The divine self comes replete with its own environment just as the human self had. This means that heaven has persisted in our higher mind, even while the lower part of our mind is preoccupied with the world. Our true reality is left untouched and thus unblemished by the world. Here, then, is further scriptural support for the idea of an unfallen or undescended soul.[389]

The stories of Enoch and Elijah, who according to the Hebrew Bible were "translated" into heaven, reiterate that death is not a requirement to enter heaven. It is said of Enoch that he "walked with God: and he was no more; for God took him" (Gen. 5:21-24). Many Jewish and Christian traditions take this to mean that Enoch was lifted into heaven without dying. Thus, he became an early mediator between the human and divine worlds. Additionally, "Elijah ascended in a whirlwind into heaven" (2 Kings 2:11). Death, then, is not a requirement for reaching heaven, for in fact death as a concept does not exist in heaven. Heaven is the state of mind whereby all is life and no opposition exists. All is good, as God declared it from the beginning, and all is loving and loved because this is understood. We

---

[388] Augustine, *Confessions*, IX.10.24, *NPNF* 1:137.
[389] See also the section in Chapter 7, "The Undescended Soul," a concept originating with Plotinus.

will therefore be like those who "touched heaven while standing on the earth" (Wisd. 18:16). For our true being, the one God shares with us, is already "shining in the vault of the heavens!" (Eccles. 43:8).

Oneness

We have mentioned that one of the great themes of the Bible is *"exitus-reditus,"* procession and return, and have pointed out this great theme is related to another great theme: the idea that God is one. Oneness became the prevailing theme of Judaism: "Hear, O Israel: The LORD our God, the LORD is one" (Deuteronomy 6:4), repeated often in practice. God is one in himself, fully integrated, as per the doctrine of divine simplicity, but what we often fail to realize is that this means he is one with his creations and his creations remain one with him. They are one simply because they share the same essence, and if they are one, they *must* share the same essence. True oneness, like true participation, requires it.

Jesus declares the oneness of God with his creations at the climax of his teaching in John's gospel. First, it is foreshadowed in John 14:

> Judas (not Iscariot) said to him, 'Lord, how is it that you will manifest yourself to us, and not to the world?' Jesus answered him, 'If a man loves me, he will keep my word, and my Father will love him, and we will come to him and make our home with him.' (John 14:22-23)

Here, our oneness with Jesus and the Father is based on our common capacity to love: To love at all is to invite an awareness of oneness with God, with Jesus, and with the world. It is also to share an essence and loving nature. In John 17, Jesus prays for the oneness of all "who will believe" with himself and the Father:

> I ask not only on behalf of these, but also on behalf of those who will believe in me through their word, [21]that they may

all be one. As you, Father, are in me and I am in you, may they also be in us, so that the world may believe that you have sent me. ²²The glory that you have given me I have given them, so that they may be one, as we are one, ²³I in them and you in me, that they may become completely one, so that the world may know that you have sent me and have loved them even as you have loved me. ²⁴Father, I desire that those also, whom you have given me, may be with me where I am, to see my glory, which you have given me because you loved me before the foundation of the world. (Jn. 17:20-24)

Everyone will believe when the truth is plain as day. Jesus is speaking universally here about all those who will simply "believe" what he is saying "through their Word," though their own individual portion of Logos, therefore of reason, and therefore of eternal being. It is this eternal being within each being that believes and knows firsthand for them until they can accept their own truth.

His prayer is universal: "that they may all be one" in the same way that he himself is one with the Father (v. 21). He is praying that they may know the same love (v. 23), the same glory (v. 22), and therefore the same essence. The closeness and intimacy of this love is indicated by the mutual indwelling (Greek, *perichoresis*) of the loving parties, each spoken of as being "in" the other. Such perichoresis and coinherence would seem to demand a oneness of essence even more than does participation in God.

The perichoresis is specified in v. 21: "As you, Father, are in me and I am in you, may they also be in us." The boundary lines that we hold sacred are illusory to God and his spirits. He holds his creations in his mind forever and they are suffused with him. The oneness of divine beings, it seems, is known and experienced equally by all sides or participants.

Note that God loves humankind in the same way he loves Jesus: "I in them and you in me, that they may become completely one, so that the world may know that you have sent me and have loved them even as you have loved me" (v. 23). This reinforces that we share the same ontology, the same kind of being, and it suggests that we share a preexistent sentness with Jesus.

Jesus teaches that those who learn from him will become "completely one" (v. 23) with the Father, sharing the same glory and love Jesus himself shared with the Father "before the foundation of the world" (v.24). With the use of this phrase — "before the foundation of the world"— we are going well beyond the idea of oneness as mere shared belief or even shared volition. The oneness described here is with all creation, even primordial. We have entered into the realm of ontological oneness, oneness of being, a oneness so close that nothing can get between it and so complete that it encompasses all beings. Because the mutual indwelling is the same from any side and any participant in the relationship, an ontological sameness, a sameness of being or essence and a full awareness of such sameness, is not only suggested, but demanded.

By the fourth century this extraordinary conception of oneness had been relegated to the three persons of the Trinity, with the rest of humankind excluded. But we should not lose sight that Jesus' prayer in John 17 declares that the glory, the love, and the oneness thereof is inclusive of every individual being. This is a oneness wherein each party retains their subjective sense of being, their individual agency, yet exists in and for and *as* the other. Only the inner being, the mind with heart, can experience such mutual indwelling. Bodies cannot truly merge but only juxtapose; only mind and heart truly join in our most ecstatic and loving moments. With love, and the glory perceived in another, mind and heart leap across all formerly solid barriers (including difference, distance, space, and time) quite easily, spontaneously and naturally. Any time we love or bless, in fact, the whole of heaven rejoices with us because, due to divine oneness, every being receives it. If we can join with those close to us, we *are* doing it, in essence and reality, with everyone.

The mind naturally seeks its natural oneness with God. Philip had earlier asked Jesus, "Lord, show us the Father, and we shall be satisfied" (Jn. 14:8), which provided Jesus an opportunity to explain his relationship to the Father:

> I am in the Father
> and the Father is in me. (John 14:10)

Jesus explains his own relationship with God via the same kind of mutual indwelling human beings are said to have with God in Jn. 17. The relationships are described in the exact same terms. As with his glory and his love and his joy, three essential aspects of his being, Jesus does not reserve *anything* for himself only. After all, he had said, very graciously:

> All that the Father has is mine;
> therefore I said that he will take what is mine
> and declare it to you. (John 16:15)

Like God, Jesus holds nothing back in his giving. He seeks to share all he has *and is* with us, his entire being, his essence, his essential relationship with God — this is what it means to share his love, his glory, and his joy — thus to be saved and restored.

This is precisely why we do ourselves a disservice to think that he has something we do not or cannot have. It is right to exalt him, yet he does not seek praise from human beings, but rather fellowship with fellow gods. It is to this end that he has already identified with the least among us. Even as the regal Son of Man appearing in his glory, he *identified* with every last person. Therefore, "as you did it to one of the least of these my brethren, you did it to me" (Mt. 25:40). The oneness here is total and extreme.

Such mutual identification is reinforced by Jesus' teaching about his interchangeability with those he sends out into the world (as he was sent). He tells his disciples: "He who receives you receives me" (Mt. 10:40). Such a statement reduces any ontological distantiation between them. It speaks instead of a kind of corporate oneness among *all* people, Jesus included, and *all* spiritual beings, ourselves included. Thus, wherever two or three are gathered, he is there (Mt. 18:20) and we are there. Whenever two minds agree, he is there (Mt. 18:19) and we are there. In the least and lost of this world, he is there and we are there. The oneness even to the fullest extent with God is mutual.

For us to be one with the Father as Jesus is one with the Father would mean that we share the same type of being with both Jesus and the Father. And to share the same type of being is to share the same essence, substance, and nature. Oneness with God like participation with God requires sameness of essence. We can know this oneness even while embodied in a physical world, but we cannot know this *as* bodies inhabiting a physical world. Therefore, we must have more than one possible way of being and knowing within our mind.

One in the Son and Christ

As with deification, the Bible speaks of oneness using various mediating images. We have seen how sonship (thinking of ourselves as children of God and beings like God) works as a deifying image, drawing us closer to our transcendent Father not by drawing him down but by believing ourselves to be raised up to his level of being. In this section, we will explore how such sonship, seen in light of the oneness we have been discussing, grants us a sense of oneness that encompasses not only God but all creation.

We have mentioned that the phrase "the Son of God" was employed to express a corporate or collective being shared by many beings or souls. We have seen that Jesus associates immortality with belief in "the Son": "He who believes in the Son has eternal life" (John 3:36). Belief in the Son is more than intellectual assent to Jesus himself, or any external being. It is an entirely new level of being within ourselves, an ontological reality and identity we all might experience. God knows his creation as one because he is one. This is why God says in Isaiah 48:12, "When I call to them, They stand forth together."

The sayings about the Son apply, not only to Jesus, but to all who learn from him. This special relationship was once reserved for kings like David and Solomon, and we have seen that it was applied to angels and Israel eventually, but Jesus says all who believe in the Son come to share the Son's eternal life and relationship with God. As John says: "He who has the Son has life" (1 Jn. 5:12).[390] This is the same permanent life in oneself that John referenced in his gospel:

> For just as the Father has life in himself, so he has granted the Son also to have life in himself. (Jn. 5:26)

To believe in the Son is to become the Son, thus to realize that we have been given life in ourselves. As we conform to our own innate and personal sonship, we naturally participate in this one being or family composed of many beings.

Jesus as Son of God is the image of this Son that humans are growing into, that is, remembering. Everything that is said about "the Son" has application to ourselves as not only participants but equals in this greater sense of being with its Godlike parameters. Like "the Logos" or "the Word," "the Son" is at root a sense of collective being that came to be known as the second person of the Trinity.

This interpretation gives new meaning to the familiar passage, "For God so loved the world that he gave his only Son, that whoever believes in him should not perish but have eternal life" (John 3:16). The passage is talking about believing in the universal Son *in oneself and others*. It is an "only" Son because it is one. Jesus becomes, not exclusively this Son, but rather a true representation and image of this Son for all who would partake in this greater sense of conjoined being and its immortal nature.[391] He becomes an archetype for all those who would believe and then come to partake in the same eternal life and happiness. Hebrews 1:3 states: "His Son is the radiance of his glory, the very image of his substance." The Son is the part of our being that emanated directly from God. Human beings *are*, beneath the surface, the glory and radiance of God. Does this mean that they share the same substance and life in themselves? Here again is a confirmation of ontological identity, and

---

[390] Cf. 1 Jn. 3:36; 4:9.
[391] See esp. John 6:29-58 wherein Jesus calls himself "the bread of life" leading to eternal life for all who believe in his sentness.

universal restoration as well: one essence we share with all other beings, including God.

Origen expanded on Paul's analogy of all people sharing the same spiritual body to express his belief in a kind of *world soul* or collective being composed of all souls:

> [A]s our one body is provided with many members, and is held together by one soul, so I am of the opinion that the whole world also ought to be regarded as some huge and immense animal, which is kept together by the power and reason of God as by one soul.[392]

This "world soul," like the Son and the Word, is the sum of all souls. It is not an animal so much as it is a spiritual being comprised of many spiritual beings. Although we think of ourselves as individual minds inhabiting individual bodies, on another even higher level we work together as one great interconnected being, the Son of God, with a power and life in ourselves like our Father's.

Plato had envisioned a world soul (Gk., "psychè kósmou"; Latin, *anima mundi*), a soul or mind of the cosmos, related to the demiurge and the seven planets.

> Thus, then, in accordance with the likely account, we must declare that this Cosmos has verily come into existence as a Living Creature endowed with soul and reason ... a Living Creature, one and visible, containing within itself all the living creatures which are by nature akin to itself.[393]

When all beings are spirit, their oneness is self-evident. It is only when they entered bodies, even protozoic bodies, that competition became the order of the day. Plato associates the world soul with the demiurge, thus associating the creation of the world with ourselves. We are the makers, not only of the world systems under

---

[392] Origen, *De Principiis (On First Principles)* 2.1.3. (*ANF* 4:269).
[393] Plato, Timaeus 30b–d. W.R.M. Lamb, trans. *Plato* (1925).

which we now live (and often cannot see beyond), but also of the material world itself.

If indeed all souls comprise one greater being, then those who realize this would no longer be driven solely by self-interest because they would see themselves in others and others in themselves. Each being becomes more significant in our eyes, more cherished, more essential, as we realize their happiness and inner well-being is our own, and ours theirs. Our loving thoughts would go out like angels to help and protect them.

Along similar lines, let us explore another mediating image that we have only touched on previously. And that is the ultimate *Christhood* of believers. In his Letter to the Galatians, Paul tells his audience: "you are all one in Christ Jesus" (Gal. 3:28). Their oneness in Christ is more than flowery words and more even than community-building. It expresses a different ontological reality and identity for us as much as sonship does. Paul expounds upon this oneness in his later letters, saying: "Now you are the body of Christ and individually members of it" (1 Corinthians 12.27) and:

> [S]o we, who are many, are one body in Christ, and individually we are members one of another. (Romans 12.5)

Paul is using the word "body" figuratively in the passage above, for as he says elsewhere, "The body is not meant for immorality, but for the Lord" (1 Cor. 6:13) and "while we are at home in the body we are away from the Lord" (2 Cor. 5:6). The physical body hides our true immortality and oneness with the Lord,[394] reminiscent of how Adam and Eve hid from God among the trees in the Garden in Gen. 3:10.

To be "individually members one of another" indicates the same kind of mutual indwelling or perichoresis we saw in John 17, suggesting a loss of the boundary lines of temporary embodiment we have drawn around ourselves to exclude others. Paul informs us

---

[394] Paul contrasts our physical body with a more "spiritual" or "pneumatic" body in 1 Cor. 15:44 ("It is sown a physical body, it is raised a spiritual body. If there is a physical body, there is also a spiritual body"). He speaks of them as two separate bodies, but the spiritual body might more precisely be termed a "being."

that we are distinct individual minds who are, remarkably, also parts of one greater being called "Christ," a Greek word that means "the Anointed." It has roots in the Hebrew messiah or Savior concept in the Bible and shares a root with the English word used for baptism or any "anointing": "christening." The concept had by Jesus' time long been associated with preexistence via the concept of "sentness," the idea that the messiah was waiting in heaven to be sent by God into this world to raise this world to a new level of thinking and being and to distinguish definitively between good and evil.

Paul compares our oneness in Christ to the Eucharistic meal, or Holy Communion, saying: "Because there is one bread, we who are many are one body, for we all partake of the one bread" (1 Cor. 10:16-17). It is the oneness and sameness that is emphasized here. Paul expands upon the sacraments' deeper meaning later in the same letter:

> For just as the body is one and has many members, and all the members of the body, though many, are one body, so it is with Christ. [13]For by one Spirit we were all baptized into one body -- Jews or Greeks, slaves or free -- and all were made to drink of one Spirit. [14]For the body does not consist of one member but of many. (1 Cor. 12:12-14)

Both the Eucharist and our baptism "by one Spirit" are signs of an underlying oneness of being, one that has nothing to do with surface distinctions and divisions like social or ethnic class. This is not a mere congregational oneness because while it may begin with believers, it expands from there to include *all* people, regardless of their beliefs and practices, ecclesial or otherwise. This is how Christ saves the entire world — through *our* renewed perception and revelation of unity. And it is not a mere community or regional oneness because it includes *all* spiritual beings. Such is our oneness, in fact, that it results in shared thought and feeling: "If one member suffers, all suffer together; if one member is honored, all rejoice together" (1 Cor. 12:26). We begin to think and feel together as one being. Often such empathy begins with a few trusted persons through whom we learn of oneness, but it generalizes naturally onto others once the floodgates are opened.

Minds are not partitioned as the existence of bodies would make it appear. Thoughts and feelings flow freely despite the presence of bodies. After all, if we as individual spirits are said to comprise a sense of unified being, and if this oneness extends even to God — as in "But he who is united to the Lord becomes one spirit with him" (1 Cor. 6:17) — then there is nothing to separate us from *any* mind or heart, or *any* being, even God, except the artificial walls we impose upon our thinking. He is famously abstract: able to commune with all beings at once. This is the source of his omniscience and omnipresence, his all-knowing nature and his ability to *be* everywhere at once. We are already interconnected at this deepest level, but we have decided to deny this fact to forge our own circuitous path. This denial is the source of all our problems.

Paul exclaims: "in Christ shall *all* be made alive" (1 Cor. 15:22, my italics). Christ *is* life itself, the true life of "all." Thus, Paul is speaking to everyone, even nonbelievers, when he says: "Do you not realize that Jesus Christ is in you?" (2 Cor. 13:5). This is a more serious responsibility than we had assumed. We have seen that we share sonship with him, that we are all children of God, one with God and with one another, and what that means, what a weighty responsibility, a tremendous freedom, and a supreme power that entails.

The Pauline tradition continues in this vein: "When Christ who is our life appears, then you also will appear with him in glory" (Colossians 3:4). The idea that Christ is "our life" and that we "will appear with him in glory" indicates that this is our true being. This is reaffirmed by John's statement that by the time we see him, we will already be like him (1 Jn. 3:2). Overall, Paul speaks of this Christhood as a "new creation," different from the one we know as human beings:

> From now on, therefore, we regard no one from a human point of view; even though we once knew Christ from a

human point of view, we know him no longer in that way. ¹⁷So if anyone is in Christ, there is a new creation: everything old has passed away; see, everything has become new! (2 Cor. 5:16-17)

Knowing Christ from "a human point of view," we did not know him at all — not the way he knew himself. It is only by becoming what he is that we know him. Only by knowing ourselves in the same way he knows himself will we truly know him. The transcendence of our old, narrow way of thinking encouraged by this passage is obvious and total. This "Christ" that we inhabit via mutual indwelling and simple desire to do so allows us to see all things from a transcendent, more-than-human point of view. We represent a "new creation," which, as we have been saying, is not really new, but original and most ancient. But it is "new" to our human point of view.

Paul is speaking not only of a relative parity between believers and Christ, but of a true oneness of being whereby they realize they are part of him, part of a greater being than they had formerly imagined for themselves. What this means in heaven is that our minds are abstract and interconnected with all other beings. What it means on earth is that we may truly be called Christs, saviors, to one another as they are to us.

In the Hebrew Bible, Noah saved a remnant of humans and animals from the flood. Moses saved the Israelites from slavery in Egypt. The kings of Israel were considered anointed saviors, messiahs in Hebrew, Christs in Greek, beginning with the first two, Saul and David. Isaiah 45:1 had declared Cyrus the Great of Persia to have been a Savior, a messiah, a Christ, because he had liberated the Jewish people from exile in Babylon and tolerated their religious traditions. Many of the prophets themselves were anointed. Thus, Isaiah (61:1) says: "The spirit of the Lord God is upon me, because the Lord has anointed (*mashach*) me." 1 Chronicles 16:22 states: "Do not touch my anointed ones (*mashiyach*); do my prophets no harm." [395] There are plural saviors here. Nehemiah 9:27 states: "according to your great mercies you gave them saviors who saved

---

[395] Repeated in Psalm 105:15.

them from the hands of their enemies." Obadiah 1:21 states that "Saviors shall go up to Mount Zion to rule Mount Esau; and the kingdom shall be the Lord's."[396] Jeremiah 3:15 promised that God would send many shepherds to tend to his flocks: "I will give you shepherds after my own heart, who will feed you with knowledge and understanding." Also, Jer. 23:4, who prophecies a true universalism: "I will raise up shepherds over them who will shepherd them, and they shall not fear any longer, or be dismayed, nor shall any be missing, says the Lord."

Perhaps then there are meant to be many saviors after Christ, part of Christ, and part of his work in any world. Perhaps all is orchestrated toward this end, particularly if *all* are to be saved. Indeed they are already aspects of Christ, our saviors in this world, part of the one great interconnected being, just as they are meant to be sons and daughters, part of the one great Son, and gods, part of the one great God. We cannot easily discount at least the possibility, particularly considering that they are predestined to be deified and deify others in the process.

Conclusion

Like everything else about God, his patience is infinite. Thus, it is unfathomable in the world and in time. We as human beings cannot even begin to understand it. Only a mind that has risen fully above the world to experience timeless reality can begin to understand it. Thus, when we see it written, plain for all to see, that God's intention is to save *all* his creation, we cannot believe it possible. Our own judgments and presumptions favoring judgment, condemnation and exclusivity stand in the way. When we see it written that God "is patient with you, not wanting any to perish, but all to come to repentance" (2 Pet. 3:9), we believe this to be an idle wish on God's part, a hope against hope, not the statement of an omnipotent God whose will *must* be done.

---

[396] Alternate translation in the NRSV.

Only a fully restorative return to a full godhood does justice to God, the Creator of perfection, and to his perfect creation. There can be no greater unearned grace than our original perfect creation by God. We did nothing to earn our perfect timeless being; we do more, frankly, to earn our "unearned" salvation, our restoration, our secondary and necessary grace. Thus, the dichotomy between grace and nature does not hold. We are graced with an eternal nature.

Only a fully restorative, ontologically-based deification lends itself to a complete and total oneness such as that specified in John 17. If true participation requires sameness of being, essence and nature, then true oneness requires them even more. If we are one with all beings, and they are one with us, then we all share the same basic nature. If we are one with God as well, then this one basic nature must be his as well.

The great and universal restoration, the *apokatastasis*, like the world-ending *eschaton*, is both present and future. We experience it individually in the most present of moments, while in time the full restoration seems to await the full return of every soul. With each experience of it, or contemplation of it, we see the parts begin to interconnect which gives us glimpses of the whole. We begin to realize how great a sense of being can be and how all-inclusive it is. We learn what equality means as we discover gradually and organically our oneness with all beings.

Origen envisioned the end as a return to the beginning, deification as a restoration of the mind's original condition. Yet he boldly supersedes what has come to be known as a doctrine of "conditional immortality."[397] There is no conditional immortality; there is only ontological immortality. It is characteristic of our being or it is not. God is nothing if not thoroughly consistent. What God gives is truly given, freely given, and forever *ours*. The mind he gave us is entirely free to receive and remember its divine reality whenever we want it, or to hold it off and wait. What *seems* conditional is when we decide to accept what is true. Yet, once we do accept it, we realize the outcome was inevitable — just because it is true.

---

[397] See Bauckham 1978: 47.

Evil and carelessness will dissolve back into the nothingness from which they sprang. Origen relates this to an idea never far from his mind, that God will be "all in all," stating:

> God will be all, for there will no longer be any distinction of good and evil, seeing evil nowhere exists; for God is all things, and to Him no evil is near.[398]

Not even the slightest trace of lovelessness can subsist in the presence of God, truth, reality, or our true selves. This is why it needs to be separated out from our minds. For both God's love and the object of God's love must be eternal, and the same is true of ourselves and all we love.

Although we are individually children of God, all together every child comprises one Son, reflecting the oneness of God himself. This is why we *must* work together, even without conscious agreement, and why *not one part* may be excluded from the greater whole. Because "the Son" can be thought of as the original or higher Self within each human being, we are able to find the same Child of God in others as well as ourselves. Because we are drawn back to the original oneness of being, there is cooperation and total inclusiveness even if it is unconscious. The divine image and sonship we see in others is the exact same we find in ourselves; in fact, it is by seeing it in *any* other that it reveals itself in us and then in all the world.

---

[398] Origen, *De Principiis* 3.6.3. (*ANF* 4:345).

CONCLUSION:

WHERE HUMANITY MEETS DIVINITY

We have been searching in our study for the underlying structure of mind indicated by the idea of deification. We have traced both ideas back through the patristics and back further still to their sources in the Bible. We have pointed out similarities and contrasts with the prevailing philosophical and extracanonical teachings of the day. And at the same time, we sought to explain what this all means experientially to the individual mind.

My argument throughout this book is that deification and therefore salvation is as sure and certain as God. That is because deification is a *restoration* of godhood we already possess rather than a future *acquisition* of godhood, or even a *transformation* into godhood. We are not newly made into gods or changed into gods from something else. We either began as gods or we did not. The gulf between human and divine natures is too wide to cross, and the complications too enormous, for such a revolutionary transformation. This problem is resolved if only the mind needs transformed, and back into the godhood it originally had. We are gods now, walking about in the flesh, but fail to realize it.

How are we already gods when we are also human beings? One part of this uneasy alliance has been added to the original part. The question is which came first, not so much in time (although that, too) as in primacy of being. Does the transitory part come first, followed by the eternal part, or does the eternal part come first because, being timeless, it is as eternal going backwards as it is going forward? Which is contingent or dependent on the other?

The original part of the human being is the divine image, the sonship, the god within. That is who we are eternally as creations of God. *We* added the creaturely part to supplant the divine part, to replace it and substitute for it, to dissociate from the divine part and utterly forget it. It was a way of convincing ourselves that we are not the gods God created us to be. Because we forgot both God and ourselves so diligently, we grew to fear both as if we did something horribly wrong, but cannot remember what it was, or how or when. Only the vestige of distorted guilt remains.

While most patristics did believe that humans were destined to restoration of the paradisal state of the original creation, they differed on exactly what that original state was. There is a proclivity even among patristics to see our *current* limited state as our created state of being, so that grace must now be added to transform it into a new and entirely different state. However, this unnecessarily complex process of transformation from one kind of being to another, infinitely higher, is avoided by simply positing a perfect creation that fell. What else would a flawless, entirely spiritual God create except perfect, complete, and independent spiritual beings like himself? What else would he *know* to create? There is nothing else *to* know.

We have seen that Jesus used the term "gods" to apply to human beings, and at the same time equated "children of God" with these "gods."[399] We have seen how early Christian theologians, Justin and Irenaeus among them, found in this proclamation by Jesus the real *telos* of Christianity, its ultimate aim and overarching purpose, which was for human beings to "become gods." Only this could truly save. They found this idea taking shape in the Hebrew Bible, particularly in the Book of Genesis which states that "God created humankind in his image" (1:27), a tantalizing clue that there is something more truly wondrous, even majestic about human beings than the world lets on.

We have observed that Irenaeus introduced into theology the exchange formula for deification circa 170 CE, an encapsulation of Christianity saying that Jesus became human so that humans might become gods. This was the essence, to him, of both Christianity and its teaching of deification. We have seen that nearly every patristic writer after him for the next 1,500 years offered their

---

[399] Jn. 10:34-35, which cites Ps. 82:1, 6-7.

own version of the exchange formula: God (or a god, i.e., the Word) became human so that humans might be gods. The question is, how does it operate? Did Jesus' incarnation into a body trigger a kind of mechanistic spiritualization of material substance, or is it simply through doing his words that we become gods? Jesus himself says it is about doing his words, and more specifically states that we become children of God (therefore gods) when we allow ourselves to love like God.[400] Thus, we become gods from the inside, through a divine emotion we already possess but have denied and repressed.

We have seen that human beings are able to partake in the essential nature (*ousia*) of God (1 Pet. 1:4). This means we have all been given a share of *his* being, and not a partial share, miraculously, but each a complete share. He created us out of himself, a natural extension of his being, an increase in infinity. If we were created in the divine image, as gods and as children of God, meant to partake in his essence and being, then why do we not realize this now? If we started out as gods, which *must* be true considering who God is, his timeless nature and his perfect thoughts, his goodness and his love, then we have fallen so far from our former transcendent identity that we now stand outside it. We should be careful not to assume the fallen state is our true state, no matter how self-evident it may appear. It is more a privation of our original timeless state, born into time and thus incomplete, always in the process of becoming, never quite stable, temporary, and having nowhere here to rest its head. This is not the original being created by God to relate to him. Yet, it must exist somewhere, this original perfect creation, within our innermost being, our mind and heart and essence, because the eternal and perfect God placed it there.

It is difficult for most people, including theologians, to believe that God created very different kinds of beings than nature manifests. Yet, is it not even more difficult philosophically to accept that God would have created creatures so very *different* from himself? God's perfection demands that all God's thoughts be perfect and remain transcendent as he. So, where among his perfect thoughts was there space for a creation that was unlike him in nearly

---

[400] Mt. 5:44-45; para. Luke 6:35.

every way: limited, dependent, incomplete, and subject to corruption, decay, and death? God had no hand in any of this, God did not create *us* for any of this, and so, God did not create us human, nor animal, nor creaturely, but rather as gods, divine beings like himself.

Consider that only beings who are perfect and complete would be able to join with God as one and experience true godhood. We were given more than the potentiality for perfection because God abides in timelessness, without need of development and thus of potentiality. We must therefore have been given the complete perfect reality from the timeless beginning, which means we have always had it and always will.

It only makes sense that this flawless and divine creation still exists within our mind and that it precedes and preexists our physical manifestation, our world, and everything we think we know. But, because we have buried it so deeply in ourselves, we have placed ourselves in a position where we need to consent for it, ask for it, search it out, and remain vigilant for its answer, so as to slowly and organically activate our own essential transcendent reality. The slow and gradual nature of the change is a paeon to our resistance. This process of recovery of the lost reality must be separate and distinct from the original perfect creation.

The Holy Spirit orchestrates this secondary process on an intricate basis, using the things and beings of the world, including scripture, relationships, and everyday situations, to elicit by degrees our own inner spirit. It activates our inner spirit which we find is already joined in its purpose. The devil is the stumbling block, the prosecutor run amok, the accuser in our mind, magnifying our faults and those of others so that our original innocence remains overlooked. The Holy Spirit, orchestrator of natural religion for all the world from its beginning to its end, is our Advocate, Comforter, and nonjudgmental Counselor. It is our appeal to reason, to honesty and openness, to responsibility, our own, and universality, also our own. As such, it is our reminder of original innocence and transcendence whenever we are tempted to forget, and keeper for us of our true Self until we can again appreciate it.

If God creates only perfect beings, then he creates equal beings, beings that are equally and maximally perfect. As our changed perception, shorn of past judgments, preconceptions, and temporary differences allows us to glimpse perfection in imperfection, we learn of the true justice of God, his infinite mercy, fairness, and kindness to all. At the same time, we learn that no one but ourselves withheld both this higher perception and knowledge from ourselves. It is only we, as gods, who could have deprived ourselves of godhood.

As the shared substance between Father and Son became the crucial emphasis in Christian theology in its fourth century, a distinction between Jesus' sonship and our own was unfortunately stressed with it. As Jesus became singularly God, we became increasingly only human, even when there was common agreement that Jesus had become human so that we might become gods and share in the divine reality. We became bystanders instead, on the outside looking in. Jesus was pedestaled to the point that we no longer shared anything with him. And our own sense of godhood suffered accordingly.

Most patristics believed that immortality is *earned* via a virtuous life, rendering it conditional, while a fully restorative deification would say that immortality is instead *realized* via a virtuous life because it was fully given in the timeless beginning. The mind's natural sense of immortality is evoked and becomes self-evident through the moral sense to see others (however different in the world) as like ourselves, but the reality had been fully given at our creation. We are asked to believe only what is already true. Jesus' simple prescription for experiencing eternal life was to love God with the entirety of one's being and love one's neighbors as oneself.[401] It is the same prescription for becoming (or realizing ourselves to be) children of God.

We have argued that when God gives, he gives fully (perfectly) of himself; he gives everything, all at once, to all beings, all his children. And so, when he created us in his image, he gave us everything we could ever want, including immortality and eternal

---

[401] As in Luke 10:25-28 and parallels.

life. And this life-in-itself that he has given us is unconditional and non-rescindable. The *only* condition is whether we accept it or not. But even then, we do possess it even if we believe we do not.

Logically speaking, *either* God created beings out of nothing (*ex nihilo*) or out of Himself (*ex Theos*). These are the two possibilities of creation, not that God was limited thereby. If God created out of himself, then we, his creations, carry something of eternal God within us now, no matter how far from his reality we may roam. And, because it begins in his most holy Mind, all God's creation remains rooted within the Mind of God, which for us means that it can never really be lost. It is held safely for us in heaven. Our original reality awaits only our acknowledgement. Its reality remains safe in God, for however long we are away.

We should not disparage the moral and ethical approaches to deification by relegating them to subordinate categories leading to some supposed "analogical" godhood. After all, we have seen that Jesus' teaching centered on such moral assimilation (i.e., the capacity to love like God) as *the* way to realize sonship, which sonship represents (even by its name) an ontological relationship and a living potential within ourselves, a true godhood, meant to be fully realized and thus restored, and these are qualities that we received from our Father long *before* the foundation of the world.

We have argued that the self-evident dual nature of human beings, whereby each side of ourselves is opposed to the other, must be traced back to a dual creation, an original perfect creation followed by a fallen creation. The early Christians believed the world itself is run (even inadvertently) and ruled over by evil, whether death or the devil, and so this split we find both in the world and ourselves indicates the addition of a second creator, a demiurge, and that demiurge cannot be God, nor the Word, nor Christ, nor the Spirit; it can be no other than ourselves as fallen gods, working collectively to produce and inhabit a reality that does not include God. But this collective and consensual demiurge can only do so much; it cannot change reality itself, but only present a shadowy and ultimately illusory and unsatisfying alternative. Yet even in this, because we are gods, created by perfection, even fallen, there remain remnants of perfection, made perceptible to us by our belief in them.

We have seen that the real part of our nature remains transcendent; that is, it remains complete and perfect despite the rags of illusion with which we have cloaked ourselves. This unfallen and unshaken part is the undescended soul, our protective higher mind, which remains in heaven with God and part of God in accord with God's unbreakable will. It is the core of sanity that remains forever as it ever was, a true foundation for our mind, a sanity and stability to which we long to return. It is then, like love and relationship with God, already there in heaven, contemplating the infinite reality it shares with its Creator and all creation.

God's creation, eternal like himself, spirited like himself, remains as it ever was. Its changelessness is part of its divine simplicity and its organic naturalness to us, despite the introduction of unnatural complexity into our minds and into the world. This original creation had purest being long before time began, and will retain purest being long after time has run its course. It is preexistent, as eternal as God, from outside of time, and has primacy over anything in time. It is our joy and our true "life."

Truth manifests in the world in many different ways, but it does not belong to the world. Faced with truth, the world and self made for deception recede into the background of our awareness. Consciousness itself is shown to have very little relation to the truth in our mind simply because it was intended to keep it out. The world does not end in the face of truth, but it does recede for the moment it takes to notice its secondary nature, putting it in proper perspective. No longer is the world the seat of reality; that was reserved for *us*.

What does it take to change a mind? Although it very well may happen in an instant, it takes more than we might realize, because the mind is beholden to preestablished thoughts with long-term consequences. Once it is "set" on a certain way of being, it becomes very resistant to change. It needs to "repent," to admit its ignorance, which incidentally is a reclamation of its power to decide, and come to "believe" with atypical evidence in a different way of being, if it is going to uncover the knowledge of God. Its new belief will inspire study and a surveyance ultimately of every aspect of its belief system. And this is how its new belief will help it reset itself gradually over time.

Legalistic theories about salvation, particularly those related to sacrifice, were distant and ancient even in Jesus' time. Jesus insisted we should exceed the standards of ancient times. We need to find the new standards, rooted in God as we are, if we are going to begin to see salvation from the higher vantage point. Jesus proposed that love is the standard because it brought about a more substantial relationship with God, as his children, beings like him, than legalistic or sacrificial theories ever dreamt of.

God does not induce nor even encourage fear, but total love. He cannot be both at once because of their oppositional nature. He must therefore be one or the other. As much fear as we apply or project onto him diminishes the love he actually is, giving us the wrong impression of not only him but also ourselves and humankind in general. The fear is our own; the love is all his, but what is his is ours, if we can accept it.

APPENDICES

Restoration and the Patristics

Many theologians ancient and modern walk right up to the line of an innate divine element in human beings, only to pull back at the last moment. They make some interesting contortions to refrain from viewing deified human beings as actual gods, although they do call them "gods" in the way Jesus had in John 10. For some of them, even in the afterlife there is no real godhood, but instead an inexorable striving towards it, which continual striving without resolution might seem to resemble hell rather than heaven.

Most of the inconsistencies among the church fathers as regards the true nature of our deification stem from the many qualifications they had to weave into it to combat the hydra-headed Gnosticism and other doctrinal challenges. Their own reasoning was contorted at times when faced with such questions. As the Gnostics were in general more aligned with Platonic thinking, the patristics took it upon themselves most often, despite their learnedness in the intricacies of such philosophy, and despite their having awarded posthumously to Plato and Plotinus an honorary Christian salvation, to veer away from it in haphazard reactivity and thus to lose themselves in philosophical quandaries and dead ends.

And so, on the one hand, we are so close to God that we are said to be "like him" and eternally united with him. Yet, on the other hand, the divine element cannot fully overcome our "creaturely nature." On the one hand, we were created in God's image, and yet we are to some theologians only images of images, imperfect copies lest God's perfection somehow be depleted like ink in a printer. Irenaeus upholds the assumption that only God is uncreated; everything created must therefore be inferior to him. Yet the fact that God "could have" created perfect beings like himself means that there is no necessity to Irenaeus' belief. It is dependent upon a supposed whim of God which is otherwise uncharacteristic of him. Nispel quotes Irenaeus: "Inasmuch as they are not uncreated, for this reason do they come short of the perfect." Nispel comments: "Since mankind was not uncreated and therefore not perfect, a process leading to perfection was required."[402] Even the illustrious Clement of Alexandria was hesitant in this regard.

There are simple answers to all these concerns. If God created us to be like himself and in his image, then we in some sense share his essential goodness. As love is his goodness and his essence, the gift of his love as our being at creation is a giving of *himself* in a literal way. Moreover, if our godhood was given fully at the moment of our creation, then it must still be available to us. A gift of God's self is the epitome of irrevocable and permanent. "For the gifts and the call of God are irrevocable" (Romans 11:29). Our true godly self is always with us even if we teach ourselves not to notice. And what is restored to us as our "deification" is the full identification with this godhood. It is not, as has so often been assumed, something new that is added to us, nor a total transformation from one nature to another. Rather, it is the restoration of an original identity we have relinquished and denied. This solution combines elements of Eastern father Origen and his followers like Gregory of Nazianzus with some elements from Western fathers (like Hilary, Augustine, Anselm, and Thomas Aquinas), all of whom left room for a shared essence between humankind and God.

Early Latin theologian Tertullian saw the flesh as chronologically prior to the soul, which highlighted the flesh as the focus of salvation as well as of divine reality itself. In my view, this is rendered most unlikely by considering the priority of spirit or soul based on its eternal timelessness; it remains outside of time *despite* the manifestation of the body.[403]

---

[402] Nispel 1999: 299, citing Iren., *Adv. Haer.*, 4.38.1.
[403] Tertullian, *De Resurrectione mortuorum* 53.12 (CCL 2 999.40-45); Scully 2011: 127.

Tertullian writes that body and soul are created at the same moment and in the same way, with each human birth, which makes him an early champion of creationism, but he seems to leave open the possibility that the soul is first. Givens comments on Tertullian's equivocation: "Such vacillation and caution reveal a church in which burgeoning heresies made orthodox boundaries imperative, even as scriptural resources often proved inadequate to the task."[404] I have attempted to show that it is not scriptural resources that prove inadequate, but almost always our self-constrictive interpretation of them. This still fledgling church included his contemporaries Irenaeus and Clement, soon to be followed by Origen. Each had their own way of answering these questions, while responding to Gnostic and Middle Platonic points in these formative years of the church.

Early Gnostics and proto-Gnostic Christians like the Egyptians Basilides and Valentinus raised some valid questions and points about the nature of the world and God and ourselves. Valentinus' Gospel of Truth is a succinct, poetically philosophical summation of deification as a return and rest of souls in the Pleroma or "fullness" of divine reality. As we have seen, the scriptures contain their own proto-gnostic concepts, expressed with different imagery and less mythology. The questions that arose were similar for both church and these proto-gnostics. Is the world as we know it really worthy of being called the creation of a perfect and loving God? Is it not in its current condition more reminiscent of the fall, thus a fallen world? The personified God of the Hebrew Bible was not always to be taken literally because of some of the motives imputed to him in those ancient texts. Just as Plato and the pre-Socratic philosophers moved beyond the humanlike personality-driven gods of Homeric mythology, so would Judaism and Christianity need to do the same.

It was common among thinkers in the ancient world to believe that spirit was a more refined type of matter, like "aether," thought to have been lighter than air. This interpretation, while helpful to the ancients in responding to the proto-Gnostics and docetists,[405] for instance, does not match the New Testament

---

[404] Givens 2010: 90.

[405] Early Christians and Gnostics who believed Jesus never really took on flesh.

evidence. The materialistic view was promoted by Irenaeus, Tertullian, Athanasius, and Basil the Great. Cyril of Alexandria also rejects Origen's anthropology and his vision of human beings as fallen minds who can rise back up to their original state of being. The ontological divide was deepening and the emphasis on the deified flesh of the incarnate Logos entered to supplant it.

A more spiritual or noetic view similar to Origen's was taken by Gregory of Nazianzus, Gregory of Nyssa, Eusebius (the early church historian), Diadochus, Evagrius, Didymus, and a few others. Gregory of Nazianzus followed Origen in postulating an innate propensity toward God within the human being.[406] This does not come from our creaturely nature, but rather from the divine "breath of God" from Gen. 2:7. His friend Gregory of Nyssa insisted that:

> To allow participation in God, there must, of necessity, be something in the nature of the participant which is akin to that in which it participates. This is why Scripture says that man was born in the image of God. It was surely that he could see as like does to like. For the vision of God is unquestionably the life of the soul.[407]

For Nyssa, this natural kinship with God comes from both the inborn divine image (Gen. 1:27) and the breath of God which birthed the soul (Gen. 2:7).

In the succeeding centuries, the influential theologian known as Pseudo-Dionysius returns to Origen's idealistic idea that human and divine nature meet and connect in the mind. The only question is the degree of overlap. Maximus later speaks of *logoi* (minds) in order to rehabilitate Origen and Nazianzus, leaving open the possibility of thinking of human beings as multiple *logoi* or pre-existent minds.[408] Maximus distinguishes between the image and likeness in such a way that we do have eternal being by nature, but

---

[406] See McGuckin 2007: 102.
[407] Gregory of Nyssa, *Discourse on Children. Gregorii Nysseni Opera*. Ed. E Muhlenberg. Leiden. 1996.Vol. 3.2. p.79; McGuckin 2007:108.
[408] Russell 2004: 274.

we also have free will as to whether or not to participate in it.[409] Such a statement is fully consistent with a fully restorative deification.

We have noted that Augustine distinguishes between deification by grace versus by nature in his interpretation of Psalm 82:6 ("I have said, You are gods, and all of you sons of the Most High").[410] Despite this direct statement reiterated by Jesus in Jn. 10, in Augustine's opinion only Jesus is a true Son of God; everyone else is *made* a god by way of grace, which would seem to preclude an essential, substantial connection. Ordinary humans can only hope to receive a secondary connection through him. Only thus would we become "co-heirs with Christ." In this part of his vast theology, he follows the trend of most Eastern patristics like Athanasius.

To say, with Augustine and Irenaeus, that humans are deified by grace and not by nature is to say that human beings begin with a different substance or essence from their Creator. But this begs the question: From where have they derived this different substance or essence? The answer must be either from God or from themselves. If from God, then God created imperfect and incomplete beings *unlike* himself in the faint hope that they might later become gods. If from ourselves, then this allows God to have created perfect, complete, mature and self-responsible beings who nonetheless misused their power of free decision to become imperfect. This latter view makes clear that any imperfection must come from ourselves, not from God.

If human beings were truly created in the divine image, then how can they have acquired this different essence? Would a divinely simple God have created a confused and confusing dual nature? Must not the different essence come from elsewhere than God? If it does not come from God, the secondary and contingent nature must come from ourselves. We are the demiurge — creators of a different nature and reality than the perfect ones we were graced with.

Augustine's interpretation forces him to differentiate between Jesus' sonship and our own:

---

[409] See Russell 2004: 265.
[410] Augustine, *Enarr. in Ps. 49,2* (PL 36,565); Fokin 2014: 215-16.

The Only begotten Son is like Him by birth, we are like Him by seeing. For we are not like in such sort as He, Who is the same as He is by Whom He was begotten: for we are like, not equal: He, because equal, is therefore like. And we have heard who are the gods that being made are justified because they are called the sons of God.[411]

As with the Eastern fathers, Augustine needs Christ to be divine by nature because, again, this "is a necessary condition of the deification of other people who become gods by grace and adoption without being true gods."[412] So, Christ and humans need to be different in nature simply to uphold this lacking model of deification.

As far as restoration itself goes, for most of the patristics, as Ortiz writes, "We are restored to our first state, but then go beyond it because we are united to Christ's divinity."[413] In a fully restorative view, to the contrary, our first state is *already* united with Christ's divinity, as established by God before the world ever existed. God did not create us incomplete and in need of development, but rather, perfect and complete. Something is ultimately added to the original state of being, but it is not therefore divinity. *That* we already had by virtue of having been created in the divine image. What is added is rather any love that we experience while we are here, which has a reality of its own and in a sense a life of its own, as well as the Holy Spirit, created after the fall as a free guide to lift us back to our highest reality, as protector and guarantor of the universal restoration and ultimately an adopted sibling.

For most of the patristics and early Christian theologians following Irenaeus and Augustine, the differences between humanity and divinity were insurmountable. They sometimes (particularly in the East) extrapolated from this that a certain distance would remain forever. To retain the proper balance between God's closeness and transcendence, we must see things differently. Our closeness to God depends on our likeness to him and

---

[411] Augustine, *Enarr. in Ps.* 49,2 (PL 36,565); Fokin 2014: 215.
[412] Fokin 2014: 215-216.
[413] Ortiz 2019: 18.

our sharing in the same essential being. To overcome the distance between Godhood and humanity, either we must define God downward — as closer to human — or we must define ourselves upward — as closer to divine. Although God as pure being does not change, *our* conception of God is still evolving — as it should be. And as that changes, or grows more realistic, our conception of who *we* are must change with it. It is just this change in our assumptions about ourselves and God that makes a preexistent cognitive deification possible, which is remembered as it is learned.

Deification eases, if not completely erases, the boundaries we have imagined to exist between humanity and divinity, not by drawing divinity down, but rather by elevating and expanding our conception of humankind. It provides a new significance to human life itself by re-orienting it towards divinity as its teleological end, its overarching purpose and meaning. The scriptural ideas that human beings were created originally to be children of God, that they were made in the image of God, that they were intended to participate with God, and that they can experience "eternal life" here and now are major mediating concepts for how deification transforms our understanding of humanness and thus humanness itself.

Categorization of Approaches

We need a new category for a fully restorative, ontologically based deification. It is *realistic* in the sense that we are actual gods, which cannot be said for many past interpretations of deification. It is *ontological*, in that we share the same essence and nature, the same order of being as does God. This is per God's will, and reveals his utter goodness and love for us, that he seeks to share even himself with us. It is *participative*, depending on our assent and cooperation, which is truly the only condition placed upon it. It is *contemplative* in that it involves a growing awareness of the depths of God via our own spiritualization. It is *moral* and *ethical* because it belongs to everyone in full and equal measure, and we are taught to treat one another with the dignity and care such a belief entails. And it is *practical* in that it involves our gradual assimilation to a new way of living with new guiding values as well as ever-present internal help. I hope to have shown also that the fully restorative approach is *experiential* or meant to be experienced subjectively, which increases its immediate significance, by degrees of increasing glorification. Furthermore, this approach is *universal* in expecting a restoration of all things, a coming together of all equal resanctified beings in peace, each as great as the other, but greater still as a whole, in a completely harmonious and perfectly organic oneness.

There were other forms of deification around the same region of the ancient world before the Christian came along. Roman *apotheosis* or elevation to divine status was mostly limited to emperors, national heroes, or exceptional athletes, usually only after death. It was not meant for the populace at large, and was based on quite different underlying principles. And an ancient Greek form, going back to Plato, was limited to philosophers (specifically those who had led three successive lifetimes of contemplation, an idea which demands reincarnation or *metempsychosis*). The Hermetic mystery religions were more democratic, inviting initiates of all stripes to experience in dramatic fashion the lowliness of the lone naked human contrasted with the higher interconnected spiritual realm only to culminate in the discovery of the divinity in oneself.

The Christian idea of deification was universal and populist from the start, available to everyone and anyone, from ordinary people to the most marginalized in society. (In fact, those most ostracized by the world would get there first.) One need not have been an emperor, a national hero, nor a philosopher on the third lifetime of contemplation to be a god. Nor did one need to undergo a dramatic secret rite. It was much more freely available than formerly thought. All they really had to do was to learn how to love — like God loves — and to learn to think of themselves and others as perfect — as God is perfect. They did not need to change reality, only their minds about reality.

We have noted that Norman Russell's exhaustive *The Doctrine of Deification in the Greek Patristic Tradition* (2004) lays out an intricate roadmap of the development of theosis in the East. One quarrel is that he also presents a highly disputable classification of the different forms of deification. Russell begins with three major categories: *nominal, analogical, and metaphorical*.[414] The nominal godhood is a mere appellation or title of honor (as with Roman emperors and some national heroes of the time, usually applied only after death). All Christian (and Greek philosophical) approaches are then classed in the "analogical" and "metaphorical" categories. The typological categories are generally confusing and limited from the start.

Russell's 'analogical' category 'stretches' the nominal: Moses was a god to Pharaoh as a wise man is a god to a fool. As such, this seems to be merely a linguistic category. However, Russell includes in this category the idea of humans becoming sons and gods 'by grace' in relation to Christ who is Son and God 'by nature,' despite arguing that nearly every patristic believed this. Neither of these categories is true deification in either a transformative or restorative sense, and so to place becoming sons and gods by grace into this analogical category is automatically to render it merely linguistic as well (which I hope to have shown is not the case).

---

[414] Russell 2004: 1-3 is where he explains his initial classification system. He has since revised his typology in both his 2009 book and in subsequent articles.

The third major category, the metaphorical, is further divided into ethical and realistic, and the realistic is subdivided into ontological and dynamic. Russell's ethical approach involves contemplation for the purpose of *homoiosis*, or attaining *likeness* to God by sharing his virtues (goodness, beauty, love, equality, justice, etc.) through moral and ascetic practices. Russell associates this ethical approach with the early Alexandrians — Origen and Clement, as well as Ignatius of Antioch and to some extent Gregory of Nyssa, Evagrius, and the Desert monastic tradition. While these theologians include process elements of this sort of *homoiosis*, the content of their approaches can in no way be confined to this "category" which is actually a method shared by many approaches, including the fully restorative.

Russell points out that the most developed systems of deification (in his opinion, Cyril's and Maximus') integrated both ethical and realistic senses.[415] I believe this is true of any developed system of deification. A fully restorative deification likewise involves "ethical" deification as a process element, a way to realize the goal of godhood through reattaining the divine image by choosing to render oneself like God via imitation, elicitation, and cultivation of the Godly virtues within ourselves. It is essential in the teaching of Jesus that to love like God is to be like God. Augustine and Maximus emphasize this way of love to great extent in their systems, and I think this element should be highlighted by having its own category as a process element that leads to recognition of an ontological oneness as we, like God, may *identify* with love, the basis of our union and shared essence with God and all divine beings.

We should differentiate *physically* transformative views such as that which Harnack objected to in Athanasius from a *cognitively* transformative model such as I have presented. Again, there is nothing inherently bad about imaging the exchange formula as an exchange of human for divine substance except that it is unnecessary. The exchange formula can be viewed instead simply as a way of exchanging one state of *mind* and therefore *being* for another, which then causes us to think of mind and body totally

---

[415] *See* Keating 2015: 273.

differently. The body and its operation is but a small part of the mind's capability, yet we have given it outsized influence.

Russell's *realistic* approach emphasizes transformation and participation in God, but, confining himself to the East, he does not include in this Anselm's and Aquinas' participation in essence. This leaves it lacking, and not truly realistic from both God's and our own vantage points. We need at least one category for real ontological connection and true similarity of being. "Realistic" should be narrowed down to its core meaning of denoting true, ontologically based godhood, wherein it is truly "realistic" whereby gods are truly "gods" because they began as such.

Russell's *ontological* category, subordinated to the realistic, involves participation, adoption, the indwelling Holy Spirit, and the Trinitarian relationship(s). But even with all this, it is lacking in the sense that it is not truly ontological if it does not originate with our being composed of or acquiring a truly divine nature. And the Trinity must include human beings if it is going to have application to a human being's ontological nature, which it does have in our fully restorative model because of our identification with the Son.

Russell does not envision a category that would encompass a full return to actual godhood. Such a fully restorative approach would be truly both "ontological" and "realistic" in that it posits a real godhood that is innate to us, not based on transformation of substance. It is "ontological" in that it involves a real participation in and likeness to God, including a shared essence of being and attributes, but it does so in ways that go beyond the world and even the church. It spans many of Russell's categories and so, it requires a new category of its own.

It can be said that *all* forms of deification employ "analogical" and "metaphorical" expression, including the restorative because its ontological and imperceptible character was initially expressed through mediating images (like sonship and the divine image). However, these mediating images usually relate to a shared essence and nature that is often denied in Eastern approaches. Keating points out that "analogy is part and parcel of how we describe 'realistic' participation in God,"[416] which necessarily obscures both categories as Russell used them in 2004.

I would point out that in no way should the realistic category be subsumed by a "metaphorical" category. Russell's overarching description of deification as a "metaphor" [417] (even while categorizing most of its usage in the Byzantine tradition as "realistic" or "ontological") greatly confuses the categorical issue. Even the Pauline and Johannine traditions of deification are said to be "metaphorical."[418] I have sought to show throughout this book that they, too, are both realistic and ontological ideas even if *expressed* metaphorically, as with Jesus' teaching in parables about the kingdom of God.

Litwa gets to the crux of the issue: "In none of the three ways of deification that he outlines (nominal, analogical, and metaphorical) does Russell think that the deified Christian is *actually* made a God." [419] He notes that most modern researchers and theologians view Christian deification as "nothing more than becoming truly human." This is why it is called "metaphorical" as opposed to "literal."[420] I share Litwa's opinion that "ontological" or "realistic" deification should be a primary category, not subsumed (as it is in Russell) by an overarching metaphorical categorization. In this way, the three major categories should be nominal, analogical, and ontological (or realistic), ascending in degree according to how much a person *actually* becomes a God.

Nearly every patristic saw deification in terms of restoration of what was lost when humanity fell. But precious few of them saw it as a restoration of full godhood. We need a fully restorative-ontological category for those few (mostly Origen and those who followed his logic) who see both our origin and ultimate destination as being full God-derived godhood. It includes analogical and ethical process elements as do most ancient types of deification. This is

---

[416] Keating 2015: 271.
[417] Russell 2004: 8.
[418] Russell 2004: 11.
[419] Litwa 2012: 9.
[420] Litwa 2012: 285.

necessary because of the inherent gulf between humanity and divinity. These ubiquitous analogical and ethical elements, which are truly distinct from one another, must yet be seen to be nearly universal in most ancient types. In other words, Christian deification is never *just* an analogy, and never comprised *solely* of ethical elements. Such categories, then, are partial and descriptive, not encompassing of any one form of deification. Christian deification, even in its earliest stages (with Jesus, Paul, and John) was a complex of mediating images with a large but largely unwritten philosophy behind them and ethical practices already associated with them. It is up to us to detect and draw out the underlying philosophy on the basis of the images themselves, their consistent use, and the ethical practices associated with them. Preexistence is expressed in the Bible but it is not systematically developed, unless we can accept the mediating images as composed, often, of layers of meaning (which metaphors most often are). Sometimes the secondary and tertiary aspects of their intended meaning are lost to time, which is in part why the world's recent discovery of ancient extracanonical texts such as the Gnostic find in Nag Hammadi and the Dead Sea Scrolls found in Qumran can be so enlightening to the modern reader.

Litwa sees Russell's listing of the "ontological" and "realistic" as subcategories of the metaphorical to be an attempt to "explain away" the 'otherness' of deification and the newness of being it holds out to humankind. He notes that "Russell (following Bigger), reduces participation to a mere 'relation' of two beings 'of diverse ontological type.'"[421] While many patristics and modern scholars do seem to pull back from envisioning true ontological similitude between God and his souls, this is most often done out of need to protect what they view or viewed as orthodoxy rather than a conclusion derived purely out of deductive or inductive reasoning.

A fully restorative, ontologically-based deification has for the most part escaped analysis thus far. In the East, Origen is probably closest to it, but even he verges on the physical at times. Following him to a large extent are the Cappadocians Gregory of Nazianzus and Gregory of Nyssa, along with Evagrius, Eusebius, Didymus, and a few

---

[421] Litwa 2012: 9.

others. Maximus does seem to be a great consummation of the intricacy of approaches, yet even he holds back when it comes to ontological identification. The West is on the whole more inclined to such ideas from Hilary, Augustine, Anselm, and Aquinas. I think that it is about time we come to the realization that, when God creates, he creates gods. This is what he creates because it is what he knows. Everything he knows goes into each, so that each individual creation contains the whole, yet it has its own mind, with its own agency for decision and experience.

The Essence-Energies Distinction

The essence-energies distinction has been proposed as an essential component of the Eastern doctrine of theosis.[422] Those who uphold such a distinction claim that while human beings can participate in the *energies* of God, they cannot participate in the *essence* of God, which remains forever shrouded in transcendence. In this, I believe they took a good point too far. They have also used this distinction as evidence that Western deification is somehow inferior to its Eastern counterpart which holds this distinction. Recent scholars have pointed out that, contrary to this assertion, not many Eastern patristics have taught such a distinction.

The issue initially arose when Gregory Palamas (1296-1359) stood up for a group of monks from Mount Athos, whose contemplative prayer centered on seeing "the uncreated light" of God, which they believed was the same light that suffused Jesus at his transfiguration. It was to such experiences of transcendent light that Palamas associated Maximus' idea of "the energies" of God. The light they experienced was not God himself in his essence, Palamas argued in response to accusations, but only his emanative energies, a manifestation of God meant for human comprehension.

Palamas' explanation of this experience was criticized at the time by the Western nominalist Barlaam, who argued that Gregory was committing the old Messalian heresy that God could be seen with physical eyes. Neither side saw the applicability of Aquinas' idea that "the beatified intellect can 'see' the essence of God."[423] Indeed, this was the nature of Barlaam's charge against him.

The entire debate may prove moot in the end. Keating takes issue with Gavrilyuk's contention that the essence/energies distinction is necessary for a "more developed theology" of deification. He notes that "most of the Greek Fathers make no explicit distinction between our participation in the energies, rather than in the essence, of God."[424] This is particularly true of Athanasius

---

[422] See for example Hallosten 2007: 284.
[423] Gavrilyuk 2009: 650.
[424] Keating 2015: 277.

and Cyril of Alexandria, two of the main systematic theologians of Eastern deification. Nor is it ubiquitous even among modern Eastern Christian theologians. Whereas Lossky and many after him depend upon it (e.g., Christos Yannaras), others like John Zizioulas have "dared to criticize the almost-canonical theology of Vladimir Lossky."[425]

Gregory Palamas' distinction between the essence and energies of God,[426] like Lossky's in the early 1900s, was for the stated purpose of trying to retain and "protect" both the transcendence and unique personhood of God.[427] Palamas developed Maximus' essence/energies distinction as a kind of compromise position so that God might remain utterly transcendent even as he shares himself with human beings. Finch concludes: "Palamas only wishes to say with his teaching that God does not remain within himself alone, but wills to exist also for us and that both are not simply identical. He also intended to say that the operations of God in the world are fully God, rather than some created intermediary."[428] Finch points out that the Palamite essence-energies distinction is like Aquinas's between being and existence.[429]

The issue was rekindled in 1925 when an Augustinian friar (Martin Jugie) accused Palamas of having taught heresy by making a 'real distinction' between the divine essence and the divine energies; Lossky, Etienne Gilson and others came to Palamas's defense. Charges of pantheism were averted because the finite being of the

---

[425] Olson 2007: 189. Zizioulas' book *Being as Communion* (1997) has been well-received by "Protestants and Catholics alike," though some in his own Eastern tradition find him "a maverick, if not a heretic" (Olson 2007: 189).

[426] "The theology of St. Gregory Palamas is marked by its special polemical context, which focused on the question of knowing and experiencing God through his energies and on the experience of mystical prayer. This, in turn, fits very well with a pre-understanding of deification as meaning primarily participation in divine life" (Hallonsten 2007: 284).

[427] Olson 2007: 191.

[428] Finch 2007: 243.

[429] Finch 2007: 233.

divinized creature remains finite and the infinite being of God remains utterly unchanged.[430]

Palamas and his fellow monks were simply attempting to explain their experiences of light within the rules set for them by the orthodoxy that criticized them. What gets lost in such theological controversies is the idea that the experience of the light itself is of primary importance. The discursive interpretation always is secondary. In other words, we do not really know whether the light experienced by these medieval monks was created or uncreated, whether it was a mediated aspect of God or God himself.

They interpreted it as the same light the disciples saw on Mount Tabor in the transfigured Christ, "the uncreated splendor with which 'the righteous will shine like the sun' (Mt 13:43)."[431] We might consider it created light rather than uncreated, even a symbol of primordial beginnings, but we can certainly understand that its experience was extraordinary enough that it seemed to those medieval monks like a window into another reality altogether. It was simply their form of contact with divinity, the image in which God was shown to them at that particular stage of their progress, perhaps perfectly in accordance with their capacity to understand (and not fear) at the time. And let us not forget that the vision of the Face of God (thus his essence) was the ultimate experience for Aquinas, albeit not a physical perception, and was the consummation of purified perception as it cedes to knowledge.

It is true that we as human beings have a limited capacity to understand anything about God in his timeless and transcendent reality. However, we have another mind, the mind of the divine being patterned after God, which part of ourselves understands everything perfectly. In time, God seems to evolve, but this is because of how slowly we accept its unfolding revelation. This is why great leaps in understanding often follow great experience, experience that dogma can never quite circumscribe. The highly anthropomorphized God of the Hebrew scriptures is of course different from God in his essence, and this is part of what Gregory

---

[430] Finch 2007: 242.
[431] Finch 2007: 235.

Palamas was trying to express. Moreover, God in his essence is detectable in God's statement to Moses, "I am that I am," and even more strongly when God confers to Moses his own shining countenance. We have no way of knowing how much the monks of Mt. Athos had experienced just a part of this true essence of God as relayed to Moses. In that case, the experience of the energies would be significant glimpses along the way toward experience of the essence.

Such religious disputes often spill over into politics as sides entrench in their positions. Where once Palamas and his supporters suffered imprisonment and persecution, the tables eventually turned and the Palamites regained power and bishoprics. Despite continuing debate over the centuries, Palamism has remained the prevailing and politically sanctioned view in the East. The (largely Catholic) West has continued to criticize the distinction, primarily insofar as they claim it violates the principle of divine simplicity, whereby the attributes of God are identified with his energies, and God is one with his attributes.

In my view, the distinction between essence and energies holds only from the human standpoint. This retains divine simplicity from the divine vantage point, which is infinitely higher, and where there is no such distinction. I would think that the experience itself is interpreted immediately by the experiencer in heaven, while on earth, the experience is distinguished from the interpretation, and so, seems separate from the interpretation, as thoughts seem separate from the one who thinks them, yet in heaven remain one.

But the Palamites are absolutely correct that the experience is most essential to our deification. Such experiences of light are to be expected in the process of deification as, at the very least, emblematic of stages along the way. The experiencer will interpret them in an evolving way as they spiritualize, but the experience itself should not be disparaged thereby. And, in the end, although no human being has ever seen God in his essence, every human being will be graced to see, with their mind, the Face of God and therefore God in his essence as he runs to embrace his beloved children.

BIBLIOGRAPHY

Acardi, James M. (2020). *"Homo adorans: exitus et reditus* in theological anthropology." Scottish Journal of Theology 73:1 February.

Anselm of Canterbury. *Proslogium* (1903; 1926 reprint ed.), translated by Sidney Norton Deane. Chicago: Open Court Publishing Company. (Via Fordham University Center for Medieval Studies. Retrieved 3/20/2022).

Ante-Nicene Fathers. Ed., Alexander Roberts. Vols. 1-5. Buffalo: Christian Literature, 1886-1905.

Aquinas, Thomas. *Summa Theologiae of St. Thomas Aquinas.* Translated by The Fathers of the English Dominican Province (Second and Revised ed.), 1920.

_____. *Super Evangelium S. Ioannis lectura*, 6th edn., ed. R. Cai. Turin and Rome: Marietti, 1972.

Athanasius. *Contra Arianos.* Translated by Philip Schaff. *Select Writings and Letters of Athanasius.* Archibald Robertson, ed. *Nicene and Post-Nicene Fathers*: Second Series, Vol. 2, 04. Grand Rapids, MI: Wm. B. Eerdmans Publishing Co., 1891.

Augustine of Hippo, *City of God.* Translated by Marcus Dods. From *Nicene and Post-Nicene Fathers*, First Series, Vol. 2. Edited by Philip Schaff. (Buffalo, NY: Christian Literature Publishing Co., 1887.).

_____. *Confessions.* Translated by J.G. Pilkington. From *Nicene and Post-Nicene Fathers*, First Series, Vol. 1. Edited by Philip Schaff. (Buffalo, NY: Christian Literature Publishing Co., 1887.)

_____. *The Enchiridion.* Trans., Albert C. Outler. Grand Rapids, MI: CCEL, 1955.

_____. *Expositions on the Psalms.* J.E. Tweed, trans. From *Nicene and Post-Nicene Fathers*, First Series, Vol. 8. Edited by Philip Schaff. (Buffalo, NY: Christian Literature Publishing Co., 1888.) (Revised and edited for New Advent by Kevin Knight. http://www.newadvent.org/fathers/1801.htm).

_____. *On the Trinity.* Arthur West Haddan, trans. From *Nicene and Post-Nicene Fathers*, First Series, Vol. 3. Edited by Philip Schaff. (Buffalo, NY: Christian Literature Publishing Co., 1887.) (Revised and edited for New Advent by Kevin Knight.)

_____. *Sermon 23B*, in *Sermons*. Trans. Edmund Hill. NY: New City Press, 1997.

Basil the Great. *On the Human Condition.* Translation and Introduction by Nonna Verna Harrison. St. Vladimir's Seminary Press: Crestwood, NY, 2005.

Billings, J. Todd . (2008). *Calvin, Participation, and the Gift: The Activity of Believers in Union with Christ.* Oxford: Oxford University Press.

_____. (2005). "United to God through Christ: Assessing Calvin on the Question of Deification" in *The Harvard Theological Review*, Vol. 98, No. 3 (Jul.), pp. 315-334.

_____. (2007). "John Calvin: United to God through Christ," in *Partakers of the Divine Nature: The History and Development of Deification in the Christian Tradition.*

Blatz, B., trans. *The Coptic Gospel of Thomas*, W. Schneemelcher, ed., *New Testament Apocrypha*, English translation by R. McL. Wilson, James Clarke & Co. Ltd.; Westminster/John Knox Press, Cambridge; Louisville, 1991, 110-133.

Bonner, Gerald. (1986). "Augustine's Concept of Deification" in *Journal of Analytic Theology*, Vol. 3, May 2015; reprint of JTS 37.2.

Braaten, Carl E. and Robert W. Jenson, eds. (1998). *Union With Christ: The New Finnish Interpretation of Luther*. Grand Rapids, MI: Wm. B. Eerdmans Publishing Company, 1998.

Buda, Daniel. (2013). "Some aspects of Adolf von Harnack's criticism on Orthodox tradition." *HTS Teologiese Studies/ Theological Studies* 69(1), Art. #1949, 6 pages. http://dx.doi.org/10.4102/ hts.v69i1.1949.

Calvin, John. *Commentaries on the Catholic Epistles.* John Owen, ed. and trans Grand Rapids, MI: Christian Classics Ethereal Library. [http://www.ccel.org]

Charles, R.H. *The Apocrypha and Pseudepigrapha of the Old Testament.* Oxford: Clarendon Press, 1913. (Scanned and Edited by Joshua Williams, Northwest Nazarene College (retrieved 12/25/2023)).

Christensen, Michael J., and Jeffrey A. Wittung, eds. (2007). *Partakers of the Divine Nature: The History and Development of Deification in the Christian Traditions.* Madison/Teaneck: Farleigh Dickinson UP, 2007.

Christensen, Michael. (2008). "The Problem, Promise, and Process of Theosis," in *Partakers of the Divine Nature*. Eds., Michael Christensen and Jeffrey Wittung. Grand Rapids: Baker Academic, 23–31.

Clement of Alexandria. *Ante-Nicene Fathers*. Ed. Alexander Roberts. Vol. 2. New York: C. Scribner's Sons, 1905. Print.

Collins, Paul M. (2010). *Partaking in Divine Nature: Deification and Communion.* London/NY: T & T Clark/Continuum.

Cooper, Adam G. (2014). *Naturally Human, Supernaturally God: Deification in Pre-Conciliar Catholicism.* Augsburg Fortress Publishers.

Couenhoven, Jesse. (2005). "St. Augustine's Doctrine of Original Sin" in *Augustinian Studies* 36:2, 359–396.

Decock, Paul B. (2011). "Origen: On Making Sense of the Resurrection as a Third Century Christian" *Neotestamentica*, Vol. 45, No. 1, pp. 76-91.

Dillon, John. (2020). "Plutarch, Plotinus and the Zoroastrian Concept of the *fravashi*," in B. David (ed.), *Passionate Mind: Essays in Honor of John M. Rist,* Academia Verlag: Baden-Baden, 181-190.

Dionysius the Areopagite. *On The Divine Names and the Mystical Theology*, C. E.

Rolt, ed./trans. Montana, U.S.A.: Kessinger Publishing Company, 1920.

Doresse, J., trans. *The secret books of the Egyptian Gnostics: An introduction to the Gnostic Coptic manuscripts discovered at Chenoboskion.* Viking/Hollis & Carter, New York/London, 1960.

Drever, Matthew. (2014). "Deification in Augustine: Plotinian or Trinitarian?" in Khaled Anatolios, ed. *The Holy Trinity in the Life of the Church.* Grand Rapids, MI.: Baker Academic, 101-12.

Finch, Jeffrey. (2006a). "Irenaeus on the Christological Basis of Human Divinization" in Finlan, Stephen, and Vladimir Kharlamov, eds. *Theosis: Deification in Christian Theology.* Cambridge, UK: James Clarke & Co., 86-103.

_____. (2006b). "Athanasius on the Deifying Work of the Redeemer" in Finlan, Stephen, and Vladimir Kharlamov, eds. *Theosis: Deification in Christian Theology.* Cambridge, UK: James Clarke & Co., 104-121.

_____. (2007). "Neo-Palamism, Divinizing Grace, and the Breach Between East and West" in Christensen, Michael J., and Jeffrey A. Wittung, eds. *Partakers of the Divine Nature.* Madison/Teaneck: Farleigh Dickinson UP, 233-243.

Finlan, Stephen and Vladimir Kharlamov, eds. (2006). *Theosis: Deification in Christian Theology.* Eugene, OR: Pickwick Publications.

Finlan, Stephen. (2007). "Can We Speak of *Theosis* in Paul?" in Christensen, Michael J., and Jeffrey A. Wittung, eds. *Partakers of the Divine Nature.* Madison/Teaneck: Farleigh Dickinson UP, 68-80.

_____. (2011). "Deification in Jesus' Teaching," from *Theosis: Deification in Christian Theology*, Volume 2; Kharlamov, ed. V. Wipf & Stock, 2011.

Fokin, Alexey R. (2009). "The Relationship Between Soul and Spirit in Greek and Latin Patristic Thought," *Faith and Philosophy: Journal of the Society of Christian Philosophers*: Vol. 26 : Iss. 5 , Article 11.

_____. (2014). "The Doctrine of Deification in Western Fathers of the Church: A Reconsideration" in *Fur Uns und Fur Unser Heil: Soteriologie in Ost und West.* Innsbruck: Verlagsanstalt Tyrolia, 2014, pp. 207-220.

Forger, Deborah. (2018). "Divine Embodiment in Philo of Alexandria" in *Journal for the Study of Judaism* 49 (2018) 223-262.

Foster, Kenelm, ed. (1959). *Life of Aquinas* on archive.org (retrieved 2/23/23).

Gavrilyuk, Paul. (2022). "How Deification was Rediscovered in Modern Orthodox Theology: The Contribution of Ivan Popov" in *Modern Theology* 38:1 Jan., pp. 100-127.

_____. (2009). "The Retrieval of Deification: How a Once-Despised Archaism Became an Ecumenical Desideratum" in *Modern Theology* 25:4 Sept.

Givens, Terryl L. (2012). *When Souls Had Wings: Pre-Mortal Existence in Western Thought.* Oxford UP.

Glazov, Gregory. (2006). "Theosis, Judaism, and Old Testament Anthropology" in Finlan, Stephen, and Vladimir Kharlamov, eds. *Theosis: Deification in*

Christian Theology. Cambridge, UK: James Clarke & Co., 16-31.
Gorman, Michael. (2009). *Inhabiting the Cruciform God: Kenosis, Justification, and Theosis in Paul's Narrative Soteriology.* Grand Rapids, MI: Eerdmans.
Gregory of Nyssa. *Discourse on Children. Gregorii Nysseni Opera.* Ed. E Muhlenberg. Leiden. 1996. Vol. 3.2.
Gross, Jules. *The Divinization of the Christian According to the Greek Fathers.* Trans., Paul A. Onica. Anaheim, CA: A & C Press, 2002.
Haag, Herbert. (1982). "'Son of God' in the Language and Thinking of the Old Testament," in *Jesus: Son of God?* Concilium 153.3.
Hadot, Pierre. (1993). *Plotinus: or, The Simplicity of Salvation.* Trans., Michael Chase. Chicago/London: University of Chicago Press, 1993 (orig. French 1989).
Hahn, Michael S. "A Critical Assessment of St Cyril of Alexandria's "On the Unity of Christ," and its Significance for Patristic and Modern Theology" online https://www.academia.edu/7960560, (retrieved 6/23/2022).
Hallonsten, Gösta. (2007). "Theosis in Recent Research: A Renewal of Interest and a Need for Clarity." In M. J. Christensen, & J. A. Wittung (Eds.), *Partakers of the Divine Nature.* Farleigh Dickinson University Press, Cranbury, N.J.
Harnack, Adolf von. *History of Dogma.* (1901). Trans., Neil Buchanan. (Boston, MA: Little, Brown, and Company.
_____. (1908). *What is Christianity? Lectures Delivered in the University of Berlin during the Winter-Term 1899-1900.* Trans. T.B. Saunders. 2nd ed., revised. NY: G.P. Putnam's Sons, London: Williams and Norgate; orig. pub. 1901.
Hilary of Poitiers. "*De Trinitate.*" Translated by E.W. Watson and L. Pullan. From *Nicene and Post-Nicene Fathers, Second Series*, Vol. 9. Edited by Philip Schaff and Henry Wace. (Buffalo, NY: Christian Literature Publishing Co., 1899.) Revised and edited for New Advent by Kevin Knight. <http://www.newadvent.org/fathers/330211.htm>. (retrieved 01.07.2023)
Irenaeus of Lyons. "*Against Heresies.*" Ante-Nicene Fathers. Ed. Alexander Roberts. Vol. 1. New York: C. Scribner's Sons, 1905. Print.
Jacobs, Jonathan D. (2009). "An Eastern Orthodox conception of theosis and human nature" in *Faith and Philosophy*, 26(5), pp. 615-627.
Jacobsen, Anders Lund. (2008). "Genesis 1-3 as Source for the Anthropology of Origen" in *Vigiliae Christianae.* Vol. 62, No. 3, pp. 213-232.
Jung, Carl. (1970). *The Collected Works of Jung.* Princeton, NJ: Princeton UP.
Keating, Daniel A. (2004). *The Appropriation of Divine Life in Cyril of Alexandria* Oxford Theological Monographs New York: Oxford University Press.
_____. (2006). "The Doctrine of Deification in the Greek Patristic Tradition (review)" *Journal of Early Christian Studies.* Vol. 14, no. 3, Fall, pp. 389-390.
_____. (2007). *Deification and Grace.* Naples, FL: Sapientia Press.

_____. (2015). "Typologies of Deification" in *International Journal of Systematic Theology* Vol. 17, Issue 3, June.

Kerr, N. R. (2007). "St Anselm: Theoria and the Doctrinal Logic of Perfection," in M. J. Christensen and Jeffrey A. Wittung, eds., *Partakers of the Divine Nature: The History and Development of Deification in the Christian Traditions.* (Grand Rapids, MI: Baker Academic).

Kharlamov, Vladimir. (2007). "Rhetorical Application of *Theosis* in Greek Patristic Theology" in Christensen, Michael J., and Jeffrey A. Wittung. *Partakers of the Divine Nature: The History and Development of Deification in the Christian Traditions.* Madison/Teaneck: Farleigh Dickinson UP, 115-131.

_____. (2009). *The Beauty of the Unity and the Harmony of the Whole: The Concept of Theosis in the Theology of Pseudo-Dionysius the Areopagite.* Eugene, OR: Wipf & Stock.

_____, ed. (2011a). *Theosis: Deification in Christian Theology.* Vol. 2. Eugene, OR: Pickwick Publications.

_____. (2011b). "Basil of Caesarea and the Cappadocians on the Distinction between Essence and Energies in God and Its Relevance to the Deification Theme" in Kharlamov, Vladimir, ed. *Theosis: Deification in Christian Theology.* Vol. 2. Eugene, OR: Pickwick Publications, 100-145.

Kirby, Peter. (2023). "Origen." *Early Christian Writings.* <http://www.earlychristianwritings.com/origen.html>.

Lenz, John R. (2007). "Deification of the Philosopher in Classical Greece" in Christensen, Michael J., and Jeffrey A. Wittung. *Partakers of the Divine Nature: The History and Development of Deification in the Christian Traditions.* Madison/Teaneck: Farleigh Dickinson UP, 47-67.

Litwa, M. David. (2013). "We are Being Transformed: Deification in Paul's Soteriology" in *Religious Studies Review* 39:2 June.

_____. (2014). "The God 'Human' and Human Gods: Models of Deification in Irenaeus and the *Apocryphon of John*." *Journal of Ancient Christianity.* May, Vol. 18 Issue 1, 70-94.

_____. (2015). "'I Will Become Him': Homology and Deification in the *Gospel of Thomas.*" *Journal of Biblical Literature.* Jan 133 no. 2, 427-447.

_____. (2016). "You Are Gods: Deification in the Naassene Writer and Clement of Alexandria." Published online by Cambridge University Press: 21 December, online at: https://www.cambridge.org/core/journals/harvard-theological-review/article/you-are-gods-deification-in-the-naassene-writer-and-clement-of-alexandria/C80F703545F874BFF70612BFC1D92021 (retrieved 1/22/2023)

Lossky, Vladimir. (1957). *The Mystical Theology of the Eastern Church.* London: James Clarke, 1957; rep. Crestwood, NY: St. Vladimir's Seminary Press, 1976/1997.

_____. (1974). "Redemption and Deification" in *In the Image and*

Likeness of God, edited by John H. Erickson and Thomas E. Bird. Crestwood, NY: St Vladimir's Seminary Press, 1974/2001.

Louth, Andrew. (2003). "Theology, Contemplation, and the University" in *Studia theologica* I, 2/2003, 64-73.

_____. (2008). "The Place of Theosis in Orthodox Theology," in *Partakers of the Divine Nature,* edited by Michael J. Christensen and Jeffery A. Wittung, Grand Rapids, MI: Baker Academic.

_____. (2021). "Love in Dionysius the Areopagite and St Maximus the Confessor." In K. Grødum, H. F. Hägg, J. Kaufman & T. T. Tollefsen (Eds.), Love – ancient perspectives (Ch. 7, pp. 123–137). Cappelen Damm https://doi.org/10.23865/noasp.133.ch07.

Mannermaa, Tuomo. (1995). "Theosis as a Subject of Finnish Luther Research," trans. Norman W. Watt, *Pro Ecclesia* 4 (Winter): 37-48.

Marchant, Daniel L. (2011). "The Sacrifice of the Life-Giving Death The Atonement and Its Theological Presuppositions in Eastern Orthodox Soteriology." Thesis, Liberty Univ., online at: https://digitalcommons.liberty.edu/cgi/viewcontent.cgi?article=1219&context=honors (retrieved 2/13/2023)

Martens, Peter. (2013). "Origen's Doctrine of Pre-Existence and the Opening Chapters of Genesis," in *Zeitschrift für Antikes Christentum* 16: 516-549.

Maurer, Joshua and Amy Peeler (2011). "Sonship in the Bible," *St. Andrews Encyclopedia of Theology* (online; retrieved 12/25/2023).

McGuckin, J. A. (2007). "The Strategic Adaptation of Deification in the Cappadocians" in Christensen, Michael J., and Jeffrey A. Wittung. *Partakers of the Divine Nature: The History and Development of Deification in the Christian Traditions.* Madison/Teaneck: Farleigh Dickinson UP, 95-114.

McInroy, Mark. (2021). "How Deification Became Eastern: German Idealism, Liberal Protestantism, and the Modern Misconstruction of the Doctrine" in *Modern Theology* 37:4 Oct.

Meconi SJ, David Vincent. (2006). "The Consummation of the Christian Promise: Recent Studies on Deification" in *New Blackfriars* 87:1007 Jan., pp. 3-12.

_____. (2013). *The One Christ: St. Augustine's Theology of Deification.* Washington, DC: The Catholic University of America Press.

Medley, Mark. (2011). "Participation in God: The Appropriation of Theosis by Contemporary Baptist Theologians" in Kharlamov, Vladimir, ed. *Theosis: Deification in Christian Theology.* Vol. 2. Eugene, OR: Pickwick Publications/Wipf and Stock, pp. 205-246.

Meyendorff, John. (1959). *A Study of Gregory Palamas*. NY: St. Vladimir's Seminary Press, rep. 2010.

_____. (1966). *Orthodoxy and Catholicity*. NY: Sheed and Ward.

Monroe, Ty. (2015). "The One Christ: St. Augustine's Theology of Deification." (Book Review). *Modern Theology*. Apr, Vol. 31 Issue 2, pp. 357-359.

Mosser, Carl. (2002). "The Greatest Possible Blessing: Calvin and Deification" in

Scottish Journal of Theology, Volume 55, Issue 1, February, pp. 36–57.

———. (2005). "The Earliest Patristic Interpretations of Psalm 82, Jewish Antecedents, and the Origin of Christian Deification." *Journal of Theological Studies*, NS, Vol. 56, Pt 1, April, pp. 30-74.

Nellas, Panayiotis. (1987). *Deification in Christ: Perspectives on the Nature of the Human Person*. Crestwood, NY: St. Vladimir's Seminary Press.

Nelstrop, Louise. (2019). *On Deification and Sacred Eloquence: Richard Rolle and Julian of Norwich*. Taylor & Francis.

Neyrey, Jerome H. (1989). "'I Said: You are Gods': Psalm 82:6 and John 10" in *Journal of Biblical Literature*, Vol. 108, No. 4 (Winter), pp. 647-663.

Nicene and Post-Nicene Fathers (NPNF). *A Select Library of Nicene and Post-Nicene Fathers of the Christian Church*. Edited by Philip Schaff and Henry Wace. 28 vols. in 2 series. 1886–1889. Repr., Grand Rapids, Mich.: Eerdmans, 1989.

Nispel, Mark D. (1999). "Christian Deification and the Early Testimonia." *Vigiliae Christianae: A Review of Early Christian Life and Language*. (VigC) Aug; 53 (3): 289-304.

Ollerton, Andrew J. (2011). "Quasi Deificari: Deification in the Theology of John Calvin" in *Westminster Theological Journal* 73: 237-54.

Olson, Carl E., and David Vincent Meconi. (2016). *Called to Be the Children of God: The Catholic Theology of Human Deification*. San Francisco: Ignatius Press.

Olson. Roger E. (2007). "Deification in Contemporary Theology," *Theology Today* 64/2 (July), pp. 186–200.

O'Meara, John. (1984). "Saint Augustine's Understanding of the Creation and Fall" *The Maynooth Review / Revieú Mhá Nuad*, Vol. 10 (May), pp. 52-62.

Origen of Alexandria. *Commentary on the Gospel According to John*, Books 13-32. Trans. Ronald E. Heine. Washington, D.C.: Catholic University of America, 1993. 406. Print.

———. "Commentary on John, Book 1." Trigg, Joseph W. *Origen*. New York: Routledge, 1998. 103-149.

———. *Contra Celsus*. 2007. Roberts-Donaldson English translation. http://www.earlychristianwritings.com/ (Retrieved 12.12.2007).

———. "Homily 12 on Jeremiah." *Origen*. Trans. Joseph W. Trigg. New York: Routledge, 1998. 179-192.

———. *Homilies on Genesis and Exodus*. Trans., Ronald E. Heine, The Fathers of the Church. (Washington, DC: The Catholic University of America Press, 1981).

———. *De Principiis*, or *On First Principles. Ante-Nicene Fathers* Volume 4. Trans., Roberts-Donaldson. Arranged by A. Cleveland Coxe. Grand Rapids, MI: Eerdmans/Edinburgh: T & T Clark, orig. published 1885.

———. *On First Principles*. G. W. Butterworth, ed. New York: Harper & Row, 1966.

Orr, Peter. (2016). "We Are Being Transformed: Deification in Paul's Soteriology

(review)." *Themelios* Vol. 41, Issue 2, Aug.
Ortiz, Jared, ed. (2019). *Deification in the Latin Patristic Tradition*. Catholic University of America Press.
Peppard, Michael. (2011). "Adopted and Begotten Sons of God: Paul and John on Divine Sonship." *The Catholic Biblical Quarterly,* Vol. 73, No. 1 (January), 92-110.
Philokalia. Vol. 1. Palmer, G.E.H., ed. London: Faber and Faber, 1981.
Plato, *Phaedo* 75b. *Plato in Twelve Volumes*, Vol. 1 translated by Harold North Fowler; Introduction by W.R.M. Lamb. Cambridge, MA, Harvard University Press; London, William Heinemann Ltd. 1966.
Plotinus. *The Six Enneads*. Trans., Stephen MacKenna and B. S. Page. London, P.L. Warner, publisher to the Medici Society [1917-1930].
Popov, Ivan B. (2011). "The Idea of Deification in the Early Eastern Church." Trans., Boris Jakim. In Kharlamov, Vladimir, ed. *Theosis: Deification in Christian Theology*. Vol. 2. Eugene, OR: Pickwick Publications, 2011, 42-82.
Puchniak, Robert. (2006). "Augustine's Conception of Deification, Revisited" in Finlan, Stephen, and Vladimir Kharlamov, eds. *Theosis: Deification in Christian Theology*. Cambridge, UK: James Clarke & Co., 122-133.
Ramelli, Ilaria L. E. (2009). "Origen, Bardaisan, and the Origin of Universal Salvation." The Harvard Theological Review, Vol. 102, No. 2 (Apr.), pp. 135-168.
_____. (2013). "Origen, Eusebius, the Doctrine of Apokatastasis, and Its Relation to Christology" in Johnson, Aaron, and Jeremy Schott, eds. *Eusebius of Caesarea: Tradition and Innovations.* Hellenic Studies Series 60. Washington, DC: Center for Hellenic Studies.
Rist, J. M. (1967). "Integration and the Undescended Soul in Plotinus" in *The American Journal of Philology.* Vol. 88, No. 4 (Oct.), pp. 410-422.
Russell, Norman. (2004). *The Doctrine of Deification in the Greek Patristic Tradition.* Oxford Early Christian Studies. Oxford and New York: Oxford University Press.
_____. (2009). *Fellow Workers with God: Orthodox Thinking on Theosis.* Crestwood, NY: St. Vladimir's Seminary Press.
Sachs, John R. (1993). "Apocatastasis in Patristic Theology." *Theological Studies* 54: 617-640.
Salladin, James R. (2022). *Jonathan Edwards and Deification: Reconciling Theosis and the Reformed Tradition*. Downers Grove, IL: IVP Academic.
Schaff, Philip. (1867). *From Constantine the Great to Gregory the Great, A.D. 311-600*. Vol. 3. *History of the Christian Church.* Scribner.
Scully, Ellen. (2011). "The Assumption of All Humanity in Saint Hilary of Poitiers' Tractatus super Psalmos" Dissertation Marquette University online. https://epublications.marquette.edu/dissertations_mu/95 (retrieved 3/2/2023)
Sidaway, Janet. (2019) "Making Man Manifest: Deification in Hilary of Poitiers" in

Ortiz, Jared, ed. *Deification in the Latin Patristic Tradition*. Washington D.C.: Catholic University of America Press.

Starr, James. (2007). "Does 2 Peter 1:4 Speak of Deification?" in Christensen, Michael J., and Jeffrey A. Wittung. *Partakers of the Divine Nature*. Madison/Teaneck: Farleigh Dickinson UP, 2007, 81-94.

Steele, Richard B. (2008). "Transfiguring Light: The Moral Beauty of the Christian Life According to Gregory Palamas and Jonathan Edwards" in *St Vladimir's Theological Quarterly* 52, pp. 403–439.

Strachan, R. H. (1914). "The Idea of Pre-Existence in the Fourth Gospel." *The American Journal of Theology*, Vol. 18, No. 1 (Jan.), pp. 81-105.

Thomas, Stephen. (2007). *Deification in the Eastern Orthodox Tradition: A Biblical Perspective*. Piscataway, NJ: Gorgias Press, 2007.

Townsend, Luke David. (2015). "Deification in Aquinas: A Supplementum to the Ground of Union." (Book review.) *The Journal of Theological Studies*, NS, Vol. 66, Pt 1, April, pp. 204-234.

Tripolitis, Antonia. (1978). *The Doctrine of the Soul in the Thought of Plotinus and Origen*. Libra Publishers.

Watzek, Margaret M. (1986). "The Theological Anthropology Developed in Origen's Interpretations of Genesis 1:26-30 and Genesis 2:4-9." Master's Thesis, Univ. of Chicago, Loyola. (online: https://ecommons.luc.edu/cgi/viewcontent.cgi?article=4492&context=luc_theses; retrieved 5/23/22)

Weigel, George. (2001). *The Truth of Catholicism*. New York City: Harper Collins.

Williams, A. N. (1999). *The Ground of Union: Deification in Aquinas and Palamas."* Oxford: Oxford University Press.

Wray, T. J. and Gregory Mobley. (2005). *The Birth of Satan: Tracing the Devil's Biblical Roots*. NY: Palgrave Macmillan.

Vishnevskaya, Elena. (2007). "Divinization as Perichoretic Embrace in Maximus the Confessor" in Christensen, Michael J., and Jeffrey A. Wittung. *Partakers of the Divine Nature*. Madison/Teaneck: Farleigh Dickinson UP, 132-145.

Ware, Kallistos. (1995). *The Orthodox Way*. Crestwood, NY: St. Vladimir's UP.

Winter, Benjamin. (2013). "Souls and Soteriology: The Reception of Origen's Doctrine of Preexistence at the End of the Fourth Century." www.academia.edu/6571777 (retrieved 9/25/22).

World English Bible (2020). https://worldenglish.bible (retrieved 1/18/23).

Yannaras, Christos. (2007). *Person and Eros*. Norman Russell, trans. Brookline, MA: Holy Cross Orthodox Press.

Zizioulas, John D. (1997). *Being as Communion: Studies in Personhood and the Church*. Crestwood, NY: St. Vladimir's Seminary Press.

Zorgdrager, Heleen. (2014). "Reclaiming theosis: Orthodox Women Theologians on the Mystery of the Union with God" in *IKZ* 104, Seiten 220–245.

INDEX

1 Corinthians, 43, 65, 126, 167, 200, 203, 204, 207, 240, 249, 254, 256, 260, 273-275, 291, 292, 308, 321-324

1 John, 27, 86, 89, 90, 91, 105, 174, 197, 211, 216, 226, 236, 250, 254, 319, 323

1 Peter, 133, 210, 231, 302, 313

1 Timothy, 244, 288, 289

2 Corinthians, 42, 66, 124, 125, 131, 136, 200, 236, 240, 262, 263, 312, 321, 323, 324

2 Esdras, 62, 121, 122, 258, 300

2 Peter, 9, 14, 26, 46, 224, 225, 284, 285, 303, 325, 363

Abraham, 18, 27, 68, 69, 74-77, 93, 99, 169, 181, 186, 258, 259, 272, 289, 311

Adam, 3, 38, 39, 44, 47, 58, 59, 113, 116, 119, 129, 137, 138, 141, 142, 143, 209, 212, 213, 215, 219, 223, 226, 227, 228, 231, 235, 258, 259, 270, 275, 284, 301, 321

adopted, 18, 69, 71-76, 93, 118, 205, 341, 362

adoption, 25, 33, 69, 70, 73, 74, 76, 77, 78, 79, 116, 119, 224, 341, 346

adoptive, 18, 27, 68, 69, 70, 72, 74, 75, 76, 77, 78, 81, 93, 95, 116, 137

Advocate, 164, 166, 196, 197, 269, 331

angel, 11, 92, 93, 145, 148, 150-153, 181, 249, 273, 276, 294, 296, 301, 319, 321

Anselm, 10, 13, 15, 97, 98, 145, 213, 214, 220, 221, 222, 235, 337, 346, 355, 359

Anthony [Antony] the Great, 4, 5, 13

anthropology, 11, 13, 14, 22, 23, 93, 100, 101, 107, 131, 157, 165, 177, 339, 349, 353, 355, 358, 363

apocalyptic, 8, 29, 62, 178-181, 256-282, 299, 300-303, 309

apocrypha, 40, 91, 176, 178, 181, 182, 192, 279, 300, 356

apokatastasis, 29, 150, 283-297, 362

apophaticism, 12, 225, 237

apotheosis, 3, 8, 343

Aquinas, 10, 13, 15, 19, 45, 46, 48, 49, 72, 73, 97, 176, 177, 180, 190, 191, 235, 243, 244, 252, 337, 346, 350, 352, 355, 357, 363

Arians, 36, 37, 43, 48, 70, 71

Aristotle, 66, 202

Athanasius, 8, 11, 14, 15, 36, 43, 44, 45, 47, 58, 59, 70-72, 205, 339, 340, 345, 350, 355, 357

attributes, 5, 17, 27, 39, 46, 96, 97, 106, 135, 179, 184, 199, 200, 220, 221, 237, 238, 240, 249, 251, 252, 254, 283, 346, 353

Augustine, 1, 10-20, 28, 37, 39, 43-46, 51, 58, 72, 97, 98, 116, 123, 129, 130, 135, 138, 143, 150, 151, 156-159, 162-164, 175, 176, 185, 211, 213-219, 223-225, 227, 228, 239, 263, 295, 297, 308, 309, 312, 313, 339, 340, 341, 345, 352, 355-362

autonomy, 60, 133, 143, 144, 155, 220, 238, 293

awareness, 6, 21, 38, 40, 53, 58, 61, 63-67, 84, 85, 122, 139, 155-157, 170, 186, 189, 191, 193, 202, 203, 217, 224, 243, 260, 264, 265, 281,

297, 307, 310, 311, 314, 316, 334, 343
baptism, 6, 91, 196, 213, 234, 238, 322
Baptist, 14, 171, 172, 186, 194, 195, 296, 306, 361
Basil, 13, 36, 142, 164, 339, 355, 359
begotten, 2, 3, 16, 18, 21, 23, 27, 44, 45, 68, 69, 73-75, 77, 80, 81-91, 94-97, 113, 115, 134, 137, 150, 178, 244, 341
belief, 1, 2, 8, 20, 21, 37, 44, 50, 60, 63-67, 73, 75, 80, 86, 88, 94, 114, 167, 170, 171, 202, 204, 210-212, 230, 233, 239, 246, 247, 261, 271, 280, 282, 286, 289, 292, 314-316, 318, 319, 322-3, 334, 338, 346, 351
Berdyaev, 10
bipartite, 23, 135, 218, 225, 245
body, 4, 5, 11, 26, 38, 43, 44, 52, 53, 57, 66, 67, 100, 112, 114, 122, 123, 125-131, 136, 147, 153-167, 169, 175, 177, 179, 181, 186, 199, 200, 208, 211, 216, 236, 249, 267, 272-275, 277, 279, 294, 312, 320, 321, 322, 330, 338, 345, 346
Bonner, 11, 223, 356
Book of Enoch, 181, 258, 259, 300, 302
born again, 16, 86
breath, 5, 47, 57, 58, 60, 114, 178, 193, 196, 339
Calvin, 1, 10, 13, 15, 19, 173, 213, 224, 225, 356, 361
Cappadocians, 13, 71, 205, 359, 360
Catholic, 2, 10, 11, 13, 213, 351, 356, 361, 362, 363
Catholicism, 45, 356, 363
Christ, 3, 9, 11, 12, 16, 39, 42-44, 48, 49, 70, 75-77, 79, 81, 88, 123, 129, 132, 151, 161, 162, 175, 198, 203, 204, 207, 234, 240, 245, 253, 263, 264, 286, 290, 292, 321-325, 340, 341, 344, 352, 356, 358, 360, 361
Christensen, 13, 238, 356-360, 363
Christhood, 29, 43, 294, 295, 321, 323
Christification, 43, 207
Christology, 22, 23, 25, 44, 157, 357, 362
Clement, 4, 15, 35, 36, 37, 39, 43, 44, 57, 164, 238, 293, 305, 337, 338, 345, 356, 359
collective, 91, 118, 190, 207, 213, 240, 263, 281, 292, 304, 318, 319, 320, 333
Colossians, 41, 168, 175, 240, 263, 323
common good, 200, 233, 248, 258, 294, 304
completion of being, 20, 23, 24, 31, 50, 51, 57, 116, 117, 120, 155, 169, 177, 231, 256, 265, 311, 315, 316, 329, 330, 331, 340, 341
complexity, 25, 44, 98, 153, 156, 231, 334, 353
conflict, 55, 91, 96, 98, 105, 112, 122, 130, 134, 135, 141, 182, 230, 290, 305
contemplation, 5, 10, 29, 43, 44, 57, 150, 187, 237-244, 253, 254, 343, 345, 347
councils (church), 2, 18, 19, 85, 165, 295 (*see also* divine council)
created, 4, 13, 23, 26, 37, 38, 39, 41, 48, 50, 53, 54, 55, 56, 59, 60, 62, 73, 79, 99, 106, 107, 108, 113-126, 135-138, 140, 145, 146, 159, 161, 164, 173, 194, 195, 222, 223, 225, 244, 272, 278, 329, 336, 340, 341, 342, 351, 352
creation, 2, 12, 23, 27, 37, 48, 49, 53, 55-60, 67, 72, 78, 94, 108, 109, 113, 115, 118, 121, 123, 126, 128, 137, 138, 140, 141, 146, 149, 153, 154, 156, 157, 159, 160, 167, 174,

175, 177-179, 184, 188, 190, 217, 218, 222, 224, 226, 231, 245, 251, 263, 275, 285, 291, 295, 326, 332, 337
creationism, 164, 165, 338
Creator, 13, 27, 34, 50, 99, 120, 140, 223, 326
cross, 28, 46, 135, 203-210, 232
crucifixion, 203-210, 232, 273, 301
Cyprian, 13, 43, 44
Cyril, 11, 15, 71, 164, 339, 345, 351, 358, 359
Damascene, 9
Daniel, 257-259, 299
death, 27, 35, 38, 48, 53-57, 63-66, 77, 78, 95, 100, 108, 109, 110, 114, 121, 122, 130, 133, 137, 141, 144, 145, 169, 187, 198, 203, 207-215, 219, 228, 232, 235, 259, 261, 262, 271-274, 278, 280, 281, 291, 292, 298, 299, 301, 309, 313, 331, 343, 344, 360
deathless, 35, 53, 59, 60, 63, 64, 210, 261, 271, 273, 274
decision, 19, 39, 49, 50, 54, 57, 60, 83, 84, 112, 113, 116, 118, 128, 135, 142, 143, 144, 148, 149, 154, 158, 161, 163, 166-168, 173, 179, 212, 218, 219, 227, 240, 254, 257, 270, 279, 293, 297, 323, 326, 334, 340, 348, 354
depths, 20, 24, 70, 135, 155, 170, 200, 204, 226, 266, 286, 343
Descartes, 185
detheologize, 25
devil, 108, 109, 110, 144, 168, 209, 227, 298, 300-305, 331, 333
Diadochus, 39, 51, 339
dialectic, 29, 183, 237
Didymus, 51, 296, 339
Dionysius, 15, 71, 237, 251, 253, 339, 357, 359, 360

dissociated, 28, 60, 94, 136, 148-150, 155, 156,184, 193, 195, 223, 230, 235, 237, 298, 312, 329
divine council, 35, 241, 302
divine image, 10, 16, 18, 21-23, 37-41, 44, 47, 50, 57, 60, 62, 63, 71, 71, 96, 106, 107, 113, 124, 128, 138, 149, 153, 160, 175, 182, 201, 202, 207, 212, 214, 217, 228, 234, 235, 240, 245, 247, 248, 278, 279, 293, 308, 318, 319, 327, 328, 330, 332, 336, 337, 339, 340, 341, 346, 352, 354, 360
divine nature, 16, 26, 44, 46-50, 71, 107, 130, 138, 190, 192, 208, 212, 214, 224, 231, 238, 244, 248, 328, 339
divine simplicity, 27, 44, 55, 96-99, 106, 249, 283, 314, 334, 353
divinization, 8, 16, 44, 173, 253, 352
double love command, 12, 83, 104
dream, 143, 157, 191, 259, 284, 285
dual nature, 23, 59, 116, 129, 130-136, 157, 158, 333, 340
Eastern orthodoxy, 2. 4-10, 12-19, 45-49, 58, 66, 142, 184, 199, 210, 219, 223-225, 228, 237, 241, 242, 337, 340, 341, 344, 346, 350, 351
Ecclesiastes, 40, 61, 110, 298, 314
Ecclesiasticus, 39
Eden, 127, 142, 276, 310
Edwards, 14, 363
Elijah, 172, 193, 258, 260, 278, 313
Elowsky, 59, 126
energies, *see* essence/energies
Ephesians, 74, 79-81, 132, 151, 156, 161, 168, 175, 201, 263, 289, 302, 311
equality, 18, 42, 70, 72, 96, 97, 104, 105, 107, 110-112, 120, 124, 125, 128, 137, 146, 151, 172-3, 182-184, 191, 198, 200, 201, 215, 244, 246, 247, 249, 253, 273-4, 286,

366   *Index*

315, 319, 326, 332, 341, 343, 345, 353

eschatology, 22, 29, 178, 180, 256-264, 268, 280, 309, 326, 349

essence, 2, 11, 13, 15, 18, 21, 22, 26-28, 40, 46-51, 60, 66, 68, 69, 71, 72, 73, 77, 89, 98, 100, 105-107, 151, 156, 161, 176, 199-201, 210, 223, 238, 243, 244, 249, 250, 286, 307, 308, 314-318, 320, 326, 329, 330, 337, 340, 342, 343, 345, 346, 350-354

essence/energies, 11, 14, 18, 30, 199, 244, 350-354

Essenes, 300

eternal life, 2, 17, 24, 26, 40, 52-67, 100, 104, 150, 169, 210, 212, 222, 242, 255, 261, 274, 278, 280, 281, 301, 318, 319, 332, 342

eternity, 40, 57, 61, 62, 92, 130, 131, 136, 137, 145, 176, 181, 245, 273

Eucharist, 5, 6, 234, 322

Eusebius, 51, 296, 339, 362

Evagrius, 39, 51, 165, 294, 295, 296, 339

evil, 20, 62, 67, 82-84, 89, 90, 112, 121, 128, 134-136, 142, 144, 185, 186, 191, 214-219, 225, 227, 228, 256, 264, 276, 281, 291, 297, 299-301, 304, 305, 308, 309, 327, 333

exchange formula, 3, 11, 23, 26, 32, 41-46, 48, 66, 69, 72, 169, 205, 329, 330, 345

exitus-reditus, 283, 284, 314, 355

Exodus, 69, 91, 99, 127, 362

experience, 4, 10, 16, 19-30, 39, 40, 47, 48, 52, 60, 63-67, 73-76, 82, 88, 90, 99, 102, 103, 106, 107, 111, 113, 126, 132, 134, 136, 140, 141, 146, 148, 153-157, 162, 163, 180, 185-6, 189, 190, 192, 200, 204, 208, 210, 215, 219-224, 234-256, 259, 260, 262, 265, 266, 272,

280, 294, 297, 307, 315-318, 325, 326, 331, 332, 341-343, 348-354

Ezekiel, 219, 257, 278

Ezra, 62, 121-22, 258, 259, 300, 307

fall, 3, 21, 27, 35, 37-39, 57, 59, 60, 62, 65, 67, 90, 94, 98, 108, 110, 116, 126, 128, 132, 136, 138, 140-159, 162, 166, 188, 191, 195, 212, 215-221, 224, 226-8, 296, 303, 312, 330, 333, 334, 338-9, 341

family, 18, 51, 68-70, 73, 75-77, 84, 85, 103, 172, 173, 258, 284, 319

Finch, 8, 14, 209, 351, 352, 357

Finlan, 7, 10, 13-14, 84, 265-267, 357

fire, 145, 172, 196, 256, 276, 305-308

flesh, 4, 35, 43, 45, 53, 55, 58, 66, 71, 73, 78, 86, 87, 122, 130-134, 136, 182, 197, 199, 214, 270, 273, 281, 328, 337, 339

Fokin, 151, 340, 341, 357

foreknowledge, 161, 172-177, 187

forgiveness, 84, 186, 204, 206-208, 211

foundation(s), 2, 9, 15, 23, 28, 32, 36, 41, 56, 57, 79, 98, 156, 161, 168, 174, 175, 178, 181, 187, 202, 203, 212, 223, 234, 236, 286, 297, 308, 315, 316, 333, 334

freedom, 21, 38-9, 57, 60, 65, 67, 75, 78-9, 83, 93-95, 97, 115, 116, 118, 128, 138, 140, 143, 146, 148, 156, 161, 163, 166-7, 173, 181, 187, 192, 198, 205, 212, 217, 218, 222-224, 237, 250-1, 255, 270, 286, 297, 323, 325, 340, 341

free gift, 65, 67, 84, 138, 140, 141, 217, 218, 222, 224

free will, 57, 60, 83, 212, 340

Freud, 226

fullness, 74, 80, 132, 135, 140, 176, 195, 222, 231, 265, 288, 290, 297, 338

Galatians, 66, 74-78, 80, 207, 321

Gavrilyuk, 8, 9, 13, 18, 350, 357
gender, 30-33
Genesis, 37-41, 47, 57, 60-62, 69, 75, 113, 121, 123-127, 129, 141, 143, 144, 160, 163, 178, 192, 194, 215, 226, 227, 228, 243, 245, 258, 259, 278, 285, 302, 303, 313, 321, 329, 339, 358, 360-363
Givens, 128, 148, 162-64, 179, 181, 184, 185, 187, 338, 358
glorification, 15, 16, 22, 28, 59, 78, 115, 129, 174, 204, 205, 207, 235, 236, 243, 285, 343
glorified, 76, 77, 115, 129, 174, 175, 200, 243, 281
glory, 41, 70-73, 77, 78, 88, 90, 110, 131, 165, 169, 170, 174, 176, 200, 203, 204, 212, 218, 236, 243, 244, 267, 273, 274, 276-278, 286, 287, 296, 310, 315-317, 319, 323, 354
Gnosticism, 29, 50, 66, 69, 108, 114, 134, 141, 182, 184, 187, 205, 259, 278, 293, 336, 338
Gospel of Truth, 338
grace, 12, 20-22, 25, 27, 28, 49, 60, 67, 71, 72, 79, 88, 89, 94, 136, 138, 140, 163, 184, 187, 191, 205, 212-214, 217-219, 221-223, 225, 236, 244, 282, 295, 326, 329, 340, 341, 344
Greek, 1, 3, 4, 7, 9, 11, 12, 14-17, 35, 46, 66, 75, 88, 100, 101, 146, 179, 183, 194, 200, 202, 207, 224, 256, 284, 299, 303, 315, 322, 324, 343, 344, 350, 358, 359, 362(see also Hellenism)
Greek philosophy, 3, 4, 7, 66, 183, 202, 207, 344
Gross, 8, 9, 358
guardian angel, 151-52
guilt, 66, 85, 144, 147, 163, 164, 187, 204, 206, 214-217, 219, 226-230, 232, 254, 268-270, 306, 329
Guthrie, 69

Hamerton-Kelly, 178-181
Harnack, 6-8, 14, 180, 345, 356, 358
healing, 181, 199, 200, 205, 208, 211, 252, 277, 285, 293, 304
heart, 31, 38, 48, 50, 62-64, 66, 77, 83-4, 92, 94, 98, 101-104, 107, 110-11, 121, 122, 124, 126-128, 131, 132, 134, 136, 142, 165, 177, 189, 191-194, 198, 211, 216, 218, 222, 226, 232, 239, 241, 242, 250-252, 257, 264, 265, 270, 273, 275, 289, 296, 303-4, 306, 310, 316, 323, 325, 330
heaven, 16, 20, 24, 29, 41, 79-85, 92, 100, 103, 105-6, 109-111, 123, 125-127, 134, 150-152, 155-157, 160, 168, 170-173, 178, 180-1, 187, 194, 196, 209, 225, 232-3, 236, 238-240, 252-3, 256-7, 259, 263-265, 272, 274, 276-7, 281, 286, 289, 296, 299, 303, 306-7, 309, 310-314, 316, 322, 324, 333, 334, 336, 351
Hebrew Bible, 8, 31, 61, 91, 98, 164, 176-182, 192-195, 202, 257, 297-300, 303, 324, 329, 338 (see also Old Testament)
hell, 29, 61, 109, 110, 112, 173, 256, 257, 297-310, 336
Hellenism, 6-9, 50, 53, 123, 256
Hermetic, 9, 343
Hilary, 10, 14-16, 48, 72, 128, 129, 263, 264, 267, 337, 358, 363
Hippolytus, 3, 4, 52
Holy Spirit, 28, 56, 77, 92, 94, 122, 188, 192-202, 211, 216, 217, 269, 277, 290, 292, 304, 306, 322, 331, 333, 341, 346
Hosea, 34, 91
human spirit, 177, 178, 192, 193, 199, 200, 202
illumination, 16, 205

illusion, 56, 59, 65, 66, 109, 112, 137, 138, 144, 156, 169, 202, 261, 273, 280, 293, 312, 315, 333, 334
image of God, 12, 21, 37-41, 47, 100 128, 240, 339, 342 (*see also* divine image, divine nature)
imitation, 43, 235, 238, 245, 253, 345
immortality, 4, 5, 16, 23, 26, 28, 33, 35-38, 45, 52-68, 96, 114, 115, 118, 124, 137, 138, 184, 201, 207, 210, 211, 219, 238, 242, 271, 272, 275, 280, 293, 318, 319, 321, 326, 332
incarnation, 3, 8, 39, 45, 54, 195, 205, 209, 232, 259, 330, 347, 348
incorruptibility, 4, 8, 37, 39, 40, 46, 54, 58, 62, 119, 124, 137, 242, 293
inner man, 94, 124, 126-128, 134
inner nature, 66, 124, 131
intertestamental, 39, 61, 91, 92, 121, 164, 182, 194, 299, 301, 302
inviolate, 104, 157, 272, 281
Irenaeus, 3, 4, 8, 11, 14, 15, 23, 33, 38, 39, 41, 43, 45, 54, 55, 59, 68, 69, 70, 74, 97, 114-119, 136, 137, 138, 194, 209, 238, 242, 329, 336-341, 357, 358, 359
Isaiah, 62, 91, 100, 171, 173, 206, 239, 257, 258, 287, 299, 303, 305, 306, 318, 324
Jacobsen, 124, 125, 358
Jeremiah, 93, 161, 171, 176, 186, 193, 257, 258, 294, 306, 325, 361
Job, 40, 92, 178, 193, 215, 216, 301-303
Joel, 197, 257
John, 9, 10, 13, 15, 26, 27, 32, 39, 48, 51, 64, 68, 71, 73, 86, 93, 94, 98, 99, 101, 103, 104, 105, 108-110, 113, 122, 134, 141, 150, 151, 160, 161, 167, 169, 170-173, 186, 194-197, 208, 236, 242-247, 250, 261, 262, 268, 270, 274, 276, 278, 286, 287, 289, 290, 295, 305, 308, 311, 314, 315, 317, 318, 319, 326, 329, 336, 351, 356, 357, 359, 360, 361, 362, 364
joy, 20, 57, 60, 62-3, 84-5, 88, 90-1, 98, 107, 128, 136, 142, 157, 178, 191-2, 199, 216-17, 221-223, 228, 232, 281, 288, 297, 310, 311, 317, 334, 354
judgment, 35, 63, 65, 111, 112, 134, 147, 187, 196, 204, 206, 207, 228, 232, 250, 261, 281, 301, 304, 308, 325, 331, 332 (*see also* last judgment)
Jung, 31, 240, 358
juridical, 17, 28, 207, 234
justice, 84, 96, 107, 123, 125, 128, 135, 146, 161, 164, 166, 171, 184, 199, 206, 215, 249, 255, 281, 293, 294, 296, 300, 326, 332, 345, 353
justification, 15, 17, 28, 174, 175, 194, 207, 208, 213, 223-225, 268, 269, 358
Justin, 2, 33, 38, 53, 55, 207, 329
Keating, 9, 11, 16, 345, 346, 347, 350, 359
Kerr, 13, 221, 222, 235, 359
Kings, (Book of), 193, 313
Kharlamov, 7, 9, 14, 113, 137, 359
kingdom, 16, 24, 28, 29, 63, 64, 86, 87, 109-111, 132, 162, 168, 177, 182, 197, 204, 205, 208-210, 256, 260, 261, 264-268, 278, 280, 289, 292, 305, 310, 311, 325, 347
knowledge, 5, 16, 19, 38, 41, 45, 57, 60, 63-65, 69, 73, 86, 100, 102, 107, 125, 144, 157, 168, 170-1, 174-5, 181, 183-185, 200, 204, 211, 216, 231, 237, 239, 240, 242-3, 243, 249, 252, 288, 291-2, 300, 305, 310, 312, 325, 332, 335, 352
lake of fire, 256, 276, 308
last judgment, 29, 147, 256, 259, 261, 268-271, 280, 281, 299

Latin, 11, 12, 14-17, 33, 48, 88, 224, 305, 320, 337, 357, 362
law, 29, 32, 34, 62, 74, 75, 77, 80, 130-133, 189-191, 193, 194, 198, 201, 202, 206-208, 212, 232, 241, 249, 279-281, 286, 301
Lenz, 13, 184, 359
likeness, 2, 4, 16, 18, 21, 26, 35, 37-43, 46, 57, 60, 68, 72, 73, 96, 113, 133, 138, 173, 191, 199, 207, 214, 244, 265, 278, 293, 313, 339, 341, 345, 346, 360
limitation, 17, 19, 21, 47, 50, 55, 63, 65, 73, 83, 94, 95, 100, 101, 107, 109, 113, 117, 118, 125, 127, 128, 130, 131, 141, 143, 145, 147, 154, 156, 162, 167, 169, 181, 191, 213, 217, 219, 220, 223, 232, 233, 237, 238, 241, 250, 254, 255, 261, 165, 281, 309, 311, 329, 331, 333, 343, 352, 353
limitlessness, 95, 106, 167, 243, 297
Litwa, 9, 100, 151, 182, 240, 279, 347, 359
logika, 36, 123, 124
Lossky, 8, 351, 352, 360
Lot-Borodine, 10
Louth, 10, 237, 360
Luke, 24, 30, 41, 63, 83-85, 104, 110, 180, 194-196, 199, 201, 208, 222, 241, 246, 260-1, 264-5, 272-3, 277-8, 286, 296, 301, 304, 307, 312, 330, 332
Luther, 1, 10, 13, 15, 19, 212, 224, 356, 360
Marchant, 114, 115, 360
Martens, 123, 126, 127, 160, 291, 360
Mary Magdalene, 30, 273
Matthew, 20, 41, 45, 63, 68-9, 81-84, 103, 104, 109-111, 120, 122, 134-5, 151, 168, 171-2, 195-6, 199, 201, 207-209, 222, 229, 232, 234, 238, 241, 249, 261, 264-266, 268, 271, 277-8, 286, 289, 296, 304-306, 310-312, 317, 330
Maximus, 6, 11, 13, 15, 36, 39, 60, 72, 199, 251, 339, 345, 350, 351, 360, 363
McGuckin, 12, 13, 16, 47, 58, 71, 251, 339, 360
Meconi, 9, 11, 12, 360, 361
mediating image, 2, 10, 17, 22, 24, 26, 33, 43, 68, 73, 173, 223, 232, 233-235, 240, 275, 318, 321, 346, 348, 349
messiah, 91, 207, 258, 322, 324
metaphorical, 9, 10, 71, 80, 136, 165, 307, 344-348
Methodius, 166, 259, 296, 345
methods, 5, 9, 22, 23, 25, 28, 42, 237, 348, 349
Micah, 206
midrash, 8, 9
mind as a separate reality, 38, 86, 157, 159, 160, 177, 180, 276, 300
monotheism, 36, 185, 209, 283
morality, 3, 5, 10, 17, 54, 132, 162, 174, 264, 292, 301, 305, 321, 332, 333, 343, 345
Moses, 34, 69, 99, 181, 185, 230, 242, 243, 246, 258, 259, 272, 278, 324, 344, 353
Mosser, 7, 37, 114, 119, 224, 361
mystery, 6, 9, 147, 164, 203, 210, 246, 249, 251, 252, 343
Narbonne, 152, 155
natural theology, 28, 90, 93, 188-192, 201, 202
Nazianzus, 11, 15, 17, 41, 47, 51, 58, 71, 164, 205, 296, 337, 339
Nellas, 10, 220, 361
Neoplatonism, 50, 150
Neyrey, 35, 274, 361
Novatian, 14, 48
Nyssa, 11, 15, 47, 51, 71, 129, 164, 205, 237, 243, 253, 293, 296, 306, 339, 345, 358

Old Testament, 14, 31, 34, 60, 118, 176, 177, 279, 283, 293, 294, 297, 300, 356, 358 (*see also* Hebrew Bible)

Ollerton, 224, 361

oneness, 29, 31, 37, 48, 49, 63, 98, 110, 111, 142, 176, 200, 207, 236, 241, 251, 258, 283, 288-290, 292, 314-327, 343, 345, 352, 353

ontology, 9, 13, 14, 18, 21, 23-25, 27, 29, 46, 50, 53, 55, 58, 64, 65, 68, 72, 74, 76, 77-79, 81, 84, 88, 89, 91, 93-4, 107, 110, 112, 131, 134, 156-7, 159, 170, 209, 221, 238, 265-267, 272, 281, 316-319, 321, 326, 333, 339, 343, 345-349

Origen, 8, 11, 15, 23, 27-8, 36, 43, 47, 51, 56-59, 70-1, 115, 122-128, 135, 145-148, 150-51, 159-162, 164-167, 181-183, 205, 209, 215, 217, 219, 227, 242, 243, 275, 276, 281, 283, 284, 290-296, 305, 306, 308, 320, 326, 327, 337-339, 345, 347, 348, 356, 358-363

Origenist crises, 165-166, 187, 294

original sin, 28, 72, 129-130, 212-226, 229, 294, 356

Ortiz, 14, 48, 267, 341, 362

outer nature, 66, 122, 124, 127-132, 134, 135, 154

Palamas, 11, 13, 15, 45, 49, 199, 244, 350-353, 361, 363

paradise, 44, 59, 119, 121, 127, 141, 142, 173, 232, 236, 276, 284, 305, 310, 312, 329 (*see* Eden, heaven)

participants, 26, 46, 50

participation, 2, 13, 16, 26, 35, 44, 46-50, 53, 60, 71, 92, 143, 155, 166, 173, 195, 207, 213, 219, 228, 235, 240, 244, 248, 249, 253, 285, 314-319, 326, 339, 340, 342, 343, 346, 347, 350, 351, 352

past, 19, 20, 56, 66, 75, 90, 100, 169, 179, 180, 181, 183, 187, 276, 304, 332

Paul, 10, 13, 18, 22, 24, 27-8, 30, 41-43, 61, 64-66, 68-9, 74-81, 93-4, 124, 126, 128-134, 137, 141, 154, 161, 167, 172-175, 179, 189-191, 197-201, 203-207, 216, 217, 219, 230, 232, 236, 239-241, 245, 249, 253-257, 259, 260 262-3, 267-270, 273-275, 285, 286, 288-290, 301, 308, 310-312, 320-324, 347, 348, 357, 358, 359, 362

Pelagius, 163, 187, 212

perfection, 16, 18, 20, 23-4, 27, 29, 30, 35, 38, 48, 50, 68, 70, 72-3, 82-3, 96, 98-9, 103, 105-108, 111, 113, 115, 117, 119, 120, 122-3, 127-8, 131, 137-8, 140-146, 149, 154, 171, 174, 178, 193-4, 203, 216-218, 220-222, 231-2, 238, 250, 254, 263-4, 270, 283, 285, 290, 309, 312, 326, 329-338, 340-344, 352-3, 359

Peter, 14, 26, 46, 58, 133, 210, 224, 225, 231, 250, 259, 278, 284-5, 290, 301, 302, 304, 309, 313, 363

phenomenological, 234, 349

Philippians, 42, 239, 287, 310

Philo, 123, 179, 181, 357

Philokalia, 4, 5, 36, 362

philosophy, 2-4, 7, 8, 10, 13, 14, 18, 33, 35, 42, 50, 71, 102, 106, 116, 119, 129, 150-152, 155, 159, 160, 183-185, 188, 202, 207, 246, 263, 299, 300, 328, 330, 336, 338, 343, 344, 348, 349, 359

physical, 8, 22, 31, 38, 43-45, 53-59, 63, 65, 67, 72, 73, 81, 96, 101, 102, 118, 121, 125-130, 142, 144, 150, 156, 159, 160, 165, 166, 168, 177, 178, 180, 183, 197, 228, 230, 242, 262-3, 272-275, 280, 281, 293, 298, 313, 318, 321, 331, 345, 348, 349

Plato, 8, 50, 57-58, 61, 126, 129, 135, 136, 150-152, 157, 162, 179, 180, 181, 183-185, 202, 238, 240, 297, 320, 336, 338, 343, 362
Plotinus, 45, 50, 72, 129, 150, 152-155, 163, 175, 202, 237, 313, 336, 356-358, 362, 363
Popov, 8, 14, 59, 243, 248, 357, 362
prayer, 82, 98, 186, 196, 211, 234, 235, 237-242, 244, 266, 278, 296, 314-316, 350, 351
predestination, 22, 78, 79, 150, 172-176, 204, 252, 285, 325
preexistence, 22, 28, 42, 44, 46, 56, 57, 61, 70, 78, 79, 93, 110, 122, 123, 126, 128-9, 147, 150, 159-187, 194-196, 213, 215, 217, 219, 226-228, 246, 284, 285, 295, 296, 312, 316, 322, 331, 334, 342, 347, 348, 364
present (timeless), 19, 66, 81, 89, 99, 100, 120, 127, 169, 177, 180, 188, 193, 197, 238, 259, 260, 261, 343
present future, 180, 259, 264
problems (existential), 55, 63, 64, 73, 75, 107, 115, 122, 130, 140, 141, 144, 147, 149, 168, 185, 206, 214, 215, 223, 226, 229, 231, 232, 254, 323, 328
prodigal son, 84, 152, 254
projection, 112, 143, 204, 206, 219, 226, 228-230, 232, 268-271, 287, 288, 335
Protestantism, 1, 2, 6, 10, 11, 42, 351, 360 (*see also* Reformed)
Proverbs, 40, 61, 110, 178, 192-193
Psalm 82, 7, 9, 33-37, 70, 104, 141, 340, 361
Psalms, 7, 9, 11, 12, 32-37, 43, 45, 55, 70, 72, 91, 104, 123, 141, 177, 192, 215-218, 223, 239, 241, 242, 298, 310, 324, 329, 340, 341, 355, 361, 363
psyche, 148, 155, 263, 320

psychological, 19, 27, 31, 50, 101, 148, 155, 168, 226, 229, 257, 263, 265-267, 274, 298, 304, 305, 307, 320, 349
Puchniak, 11, 14, 135, 362
punishment, 61, 142, 144, 173, 174, 205, 213, 215, 216, 223, 229, 231, 293, 294, 305, 308, 309
purification, 15-17, 28, 132, 162, 205, 223, 224, 237, 267, 289, 293, 294, 305, 308, 352
Pythagorean, 9, 184, 185
qualities, (*see* attributes)
Rahner, 13
realistic, 9, 343, 345-347
realization, 1, 22, 27, 40-42, 53, 59, 60, 67, 76, 83-85, 90, 93-4, 98, 103-4, 109-111, 113, 138, 144, 147, 149, 151-153, 155, 167, 174-176, 180, 186, 188, 189, 195, 198, 204, 211, 231-2, 234, 238, 245, 257, 259-261, 266-7, 269, 271-274, 287-8, 295, 297, 310, 311, 314, 319, 321, 323-4, 326, 328, 330, 332, 333, 345, 348
realized eschatology, 29, 256-264
recapitulation, 3, 38, 39, 115, 129, 137, 141, 209, 235
Reformed, 1, 10, 15, 42, 129, 212, 217, 296, 363 (*see also* Protestantism)
reincarnation, 172, 343
relationship, 4, 17, 18, 24, 34, 36, 48-51, 68, 69, 71-2, 79, 81, 84, 85, 88, 90, 97, 103, 106, 107, 167, 187, 199, 207-211, 218, 224, 229, 230, 232, 238, 242, 253, 261, 291, 307, 313, 316-319, 330, 331, 333-335, 344, 346
restoration, 16, 18, 19, 21-2, 26, 28-30, 38-40, 46, 50-1, 53, 58-9, 69, 29, 50, 51, 58, 65, 73, 79, 98, 106, 113, 119, 129, 138, 144, 149,, 159, 162, 188, 203, 212, 213, 216, 217,

372 Index

219, 221, 222, 224, 226, 232, 240, 243, 252, 254, 260, 263, 283-285, 290-297, 307, 312, 317, 320, 326, 328, 329, 332, 333, 336-342, 343-349

resurrection, 20, 26, 29, 52-54, 58, 59, 62-65, 129, 138, 151, 166, 205, 210, 232, 256, 257, 259, 261-263, 271-275, 278, 302, 348, 356

revelation, 19, 22, 26, 31, 34, 78, 89, 102, 131, 136, 138, 157, 165, 171, 177, 188-190, 196, 197, 238, 249, 252, 256, 280, 289, 294, 312, 322, 349, 351, 353

Revelation (Book of), 29, 257, 258, 276, 277, 285, 304

Romans, 41, 43, 64-66, 74, 76-80, 93, 95, 124, 125, 130, 133, 136, 141, 161, 172-189, 190, 198, 199, 205, 207, 215, 217, 219, 249, 269, 270, 285, 321, 337

rooted, 152, 231, 234, 265, 284, 285, 289, 333, 335

Russell, 6, 9, 10, 11, 12, 14, 44, 46, 53, 70-72, 155, 313, 339, 340, 344-347, 362

sacrosanct, 128, 148, 173, 187, 281

salvation, 1, 2, 4, 11, 12, 15-17, 22, 28, 38, 48, 58, 132, 138, 156, 167, 174, 195, 203-233, 250, 252, 258, 262, 284, 286, 295, 296, 306, 307, 309, 326, 328, 335-337, 358, 362

Samuel, 69, 91, 177, 259

sanctification, 15, 16, 28, 32, 161, 205, 217, 224, 237, 289, 307, 343

Satan, 209, 226, 300-305, 363 (see also the devil)

Savior, 209, 289, 322, 324

saviors, 324-325 (see also messiah)

scripture, 3, 7-9, 17, 19, 21, 26-7, 29, 31-37, 39, 46,-7, 50, 52, 80, 123, 128, 131, 145, 150, 164, 173, 183, 188, 212, 215, 228, 234, 249, 259, 284, 293-296, 313, 331, 338, 339, 342, 349, 353

second self, 153, 155, 175

sex, 212, 216, 226, 302

Sheol, 61, 257, 297-300

Sidaway, 14, 48, 72, 263, 267, 363

simplicity, 25, 27, 44, 53, 55, 65-6, 68-9, 73, 75-6, 88-90, 93-4, 96-99, 105-6, 117, 128-9, 135, 140, 174, 191, 201, 202, 210-212, 217, 222-224, 228, 230-232, 234, 238-9, 243-245, 249, 250, 252-3, 261, 268, 271-2, 274, 280, 283, 294, 314, 324, 329, 330, 332, 334, 337, 340, 345, 347, 353

sin, 64, 65, 77, 89, 90, 115, 130, 131, 141, 198, 206, 212-226, 227, 229-232, 235, 294

Soloviev, 10, 14

Son of God, 45, 59, 69, 88, 89, 91, 116, 117, 153, 169, 194, 211, 247, 256, 262, 292, 318-320, 340, 358

Son of man, 69, 116, 149, 180, 209, 222, 256, 260, 261, 307, 317

sons of God, 21, 24, 30, 31, 33-38, 45, 68, 70-73, 75, 82-84, 91-93, 104, 116, 175, 198, 223, 238, 247, 249, 253, 271, 273, 300-304, 325, 340, 341, 344, 362

sonship, 9, 10, 12, 16, 18, 25, 27, 29, 35, 37, 48, 51, 64, 68-95, 103, 116, 119, 137, 172, 173, 196-198, 207, 211, 223, 224, 235, 238, 245, 250, 261, 285, 304, 318, 319, 321, 323, 327-8, 332-3, 340, 346, 360, 362

soul, 4, 5, 11, 27, 29, 38, 44, 47, 50, 52, 53, 57, 58, 61-63, 71, 83, 92, 109, 123, 146-7, 150-156, 157-159, 161-165, 172-174, 177-8, 181, 184, 191, 196, 213, 220, 221, 228, 240, 243, 248, 287, 393-4, 296, 301, 313, 318, 320, 321, 326, 334, 337-339, 357, 358, 363 (see

Being Gods 373

also undescended soul, world soul)
spiritual man, 126, 127, 209
study, 93, 94, 239, 240, 242, 254, 312, 335
subjectivity, 2, 24, 38, 40, 47, 60, 63, 64, 66, 67, 88, 102, 104, 107, 153, 200, 204, 234, 235, 244, 265, 267, 307, 316, 343, 348, 349, 351
substance, 9, 22, 43, 44, 48, 69, 86, 122, 126, 159, 162, 177, 236, 308, 318, 319, 330, 332, 335, 340, 345, 346, 348
Talmud, 181
Tatian, 38, 242
telos, 2, 6, 41, 290, 329
Tertullian, 10, 14, 15, 33, 34, 48, 57, 58, 337-339
Theodore, 59
Theophilus, 45, 51, 54, 59, 113, 114, 116, 137, 165, 166, 194, 242
theosis, 1, 7, 14, 17, 224, 344, 350
Thomas, 30, 31, 182, 259, 273, 278, 279, 304, 356, 359
time, 36, 56, 57, 63, 99, 100, 101, 110, 118, 119, 121, 124, 145, 150, 153, 159, 160, 165, 166, 169, 174, 177, 180, 187, 193, 204, 243, 285, 316, 325, 326, 328, 330, 334, 337, 353
timeless, 22, 40, 56, 57, 66, 67, 79, 99, 100, 107, 120, 124, 126, 131, 134, 145, 150, 159, 160, 165, 166, 169, 171-173, 176, 177, 187, 231, 260, 285, 325, 326, 328, 330-332, 337
Torah, 34, 35, 179, 181
Townsend, 13, 49, 72, 73, 243, 252, 363
traducianism, 165
transcendence,
of human beings, 6, 24, 33, 40, 51, 63, 68, 70, 79, 82-3, 87, 89, 93-96, 100, 103-107. 113, 150, 152, 156, 157, 169, 170-172, 175-6, 186-7, 190, 193, 195, 199, 204, 208, 226, 234, 236, 247, 251-253, 259, 262, 266, 269, 277, 280, 282, 291, 310, 318, 324, 330-1, 334, 354
of God, 13, 71-2, 82, 96, 99, 100, 102-104, 118, 165, 177, 192, 253, 279, 280, 287, 318, 341, 350, 351
of Jesus, 245-248, 262, 286
transfiguration, 16, 232, 273, 278, 350, 352
Trinity, 97, 98, 194, 316, 319, 346, 355, 358
two natures, 23, 27, 29, 47, 65, 66, 94, 129, 134 (*see also* bipartite)
undescended soul, 150-156, 157, 313, 334
union, 13, 14, 30, 48, 51, 129, 142, 168, 182, 211, 221, 252, 253, 290, 345, 363
universalism, 3, 22, 25-6, 28-9, 33, 40, 62-3, 68-9, 74-5, 78-9, 80, 82-84, 91, 93, 99, 104, 106, 167, 174, 191, 196, 202, 219, 240, 245-6, 251-2, 258, 281, 283-297, 309, 311, 315, 319, 320, 325-6, 331, 343, 344, 347
Valentinian, 9, 69, 114, 118, 119
Valentinus, 338
values, 12, 110-112, 132, 135, 142, 191, 246, 290, 292, 343
via negativa, 237, 262
Virgin Mary, 58
virtues, 5, 11, 43, 46, 96, 132, 186, 187, 238, 239, 248, 249, 345 (*see also* attributes)
Vishnevskaya, 13, 249, 251, 363
vision, 11, 13, 16, 24, 29, 47, 48, 84, 99, 102, 111, 115, 124, 154, 155, 181, 189, 235, 238, 240, 242-245, 251, 257, 258, 267, 269, 276, 278, 285, 287, 288-290, 300, 312, 320, 326, 339, 352
vision of God, 115, 242, 243, 278

volition, 57, 84, 316
von Balthasar, 11, 39
Ware, 10, 363
Wesley, 1, 10, 13, 15, 224
Western tradition, 2, 5, 8-22, 28, 29, 37, 39, 45-48, 57, 58, 66, 70, 72, 97, 129, 185, 199, 210, 212, 213, 233, 224, 242, 263, 305, 337, 350, 355, 357
Williams, 13, 363
Winter, 166, 167, 363
Wisdom, 8, 40, 60-1, 92, 97, 178, 179, 186, 194, 200, 202, 179, 186, 194, 200, 202-204, 216, 239, 262, 280, 290, 299, 300, 314

Word of God, 3, 32-37, 41, 43-45, 49, 54, 69, 71, 88, 110, 116, 122, 123, 168, 179, 194, 244, 280, 290, 314, 315, 319, 320, 330, 333
world soul, 240, 318
yearning, 51, 78, 175, 180, 181, 188, 216, 217, 239, 252, 269, 310
Zechariah, 177, 195, 257, 258, 278, 299
Zizoulas, 10, 351, 364
Zorgdrager, 11, 364
Zoroaster, 185, 264
Zoroastrianism, 185, 256-58, 264, 299, 300, 356

Christian Theology by Michael Roden:

Jesus and Ourselves: An Alternative Understanding of Christianity

A Church Not Made with Hands: Christianity as Spiritual Experience

The Enlightened Christian: A Psychological Interpretation of the Bible

www.ingramcontent.com/pod-product-compliance
Lightning Source LLC
Chambersburg PA
CBHW071657170426
43195CB00039B/2214